How Language Makes Meaning

Language's key function is to enable human social interaction, for which people are motivated to engage by powerful brain mechanisms. This book integrates recent work on embodied simulations, traditional meaning-making processes and a myriad of semantic and other meaning contributors to formulate a new model of how language functions, following a pattern of conjoined antonymy. It investigates how embodied simulations, semantic information, deviation, omission, indirectness, figurativity, language play, and other processes leverage rich meaning from only a few words by using inherently biological, cognitive, and social frameworks. The interaction of these meaning-making components of language is described and a language-functioning model based on recent neuroscientific research is laid out to allow for a more complete understanding of how language operates.

Herbert L. Colston is Professor and Chair for the Department of Linguistics at the University of Alberta, Canada.

How Language Makes Meaning

Embodiment and Conjoined Antonymy

Herbert L. Colston

University of Alberta

CAMBRIDGE
UNIVERSITY PRESS

CAMBRIDGE
UNIVERSITY PRESS

University Printing House, Cambridge CB2 8BS, United Kingdom

One Liberty Plaza, 20th Floor, New York, NY 10006, USA

477 Williamstown Road, Port Melbourne, VIC 3207, Australia

314-321, 3rd Floor, Plot 3, Splendor Forum, Jasola District Centre, New Delhi - 110025, India

103 Penang Road, #05-06/07, Visioncrest Commercial, Singapore 238467

Cambridge University Press is part of the University of Cambridge.

It furthers the University's mission by disseminating knowledge in the pursuit of education, learning and research at the highest international levels of excellence.

www.cambridge.org
Information on this title: www.cambridge.org/9781009246026
DOI: 10.1017/9781108377546

First published 2019
First paperback edition 2022

A catalogue record for this publication is available from the British Library

ISBN 978-1-108-42165-2 Hardback
ISBN 978-1-009-24602-6 Paperback

Cambridge University Press has no responsibility for the persistence or accuracy of URLs for external or third-party internet websites referred to in this publication, and does not guarantee that any content on such websites is, or will remain, accurate or appropriate.

My words are a bridge
with load limits;
sturdily enough made
but there are some weights
just too much, just too heavy
that still insist on crossing.

—Michael Penny, poem 12, *Outside, Inside*

My mind watches my mind
being a mind.
In the standing back things are clear,
an attitude immeasurable
towards something watchable
though not knowing what.

—Michael Penny, poem 16, *Outside, Inside*

I walk on small roundish feet
on a small roundish planet
and what pushes up through my feet
pulls down my thoughts.
I am earth-bound, because I believe
it's gravity which makes me profound.

—Michael Penny, poem 170, *Outside, Inside*

Contents

Contents

Tables

Preface

Imagine a pianist playing a song. She is very skilled – mastering the strike and fade of each note – some crisp, some smoky. Holding each key for the ideal length. Sequencing the chords in precise order. Allowing some notes to overlap, spreading others out – pausing perfectly in between. Melding and swaying the tapestry of tones for a lilting melodic appeal. Enhancing and softening the overall intensity, speeding and slowing the tempo, building to crescendos, and then savoring their aftermath. Tickling your ear with a glissando at one moment and awing it the next with an audio-psychedelic wall of sound.

If you've ever heard and appreciate really good piano music and its playing, in any genre, you know how good an experience this can be.

But imagine this particular piano is special. Instead of each note causing only an auditory experience, imagine they trigger something much fuller. When played, each individual note forces a hearer to relive, if only briefly, a small but specific concrete experience in their past life. Some experiences are things seen or heard. Others are physical feelings or movements. One note, for instance, instantly conjures the experience of *honey* – its earthy but light sweetness, its amber color, its lava texture and viscosity, the way it can be creamy or crystally or sticky – the resistance it gives a spoon when you scoop out a dollop. Another note recalls the experience of *pulling*, as in drawing something heavy toward yourself. The way your arms are extended in front asymptotically, hands tightly gripping, back bowed forward, feet planted firmly, supplicating for the pull. Then the exertion, the pulse of strength, the head back, the legs anchored, and the clenching force of all your muscles as you extract the thing from its mount.

Another note gives you *tomatoes*. Still another, a deep inhale *sniff*. One note conjures *metal*. Another the color *salmon*. Still other notes give you *guitar, lightbulb, tree, ant-stepping, strolling, pillow, cold, sliding, reaching up, orange* (the color or fruit), *sky, milk, woman, sitting, mic stand, thumb, fried eggs, pickles, roof, nausea*, and so on, seemingly endlessly, through all the vivid bits of your past sensory and motor experiences.

Pretty amazing, isn't it? A piano like this would be nothing less than a virtual reality machine, and a full-bodied one at that. By playing the keys of the piano in a particular sequence and style, the pianist can make you relive entire past life episodes, or experience altogether new ones. It's also remotely controlled – it can be used on you from within the room or across a valley, or even from a recording, just so long as you can hear the notes.

Perhaps even more amazing, nearly all modern humans who have ever lived own such a piano and play it nearly every day of their lives. Indeed, nearly all of us are virtuosos. We also hear other people's piano music much of the time and experience vast new realities because of it. Most of us can even read piano music off a page, although this is a relatively recent development in human history. Many people can even compose music onto a page, but not everyone is good at it.

This piano is language. I've been "playing" it for you since you opened this book. You've been "hearing" the music and experiencing the meaning it has wrought for you.

There is a slight difference, though, between our magic piano and language. Language doesn't actually give you all these experiences in the full intensity described here. Language doesn't completely take over your body, moving you avatar-like at the will and whim of the piano player. It doesn't slip you into an hallucination trance where you lose all sensory contact with the present, surrendering completely to the sensory and movement illusions rendered for you by the words.[1] It instead does something a bit less taxing than that, but also no less amazing – *it gives you meaning*. But it does so *under the table*.

Language achieves meaning because the brain regions associated with all those sensory and motor and possibly other past experiences are indeed activated by language. Those activation patterns are also extremely similar to ones occurring during real experiences (e.g., *actually* seeing a giraffe or *genuinely* paddling a canoe). But the brain regions are mostly and temporarily cut off from your body when they're activated by language, much like what occurs during REM sleep dreaming. Your brain looks like you're seeing a giraffe or paddling a canoe, but you aren't. So you are given a state of enriched meaning by encountering language such as, *running up a set of narrow, creaky wooden stairs in an old downtown office building, to arrive at a dingy, bare-lightbulb-lit, institutional green-painted landing, with arched black and gold letters spelling, "Sam Tracey, Private*

---

[1] There may be exceptions to this general truth in the case of certain religious experiences, trance states, or hypnoses brought on by language. Or even just very captivating language that triggers powerful mental imagery which shrouds present sensory or motor experience.

Detective," peeling off the old frosted-glass office door, without really having experienced or hallucinated running, hearing, seeing things, etc. Language is essentially a form of *direct deposit*; you get the meaning without having to handle the cash.

You thus end up, when hearing or reading language, in a state something like *as-if-I-just-sorta-experienced* X when you hear the tune for X. Moreover, this *as-if-I-just-sorta-experienced* experience itself *IS* meaning, or rather one large part of it. You have not just *done* X. You have not *hallucinated* X. But you do have a vivid and full *understanding* of X, enriched by all your past experiences of the parts of X brought up by the *embodied simulations* triggered by the language describing X.

So if embodied simulations are only part of how a language makes meaning, what then are the other parts of meaning? What more is there than the mere *as-if-I-just-sorta-experienced* experience of X, enabled by embodied simulations? One additional part is that, despite what was just described about most language, *some* of those embodied simulations might *indeed* rise to something like the level of the takeover described of the magic piano. Some sensory simulations can be especially strong, to the point where you experience something like actually seeing things. Very novel, rich, or vivid language can take your comprehension nearly to this level of sensory takeover in the form of poignant mental imagery (Rasse, 2017; Hakemulder, Kuijpers, Tan, Balint, & Doicaru, 2017). Vivid, near-to-real experiences can also occur through other senses and described motor activities. Strong emotions can certainly be triggered by language as can other experiences (e.g., things strongly associated with mental or movement images).[2]

Whether such a takeover occurs depends in part on a number of factors. The speed of language delivery is one. The stealthiness of the delivery can matter as well. Language delivered with timing arranged to allow the rich full sensory and motor embodied simulations to peak can aid their potential maximization at takeover. Sequencing the peaks of several embodied simulations so they mesh perfectly – for instance, one embodied simulation rising at the ideal fading point of a previous one – can maximize their impact as well as afford meta-meanings from their blending and juxtaposition. If language is monotone or delivered in too rapid-fire a pace – with one embodied simulation wiping out a previous one before it can peak – then less than full sensory takeover will occur.[3]

---

[2] All one need do to see this is to recall experiences where a speaker "put an image into your head" perhaps of the too-much-information variety, of which you cannot rid yourself.

[3] These parameters also affect the quality of meaning derivation under normal comprehension circumstances, when simulations are not producing "takeover."

Other parts of meaning stem from the syntactic or morphosyntactic structures in which the simulation-triggering morphemes, words, or phrases are embedded – the chords, stanzas, refrains, and choruses if you will, that arrange the notes in the piano music (Bergen, 2012). These structures corral the sequencing, spacing, blending, repetition, inter-weaving, and other choreography of the words/notes/simulations you encounter. In this sense, the morphosyntactic structures contribute meaning of their own by both honing *how each* individual embodied simulation progresses, and affording nuanced meaning themselves through the *melding of multiple* embodied simulations (e.g., a piano chord of F-sharp played amid an ascending sequence is very different than just the individual note F-sharp played alone).[4]

The account of language presented thus far has emerged in essentially the last couple of decades. Prior to that, many scholars, in fields from philosophy to cognitive science, had struggled with the idea of meaning, attempting for centuries really to describe and explain it. But only recently have we gained some serious traction. The rise of the idea of embodied simulations as briefly just described, as essentially the crux (or more accurately *a* crux) of how meaning works in language, has been a bit of a revolution (Aziz-Zadeh, 2013; Barsalou, 2010, 2016; Bergen, 2012; Boroditsky & Ramscar, 2002; Boulenger, Hauk, & Pulvermuller, 2009; Casasanto & Dijkstrka, 2010; Chatterjee, 2008, 2010; Colston, 2017a; Dove, 2009; Fernardino, Contant, Binder, Blindauer, Hiner, Spangler, & Desai, 2013; Fischer & Zwaan, 2008; Gallese & Lakoff, 2005; Gibbs, 1994, 2006; Glenberg, 2010; Glenberg & Kaschak, 2002; Hauk & Pulvermuller, 2004; Kable, Kan, Wilson, Thompson-Schill, & Chatterjee, 2005; Kable, Lease-Spellmeyer, & Chatterjee, 2002; Kemmerer, Castillo, Talavage, Patterson, & Wiley, 2008; Mahon & Caramazza, 2008; Pecher & Zwann, 2005; Raposo, Moss, Stamatakis, & Tyler, 2009; Richardson, Spivey, Barsalou, & McRae, 2003; Saygin, McCullough, Alac, & Emmorey, 2010; Wallentin, Nielsen, Vuust, Dohn, Roepstorff, & Lund, 2011; Wallentin, Ostergaard, Lund, Ostergaard, & Roepstorff, 2005; Watson, Cardillo, Ianni, & Chatterjee, 2013; Zwaan & Taylor, 2006).

Embodied simulations provide us with a gold standard by which to understand language as a form of currency in human communication/ interaction. According to a gold standard, the value of a unit of currency is

---

[4] Or, to invoke yet another metaphor – that of a food recipe. The ingredient list in a recipe is only part of the picture; the preparation portion matters crucially as well. Embodied simulations are like the ingredients in this metaphor; the syntax/morphosyntax is then the sequence of procedures done on the ingredients to complete the recipe.

anchored to the genuine value of the amount of gold the currency note represents. In the same way, words or phrases have meaning in part because they are anchored to the embodied simulation(s) they trigger in a person's mind.

But just as the "genuine value of the amount of gold" is *itself* part of a much more complex human system, so are embodied simulations part of something much bigger. The *wealth or value* of gold is dependent on many phenomena like rarity, relative rarity, the *perception* of rarity, competitiveness, ownership, entitlement, possession, exclusion, prestige, aesthetic appreciation, unusualness, value, wealth, association, and many other notions, all of which are inherently social constructions arising from the intersection of the material world and human interaction. As this book will hopefully demonstrate, so too are embodied simulations only a part of a much broader framework used to achieve meaning.

The main additional part of language to be treated in this book is, in a way, the counterpart to embodied simulations. The shared experience wrought by the magic piano can only go so far. An additional "side" of language is needed to indoctrinate embodied simulations amid the myriad of preexisting human *communication* systems. This other side must also usher embodied simulations through the myriad of human *interaction* systems, social and otherwise, which motivate how and why we are together with one another. This other side must finally *fill in* where embodied simulations fall short – giving us a sense of having gainfully exchanged meaning when the actual conscious sharing may have been more skeletal.

This book will attempt to position embodied simulations, and how they leverage lots of meaning from a little language, amid broader, inherently biological, cognitive, and social frameworks. As the value of gold is really only part of the picture of how a currency works, so too are embodied simulations and their morphosyntax only part of the picture of how a language works.

Acknowledgments

How Language Makes Meaning: Embodiment and Conjoined Antonymy owes its existence in part to David Attenborough. I've been a fan of his as long as I can remember. His passionately intellectual presentations of wondrous and often new, at least to my experience, revelations of the natural living world have always amazed me. He became a star of nature documentaries, so fascinated by and apparently knowledgeable about the phenomena he presented that many people took him to be an actual biologist.

Later in his career he hosted a new program about the Great Barrier Reef off northeast Australia, broadcast in January 2016 on CBC TV in Canada (Geffen et al., 2015). One of the key themes of the program was the interaction between land and sea, which enables growth and formation of the reef. As the continental shelf in this region of Australia/the Pacific Ocean is both very large and very shallow – as well as very warm – relatively minor changes in sea level can convert a huge area back and forth between dry land and sea. This can also occur in a relatively short period of time. Indeed, on the program Mr. Attenborough learns himself just how young the current reef actually is. Oral histories have demonstrated people's knowledge and memory of its beginning – a warming climate since the last ice age re-submerged the area, allowing the reef in its current form to develop.[1] Corals thrive in this warm shallow sea environment, and they've produced the largest and most complex structure ever built by known living beings. This structure also enables thousands of other species to exist, including many that don't actually reside on or near the reef, but whose populations depend on visiting it.

In some ways, this careful balance and interaction between land and sea – seemingly oppositional planet surfaces and environments – and what the balance/interaction supports, resembles the likewise seemingly opposed parts of language this book discusses. In order for the Great

---

[1] And as a tragic side note, warming sea temperatures may also allow now-living humans to witness its death.

Barrier Reef to develop, a large relatively level land area is needed.[2] But this land must be submerged under a warm shallow sea. The area also must be adjacent to deep water channels where sea nutrients settle. But strong local currents are also required to churn up those nutrients on which the coral ultimately can feed, at least in part.[3] Those currents are in turn enabled by the land structures in and around the seas, which channel the broader ocean currents in ways that ideally stir the sediments and send them toward the reef. So land and sea are mutually dependent on one another to enable the reef's existence.

This is much like the interdependence of the different contributing mechanisms required for a language to work. On one level, you need some signal-like components that can trigger communicable, largely shared hunks of meaningfulness in people. This source of meaning needs to be as consistent within and between individuals as is possible. Call this the oft-heard and so-called *objective* meaning if you will. This meaning contribution is enabled because the signals trigger preexisting parts of our cognitive functioning which will reverberate similarly in people. These "embodied simulations," predominantly sensory and motor in nature, but possibly also involving other areas (e.g., emotions) provide many of the raw ingredients for constructing meaning.

But this system is by nature a bit messy and inexact, in part because it's cobbled together from other systems that arose earlier to do different things (e.g., the sensory and motor cortical regions controlling perception and action). So other systems must be in place to either hone "symbolic" imprecision or to bolster, prop up, or "rig" things somehow so that meaning exchange and cognitive alignment can happen nonetheless – or can happen well enough at least to warrant cognitive evolution continuing in this direction. These other cognitive systems must also liaise with still other older human communication systems as well as the extensive neuro-social systems that connect us (Lieberman, 2013).

But as with sea and land being mutually dependent in order to enable the Great Barrier Reef, so too are the different language subsystems mutually dependent. The non-"symbolic" parts are not merely serving the inexactness of the "symbolic" ones. The non-"symbolic" half of language brings something all its own to the mixture of meaning, without which language as we know it would not work. It is this relatively stealthy portion of meaning, how it functions, and why it has avoided in part the level of attention of the more "symbolic" portion, that this book is about.

[2] Level in that it holds a relatively consistent height above (below) sea level, rather than having no contoured surface features.
[3] Coral actually feed on the algae they host within their bodies, which in turn feed directly on the sediment nutrients. Coral additionally feed directly on other animals (zooplankton).

As Richard Attenborough demonstrated in the CBC program, the water/ land interaction isn't just interesting in that it enables coral to build a living structure visible from space. It also enables thousands of other species to exist. So too is it with language – the interaction of the two major meaning contributors has enabled not just our means of communication. It has built our cultural and technological worlds to amazing levels, unlike anything else we know of in nature.[4] This book attempts to describe this complex interaction and the vast, complicated modern human existence it has enabled.

I, of course, have many other people to thank for this book. I'm grateful to the editorial, production, and other people at Cambridge University Press and their affiliates, including Matthew Bennet, for entertaining the initial idea development of this project and Stephen Acerra for his follow-through. My many colleagues and friends with whom I've engaged in multiple delightful discussions and arguments on ideas put forth here. Among those I have to thank are Angeliki Athanasiadou, John Barnden, Greg Bryant, Raymond W. Gibbs, Rachel Giora, Juhani Jarvikivi, Albert Katz, Eleanor Kinney, Gary Libben, John Newman, Elena Nicoladis, Maity Siqueira, Gerard Steen, and Carina Rasse.[5]

Gratitude is also deserved by Morgan Colston for tolerating my frequent hyperactive blatherings on all things figurative, semiotic, ironic, and essentially everything else.

I'm indebted to the staff and other colleagues at the University of Alberta for their endless efforts enabling this work, including Elizabeth French, Joanne McKinnon, Vanessa Ianson, Michael O'Driscoll, and Steve Patton.

Penultimate thanks go to the generous support of the University of Alberta and the Department of Linguistics, SSHRC, the Killam Foundation, and the research colleagues and support people at the Centre for Comparative Psycholinguistics and the Faculty of Arts, who all make this worth doing.

My final gratitude goes to my mother Marlene Colston. My assimilation of her sound and stoic, frequent advice, "You gotta do what you gotta do," not only provides sustainment through the many "crunch times," but it's also a clever colloquial tautology coupled with structural components of asyndeton with hints of phonetic reduction leveraging a variety of complex intertwined cognitive, social, and emotional pragmatic effects including …

[4] And something also visible from space. Not only is the night side of our planet strewn with pools and canals of lighted cities, our ever-expanding electromagnetic bubble of broadcast language, along with everything with it, will likely make our first contact beyond the planet, if one ever occurs, should anyone be listening.
[5] A special thanks to Carina Rasse for discussions on several ideas contained in this work and for inspiring me to complete it.

A Note on Examples

The discussions in this book contain reviews and mentions of original research studies, observational, corpus, and archival language data, as well as many examples. The latter were selected from a very wide variety of sources including many genres of popular culture (e.g., movies, television programs, novels, advertisements, song lyrics, even cartoons). The latter may obviously have a caricature quality to them, which may actually benefit their intended roles as illustrative examples – occasionally enhancing the very mechanisms or processes they're presented to demonstrate. And as pop cultural material, they're often accessible through Internet and other widely available sources, so they have a ready accessibility to a broad populace. And, indeed, many people may already be familiar with some of the examples because of their popularity, which aids the demonstrative purpose.

But, of course, their scripted nature can make them differ in certain ways, some of them important, from more "authentic" language – either the abstract notion of all the "authentic" language out there since humans have had language or the narrower recorded bits of it. But "authentic" language taking place among unrehearsed interlocutors, creating language from scratch in genuine, live, experienced-in-situ contexts may obviously differ from more scripted examples. I've often maintained that there is nothing inherently more pure, uncontaminated, or just generally better about these "authentic" sources of data. All language takes place in particular contexts, with particular parameters, constraints, and characteristics – even scripted language. So I view these as just different arenas where language can reside, with each being worthy of study. But it holds that the differing characteristics of "authentic" versus more scripted language sources can have great importance to scholars' different research questions.

So I alert the reader to the fact that the examples are not necessarily offered as data qua data, but rather as handy ways to illustrate the language phenomena being discussed. As to the level of representativeness the examples bring for similar phenomena in "authentic" language usage, on the one hand we don't always know the prevalence and nature of some of those phenomena in the big universe of "authentic" language usage. So such a representiveness assessment isn't always currently possible. Moreover, the topics covered in the book are often quite difficult to measure for broad prevalence and nature – many of them are not even part of deposited language artifacts (e.g., written words or recorded/transcribed speech or sign), since they take place in camera. And if they are accessible as artifacts, how to quantify those prevalences and natures is a notoriously thorny problem (Colston, 2015). But, given how the popular examples were scripted for ready comprehension, interpretation, and pragmatic effect production in hearers, viewers, and readers, as popular cultural material, they must at least adhere to some general operational parameters of the broader phenomena in that "authentic" universe, or they wouldn't have made it into their various canons.

And lastly, some of the phenomena discussed in the book don't necessarily exist completely in the more "authentic" arena as their very nature makes them belong more or mostly to the relatively scripted world. Satire, parody, and even ad-libbed acting and improv comedy to a degree, along with many other phenomena, are products of language scripting. Yes, speakers may use some imitative practices in their "authentic" live speech, approaching and perhaps even achieving parody, for instance. But in so doing they are de facto becoming scripted in a sense since they must adhere to some established style or known pattern to achieve the parody – i.e., following a script. And even writing almost approaches a pure scriptedness given its slower, more contemplative production process and obviously its revisability. Moreover, the so-called pure, "authentic" forms of language themselves contain many instances of scriptedness, ranging from phatic language to any bit of language a person has used before and so may have honed its content or delivery. And even in cases of purely novel language, some scriptedness can arise if a person is intensely focused on what they're saying and how they're saying it – i.e., *choosing their words carefully*.

So the borderlands between "authentic" and scripted language in my view are already quite fuzzy. And some forms of almost exclusively scripted language (e.g., satire, impressions, mimicry) belong just as much to our language culture as live, impromptu conversations between live speakers, residing in many genres of language usage (e.g., story-telling, singing, prayer, historical or mythological reenactments, theatrical performances, oral genealogical recitings). And finally, many instances of "authentic" language usage itself also have scripted characteristics to them (e.g., borrowing and speaking a turn of a phrase that worked well for you when you heard it). So the citing of scripted works to help us understand language as a broad human phenomenon may not be as worrisome as some might hold.

1   The Coin Toss

What are little boys made of?
What are little boys made of?
Snips and snails,
And puppy dog tails.
That's what little boys are made of.

What are little girls made of?
What are little girls made of?
Sugar and spice,
And everything nice.
That's what little girls are made of.

Making Up Meaning

Heads and *Tails*

One might wonder why a book about language and meaning intended for adults would open its first chapter with an epigraph of an old nursery rhyme written for children – and a sexist one at that. The point of including the rhyme is that language and how it fashions meaning, as this book hopes to demonstrate, is much like the children in the rhyme. Both are made of other smaller bits, some of which might not appear at first as sensible constituent ingredients of the whole. On further consideration, though, the aptness of the ingredients may become more apparent.[1]

For the rhyme, most people would agree that children are not constructed from cayenne and mollusks. But many people might allow an at least metaphorical or loose semantic truth to the rhyme's claims about boys' and girls' characteristics (e.g., boys are often hyperactive ["puppy

---

[1] In the case of the rhyme, not "aptness" with respect to the claimed differences between boys and girls, but rather "aptness" in *how* the odd ingredients can invoke personality characteristics (e.g., "puppy dog tails" conjuring *liveliness* or *pep*), which could of course apply to many children regardless of their location in a gender landscape.

dog tails"] and appreciate icky things ["snips and snails"], girls can be pleasant ["everything nice"] and can have complex personalities ["sugar and spice"]). Many other people would certainly and understandably take issue with such claims. But these protests would not likely correspond to the metaphorical or semantic meaning mechanisms per se. Rather, people would probably be upset about the claimed differential and systematic alignment of these characteristics to boys versus girls, and/or that a catchy tune aimed at children perpetuates those gender stereotypes.

With regard to language, the main idea of this book is that the way language conveys meaning is best conceptualized as a balance between two primary sets of ingredients (rather than the three supposed ingredients for a child) which are effectively both oppositional and codependent at the same time. On one side, we have a system where words and phrases correspond to other things semantically, syntactically, and semi-symbolically. The lexical item "tree," for instance, refers to something conjured in our heads, **tree**.[2] This in turn corresponds to something in the external world, TREE. Such a correspondence has been discussed in various ways throughout the history of thought about language. For instance, by one simple account, spoken or written words are symbols ("tree") for real things (TREE). Other accounts get more elaborate (see the next section, "Heads").

This semantic/syntactic/symbolic (or hereafter: sem/syn/sym) ingredient, or portion, or perhaps half – as we'll see – of linguistic meaning has undergone a great deal of discussion in many disciplines.[3] Recent accounts basing it on embodiment have also attracted considerable attention in the form of intense theoretical debate and escalating empirical evaluation (see later in this chapter and citations in the Preface). Although these ongoing theoretical arguments and empirical studies concerning embodied simulations are fascinating in themselves, that work will *not* actually be the focus of the present book – this first ingredient of linguistic meaning, despite its laudable recent development, is not being evaluated here.

The other main set of ingredients of linguistic meaning, however, has received less attention. At best, some of its component parts have been developed in a piecemeal fashion. But they've rarely been discussed

---

[2] The following notation will be used to distinguish between lexical items, mentalese entries, concepts, embodied simulations, and real-world entities, respectively: "tree," M-"tree," **tree**, T*R*E*E, and TREE.

[3] The semantics arises from lexical references as well as morphosyntax, which can contribute meaning through guiding which of several different senses of things in the external world are invoked by lexical references (e.g., a noun, "climb a tree," a modifier, "a tree climb").

collectively as a broader category of meaning contribution, with things in common and a consistent motivating framework.[4] They've also not always been considered on par with, and in some ways *necessarily complementary* to, sem/syn/sym meaning. The nature of these other main ingredients, and the relationship between these two "halves" of linguistic meaning, constitute the main theme of the present work. To begin to lay the foundation of this idea, first briefly consider the sem/syn/sym side of the coin in a little more depth.

Heads

Beyond the relatively simple notion that symbolic meaning involves merely symbol and symbolized, another more detailed approach argues that a word ("tree") corresponds to an entry in the language-of-thought or mentalese (M-"tree"). This entry also shares the meaning of "tree" but without word-like components (e.g., pronounceability, a written or signed form). The mentalese entry also in turn corresponds, *somehow*, to the concept **tree**. Such concepts have been claimed as fully or partially innate (e.g., arguably, the **solidity** of objects), or acquired through experience (e.g., learning that "hot," **hot**, HOT things "burn," **burn**, BURN, or that a male biological full sibling is one's "brother," **brother**, BROTHER). Still other concepts have been claimed to be acquired externally but with an innate predisposition *to become* acquired (e.g., the human "face," **face**, FACE).

The operative word here, though, is *"somehow"* – *somehow* a mentalese entry must be connected to a concept. One of the shortcomings of accounts based on the notion of mentalese or something similar, however, is the lack of a clear idea about such a connection. By what means can we connect a mentalese entry, M-"tree," with a concept, **tree**, other than they just go together through repeated but arbitrary association?

One remedy would be to just reduce the two into a single entity – somehow collapse mentalese and concepts into just the latter. But then we're still left with the problem of, *what is a concept?*[5] Is it just a unitary idea, a notion, a mental representation? If so, then how are concepts formed? Where do they come from? How are they distinguished and categorized? How are they manifest in the brain, etc.? We essentially have no means of *grounding* meaning easily in this kind of account without answers to these questions.

---

[4] With some noted successful exceptions (e.g., Relevance Theory).
[5] An insightful question posed to me during my Ph.D. qualifying exam (thanks, Ray), which I've since had the pleasure of passing along to others (you're welcome, Kristina).

According to a more recent approach, though, words ("tree") correspond to one or more of a set of *embodied simulations* we can run (T*R*E*E) (Gibbs, 2005; Bergen, 2012). These simulations themselves are our sensory and motor experiences with TREES stored as generic patterns of neural activation typically in the areas of the brain responsible for sensory and motor processing. The patterns occur *authentically* when we actually interact with real TREES (e.g., when seeing TREES, climbing them, pruning them, chopping them, walking amid them, hearing them). But the patterns can also be *simulated* without peripheral sensory or motor activation as occurs when we *imagine* things like TREE. This embodied view is very promising in its ability to ground meaning in ways that are convincing biologically,[6] evolutionarily,[7] and neurologically[8] – ways that ring true when contemplating the subjective (as well as shared) experience of meaning.

Grounding meaning in embodied simulations also succeeds when we consider the many decades' worth of research in an array of areas of cognitive psychology which address embodied simulations without having necessarily sought to investigate them as such. This research aligns nicely with the idea of embodied simulations underlying certain perceptual and cognitive functioning and their characteristics (e.g., imagination, mental imagery, mental rotation, representational momentum, priming, the Perky Effect). A great deal of recent research has also determined the extent to which embodied simulations play a direct role in language processing proper (see Bergen, 2012 for a review of both the research aligning with cognitive and neuropsychology, and research demonstrating embodied simulations playing a role in language processing).

Each of these approaches – simple symbolism, mentalese, and embodied simulations – thus delineates through different means the ways in which a fixed speech signal or written form (or sign) points to, stands for, represents, or *means* somehow things in the world – often mediated by the mind doing that referring. They each thus attempt to tackle *how* those speech signals/written forms/signs achieve sem/syn/sym meaning.

But the other-side-of-meaning is much less well delineated. The relationship *between* the aforementioned sem/syn/sym side and this other-side

---

[6] "Biologically convincing," in that the fairly well-established mechanisms involved in sensation/perception and motor functioning provide a readily available set of ingredients with which to construct meaning.

[7] "Evolutionarily convincing," in that it makes sense that later evolving cognitive capacities (e.g., language) would have usurped already existing ones (e.g., sensation/perception, motor functioning).

[8] "Neurologically convincing," in that it is well-established that activation in brain regions that support *actual* sensation/perception and motor functioning occurs when those same percepts and motions are imagined, witnessed, or *contained in language being processed*.

-of-meaning is also not as thoroughly considered or discussed. Indeed, one could argue that the other-side-of-meaning and the relationship between the two sides is often miscast.

Tails

This other-side-of-meaning is in a way oppositional to the sem/syn/sym side. The sem/syn/sym side emphasizes the degree of *success* language has achieved in that words and phrases *can* mean things. The other-side-of-meaning emphasizes the degree of *failure* of this mechanism – words and phrases *don't exactly* mean things. Sem/syn/sym meaning is loaded with imprecision, ambiguity, polysemy, and other slipperiness. People don't agree universally on word/phrase meanings. If the resolution, metaphorically, on sem/syn/sym meaning is increased, the word-to-meaning correspondences become fuzzy, much like how clouds can seem whole and unitary at a distance, but foggy, edgeless, and ephemeral up close.

But, importantly, just as the success of the symbol–symbolized relationship is limited, so too is its failure of exactness. On some level, words and phrases *do* mean something. The upshot is that:

*Language works because an **optimal** level of exactness–inexactness exists in the relationship between symbol and symbolized.*

Sem/syn/sym meaning springs from the extent to which symbol *can* indicate symbolized. But this source of meaning is limited. The remaining contribution of meaning being argued for and fleshed out by this book arises from the extent to which symbol *cannot* indicate symbolized. It thus fills in where sem/syn/sym fails. The two sources of meaning are also codependent – sem/syn/sym meaning needs something to flesh out its meaning vagary, the other side requires some kernel of anchoring to guide its progression – akin to how raindrops require a mote of dust around which to form.

This other-side-of-meaning is thus enabled essentially by the optimal inexactness with which the sem/syn/sym side operates. Regarding again the sem/syn/sym side, "tree" means TREE because, depending on which of the accounts just described one invokes – I'll use embodied simulations – we've had experiences with TREE, sensorily and motorily, that are now encoded in us as relatively fixed generic patterns of neural activation. Since these patterns are recorded (i.e., trained) neurally, they can be rerun or simulated in us when we encounter the lexical item "tree," to give us embodied simulations, $T^*R^*E^*E$. So when we hear, see signed, or read "tree," we reenact the seeing of a TREE as a $T^*R^*E^*E$ [seeing of], or the climbing of a TREE as a $T^*R^*E^*E$ [climbing of], as if we were actually seeing/climbing one in that moment. These reenactments thus take the form of activation in our corresponding brain regions which are for a moment semi-independent of the environment outside our skull (i.e., whether an actual tree is in our presence). The only difference between the simulation and an authentic encounter with something is that our eyes and muscles are a bit disengaged (to put it simply) in the simulation.

But again this symbol-to-symbolized correspondence is always a bit vague. It can change with time. It can trend off into several fairly distinct directions. For instance, the OBJECT TREE, as we've discussed TREE thus far, is invoked when we simulate the noun meaning of "tree" as in, "Look at that beautiful maple tree." But "tree" can also correspond to the act of PUTTING SOMETHING INTO A TREE, which we haven't discussed as much thus far, but which is entirely viable, invoked when we do a simulation from "tree" as a verb, as in "to tree a kite."

The correspondence between symbol-to-symbolized is also affected by the simulations preceding it as well as the way "tree" is embedded in its surrounding morphosyntax. The correspondence also may not be the same across individuals. For instance, people from Belize might simulate P*A*L*M. People from Alberta might simulate W*H*I*T*E S*P*R*U*C*E. People from Madagascar might simulate an enormous B*A*O*B*A*B, and an Inuit person who has never left their Arctic island home might only simulate print or screen images of trees.[9]

The following chapters present the argument that this very lack of perfect, one-to-one, symbol-to-symbolized, word-to-meaning correspondence enables another entire side of meaning to exist. Put simply, the slack in sem/syn/sym meaning provides or enables different sources of meaning themselves to arise – sources of meaning that wouldn't exist if language had a tighter symbol-to-symbolized correspondence.

Indeed, it is interesting to ponder whether the degree of accuracy in the symbol-to-symbolized connection is simply at some kind of functional plateau, in that getting all these minds together with a unitary lexical item "tree" can only get us so far. Other meaning components are then just whatever happen to be additionally leverageable by language. Or is it the case instead that the symbol-to-symbolized connection is *held* to its current level of precision by the value and utility of those other contributions to meaning enabled by the lack of perfect symbol-to-symbolized connection? So, to earn the value of those other sources of meaning, the symbol-

---

[9] One can also of course take this reasoning further. A retail salesperson at a shoe store might simulate a SHOE TREE. An historian might simulate a diagram of a FAMILY TREE. A generative linguist might simulate a PHRASE STRUCTURE TREE, etc.

to-symbolized meaning precision must remain at a lesser-than-maximal level.

But either way, the two sides of meaning work in tandem to build up the resulting final overall meaning which gels, if only for a moment, in the person's mind.[10] This final meaning is a complex combination of semantic content and pragmatic effects – the former comprised of embodied simulations, morphosyntax, and other semantic input, the latter resulting either from that semantic content or arising semi-independently through the multiple mechanisms that produce pragmatic effects (see Colston, 2015 for a review of how these processes "leak in" to language processing proper).

Sometimes portions of these two categories of meaning contributors are elicited under a speaker's control; other times they occur emergently. Indeed, some of the meaning that results might morph into its final form over the ongoing interaction of the interlocutors as it unfolds in time through the discourse. These portions of sem/syn/sym and pragmatic effects also combine or interact in complex ways. These braidings can also get very intricate, and can be influenced by psychological/cognitive phenomena that function in parallel to, but can also operate semi-independently from, language functioning per se. As I put it in my 2015 book, *Using Figurative Language*:

> . . . a speaker might intend a given pragmatic effect, and that effect might not occur either because it is overtaken by some other effect or issue or because a hearer just does not compute it. But the relationship between intentionality and pragmatic meaning is much more complex than that. Pragmatic effects unintended by a speaker might occur in a hearer. A speaker might intend pragmatic effect X but instead achieve pragmatic effect Y. Hearers may be particularly primed to compute some sets of pragmatic effects but not others, resulting in a systematic bias in how intentionality is skewed – only certain effects from a speaker, intended or not, get achieved, whereas others do not occur, whether or not intended by the speaker.
>
> The ways in which pragmatic effects can cascade off one another . . . also can be intentional or not. A speaker may intend a family of pragmatic effects to arise from a figurative construction, perhaps as a logical chain sequence or spreading kind of activation. These effects then may or may not actually occur, individually or as an entirety. As with individual effects, entire sets of pragmatic effects also might arise unintentionally.
>
> Intentionality can also emerge in the midst of a discourse rather than existing a priori in speakers. Speakers and hearers may begin a conversation without any particular intentions about pragmatic effects. They might instead just get talking about something rather innocuously, but then a pragmatic effect happens to occur. Perhaps one of the speakers unintentionally says something amusing.

---

[10] Or, if not in tandem, then in opposition, in competition, in cahoots, in contrast, etc. The point being that both sides of meaning are present and playing their roles.

The ensuing laughter then may instill in the speaker the more specific intention to make the other person laugh as part of the emergent camaraderie and even make the interlocutors believe that such a goal was in place at the beginning. Given the complexity of how some pragmatic effects interact with each other, a modicum of randomness also can enter into pragmatic effect computation that can assist this emergent intentionality phenomenon. (Colston, 2015, pp. 222–223)

... comprehension products, interpretative products, context, and pragmatic effects all can interact in very complex ways. They can fade and rearise and interact with schematic knowledge and potentially inaccurate memory content to influence the resulting conscious experiences of all interlocutors. Moreover, this schematic nature of memory is but one of potentially dozens of related effects concerning the malleability, alterability, inaccuracy, fallibility, and many other effects of human memory. (Colston, 2015, p. 94)

The end result of all this is an *optimal* leveraging of a maximum degree of overall final meaning being afforded at core by the individual contribution and interaction between the two basic sides of meaning.[11] But the contribution of the *non* sem/syn/sym side of meaning has not always been fully appreciated. To demonstrate, consider next how sem/syn/sym slackness has *usually* been treated.

The Disembodied Head

Symbolic/semantic inexactness or slack is taken often as a *problem* for conceptualizing language. Given the inexactness between symbol and symbolized, how do people ever align their conscious states through language? If one person says "tree," for example, when meaning **oak**, but another hears that "tree" and comprehends **palm**, how can people ever share meaning? This "problem" has been purportedly "surmounted," however, in a variety of ways.

Detection and Repair   First, people have means by which to detect and correct for this type of inexactness. In the same ways people we know personally who might be considered "two-faced," in that they say one thing to us but then something contradictory to someone else (e.g., that *each* of the given addressees is the speaker's "*one and only* BFF"), are often found out, we can also detect usually when differences in interpretation have taken

---

[11] In some cursory ways, the view proposed here resembles the old bottom-up/top-down dichotomy of language processing contributions. But the current view is much more nuanced, encompassing embodied simulations, pragmatic effects, and other effects semi-independent of language functioning that leak in to affect meaning (Colston, 2015). A much greater degree of interaction among the contributing meaning components is also allowed, as is as a degree of chaotic self-emergentness to meaning that is not solely the sum of the contributing parts but is in part driven by meaning-seeking and multiply motivated human agents.

place.[12] Any given single or small set of embodied simulations usually occurs amid a much longer discourse. This lengthier interaction affords many opportunities to detect misalignments or vagaries in meaning and then hone interpretations to more closely align.

For instance, if two non-native English speakers encounter the English lingua franca simile, "like a walk in the park," as a response to an inquiry about how a job interview went, they might arrive at very different meanings. The first person, who grew up perhaps in an Asian city with beautiful sculptured public parklands laced with lovely, rolling walking paths and lush tropical scenery, might consider the job interview something pleasant, leisurely, without difficulty, etc. The second person who grew up in a country where "parks" refer to enormous, undeveloped, steppe or savannah game preserves with no facilities, great distances, little available potable water, extreme heat, and many dangerous animals, might interpret the job interview as burdensome, frightening, dangerous, requiring much preparation, etc. But if these two individuals continue their discussion of the job interview, the fact that they've interpreted the simile differently could become apparent. They might even discover and discuss the very underpinnings outlined above as potentially producing their different initial interpretations – things like similes are often discussed when people are learning or using a lingua franca (Kecskes, 2007; Kecskes & Horn, 2007). So the interlocutors may be able to iron out their different interpretations on their own.

Contextual Momentum   The inexactness "problem" can also be overcome through the sheer weight of the text, speech, or other context surrounding an ambiguous utterance. Consider, for example, a speaker saying, "take a taxi." This phrase's meaning is not at all clear when spoken in isolation. "Take" can be simulated as active or passive, and as more or less concrete. "Taxi" can also be simulated as a process, a verb, or a noun, and the latter as real or modeled. Given these alternatives, a number of different interpretations are thus available, including among others:

1.1a   **Flag down, enter, and ride in a hired taxi to get to a destination.**
1.2a   **Accept a toy taxi as a gift.**
1.3a   **Physically grab a toy taxi.**
1.4a   **Use one of a taxi company's taxis to drive somewhere.**
1.5a   **Consider the idea of a taxi.**
1.6a   **Consider the idea of a toy taxi.**
1.7a   **Consider the process of an airplane shuttling between airport gate to runway.**

---

[12] And, as is also the case with close friendships, we might also be particularly motivated to find such discrepancies.

But the utterance when spoken would likely be surrounded by a context that could disambiguate its meaning, e.g.:

1.1b   **You are in no shape to drive.** *Take a taxi.*
1.2b   **Thanks for staying late to stock the new toy shelves. I really appreciate it. I really wish I could repay you. Hey, isn't tomorrow your kid's birthday? She likes toy cars, right? Here,** *take a taxi.*
1.3b   **I'm having trouble carrying all these toy cars. I think I'm about to drop some. Could you give me a hand and grab one? No, not that one. I've got that one.** *Take a taxi.*
1.4b   **Could you please go pick up the new meters and GPS units from Randy's Supply? It's no problem, I let employees use the cabs so long as it's for company business.** *Take a taxi.*
1.5b   **There are a lot of ugly cars on the road.** *Take a taxi.* **It's always yellow or green or something.**
1.6b   **There are a lot of other kinds of cars your kid could add to her collection.** *Take a taxi.* **She doesn't have one of those.**
1.7b   **Being a pilot isn't** *that* **hard. Parts of the job are even easy.** *Take a taxi,* **that's no harder than driving a bus.**

The challenge this core phrase poses for interpreters – which simulations should be made and how should they be made – is thus disambiguated to a large degree by the surrounding context. Consider the last example 1.7b. Prior to reading/hearing the target phrase, the hearer has already simulated P*I*L*O*T, along perhaps with some aspects of a pilot's job, either through cascading additional simulations or the activation of schemas related to piloting.[13] For instance, difficult parts of piloting might be simulated (e.g., T*A*K*E*O*F*F and L*A*N*D*I*N*G), as well as easier parts (e.g., C*R*U*I*S*I*N*G), etc. So the sense of "taxi" involving "an airplane shuttling from airport gate to runway," or something close to that semantically or schematically, has probably been already partly simulated when the hearer encounters the target phrase.

Relative Similarity in Target Content   Another repair to sem/syn/sym imprecision involves the relative similarity versus difference in embodied simulations made by different people. As an earlier example argued, people from different places on Earth would likely simulate different types of trees when hearing "tree" – arguably each person would simulate the tree(s) with which they're most familiar. This could lead to a misalignment between the comprehended meaning in a hearer, compared to the intended meaning of the speaker making that utterance. One could counterargue, though, that members of the category *trees*, despite

---

[13] Indeed, cascading subsequent embodied simulations may be part and parcel of what schema activation in the more traditional sense actually *is*.

their diversity, are much more similar overall than trees are to other sorts of things. Trees by and large are long-living plants, with woody trunks and branches, with green or greenish foliage at least part of the year, etc.[14] These and other category characteristics might provide a *good enough* alignment between speaker-intended and hearer-comprehended meaning to suffice for most purposes.

Relative Similarity in Embodied Simulations   Sem/syn/sym imprecision may also not be as severe a problem as it might seem initially if we consider the degree to which sensorimotor-based embodied simulations underlie language processing and the level of similarity in sensorimotor experiences across many people. Considering motor similarities first, people who do different physical activities for various occupational, athletic, cultural, or other purposes might certainly have different motor programs compared to other people. But an arguably great majority of similarity nonetheless remains in the general everyday physical activity of most people. Putting consideration of differently abled people aside for a moment, most people walk, stand, sit, lie down, bend, reach, manipulate objects with their hands in many ways, and in general *move* similarly. These motions are the basic repertoire of bipedal, upright humans with our particular primate skeletal and muscular structure. True, some cultural practices can alter the *frequencies* with which we move in different ways (e.g., walking arm-in-arm with other people versus walking separately). The level of detail in our embodied simulations can also vary according to those frequencies. For instance, a golfer would be equipped with a finely detailed understanding of a full upper torso rotating swing, where a hunter might be privy to the fine motor and sensory principles of spear-throwing, dart-blowing, arrow-shooting, gun-aiming, etc. But a sizeable deal of commonality nonetheless exists in the bodily motion of most people.

The same argument holds for many other bodily functions and sensations – assuming the people involved have relatively average-functioning bodies and nervous systems. Hitting your thumb hard with something heavy *hurts* similarly across most people. Of course, people might respond differently (e.g., sweating, swearing, swinging, swaying) and the severity of the sensation could vary according to peoples' tolerances for pain, level of habituation, and socialized norms about displaying pain, which themselves can affect the intensity of the internal sensation. But the *hurt* is

---

[14] Trees, like many categories, might not have a perfect set of necessary and sufficient defining characteristics, outside of a technical or biological definition, to distinguish them from other things. But trees likely do have exemplar characteristics that aptly fit most of the category members – enabling a reasonable degree of category cohesion.

probably nonetheless pretty similar in most people. Similar claims could be made for hunger, thirst, gastrointestinal sensations, and many others.

Finally, for relatively external sensation, certainly *what* people sense can vary greatly according to their surroundings. But *that* people sense, and that those sensory systems are configured similarly in general, might afford another source of at least some similarity across our species' embodied simulations. The smell of wood smoke, the sound of running water, the feel of soft animal fur, the heft of a heavy rock, etc., all would have degrees of similarity in the subjective experiences of many if not most people.

This certainly is not to say that there are no sensorimotor differences in people. Bringing differently abled people back under consideration now, along with other clear variabilities in our bodily selves (e.g., height, physical strength) and the cultural and related differences already discussed in how we move with regularity, bodily movement also clearly varies. The same holds for people with differences in their internal and external sensory abilities. Acuity of eyesight certainly varies a lot, for instance. Other differences in vision from color-blindness, dyslexia, types of partial blindness, and others are widespread. Hearing varies a lot in people. Some people have more and less sensitive senses of various kinds. Even within senses, people vary significantly. As a personal example, I am extremely well tuned to sounds in my home environment. I can tell for instance if a slight hum two floors down and across my house is slightly different from usual.[15] But I'm useless at hearing people speak directly in front of me if a room is even slightly noisy.

It might thus be pointless to argue about quantifying how much human physical movement or sensation is essentially similar versus different across most people.[16] But to the extent that there is some similarity, the "problem" of diverging embodied simulations from a single simulation- or motor-triggering utterance (e.g., "toss me that stick," "climbing the stairs," "the weather was sweating hot," "I'm starving," "it smelled like burning hair") might be lessened. One can also invoke a *similar enough*

---

[15] I once detected while half asleep a slight difference between the normal sound of the automatic test of my basement sump pump versus when it once slurped up a small amount of water from a leaky water heater. This luckily alerted me to make a crucial repair, resulting in significant cost and headache savings.

[16] Although, in a wildly unscientific survey I conducted (I asked my daughter and her mother), the level of similarity versus difference, respectively, in the motor experiences of "all currently living human beings" was put at 60/40. For sensory experiences, the ratio was reversed (e.g., 40 percent similarity, 60 percent difference). A presumed wider array of senses in people versus the variability in ways of moving their bodies was offered as the reason for the ratio difference.

argument to handle relatively minor differences in some of this variability (e.g., "climbing" bleachers versus "climbing" a steep hill).

Relative Similarity in Embodied Simulation Limitations In another subtle way people's embodied simulations stemming from motor- or sensory-related words/phrases might end up being relatively similar. The *limitations* of embodied simulations that I have described (i.e., that they don't usually result in full-blown sensory or motor take-over [see Preface], their "ghostly quality" [see Chapter 10], etc.) might be highly similar across individuals. So, if one person hears, for instance, "the clouds were feathery on a sunny day," they might simulate white water vapor patterns against a clear blue sky in a thin fanned pattern resembling a bird feather. They probably would not, however, tip their head back as if looking up at clouds and squint as if looking into a sunny sky. They also probably wouldn't hold their hand to their brow to provide shade, as we do occasionally when authentically looking up into a sunny sky. The motor and sensory simulations would probably just not go that far when this person hears the target phrase. These limitations would also likely apply to a large number and wide array of people.

Pressure of Discourse Goals on Language Functioning Another way in which the imprecision of syn/sem/sym meaning might be overcome is through the sheer contextual pressure some situations occasionally present for interlocutors. By demanding synchronized cognitive states among those interlocutors, short-term linguistic disambiguation can result. On occasion, speakers and hearers *must* align their thoughts accurately in order to achieve some goal.

For instance, imagine two adult brothers have decided to go into business together. They have a business plan and have sought financial capital to begin. They've discussed their plans with several people as well, so their intensions are not secret. Unfortunately, though, they have very little collateral to begin, and banks have been refusing them.

As their desperation mounts one of the brothers receives a phone call from an uncle neither of the brothers knows very well. This uncle is a rich business person who heard of the brothers' planned business and, despite his limited personal familiarity with them, decides to offer help. He offers to front the brothers the start-up money for their company. The uncle says he needs a fast decision on the loan, however, because he has another deal he could make instead and would have to move on that deal right away if the brothers turn his offer down. So the brother on the phone puts his uncle on hold and quickly texts his brother to ask what he thinks. The other brother is rushing to catch a plane and only has a minute to reply. He texts back, "This seems hot to me," and is then unreachable.

How would the first brother interpret this comment? What should he tell his uncle? On the one hand, if his embodied simulations give him the general meaning of "hot" as something good as in hot food, hot from being newly created, hot as newness but maybe also requiring quick action before it cools, hot as in burning brightly, etc., the brother should accept the loan offer. But if the brother's embodied simulations give him "hot" as something bad/to be avoided, as in it will burn if you touch it, it will set things afire, you need to keep a safe distance from it, etc., then the brother should decline.

The point for present purposes is that situations such as these, which pressure interlocutors to align interpretations, might reduce some of the ambiguity in the utterances. Speakers might tend to use language that produces less potential variability in the hearer's ensuing embodied simulations in the first place. Hearers might also take account of the need for limiting ambiguity in pressure-producing situations and perform embodied simulations and other language processing activities accordingly. Hearers might also enrich their interpretations by bringing more or more greatly detailed contextual and other information to bear during comprehension/interpretation such that ambiguity can be overridden.

Of course, a number of accounts encompass mind-reading and adjustable ambiguity criteria in their structure and functioning (see Chapters 5 and 8). For now, though, I've just noted that interlocutors might behave more and less ambiguously depending on the demands for clarity and interpretative alignment brought by different situations.[17]

These "repairs" made on the "malfunctions" of sem/syn/sym meaning likely have some cognitive and psychological validity. One could even attempt stretching them perhaps to account entirely for the slack in sem/syn/sym meaning. But doing so might spread their explanatory power rather thin, leaving unexplained multiple complexities known about meaning that aren't handled easily by sem/syn/sym means alone (e.g., by the contribution of target words or phrases in parallel to the sem/syn/sym contributions of the surrounding context). The repairs may also shroud other more ephemeral contributions to overall meaning, the dark matter as it were, enabled by the limits of sem/syn/sym meaning.[18]

[17] Consider how people "choose their words carefully" in some situations (e.g., being on a witness stand), perhaps more than in others (e.g., reminiscing casually about the past with friends).
[18] Dark matter provides an enormous yet somewhat opaque influence on the structure and change of matter in the universe, in the same way that *non* sem/syn/sym meaning contributes to the processes and products of language comprehension.

The earlier examples 1.1b through 1.7b demonstrated how a target word or phrase can be disambiguated by the sequence of embodied simulations preceding and even subsequent to that phrase. But disambiguation is only one small part to the meaning a hearer walks away with after encountering some language. Many other contributions to meaning can coincide with disambiguation, some coming from language processing per se, others leaking in from relevant processes that co-occur along with language processing and in turn affecting it (Colston, 2015). Among these are contributions to meaning arising from: the structures that target phrases can take, stylistic and register information, indirectness, figurativeness, linguistic playfulness, social signals indicated by target phrases and the preexisting social relationships among the interlocutors, the level of sophistication of the language, a wide array of delivery characteristics such as prosody, timing, and many others.

Making Out Meaning: A New Heading

The following chapters will attempt to make the case that, repairs to sem/syn/sym meaning notwithstanding, a whole other array of meaning contributors is operating alongside sem/syn/sym meaning when humans communicate with language. I'll save the details of these other contributions for Chapters 2 through 7. For the present, though, please consider the bird's-eye view of how different categories of contributions to meaning have been combined previously.

Any instance of language produced by a person is under-determined on at least two levels, linguistic and pragmatic. *How* to explain the end product of comprehension given these slippery meaning sources has thus been a challenge ever since the beginnings of serious thought about language. This challenge continues into our modern day of empirical and scientific attempts to figure language out. What a bit of language means, and what *saying* that bit of language means, by a particular speaker in a given context, require more than just that the language itself exists as something someone said. Meaning instead comes from something additional, *something involving the workings of the human mind encountering that language.*

Many approaches have compartmentalized and sequentialized the different meaning sources – putting linguistic sem/syn/sym under-determinism as primary (e.g., assigning references, resolving pronoun assignments, unpacking morphosyntactic structure) and necessary for enabling purportedly subsequent pragmatic elaboration (e.g., making elaborative inferences, computing ramifications, resolving indirectness or figurativeness). More recent approaches have allowed a messier mixing of the meaning sources through processes like schema activation, expectancy generation, framing, situation model funneling, and many others – generally allowing contextual input into earlier and earlier stages of language comprehension (Colston & Katz, 2005).

But the discovery of embodied simulations has provided an entirely new way of thinking about these sources of meaning. Consider how embodied simulations have changed the nature of word comprehension, to take just one example of language processing. Rather than word comprehension being a matter of looking up some kind of definition in a mental lexicon, deriving word meaning instead or additionally involves the running of one or more embodied simulations of a person's generic experience(s) with the thing(s) referred to by the word. Meaning in this sense thus has a tremendous amount of raw content in it. This content is essentially the summation or generication of all of a person's experiences with the thing(s) in question.

For example, consider the word *vinegar*. To use another personal anecdote, one of my first remembered experiences of vinegar was as a presumed remedy for the itching of mosquito bites. Whether vinegar actually reduces the swelling or itchiness of mosquito bites, or simply acts as an odiferous repellent to subsequent hungry bugs, if even that, is unknown to me. But vinegar and hot, sweaty, summer Indiana nights with children running around outdoors at twilight are undoubtedly part of my embodied simulations of "vinegar." Others, of course, involve the tart taste and smell, the mouthwatering appeal of application to fish and chips or varieties of salads, the pseudo-monthly cleaning of my water kettle, the generic appearance of a sprig of tarragon in a bottle, the apple-cider-colored plastic gallon jugs, matching oil and vinegar serving decanters, the delicate sideways jerking motion to apply vinegar to a salad, etc. So, when I hear the word *vinegar*, my cortex comes alive with neural activity that looks nearly identical to my doing or encountering parts of the above interactions (e.g., sensations and motor programs) involving actual vinegar.

The same situation holds for longer segments of language which allow greater influences of morphosyntax. Here, the final comprehended meaning is not just the looking up of several word definitions in a mental lexicon while imposing the morphosyntax (e.g., agency being revealed by a bound morpheme or word order, as in, "The vinegar soaked into the golden-fried breaded fish"). Rather, as was the case with word comprehension, the array of embodied simulations triggered by the language segment are loaded with raw sensory and motor experiences as well as associated ones which are brought to bear on the final meaning. Yes, these simulations are corralled in particular ways by the syntax and morphology. But they're present regardless of those influences and greatly enrich the set of ingredients going into the computed meaning.

It is thus not as if morphosyntax has to be completely resolved before a comprehender has obtained something richly and deeply meaningful out of the language they've encountered. These embodied simulations are meaningful in their own right, and they bring with them affective responses, associates, and schematic structures (e.g., "sunshine" is likely positive, is associated with warmth, and is part of larger meaning structures [a pleasant day] to many people. "Vomit," on the other hand, is negative, is associated with nausea, and is part of other schematic structures [sickness]).[19] The embodied simulations themselves also help guide how *sequences* of embodied simulations can abut, meld, and combine with one another.

But this enrichment of meaning brought by embodied simulations hasn't rid us of the problem of linguistic under-determinedness. We are still faced with unaccounted-for pragmatic and other content in the final meaning a hearer takes from hearing an utterance. This content comes from other influences to meaning brought about by the non-morphosyntactic structures the language brings and by psychological, cognitive, social, and other influences that take place alongside language processing.

A Head's Up

The following chapters attempt a tour of the details of these *non* sem/syn/sym contributions to meaning. We first consider the array of ways in which deviation from established patterns in language itself is meaningful or enables meaningfulness (Chapter 2). We next look at cases where language goes beyond the mere deviation from norms to involve outright intended usage of language omission, and the meaningfulness inherent in these forms (Chapter 3). We next look at deliberate instances of imprecision in language to leverage meaning (Chapter 4). We then look at more

---

[19] And yes, many of these examples are personally related, vinegar on fish and chips being an acquired taste to some – one of my first recalled experiences involved a sunny, warm, pleasant summer evening, a moderate quantity of devoured vinegary fried fish, running around outdoors, and then an unpleasant ending.

Indeed, neither the morphosyntax nor the figurativeness of an utterance necessarily require full resolution before a rich and comprehensible meaning can be derived. Consider the authentic overheard example, "If you want to run with the big dogs, you have to piss in the tall grass," said by a father to his son who opted for a beer when offered a drink of whiskey during a college graduation celebration. The father's derisive and aggressive attitude toward his son's choice of the weaker beverage are in part derivable from some of the raw embodied simulation material dredged up by the content words from the phrase.

encapsulated instances of meaning packaged in standard forms of language indirectness (Chapter 5) and figurativeness (Chapter 6). More ephemeral types of deviation are then treated in the variety of forms of language play (Chapter 7). Then we pull away from language per se for a moment to look at the multiple hardwired brain processes which motivate us to be social – indeed, arguably the very reason we have language in the first place (Chapter 8). How these different sources of meaning then come together and interact with the sem/syn/sem side is then discussed in the penultimate chapter (9). The final chapter brings the previous contributions about language and social connection together to demonstrate how language in its broadest sense actually takes a form similar to that of other important systems in nature, many built on the important notion of **conjoined antonymy**. *Why* these systems take this shape is then considered in order to shed light on why language would follow the pattern. How all of this illuminates common misconceptions about language and how it may force new ways of approaching future language research is taken up as a final theme.

2 Deviance

Well, take my meaning, and it was good;
or take my word, and it was auspicious.
—Lucian, "A Slip of the Tongue in Salutation"
(Fowler & Fowler, 1905)

Wrong Turn

Some years ago while working late at my house in Wisconsin, in the United States, where I lived at the time, I made a phone call to a local sandwich restaurant to order a takeaway meal. The restaurant was small and locally owned – run by a family. On the night in question, business was slow. Only one person was working. I'd ordered from this restaurant before and they often had only one employee running things later in the evenings on weekdays. Very early in the phone conversation before I had placed my order, the server who took my call mistakenly thought I was an acquaintance of hers who apparently had been making prank calls to the restaurant. She revealed this by interrupting me and saying, in a frustrated tone of voice,

2.1 **"Is that you again, Mike? You asshole."**

I was a bit taken aback by this, but also a bit more amused, and a bit sympathetic, instead of being offended by her comment. I could imagine readily this young woman trying to run the restaurant alone in the later evening, as I had observed directly with other employees on previous occasions. Some friend of hers is calling in to tease or annoy her for whatever reason, for ill will or good fun. She is getting frustrated with this activity, not unreasonably, while diligently trying to work. So I took no offense. I just told her who I was in a calm voice. When the woman realized her mistake, she reacted with some moderate horror. She

19

embarrassedly and very apologetically finished taking my order, told me the sandwich would be ready in twenty minutes and rang off.

Later, when I entered the restaurant to pick up my food, I saw her notice my arrival. But she kept her focus intently on the sandwich counter in front of her rather than addressing me. I could tell she was still very embarrassed, and hesitant to face me – realizing I was likely the victim of her telephone faux pas. So I approached her amusedly with a big smile and introduced myself as follows – she was the only other person present:

2.2   **"Hi.**
       I'm not Mike."

This short introduction was wildly successful. The tension visibly left the woman immediately after I'd spoken. She threw her head back and laughed aloud – very relieved to be forgiven for her error. A somewhat powerful if brief social bond existed between the two of us because of this, lasting for the rest of the brief encounter.

After exchanging smiles and my collecting the food and leaving, I thought about this pair of brief conversations on my walk back home. I had sort of intended to introduce humor into the second interaction, to let the woman know I had not taken offense from our first conversation and that everything was fine. But I had not planned what to say nor rehearsed the words prior to entering the restaurant. It all just came out spontaneously when I saw the woman standing tensely at her work counter, looking nervous and a little scared about how our encounter would go. Indeed, when I thought about the complexity of the simple construction I'd uttered and how it achieved its effects, I was a bit impressed at its concise cleverness. Not out of any degree of boastfulness on my part. On the contrary, I had surprised myself in coming up with it. But I was intrigued by what seemed to be the powerful yet stealthy underlying mechanism(s) of this brief construction and how they achieved what they did.

The construction somehow veered off an expected script. It had *deviated*. This, along with the accompanying processes of echo, double entendre, and a private key, somehow conveyed some mixture of meanings alternative to those carried by just the semantics and morphosyntax of the brief utterance. Importantly, this deviance, although surely *assisted* by the accompanying echo, double entendre, and private-key processes, also contributed a bit of meaning all its own.

It is this kind of very generic deviation or imperfect fit with expectations, and how it can alter and leverage additional meaning, which forms the main topic of this chapter. Later chapters will also grapple with related forms of deviation – first through the structure, or lack of structure, of utterances, then by standard kinds of indirectnesses. Discussion of well-established types of figurative language comes next, followed by that of more loosely organized forms of language play. But the present chapter will begin with some of the very subtle forms of communicative deviation which can leverage meaning, but that don't readily fall into these other more widely recognized categories.

Turn Table

In service encounters inside restaurants such as the one just described, the normal type of conversation flow would depend first on how the restaurant in question operates. Had the remote ordering process *not* involved grounded order identifiers like the name of the customer, an order number of some type (e.g., order number "19"), or something similar, then the customer would likely open the in-store conversation by mentioning the content or general nature of their order.[1] Perhaps one of the following utterances would be used, for instance (along with some possibly intervening small talk, depending on the discourse culture of the area and the familiarity, friendliness, and personality of the interlocutors, among many other factors):

2.3   **"Hi. I ordered the tuna club with pickle."**
2.4   **"Hi. I ordered a takeaway sandwich."**
2.5   **"Hi. I ordered a sandwich to go."**

The essential point of these constructions is to inform the server what the customer wishes to pick up. Or the constructions' designs would at least initiate a discourse to bring that information out quickly (e.g., the latter utterances, 2.4 and 2.5, for instance, would likely lead the server to ask for the specific nature of the ordered sandwich [e.g., "which one?"], at which the customer could then elaborate [e.g., "the reuben"]).

But had the earlier placement of the order involved an identifying number or other tag of some kind, or had the server taken the customer's name or business, then one of *those* would likely come up in the customer's opening remarks to the server. Of course, small talk might again intervene, but it would nonetheless be perfectly normal, in North American English, at least, for the customer to open the discourse with comments such as the following:

2.6   **"Hi. I'm Herb."**
2.7   **"Hi. Order for Herb."**
2.8   **"Hi. I had the order for Blaine's Accounting."**
2.9   **"Hi. I'm, uh, ... I placed order number 41."**

---

[1] Grounded in the sense of being in the common ground of the interlocutors.

Or some mixture of order content and the grounded identifiers might be used:

2.10   **"Hi. Bagel sandwiches for Naomi Anderson."**
2.11   **"Hi. I had the all-meat sub, order 41."**

It would thus be highly *unusual*, barring a correction of a mistake in the order, for the customer to open with a *negated* construction to indicate which order they are *not*:

2.12   **"Hi. I didn't order the chicken burrito."**
2.13   **"Hi. I'm not Juanita's Jewelry."**

or:

2.14   **"Hi. I'm not Mike."**

Unless the customer was being silly with some juvenile level of humor, or leveraging off some other small event in the local discourse – for instance, were only two sandwiches visible for customer pickup and the first of only two present customers having just said,

2.15   **"Me, I'm definitely the chicken burrito."**

prompting the second customer to use 2.12 (or again in the case of a necessary correction), no useful reason is on hand for uttering the negated constructions. So how had my deviant utterance 2.2 (or 2.14) then worked to enable not only ready and rapid comprehension by the server, but to also make her feel better about her faux pas, to lose all the tension she was feeling, to find humor in the situation, to feel some closeness toward me for enabling these things, to allow her to know who I was and what I'd ordered, etc.?

Turn a Phrase

The first thing to consider is that the woman was probably *motivated* to achieve the feelings and understandings she derived. At the time I entered the restaurant, the woman was in a situation of threat-to-negative-face (Brown & Levinson, 1987). She had made a professional mistake – a mistake another person might feel negatively toward her about. She was in turn likely feeling her own negative things (i.e., tension, dread, nervousness, regret, possibly some defensiveness held on reserve, etc.). She might also have felt fear at possibly losing her job or harming the family business should I make an issue out of her conduct on the telephone. All those negative things also had opportunity to stew for a period of time. They could have thus become amplified as she contemplated what had happened. Anything which could thus release her from these bad thoughts/feelings would probably be seized by her quickly.

Many accounts of language comprehension and pragmatics deal with situations and motivations such as this. Probably the most prominent of these is Relevance Theory (Goatly, 1997; Stover, 2011; Kovecses, 2011; Schourup, 2011; Sperber & Wilson, 1986, 1995; White, 2011; Wilson, 2011; Wilson & Sperber, 2012). This account in its briefest form, argues that deviances of the sort described for 2.2 through 2.14 trigger a *search for meaning* in hearers because the utterances have violated a sort of unspoken relevance agreement between speakers. In normal circumstances, speakers should say things which are relevant to the ongoing conversation within its context. If a speaker breaks this rule, it could just be due to error or communicative inexperience or poor language skill or something similar. Alternatively, the speaker could be authorizing the hearer to infer some additional information that would lend the original utterance the relevance it appears to be lacking. So, in the latter case, the hearer then does a bit of extra cognitive work. The hearer draws a few additional bits of meaning out of the utterance as used deviantly in the context and flow of conversation thus far. Once the modified interpretation with these new bits of additional meaning then reaches appropriate relevance – essentially, relevant enough to justify the extra cognitive work conducted by the hearer to find that relevance – the hearer's comprehension is complete.

I have argued in the past that situations like the service encounter I described are perhaps best handled by a mixture of the Relevance Theoretic-like mechanisms as well as some additional psychological phenomena that can "leak in" to language comprehension and production processes (Colston, 2015). For instance, in the situation at the sandwich restaurant, many of the motivations involving face, social interaction, emotions, and other things are deeply seated psychologically. They may thus *not* have to undergo a complex cognitive computational/inferential process such as that elegantly proposed by Relevance Theory and other accounts. These psychological processes might instead co-occur semi-independently of language processing proper, perhaps triggered in part by bits of language but also having some operational independence. And they'll interact in complex ways with language processing proper. They may even marshal, corral, direct, or motivate these Relevance Theoretic processes. And, indeed, later in the book when we consider figurative language and language play, certain figurative structures and language play processes seem to directly leverage off these and related psychological functions and the speed, fluency, and complexity with which they occur in us.

Figurative and other forms of language utilize these psychological processes because of the range of ***pragmatic effects*** that can get produced. Indeed, even the subtler forms of indirectness also handled later in the book, as well as the even simpler deviations discussed here, can leverage off these psychological functions to produce pragmatic effects. I've taken to using the term "pragmatic effects" to indicate this mixture of Relevance Theoretic "positive cognitive effects" as well as other psychological processes leaking into language comprehension proper (Colston, 2015).[2] All of these amount to meaningful internal experiences arising in a speaker during some encounter with language in a context, which extend beyond the mere semantic, morphosyntactic, and to a degree pragmatic information encoded in the language itself.

Returning now to the utterance 2.2 (2.14) and applying this mixture of Relevance Theoretic and psychological processes driving pragmatic effects, we can see how the utterance accomplished what it did when used in the service encounter situation. I'll first make no strict claims as to the order in which meaningful experiences occurred in the hearer. Such orderings are a very complex matter, as are the rise and fade rates of different pragmatic effects, how these meaningful experiences interact with one another, and where to draw lines attempting to divide one pragmatic effect from another (Colston, 2015). But we can nonetheless discuss what some of those experiences might have been. We can also discuss some of the standout processes which gave rise to those meaningful experiences.

My utterance first didn't fit the usual mold of what one says in similar situations. The server had not taken my name nor given me an order number when I'd first phoned. So my announcing my name would not have been relevant even had I *not* used the negated form. It thus seems my utterance was deviant in *two* ways – my invoking my identity when doing so would not normally have been relevant, and my invoking that identity with a negated form. As we will see, each of these deviances bears on the woman's derivation of pragmatic effects.

We can also discuss the operation of the previously mentioned double entendre, actually multiple entendre in this case, as well as private-key and echo processes. Utterance 2.2 (2.14) as used in its host context really has several slightly overlapping but still distinguishable senses – all of which, coincidentally, trace back to the actual utterance. One is the very simple surface form:

2.16   **I am not a person named Mike.**

[2] I have also called the psychological influences "cognitive side effects," among other terms (see Colston, 2015).

The second is sort of a repeat of my initial denial on the telephone that I'm not the *specific* person, Mike, who has been annoying her:

2.17   **I am not your acquaintance, Mike, who has been annoying you.**

The third is subtler, and becomes more visible if graphically hyphenating the words "not" and "Mike," to mean something like: I am the *not-Mike person* we both know about based on our first conversation. Or, put differently, if 2.16 and 2.17 are saying who I am *not*, then 2.18 is saying who I *am*:

2.18   **I am Not-Mike**

The fourth sense is then my telling the server I'm the guy who ordered the tuna sandwich:[3]

2.19   **I am the customer who ordered the tuna sandwich.**

A fifth sense could also be my saying that, in contrast to the Mike person who is demonstrably *not* a very nice guy (in pestering the woman while she's trying to work), I actually *am* a nice guy (in *not* pestering the woman, in taking the phone incident in stride, etc.):

2.20   **I am not like the annoying person, Mike (I am instead a nice person).**

The private-key part, although related to all of the above senses, is germane mainly to the 2.18 and 2.20 readings of the utterance – *I am the "Not-Mike" person*, which had been recently grounded between the server and me, and the *I am not like the annoying "Mike" person we both know about* (Clark, 1996). Since those senses had been shared and grounded between the server and me but no one else, they work as very effective private keys between us (Clark & Schaefer, 1987).

The echo component also applies to all the senses since they all involve reference to the earlier conversation. But echo might more strongly apply to 2.16, 2.17, 2.18, and 2.20, given the more explicit presence of the previously voiced Mike identity rather than the operational needs of the second conversation (e.g., my conveying what I'd ordered).

Turns Out

So we now have all the ingredients for discussing how the utterance achieved its pragmatic effects – the double discourse deviation, the several related meanings hosted in the same source utterance usage, the echo,

---

[3] This sense might require a bit of pragmatic elaboration relative to the other senses, which more closely orbit the Mike-identity proposition.

and a bit of shared meaning private to only the two interlocutors. We also know the rough psychological states of each interlocutor – the negative feelings being held by the server, her motivation to get rid of them, and my intention to alleviate those feelings for her due to my not having taken offense from the initial exchange.

It would be nice to begin by saying the twin related deviations triggered everything that comes next. But even this would be an oversimplification. The woman had looked at me when I started speaking and would have undoubtedly seen the big smile on my face and my relaxed demeanor. She may have also heard and registered my convivial tone very early in my utterance. She could have even recalled my calm reaction in the first conversation. These and other cues would have immediately been in the interpretive mix of things, likely affecting the outcome directly. Humans are extremely keen at reading emotions, gesture, facial expressions, posture, etc., in one another and indeed have difficulty not being affected by them. Especially so in situations such as the woman's where she is probably eagerly wanting to know my attitude.

But for expository enablement, let's start with the deviations. My utterance had deviated from what a customer entering such a restaurant would normally say. What would be the potential relevance then of my speaking my identity in the negated fashion I used? Earlier it was argued that giving one's identity in such a situation would be odd because the customer's identity doesn't specify which food order is being picked up (unless the order had been placed in the name of the customer). But, if giving one's identity can nonetheless specify the food order through *reminding* or *indicating* which order is being picked up, then it could work. But this more circuitous route to specifying the order should carry some additional meaning to justify the extra work being asked of the addressee. Otherwise, the speaker is just making things more difficult for no reason.

This is the crux of the mechanism of deviance. By taking the more deviant route to essentially saying (2.19), *I am the customer who ordered the tuna sandwich* – to enable the server to do her required task in the context (i.e., fulfill the order) – I am able to make the addressee attend to all or at least more of the other different senses of 2.2 (2.14), "Hi, I'm not Mike," delineated above (2.16–2.20). I am also able to leverage additional pragmatic effects through the mere usage of indirectness and through the double/multiple entendre, private-key, and echo mechanisms. This enriches the meaning being communicated to the server. Let's consider this in greater detail.

My deviance in both invoking my name and in doing so with a negated structure is not just some random form of unexpectedness. It instead echoes back to the previous conversation, where the woman had also invoked my name, but where she had also assigned me the wrong one mistakenly. So my deviances are licensing the woman to expand her derivations of possible meanings of my utterance, most of which involve my identity, which might be related to that earlier conversation. This invites her to conjure more of the 2.16–2.20 range of meanings, which all bear on that previous conversation.

One outcome of this is the conveyance of some of the tension alleviation I had intended to bring to our second interaction (e.g., *I am not the person who has been annoying you, I am instead a nice person*). This is achieved through at least three means. The first is the woman's search-for-meaning leading her to the sense in 2.20 that I'm a nice person. The second is the obvious in-the-moment demonstration of my goodwill – I'm standing there smiling at her when I could readily be angry instead. The third is the humor I've leveraged (see later in this section).

My twin deviations, again using names and with negated structure, also present a subtle double entendre (and, interestingly, one with a conjoined antonymic structure) nested within the broader polysemy shown in 2.16 through 2.20. This double entendre also gets to the heart of the interaction – who the woman mistook me for and who I actually am. With the one simple construction, I simultaneously say who I am not (2.17) and who I am (2.18), or effectively I *AM NOT* Mike and I *AM* not-Mike.

With this very short construction I allude to the earlier naming mistake by the woman, calling me someone I'm not, but I also sort of mimic her mistake by appearing to introduce myself (e.g., "Hi, I'm Herb"), but actually failing to get the identity perfectly correct, I only say directly who I am *not*. Who I *am* is said indirectly. This can add to the tension reduction in a couple of additional ways. I first bring up the woman's naming mistake, but I do so with an obvious absence of malice – effectively demonstrating forgiveness on my part. I also align myself with the woman by feigning a similar mistake of my own.

This conjoined antonymic double entendre, nested within the broader polysemy, is also at once very clever and extremely efficient ("meaning in concentrate").[4] By using it, I am saying simultaneously who I am and who I am not, I convey that I'm nice and that I bear no grudge, etc., and I bring along the coincident meanings that I'm simply not a person named Mike, and that I'm the guy who ordered the tuna sandwich, the latter meaning in part being conveyed by making this discourse infraction highly distinctive, making it easy to recall and to be aware of who I am. The cleverness

---

[4] I've often used the following phrase to describe the meaning leveraging processes on the other-side-of-meaning: "meaning in concentrate, just add brain."

inherent in packing so much meaning together in one short utterance (and in shepherding the addressee to see it all via the deviances) additionally can trigger a number of pragmatic effects.

One is the recognition of the cleverness itself – this is largely just a made-apparent characteristic of the utterance being so complex. But the cleverness can also trigger a humor reaction. Clever, indirect, and related utterances are, if nothing else, often very funny and amusing. Skirting for brevity the details of the various theories of humor available to explain this (i.e., the mere discontinuity of the utterance from expectations, the tension reduction inherent in resolving the complex meanings of the utterance, the addressee-attentiveness aroused by the novelty of the utterance, etc.), the 2.2 (2.14) utterance simply holds much potential for humor.

Recognized cleverness and experienced humor from an utterance are also often accompanied by a form of mastery display and admiration on the parts of the speaker and addressee respectively (Colston, 2015). Since clever/funny utterances are relatively difficult to construct, and are concomitantly rare, they accordingly demonstrate skill on both interlocutors' parts. The speaker appears talented in successfully producing the utterance. The addressee shows skill in correctly comprehending it.

Taking place in parallel to all this complex meaning derivation and pragmatic effect production/computation is the triggering of intimacy between the interlocutors inherent in the presence of the private key characteristic of the utterance. All of the 2.17 through 2.20 senses of 2.2 (2.14) are derivable only by the two interlocutors by virtue of their being the only witnesses to/participants in the original conversation.[5] So, not only are most of the meanings and all the related pragmatic effects of intricate high quality, but they're also private stock – held only by the interlocutors. This can accordingly catalyze the pragmatic effects discussed so far.

But it can also afford or catalyze still other pragmatic effects.[6] To illustrate, let's first return to the cleverness/mastery display (by the speaker) and admiration (by the addressee/hearer) pragmatic effect process. Not only can a speaker of a clever utterance display their skill at language and mastery of understanding situations, causing admiration from the addressee/hearer, but the positive feeling can also flow in the other direction. Inherent in the mere usage of a clever utterance is its speaker's

---

[5] Utterance 2.16 would be the one sense of 2.2 (2.14) available for other people.

[6] This is a good place to reiterate the caveat as to the sequencing and connections among meanings and pragmatic effects. An alternative way of describing the unfolding of and connections between all these processes is certainly viable. The current pattern is simply one among several possibilities.

demonstrated positive feeling toward their addressee/hearer. In a phenomenon termed *ingratiation* by one account (Colston, 2015), a speaker of a clever utterance shows their esteem for the addressee/hearer by virtue of the unveiled assumption on the speaker's part that the addressee/hearer will understand the utterance. It's demonstrated by the speaker's choice to use the utterance. The speaker would not have used the utterance otherwise. It is thus essentially a form of backdoor or wayward compliment to use a clever utterance with someone, trusting through that usage that the person will ascertain all the complexity involved.

Having such high-quality meaningfulness, involving admiration, gratitude, and other positive feelings flowing both ways between the interlocutors, coupled with intimacy arising from private-keying, echoing previously grounded content, can enhance the friendliness perceived in this interaction. It would be pretty inconsistent for a speaker to present all this quality communication in a position of moderate intimacy with their interlocutor, if the speaker were doing so due to some form of ill intent. It is far more likely that the quality and intimacy are demonstrative of the speaker's positive social stance toward the addressee.

About Turn

In addition to the variety of senses and pragmatic effects leveraged by the triggering utterance, "I'm not Mike," one other broad influence on meaning is also exemplified in this example. It invokes a category of conversation types which we have knowledge about. Accordingly we can access this generic categorical knowledge and apply it to the particular conversational situation at hand. The particular interactional category invoked in this example also results in additional meaning which happens to corroborate, in this case, the content of the accessed senses 2.16–2.20 and the computed pragmatic effects discussed thus far.

As people gain experience in using language with interlocutors, they can form categories of discourse or conversation types based on recurring patterns of interaction, which we observe and in which we participate. Akin to any form of categorization in human cognition (e.g., for furniture, vehicles, games), these categories are at once imprecise and fuzzily bounded at amplified resolutions. But they're also perceptually robust at arm's length and extremely useful to people. For instance, we have knowledge about conversational categories like small talk, shooting the breeze, and troubles talk along with many phatic categories like greetings, farewells, apologies, etc. We also form categories of talking someone up, putting someone down, flirting, being nosy, posturing, and many many others.

The one such category involved in the currently considered example is that of teasing. We have experience with teasing from both having done teasing and having been teased.[7] We've also likely observed or witnessed teasing taking place in many different and diverse contexts. Teasing has both negative and positive characteristics to it. It can result in a person feeling belittled, insulted, and otherwise negative in a large variety of related, and potentially very bad, ways. But teasing can also tilt positively. If a speaker's teasing is intended and taken as a form of benign violation – not meant to genuinely hurt but instead to demonstrate a harm that is in fact *not* taking place – it can actually make an addressee feel positively (McGraw & Warren, 2010; see also Gibbs & Samermit, 2017, for a treatment of benign violation in verbal irony).

If the addressee of the target utterance 2.2 (2.14) recognizes at some point that the utterance belongs to her category of teasing, she can then access knowledge she has stored about the characteristics of teasing (of the positive variety) and apply it to the situation at hand. On this view, conversational categories are just knowledge schemas like any other knowledge structures, with members, exemplars, prototypes, and characteristics, which have been built up over experience. Once a given instance of conversation is recognized as belonging to one of these categories, we then have much knowledge to bear on that utterance and accordingly won't necessarily have to derive it all in the moment. Categories can serve as meaningful shortcuts in this fashion, which is partly why we use them in our thinking, despite their often imprecise nature at close scrutiny.

So the addressee in the current example might have simply recognized early in the second conversation that I was teasing her through indirectly bringing up the earlier mistake she had made but also by signaling I was not making that reference to admonish her. She can then access her standard knowledge about teasing of this sort (i.e., that it bears no threat, that it is also a bit honest – not glossing over some past grievance or error but also not negatively reacting to it – a breaking of ice which can instill relief, that it is even intended with warm feeling, etc.), and apply it to the situation at hand.

Of course, accessing knowledge from stereotypical or schematized categories such as this would likely interact with the more detailed meaning senses and pragmatic effects being computed more directly from the utterance and context in situ and in the moment. And ascertaining how all those sources panned out in the current situation under consideration is very difficult to accomplish with only anecdotal evidence (although see

---

[7] Presumed a likely occurrence for most people.

immediately below). But it is likely fair to say the schematic knowledge could have played a role in the addressee's response to encountering the target utterance.

So this all thus explains how the target utterance, "Hi, I'm not Mike," succeeded at accomplishing much more than conveying the mere information about which food order I was picking up at the restaurant. Many varieties of positivity took place in the interaction (e.g., expressions of my being nice, demonstrations of my being friendly, pragmatic effects making the addressee feel good – humor, admiration at cleverness, etc. – plus the positive characteristics contained in an activated schema of teasing of the positive sort applied to the situation at hand). These were coupled with the addressee's search to find the optimal relevance warranted through the use of the deviant utterance, "Hi, I'm not Mike." All this resulted in the high degree of social bonding that occurred. The woman's preexisting state also likely contributed. Had the woman not been socially embarrassed at the onset of the second conversation she also might not have bothered to work out all the multiple meanings and then garnered the ensuing pragmatic effects. Nor might she have accessed the teasing conversational category and used the corresponding member characteristics.

One additional consideration of the difficulty in ascertaining the sequence, causal ordering, or other connections among the different senses and pragmatic effects in examples such as this is worth noting. It may be that the usual somewhat linear causal order thinking pattern we apply to understanding discourse does not apply in cases like this. It may not work, for instance, to say that the discourse deviation led to deriving a new sense of the target utterance, which then led to computing pragmatic effect A, which in turn gave rise to pragmatic effect B, and so on. Rather, these senses and pragmatic effects may be hyperlinked in a way resembling the configuration of some web pages. Consider that websites sometimes are interconnected in such a way that each page on the site has hot links to every other page on the site. Navigation is thus maximally flexible because users needn't traverse routes in a hierarchical or arterial/side-route manner. A person can instead go to any page directly from any other page. Pragmatic effects and senses may be connected somewhat like this in that their interconnectedness may be complexly intertwined. Some links might be stronger or traversed more often than others, but activation or causal-link-following may have multiple possible and even parallel or multi-parallel routes. Such an arrangement could capture the rapid cascading quality of multiple pragmatic effects and meaning senses arising when complex utterances are encountered.

This chapter has dealt with a fairly generic form of deviance in linguistic communication and how it can leverage rich meaning in interlocutors, going far beyond semantic meaning encoded in an utterance. The next chapter will focus on a slightly more focused (and oddly less focused at the same time) form of deviance. This flavor of deviance involves *omission* in speakers' utterances and how this can also leverage additional meaning in the comprehension and pragmatic effect computation processes.

3   Omission

Last night I saw upon the stair
A little man who wasn't there
He wasn't there again today
Oh, how I wish he'd go away . . .
—William Hughes Mearns, "Antigonish"(1899)

Silence Is Golden

One major category of meaning leveraging from the other-side-of-meaning involves a speaker essentially saying nothing. Consider that most modern scholars of language realize that comprehension involves running a gauntlet of sorts, between linguistic input and a mixture of context, previous knowledge, the situation model, and/or other representations of the context or preceding discourse having just taken place. Yet we still seem to have a bias toward attending mostly to the linguistic input side of this in our considerations of how meaning works (see Chapter 8 for a discussion of this imbalance). So we may not always give full credence to the idea that a speaker can leverage meaning working with *only* that context, previous knowledge, etc. background – much meaning can be conveyed by allowing those influences to do their work by themselves, with the speaker just saying nothing.

Breaking Bad

Consider for a vivid example a scene from season 5 (episode 8) of the American television program, *Breaking Bad* (Gilligan & Maclaren, 2012). In the scene, two characters are having a conversation in a coffee shop about one of the characters potentially murdering multiple crime witnesses currently in prison. The would-be murderer, Walter White, is a former high school chemistry teacher turned meta-amphetamine ("meth") drug kingpin. The men in prison are linked to Walter's industrial drug-making activities, but Walter does not know who all the imprisoned men are. Any one of them could reveal Walter's involvement in the drug operation, though, if they wanted to talk to the police. The other participant in this conversation is a woman, Lydia, who knows the men's identities. The conversation pivots around a third person (not present) – a central character, Mike, who has been keeping the imprisoned witnesses quiet by channeling money regularly to their families. Lydia is wondering why Walter now wants the list of the witnesses' names from her, given Mike's ongoing success at silencing the witnesses (the entire discourse is referred to here with 3.5, segments selected from it will be given different numbers).

3.5

WALTER: **So let's take a look at the list.**
LYDIA: *<Swallow, pause, eye-flutter, looks down.>*
WALTER: **Lydia, you've come all this way. You do have the list?**
LYDIA: **Yes, I have it.**
WALTER: **Good.**
LYDIA: **It's just not written down.**
WALTER: *<Slight pause.>* **Oh, and why is that?**
LYDIA: **It's in my head. Safer there.**
WALTER: *<Slight pause, head nod.>* **I see. Then I suggest you pick up a pen.**
LYDIA: **Not just yet.**
WALTER: *<Pause, turns head to one side, narrows gaze.>* **It was my understanding that attending to these nine names was precisely what you wanted.**
LYDIA: **Ten names now. Ten. Counting the lawyer.**
WALTER: **Yes. Ten, counting the lawyer. So, what, am I not tying up loose ends for our mutual benefit?**
LYDIA: **You're tying up loose ends, and I don't wanna be one of them. Once I give you that list, I've served my purpose, and then maybe I'm just one more person who knows too much.**
WALTER: *<Pause, slight head nod.>* **So, you put that list in my hands, and in your mind, I immediately just, murder you, just right here in this restaurant?**
LYDIA: **No. Not right here . . .**
WALTER: **Right here in this public place, immediately?**
LYDIA: **Of course not . . . that's not what I . . .**
WALTER: **Listen, Lydia. You made me promise on my children's lives that I guaranteed your safety . . .**
LYDIA: **From Mike. You guaranteed I'd be safe, from Mike** *<with emphasis>*. **There's no way he'd ever go for this. You getting rid of his guys. You wouldn't be doing this** *<pause>* **the names** *<pause>* **if Mike were still a factor.**
WALTER: *<Long silence.>*
LYDIA: **Yeah. That's what I thought.**

Silence is used multiple times in this scene, both for entire conversational turns and within utterances. It is also accompanied by some telling co-speech gestures, by both conversers but mostly on Walter's part, to hone the meanings conveyed or leveraged by the silences. Lydia's very first full turn in the conversation, following Walter's opening line, involves complete silence. In Walter's preceding turn, he had asked Lydia to reveal the list of names. Her silence in response is effectively a refutation of that request. One might ask then why Lydia didn't just respond by saying "No," or "Not yet," or "I want to discuss something else first."[1]

The reason Lydia doesn't do this is probably an interesting mixture of mere reactive behavior on her part, along with perhaps some communicable meaning – the latter possibly intentional or not. Lydia's personality, as built up in the series to this point, is very tightly wound. She seems to rarely stop thinking and worrying over things. She never relaxes. So, her not responding to Walter's request for the list could in part be just the reaction of someone with this personality – she is thinking over Walter's request, and the consequences of her acquiescing, and may be considering how to respond. She is also afraid of Walter as she reveals later on in the dialog. He is also behaving gruffly and aggressively. Her co-speech gestures corroborate all this. She first swallows. She then pauses a moment. Finally her eyes flutter and she looks down at the coffee cup she has both her hands wrapped tightly around. These all seem to indicate her thinking about, perhaps planning for, maybe strategically stalling on, but also reacting fearfully or otherwise negatively to, the consequences of her providing the list. Her final looking downward could be part of this negative reaction (people commonly look downward in response to negativity), but it could also be a signal of her relinquishing her turn. All this takes time such that Walter starts speaking again. Or perhaps he's picking up on Lydia's turn-ending signal.

But, Lydia also may be *using* the silence and gestures somewhat intentionally to leverage meaning. She could intend for the silence to suggest there is an *obstacle* preventing her from complying with the request, rather than her just being nervous. The obstacle also could be something she wishes to strategically bring into the conversation later. She could also be somewhat metaphorically indicating the obstacle with her silence – her silence response to Walter's request standing in for her reluctance to turn over the list. Her goals in this conversation, after all, involve first confirming her suspicion that Mike is dead, and then convincing Walter she

---

[1] Shortly after the scene she reveals how she can help Walter greatly increase his drug-sale profits with her assistance – effectively buying her safety.

can help him so he won't kill her. These might be best achieved if she proceeds slowly and indirectly, so Walter doesn't get defensive.

Walter seems to make this inference about the obstacle in any case, whether from Lydia's mere reaction or from a more explicit licensing on her part for him to draw that inference. Indeed, it seems, based on Walter's next turn, he's responding a bit to *both* her inference licensing and her pure reactions. He first puts some pressure on her to cease her hesitation (". . . you've come all this way . . ."). He then floats an hypothesis as to what the obstacle might be – her not being in possession of the list (". . . You do have the list?").

The next significant uses of silence, by Walter, are after Lydia says she has the list, but that it's not written down, and when she says she has the list memorized. Neither of these has a great outward appearance of intentional meaning leveraging on Walter's part. The first seems to involve Walter formulating his question as to why the list is not written. The second seems to reflect Walter assimilating the reason for Lydia having not written down the list, and possibly also agreeing with her precaution.

But the next silence usage by Walter does appear to involve meaning leveraging, along with a bit of pure reactivity. When Lydia finally does say she won't provide the list, at least for the moment, in saying, "Not just yet," Walter pauses in his response, and makes a pointed display of turning his head to his left and narrowing his gaze at Lydia. These could just indicate confusion or contemplation on his part, but when he starts speaking, and the co-speech gestures continue their momentum, it becomes apparent they, along with the silence, were signals of aggression or at least displeasure on Walter's part. Walter seems to become suspicious and a bit unhappy that Lydia might want something from him – that desire possibly being the compliance obstacle – or that Lydia might ultimately plan to never give him the list. Prior to this scene, Lydia had, in fact, wanted the imprisoned witnesses killed, which Walter knew. So he's suspecting her hesitancy now is to leverage something from him, or to fully refuse him for some reason, for which he is displeased. The silence could be used intentionally by Walter as part of this displeasure – to push back at Lydia and make her feel more afraid. Lydia has explicitly stated she is not going to give him the list, at least yet. Walter could thus be using his silence to let Lydia's paranoia work against her for a moment – making her now weigh through the consequences of *not* providing him the list when he clearly wants it, or for asking for something unreasonable in return.

Walter's next small usage of silence is also probably just a reaction on his part. After Lydia tells him why she doesn't want to give him the list – *because she thinks he'd kill her afterward* – he seems to again take a quick moment to assimilate this new information into his understanding. He is also likely preparing his response of making fun of her worry. This worry is actually not unfounded, however. Walter very likely would have proceeded to murder Lydia if she weren't successful later in her pitch to help him double his profits, or if she ultimately refused to give the list.

Modeling Silence Inferences

The final two uses of silence are the most interesting, and probably the ones most likely containing rich intentional communicative elements, especially the very last instance. For the penultimate silence, when Lydia is discussing Mike, she lays out and then fills in bits of the backbone causal structure underlying the whole situation. Lydia first states Mike's key role in that overall causal chain – he prevents Walter from murdering the witnesses (by paying the witnesses for their silence – effectively nullifying any need for Walter to murder them). But Lydia uses interspersed pauses, topical jumps, and under-specification as very clear indicators she's wanting Walter to make inferences in order to understand this causal chain situation.

She does so by first referring to the unmentioned planned murders with an ambiguous "this," and then clarifying what she intended the usage to mean (emphasis added):

3.6   **"There's no way he'd ever go for *this*. You getting rid of his guys."**

She then follows immediately with another reference, again using an ambiguous "this," but the topic has switched in the second usage to Walter's requesting the list of names. Lydia doesn't make that switch clear at first, though, as if she wanted Walter to also infer her new referent. She indicates this with a pause, and then again by eventually supplying the new referent. She also under-specifies that new referent, saying "the names" to suggest the more complete, *you're asking me for the list of names* (emphasis added):

3.7a   **"You wouldn't be doing *this* <pause> the names ..."**

She then ends her buildup with one additional pause followed by the final, key, inference-triggering utterance (emphasis added):

3.7b   **"You wouldn't be doing this < *pause* > the names < *pause* > *if Mike were still a factor.*"**

Putting the last sequence fully together we can now observe a pattern:

3.8

LYDIA: **From Mike. You guaranteed I'd be safe,** *from Mike* <*with
            emphasis*>. **There's no way he'd ever go for this. You getting
            rid of his guys. You wouldn't be doing this** <*pause*> **the names**
            <*pause*> **if Mike were still a factor.**
WALTER: <*Long silence.*>
LYDIA: **Yeah. That's what I thought.**

It thus seems in this series of referent switches, under-specifications,
and pauses, Lydia is leading up to the key information she is pursuing
(i.e., Mike's status, is he dead?). She doesn't want to ask for this knowledge directly. And she probably knows Walter would not want to provide
it directly. So she builds up to the question by moving Walter through
a series of inferences. First, an ambiguous usage of "this," followed by
a clarification. Then a second ambiguous usage of "this," which could be
confusable with the clarified referent in the first usage. The latter usage is
followed by a significant pause before the second correct referent is also
clarified. One final preceding pause is then used before the inference
trigger about Mike's status is stated. It is thus as if Lydia is doing a one,
two, three, *go* modeling process for Walter on this inference-authorizing
and inference-taking technique, so he'll know how to use it when she adds
the final emphasized piece in 3.7b.

Either this shepherding on Lydia's part was successful or Walter just
used inferencing on his own. But the final major silence, in Walter's last
turn, which lasts nearly four full seconds, is laden with leveraged meaning. Walter even accompanies his lengthy silence with a subtle blank facial
expression as if to indicate *see me not disputing your implied depiction of
events here.* He is thus authorizing Lydia to infer that Mike is indeed dead
and thus no longer "a factor." The lengthy duration of Walter's silence
could also be indicating the lengthy list of inferable consequences Mike's
death will entail. Mike's death means the witnesses will no longer receive
payoffs. This means they no longer have incentive to keep quiet to the
police. As they'll probably be seeking reduced sentences in exchange for
valuable information, and given the police are highly motivated to crack
this case, the witnesses will likely roll over. Meaning that Walter and
Lydia are now extremely vulnerable. Lydia outright confirms that she
drew at least the initial inference about Mike in her final comment,
"Yeah. That's what I thought." Evidenced in her behavior after the
copied dialog, it also looks like she computed the full inferential chain
either during the discussion or sometime after (or had derived it ahead of
time as a contingency) – she realizes she *must* now give Walter the list to
protect herself from arrest and prosecution. This additionally means she

needs to convince Walter she is valuable to his future business so he should not eliminate her too. She does both of these things subsequently – she gives Walter the list of names and she convinces him to partner with her in his drug business going forward.

This section has looked at silences, whether in the form of full conversational turns or embedded within discourse contributions, and how they can be used to leverage the other-side-of-meaning. What is interesting about these is how they involve a converser, through their implicit or explicit knowledge of how people richly function in the midst of communicating, simply allowing those functional currents, momentums, patterns, and cascades to do their own thing. The converser just says nothing, perhaps accompanied with nonverbal behavior and/or peppered with non-communicatively intentional reactive behaviors, and meaning just happens in other people, again with nothing being said.

The next section will also involve this sort of photographic-negative contribution from the other-side-of-meaning – leveraging meaning from what is not said. But the resolution is a bit lower in these processes. Rather than leveraging meaning by pointed silences, meaning is brought about instead by strategic omissions of broader potentially uttered content.

Commission of Omission

Given how the previous section was based in part on a consideration of a scene from the very popular and acclaimed American television program *Breaking Bad*, this next section will consider, although in less gritty detail, a scene from the prequel to that program, *Better Call Saul* (Gilligan, Gould, Hutchinson, Marion & Gilligan, 2018).[2] As the content of the upcoming section is also based on a much less narrow embedding of silence amid a conversation or discourse, but rather on broader omissions of content, the treatment of the example segment for consideration will also be accordingly less detailed.

Better Call Saul

In season 4, episode 9, the main character Jimmy McGill is attending a hearing to determine if he can be reinstated as a lawyer. One year earlier Jimmy had been suspended from practicing law for some illegal activities involving his older brother Charles McGill, also a lawyer and

[2] *Breaking Bad* has been widely acclaimed as one of the best television programs ever created. *Better Call Saul* has been considered by many commentators as even superior (Heritage, 2018).

an extremely respected one. Charles ("Chuck") is also a highly regarded community member. Jimmy, on the other hand, although well intentioned and big-hearted, has a more checkered past and apparent personality.

Jimmy and Chuck have a complicated relationship. The upshot of this situation for present purposes is that Jimmy, in reaction to his suspension, had struck back at his brother who had in part caused Jimmy's suspension, by anonymously getting Chuck's malpractice insurance to skyrocket, resulting in Chuck's law firm asking him to retire. Chuck, who had also been suffering from a bizarre mental illness involving a supposed allergy to electromagnetism, ends up taking his own life in part over this.[3]

Some of this history is known to the Board members at Jimmy's reinstatement hearing (although probably not the bit about Jimmy's role in the malpractice insurance increase). One of the things the Board is looking for, justifiably or not, is some form of demonstrated remorse from Jimmy with regard to his brother, if not in regard to Jimmy's own behavior. Or they'd be happy to see even a mere mention of Chuck, as evidence of Jimmy's "sincerity." Unbeknownst to the Board is the fact that Chuck had not been as esteemed and honorable a person as most people were led to believe. In fact, he had many times treated Jimmy with mean-spirited, jealous, and scheming contempt and manipulation – perhaps an angel on the surface but certainly not so in his private dealings with Jimmy.

3.9

BOARD MEMBER:	**Mr. McGill, we're ready for you now.**
JIMMY:	**Great.**
BOARD MEMBER:	**And it looks like you've completed the Pre-Prosecution Diversion Program?**
JIMMY:	**That's right, three and a half weeks ago. Actually, I believe, if you look at the supplemental materials, there's a letter from my supervisor, Brad Markham.**
BOARD MEMBER:	**Mm. Uh ah, good. He says he was impressed with your commitment. And for most of last year, you've been employed at CC Mobile?**
JIMMY:	**It's a cellphone store. And, again, there's a letter from my manager, Mr. Robert Finn. Uh, it's also in the supplemental materials.**
BOARD MEMBER:	**Mm. Says here you were part of something called the Silver Circle three months in a row?**

---

[3] Revealing this illness to the malpractice insurer was Jimmy's means of getting the premiums raised.

JIMMY:	It's a sales award. Mr. Finn and the people at CC Mobile have been very generous. You don't have to sell many phones to get in the Silver, believe me.
BOARD MEMBER:	What made you choose that particular field?
JIMMY:	Honestly, just, uh, to put bread on the table. But I would say it's given me a new outlook on client relations. I mean, after dealing with cellphone contracts, explaining statutes to my clients should be a cakewalk.
BOARD MEMBER:	Well, as the saying goes, the law is constantly changing. Have you been keeping yourself, uh, apprised of the latest developments?
JIMMY:	I've been reading the *Bar Journal*. You know, what caught my eye recently was Crawford v. Washington. Any of you follow that?
BOARD MEMBER:	That has to do with the admissibility of ex parte examinations? That was a–a Supreme Court case, wasn't it?
JIMMY:	That's right. How did it go? "The only indicium of reliability sufficient to satisfy constitutional demands is the one the Constitution actually prescribes, confrontation."
BOARD MEMBER:	Classic Scalia.
JIMMY:	I can't help but think about victims forced to confront their assailants in open court, but on the other hand, the Sixth Amendment is pretty controlling. Uh, I'm sorry. I just I get rolling on constitutional questions. Short answer, I've been doing my level best.
BOARD MEMBER:	Well, Mr. McGill, is there anything you'd like to tell us about the reasons you were suspended in the first place?
JIMMY:	This past year, that's pretty much been the only thing on my mind. And I'm humbled by the sheer stupidity of my actions. Remorse doesn't begin to cover it. I'm not gonna make excuses 'cause there's no excuse for what I did. But as I sit here, I can assure you nothing like that will ever happen again. Never.
BOARD MEMBER:	Well, all right. That would seem to be satisfactory. Um, Meg, you have something?
MEG, BOARD MEMBER:	Mr. McGill, what does the law mean to you?
JIMMY:	The law? Uh, yeah. Okay. Um, listen, growing up, becoming a lawyer was, uh, the last thing on my mind. Even if I wanted to, I didn't have the smarts or the skills or the stick-to-it-ive-ness.

But I happened to get a job with some attorneys, and I couldn't help but think, "Maybe I could do that?" Something inside me made me want to try. Now, listen, my diploma says the, "University of American Samoa Law School," and that's exactly what it sounds like. That's a correspondence school. I wish it said "Georgetown" or "Northwestern." But UAS, that's the only one that would take me. 'Cause let me tell you, I wasn't a natural. I mean, the classes, the studying, trying to pass the bar practically killed me. I must have quit ten or twelve times. But I kept coming back to it, and I'm really glad I did because when I got to work with actual clients, there was nothing else like it. Our legal system is complicated, and sometimes it could feel capricious, but it's the closest thing to real justice that we've got. And for it to work, it needs vigorous, passionate advocates. And helping my clients, you know, arguing on their behalf, that's the best thing I've ever done. And this past year I've missed the hell out of it.

BOARD MEMBER: That was very eloquent.

MEG, BOARD MEMBER: Was there any particular influence on your views?

JIMMY: <pause> Um, credit where credit is due. The University of American Samoa. Go, Land Crabs! Anything else?

MEG, BOARD MEMBER: No. Thank you.

JIMMY: No? Good.

BOARD MEMBER: I think we have everything we need. You'll be getting a letter with our decision in the next few days.

Just Sayin'

This example is very interesting as it affords a fully side-by-side comparison of what omission looks like when intended versus not. The example also demonstrates more of the complexity of language processing and pragmatic effect computation in larger, more complex discourses among people (characters) with known personalities and histories – relative to some of the items used for studying language in experimental tasks.[4] The key part of the discourse addressed here is the last question from the

---

[4] For which I've utilized as much as anyone else.

Board member, Meg, and Jimmy's response to it, where some mention of the influence of Chuck on Jimmy is expected by the Board:

3.10

MEG, BOARD MEMBER:	**Was there any particular influence on your views?**
JIMMY:	**<*Pause.*> Um, credit where credit is due. The University of American Samoa. Go, Land Crabs! Anything else?**

In this scene as it actually unfolds, Jimmy does not appear to omit mention of his brother *intentionally* in the sense of trying to communicate something, or attempting to leverage additional meaning, *via* that omission. Rather Jimmy just seems a bit taken aback by the question, and possibly aware of what the Board is looking for, but doesn't want to give credit to his brother, nor give the Board what they're seeking. Jimmy is still bearing conflicting feelings about his brother and doesn't want to be too generous to him. Jimmy had looked up to his brother and sought his love and approval. But Chuck had not respected Jimmy's law degree and even had pointedly told Jimmy near the end that Jimmy didn't mean anything to him. So, Jimmy is probably being authentic in omitting his brother as an influence at this point – Jimmy wants to just make it on his own as a lawyer now, and wants to move on from Chuck. Not attending to all that Chuck did to Jimmy, both positive and negative influences, might be one way of his doing this.

And Jimmy may be holding back a bit and not giving the board what they want on this score – thinking that Chuck's status shouldn't bear on Jimmy's reinstatement. Or, put differently, Chuck was part of the reason Jimmy got into trouble in the first place – Jimmy's law license being suspended for a year.[5] Now that Chuck is gone, Jimmy might want to be considered on his own terms. And Jimmy might feel the Board is denying him this freedom and is being unfair by bringing his brother and Chuck's lofty reputation in the community back into things. Another possibility is that Jimmy is aware of the aura around his brother, particularly in the eyes of the local lawyer community. And, given Jimmy's obvious issues shown by the suspension, he may suspect trying to convince the attorneys present of his brothers' actual failings would be a doomed strategy – they admire Chuck too much and possibly Jimmy too little.

---

[5] Jimmy committed a number of questionable acts to be sure, but Chuck was no angel himself and his refusal to grant Jimmy some of the approval and love he desired were major components in Jimmy's behavior.

Of course, an argument can be made that Jimmy *is* bitter, or is in some form of denial in not wanting to acknowledge or even see any influence of his brother. And these are, of course, all perfectly reasonable interpretable matters about Jimmy, based on what he said and how he behaved in the discourse. The Board might actively form ideas about why Jimmy is acting as he does based on all this.

But this is also a very distinct matter from Jimmy actively speaking in a way to *leverage* those ideas on the part of the Board. This is a very subtle yet crucial difference in how language works. We can observe what people do and say, and form ideas about those things. For instance, a woman might say to her husband who is offering her a piece of apple pie he just baked, "I love apple pie," and then take the piece. Here the ideas formed would probably be that the woman likes apple pie and accepted her husband's offer – coming from the statement and act respectively.[6]

But consider the same situation with the woman saying the exact same thing, but then turning and walking away and *not* taking the offered piece. Here, the ideas we form might be very different. We might take the woman's utterance meaning differently, or at least more extensively, and draw different inferences (i.e., the woman likes apple pie, but she also thinks her *husband's* apple pie is terrible, not worthy of even being called apple pie, or that she's angry with him for something, etc.). In the first case, we interpret the events and the comment. In the second case, we also interpret the events and comment, but here the comment is made intentionally to conflict with the events (i.e., to deviate, to omit, to be imprecise, etc.) in such a way as to leverage that additional meaning on our, the receivers', parts.

Returning to the *Better Call Saul* example, had things been different and had Jimmy been *purposefully* using the omission to leverage some meaning, the pragmatic effects taking place in the Board members would likely have been different. As it was, the Board ended up denying Jimmy's reinstatement, based on their interpretation that Jimmy was being "somewhat insincere" at the hearing. Interestingly, this refusal might have stemmed not so much from Jimmy's failure to mention Chuck, but rather from what Jimmy chose to mention instead – the admittedly non-prestigious institution from which he received his law training and degree.[7] It was as if Jimmy didn't want to mention Chuck, and just blurted out something else to fill the void, knowing he needed to say something and putting some enthusiasm behind it to bolster its

---

[6] Of course, inferences could also be invoked (i.e., the woman's comment being taken as acknowledgment of the man's remembering her love of apple pie, her expressing gratitude, affection, etc.).

[7] A lack of prestige Jimmy himself had just stated.

convincingness. Perhaps this *was* a bit insincere. But perhaps the Board was also probing a bit too personally, judging Jimmy's deservedness for being a lawyer by his feelings regarding his brother rather than on his having accomplished what was asked of him under the suspension. So, maybe we might consider this a subset form of omission involving an opportunity cost, or an opportunity cost meaning.

It's also very interesting to contemplate how Jimmy might have been judged had he more deliberately *demonstrated* his not mentioning Chuck to the board, *intending* for the Board to see this. Perhaps had he shown a genuine bit of irritation at their personal probing and then said his comment in 3.10 with a hint of sarcasm, as if to say, *I know you want me to mention my brother, but that's really not under the purview of your decision, and besides Chuck's influence wasn't all good so I don't want to accept it, so I'll indicate this to you by making a point of not mentioning my brother, and making my making of this point obvious.* This of course may have not been what the Board wanted to hear – Jimmy effectively telling them that his psychological state with respect to his deceased brother is none of their business, or suggesting Chuck's not being an angel caused Jimmy's somewhat understandable anger toward him. But Jimmy would have been *sincerely* conveying these points – and most interestingly, **sincerely conveying them with an indirect method from the other-side-of-meaning.**

In essence, the difference between these two responses from Jimmy, the "somewhat insincere" but not meaning-leveraged one that actually took place and a possible more sincere one based on an indicated batch of inferences authorized by Jimmy, is the set of emotions Jimmy reveals in the two cases. In the first case, Jimmy seems to be experiencing his hurt and resentment but tries to put a nice, polite spin on it that the Board doesn't buy and takes as insincere. In the second Jimmy would have shown his authentic anger, rebellious and retributive feelings, which the Board may have taken as more sincere, but likely also as a bit too angry or aggressive. So in one case he's seen as insincere – in the other, too aggressive. Jimmy simply may have been bound to lose.

Running Silent

Of course, all these different interpretations are subjective and would likely be influenced by people's projections of their own internal personalities, states, desires, senses of injustice, and many other things, onto the people and situations depicted in this scene. This is especially the case for a show with such richly developed characters and complex plot scenarios and backstories. But this actually makes an important point about attempting to study language functioning with language materials, interlocutors, and situations devoid of rich contexts and histories. Much of our language processing occurs in real-world contexts far richer than the fictional ones presented in this particular television program. Granted, the program is of a very high quality and without doubt fills its viewers with intrigue. But the show pales compared to actual people in actual situations doing language amid everything else going on. And this indeed makes the point. If we move from very simple, contextually minimal examples of omission as in the following:

3.10   SPEAKER 1:   **Hey, how was the movie?**
         SPEAKER 2:   **My popcorn was delicious.**

and try to elucidate how comprehension and pragmatic effect computation in particular take place here (i.e., *the movie was bad, the speaker is witty, the movie was really bad because the speaker won't even bother herself to address it, speaker 2 thinks highly of me . . .*), we are operating on a plane far simpler than what we can see happening even in our discussions of the *Better Call Saul* scene. If we then realize how much more complex things are in the real world, we can see how much further we might be from grappling with language operation in its genuine in situ complexity.

I hasten to add that this isn't to argue simple items and tasks have no place in our attempts to understand language. Indeed, it is very interesting to derive contender processes and functions from materials like 3.10 and then attempt to corroborate them with more authentic means (i.e., observational or corpus methods, deconstructed rich archived materials, etc.), and these levels of analysis greatly assist one another in such corroborative and other important ways (see Katz, 2017). But methods and materials and their limitations at all levels nonetheless need to be kept in mind (Colston, 2015). We might be able to identify and verify contender processes of pragmatic effects in our converging measures. But in the complex swirl of influences and mixtures of pragmatic effects in the messy world of authentic discourse, these effects can behave less than deterministically (Gibbs & Colston, 2012).

The form of leveraging meaning from the other-side-of-meaning discussed in the next chapter is when a speaker uses deviance in the form of imprecision – not allowing for a specific resolution of some utterance to rise above competing possibilities. Discussion of these kinds of deviance could arise in many sections of this book. For instance, a question about whether a speaker is being sarcastic or not, or whether a speaker is being playful or not, could appear in the chapters on figurative language and language play (Chapters 6 and 7 respectively). So for present purposes we'll restrict discussion to a simple example of semantic ambiguity.

4   Imprecision

... Through your loving
existence and nonexistence merge.
All opposites unite.
All that is profane
becomes sacred again.
    —Jalal ad-Din Muhammad Rumi, "The Alchemy of Love" (Chopra, 1998)

"Nothing You Can Say, But You Can Learn How to Play the Game"

At a backyard barbeque at a friend's home some years ago, a wide array of conversational topics was making the rounds among the twenty or so people present – most of whom were well-acquainted university colleagues, their partners, children and friends The yard, as well as the conversational participants' behavior, also resulted in an unusual acoustic situation. The yard in question was not very large – meaning the adjoining neighbor's yards were proximal and thus within easy earshot. The guests were accordingly keeping the volume of their conversations respectfully low to not disturb the neighborhood. At the same time the yard was lushly landscaped such that the vibrant flora had a dampening effect on background sounds. The outcome of this was that a person standing in the middle of the yard could effectively hear all the different conversations taking place – the voices loud enough to be heard across the yard but not so loud as to drown one another out, and with most of the background noise being squelched.

One of the people attending the barbeque was known by most of the guests to be an extreme fan of all things related to the 1960s British popular musical band, The Beatles. This person would rarely pass an opportunity to talk about anything related to the group and their lore, including fresh news items pertaining to band members. This was especially so if the person was feeling the loss-of-inhibition effects of moderate amounts of alcohol, which happened to be served at this gathering.

At one point in the afternoon, the Beatles' fan entered the yard after having been indoors for a while and approached a cooler containing chilled beverages resting in the middle of the yard. While this was happening, another guest who noticed the Beatles' fan coming into the yard raised his voice a little when introducing a new conversational topic to the group around his table, partly to gain the attention of the Beatles' fan, but also with a slightly sly intent to tease her with the topic – everyone present knowing the Beatles' fan could likely not resist taking up the topic. The utterance mentioned some bit of recent celebrity news pertaining to Paul McCartney.[1] The verbatim wording of the initiating comment is lost to memory, but it was something like the following:

4.1   **"I heard Paul McCartney was not pleased with the new**
        ***Rolling Stone* article about why the Beatles broke up."**

Essentially coinciding with the uttering of this comment, the Beatles' fan had lifted a bottle of white wine from the cooler and had attempted to pour herself another glass from it. Upon noticing no liquid coming out, she first held the bottle up to face level and shook it, and then raised it up in the air, inverted it, and peered up into the vacant bottle-neck with one eye closed, telescope-style.

She also made two sequential comments, seamlessly changing topics between them. The first comment (4.2) pertained to the bottle of wine and was said immediately following 4.1, while she was picking up and inspecting the bottle (the comment was also said a bit quietly, as if the Beatles' fan were merely thinking aloud when saying it). The second comment (4.3), without missing a beat after the conclusion of 4.2, switched to the topic of Paul McCartney, and was said with slightly raised voice as if to mirror the speaker of 4.1 and indeed to address that speaker:[2]

4.2   **"Wine . . ."**
        <Attempts to pour, then shakes bottle and holds it up to peer into it.>
        "Empty."

4.3   *<Switching reference to Paul McCartney.>*
        "And that would mean . . .?"

Another guest at the barbeque, standing a short distance away, had observed and overheard this entire exchange and, in attempting a little fun at the Beatles' fan's expense, rapidly quipped,

---

[1] Just in case – one of the surviving members of The Beatles.
[2] These next parts of the conversation are accurately recalled and verbatim.

4.4   "Somebody drank it."

resulting in some polite chuckles from the other guests and a well-deserved if amicably delivered, faux scowl from the Beatles' fan, directed at the joker.[3]

This example illustrates another general family of mechanisms from the other-side-of-meaning, which are closely related to those discussed in Chapter 2 – in leveraging off a form of deviance. But the processes discussed here have a somewhat different flavor or emphasis. They make greater usage of deviance in the form of *imprecision*.[4]

A number of different cognitive-linguistic, psycholinguistic and linguistic pragmatic theories make claims about precision in language production. As do some accounts from the philosophy of language and cognitive science. Whether coming from one of the Gricean Maxims or the "cooperative principle" in general (i.e., be appropriately specific, be cooperative in exchanging meaning), or from the idea of cognitive economy yoked to the cognitive principle (i.e., cognitive operations tend toward efficiency; linguistic claims should be valid with respect to cognitive and psycholinguistic functioning; therefore, language production should tend toward efficiency [i.e., language should be precise]), or from Relevance Theory (i.e., try to be optimally relevant in language production), among other possible sources, many accounts place high value on speakers being precise in their language production.

Of course, many of these same accounts also allow for leveraging from, riffing off, or flouting these be-precise principles, as noted in Chapter 2 for Relevance Theory (see section, "Turn a Phrase"). Indeed, many of these accounts constitute the very family of somewhat disparate but still demonstrative evidences for this thing termed presently the other-side-of-meaning (see section, "Making up Meaning," Chapter 1). But the accounts still make claims that these leverages or riffs or floutings are generally the exceptions to the rule or principle of, *be-precise*.

---

[3] Although this example appears to involve a degree of belittlement, the joker and the Beatles' fan were, in fact, friends and no offense was taken from the bout of mild teasing.

[4] Imprecision mechanisms relate to the section header as well, itself a line from the Beatles song, "All You Need Is Love" (Lennon & McCartney, 1967), since many imprecision processes are akin to a game. They often involve a speaker being imprecise purposefully in using language, inviting the hearer to sort out the intended meaning. So, the comprehended meaning arises from the gameful interaction between the interlocutors, rather than from what was actually said.

The example also illustrates something often invisible to us. When speech follows its usual precision-adhering path of topical sequencing, the extra work going on behind the scenes (i.e., topical activation and attention, and then suppression) isn't seen. But imprecisions of the sort in this example reveal those operations to us.

Moreover, as discussed in the preface and in Chapter 1, the very reason for the existence of the other-side-of-meaning, or at least one of its reasons, is the inexactness of the more sem/syn/sym side of meaning, in terms of how embodied simulations and the morphosyntax marshalling them cannot perfectly or fully align people's constructed meanings. This idea itself thus creates pressure on speakers to attempt to maximize their precision during language production.

As also claimed earlier ("Turn a Phrase," Chapter 2), little dispute is being presented here with respect to the theoretical range of mechanisms for handling precision-violating processes, at least in their broad strokes. But other more psychological or linguistically independent processes can also arise due to linguistic imprecision and perhaps interact with the linguistic precision-exception processes to give rise to content from the other-side-of-meaning – content perhaps not as widely recognized as part of how language and people make meaning. A range of these mixtures of linguistic and psychological processes, coming from various types of linguistic imprecision, make up the content of this chapter. To set the stage, let's return briefly to the opening example and how it makes use of imprecision of a certain type along with the different linguistic and psychological processes underlying it.

Double Backs

A number of types of imprecision can be invoked in this discussion of how to leverage the other-side-of-meaning. The type used by the opening example will be discussed first as it provides a nice transition from the earlier discussed forms of deviation (Chapter 2) used to leverage additional meaning, toward more purely imprecision-based practices in language production to be discussed next.

Although languages and their highly varying typologies differ greatly in the kinds of expectations they set up in the midst of processing, all languages have patterns which trigger comprehender expectations. Violations of these expectations, or deviances as they've been termed here, can then be used to leverage additional meaning. One type of these violations concerns the sequencing and suppression of topics. Topics and their sequencing follow predictable patterns in languages. Some of these sequences involve new topics being introduced, which sometimes results in previously discussed topics being suppressed. This topical waxing and waning is all essentially due to limited human attentional capacity. Only one or a very few different topics can be entertained in the attentional spans of a group of interlocutors. So, for one topic to gain attention and hold the floor, previous topics must often be suppressed to a degree.[5]

In the example exchange, the sequence of referenced topics was generally as follows. The colleague at the table first raised the topic concerning the Beatles, but he also raised it with an indication that more relevant information was unstated. The Beatles' fan, in part overlapping with that first utterance but then continuing beyond it, centered attention first on the wine bottle and its being empty, but then quickly switched to the Beatles topic. Her rapid switch to the Beatles story, as well as the structure of her turn, *added* to the suggestion that more information concerning the Beatles was potentially forthcoming. Normal expectations in American English discourse would thus be that the next contribution to the conversation should very likely maintain focus on the Beatles. Since the first two utterances concerning that topic had built up the idea that more was to be said about it, it follows that any immediately subsequent contribution should continue with the Beatles.[6]

But the joker went against that topical trend and referred in his contribution to the backgrounded topic of the empty wine bottle – he doubled back.[7] Since the Beatles topic was sort of a hot item in this discourse context at that point (the interlocutors all knowing how interested the Beatles' fan was in the topic, and the topic being raised twice by different interlocutors with each contribution indicating more information was likely forthcoming), the empty wine bottle topic had likely been suppressed, or at least abandoned, when attention focused back on Paul McCartney when the Beatles' fan uttered 4.3.

So the joker's 4.4 utterance deviated from expectations. But in doing so it also created a form of imprecision. Garden-path sentences or discourses and their doubling-back coda contributions, even by involving references that ultimately can make sense, can achieve powerful pragmatic effects. Some of these pragmatic effects (e.g., often humor) arise because the interpretive momentum at the point of the deviant contribution renders that contribution imprecise at least for a moment. It is as if the person uttering the deviation had said something nonsensical – to what is he or she referring? The utterance did not refer to what everyone witnessing the discourse had in mind. And this part is important – it is the contrast of that initial brief moment of nonsensicalness or referential imprecision,

---

[5] "Suppression" meant here in the sense of being made less cognitively or linguistically available for a moment, rather than different Freudian or other senses.

[6] Of course, subsequent contributions could continue with the suspense building taking place thus far. But at some point hearers will maximally expect the withheld or alluded to primary Beatles information to be spoken.

[7] Effectively turning the Beatles' fan's 4.3 statement into a garden path utterance.

juxtaposed to the later-occurring resolution of the reference, which creates a discontinuity, or raises tension requiring release (choose your favorite humor theory here). All of this is why these utterances are often funny (Attardo, 2009; Attardo, Hempelmann, & Di Maio, 2002; Norrick, 2003; Oring, 2011; Ritchie, 1999; Veale, Feyaerts, & Brone, 2006; Veale, 2004, 2009; Tsur, 2009).

The particular example considered here also achieved a few other pragmatic effects, partly relating to the humor achieved but partly standing on their own. In addition, the utterance leveraged a bit of social engineering, belittlement, and mastery display (see Colston, 2015). For a moment at least, the comment moderately belittled the Beatles' fan in the eyes of the audience. It accomplished this through a subtle bit of outing. In the Beatles' fan's eagerness to switch to the Beatles topic, she failed to notice that her utterance 4.3 about the Beatles also nicely followed from and fitted her initial comments and nonverbal behavior about the wine bottle. The 4.4 comment, in pointing out this linkage, effectively then revealed to everyone present what the Beatles' fan had just missed. The switching back to the wine as the referent was also probably easier for the overhearers to achieve, relative to the Beatles' fan herself, since she had been the one to make the quick leap to referring to Paul McCartney's story. She was experiencing more referential change momentum, as it were. So, the 4.4 comment also likely tripped up the Beatles' fan a bit, something for all the witnesses to see.[8]

Additionally, the nonverbal behavior of the Beatles' fan had indicated a bit of reluctance on her part to assimilate knowing that the wine bottle was empty. First, no wine came out during her attempted pour. Then she held the bottle up to eye level and shook it. Finally, she upturned the bottle over her head. Only after all this did she seem to accept and acknowledge the bottle being empty, when she uttered – the latter part of 4.2 – "Empty." So the referential doubling back to this part of the discourse after the Beatles' fan had switched to the Beatles topic reinforces this idea that the Beatles' fan didn't want to accept the bottle being empty. The comment 4.4 also accordingly alludes to the possibility that the bottle was empty because the Beatles' fan had been the one to empty it.[9] This could explain her relative slowness in noting that the bottle was

---

[8] This seems to be a fairly standard characteristic of the benign form of teasing discussed in Chapter 2: to point out or intimate a bit of imperfection on a target person's part, but to do so without malice, merely to acknowledge the reality of the imperfection but to also demonstrate acceptance of or forgiveness for it. Of course, such benign violation teasing must be done to the appropriate degree or the target or others will take offense.

[9] And as these things go occasionally, probably wanted more – hence the reluctance to assimilate the emptiness.

empty. Or even had she not drunk all the wine, the *suggestion* that she had still sort of makes fun of her delayed assimilation. Lastly, the 4.4 comment's outing may also have served to undermine a bit of cleverness the Beatles' fan had displayed. In making the adroit topic switch between 4.2 and 4.3, the Beatles' fan had demonstrated that even though her attention was directed elsewhere when Paul McCartney had been introduced in 4.1, she had noticed it and was able to turn her attention toward it deftly. So, the demonstration by 4.4 that this seemingly smooth switch had unintentionally left something behind doubly undermined a bit that display of agility.

One final point is that the 4.4 comment was delivered fairly rapidly, essentially right on the heels of the Beatles' fan completing 4.3. This contrast in processing speeds on display also served to enhance some of the gentle belittlement taking place – it could have made the joker appear masterful, thus lending value and strength to his meaning, his displayed attitude, and his leveraged pragmatic effects (see the mastery display pragmatic effect, Colston, 2015). At the same time, it could have enhanced the perceived slowness of the Beatles' fan's behavior through a contrast effect.

So, in this example, we see an utterance bucking an interpretive trend created by discourse expectations. This deviation results in an initial feeling of the utterance being imprecise referentially. Later resolution of the referent of the utterance then contrasts with the initially perceived imprecision – the utterance now makes sense. This contrast in sequenced levels of perceived referential imprecision – first high imprecision, then no imprecision – is the major source of the humor. Humor also requires this contrast to have some strength to it; otherwise, the utterance would not be funny.[10]

The type of imprecision in this opening example involved referencing. This imprecision was possible because the discourse momentum in the discussed example created a particular expectation of topicality which was then violated. So, this form of imprecision is very close to the related mechanism of deviance discussed in Chapter 2. But other types of imprecision are possible.

Imprecision can also be due to ambiguity – a discourse contribution could be interpreted with two or perhaps a few different concrete meanings, but the one particularly intended by the speaker is unclear. Imprecision can also arise because of vagueness – a discourse

---

[10] More subtle kinds of contrasts can also afford humor, given appropriate conditions. But in general a strong contrast is considered funnier than a weaker contrast (Colston & O'Brien, 2000a, 2000b).

contribution may have *many* possible meanings (i.e., referential, semantic, etc.), or even be open-ended. So, hearers don't really have an easy way
of pinpointing possible intended meanings. Imprecisions could even
involve obviously non-resolvable contributions – the contribution just
doesn't seem to make *any* sense. One example utterance will be considered under each of these types of imprecision. We'll start with a form of
imprecision of the ambiguous sort.

Ambiguity

Consider the authentic response of a speaker (A) to a claim by another
speaker (B) about something. Speaker B had made a statement whose
veracity could not be fully determined – it could have been a valid claim or
the person could have been mistaken. Speaker A then said the following
(taken verbatim from an overheard conversation):

4.5   **"Yeah, that might be true."**

Of course the intonation used and nonverbal behavior accompanying the
response could have an enormous influence on which of several possible
speaker-intended meanings would be derived. But the witnessed delivery
was conducted without any particular indications the speaker was conceding (e.g., said with a conciliatory smirk, raised eyebrows, and a slow
nod), or being ironic (e.g., said with rolling eyes, or feigned overenthu-
siasm) or anything else interesting. Rather, the speaker said the comment
with a fairly neutral intonation and little nonverbal behavior, as if to
position the intended meaning perfectly amid the various possible interpretations available.

A speaker can leverage a variety of other-side-of-meaning content from
such an intentional use of ambiguity. One is a particularly enhanced form
of mastery display. This pragmatic effect has often been discussed for
instance when a speaker comes up with a particularly novel, clever, or apt
metaphor (Colston, 2015). In so doing the speaker demonstrates
a mastery not only of language usage but also of the complexities of the
situation to which the language applies.

Consider for instance a recent utterance from a private conversation
describing possible types of questionnaire rating scales that a student
might use in an experiment, either one ranging from 0 to 7 or another
one ranging from −3 through 0 to +3:

4.6   **"One is a seesaw, the other is a ramp."**

Here the speaker is able to show both their knowledge about these rating
scale differences (e.g., the *0 to 7* rating scale implies a continuum from the

absence of something through a linearly-increasing-in-magnitude presence of something; the *–3 to +3* scale implies oppositionality, a continuum from the moderate presence of one entity, through a neutral state, to a moderate presence of an antonymous entity), as well as a deft skill in communicative brevity.

Or consider a similar example again from another authentic private conversation, about the complex methodological compromises and operational definition deliberations one must traverse when measuring human behavior, where a speaker said,

4.7   **"Measuring human behavior is like measuring a river."**

Here again, mastery over both metaphorical (or simile) language usage as well as the target-domain topic(s) can be deftly revealed in performance of a short utterance.[11]

Or consider how a speaker might demonstrate mastery by simultaneously achieving different interpretations in different addressees (e.g., a victim of a sarcastic comment is made to think the speaker was earnestly delivering praise, but an overhearer is allowed in on the subtle insult). Here, the speaker is able to craftily negotiate the construction and delivery of the utterance, along with what the speaker knows about the hearers (i.e., what they may know, their personalities, and their propensity for interpreting sarcasm) to marshal carefully customized different interpretations on the hearers' parts – all from the same surface utterance.

But mastery in the case of 4.5 arises from something slightly different – it comes from speaker A simultaneously keeping alive several different meanings of the utterance and leveraging a bit of power by not giving away which of these meanings they intend (i.e., whether speaker A is conceding something or not). Speaker A can also set in motion a sequence of perspective-taking comparisons and reconsiderations on the part of addressees or overhearers, possibly impressing them by so doing, or perhaps distracting them, or confusing them, and concomitantly weakening their power, or both.

An overhearer of 4.5, for instance, might initially take the comment as acquiescence. Speaker B would then be seen as having won the argument through being correct. But the overhearer may then note the modal in the comment, and accordingly reinterpret the comment as a stealthy disagreement or even subtle irony. The overhearer might then shift attention to speaker A, assessing whether these new meanings were really intended. Perspective may then shift again, this time

---

[11] Thanks to my students Erinne Ng and Yolane Yang for enabling these 4.6 and 4.7 constructions.

back to speaker B, with the overhearer wondering if speaker B also noticed these other possible interpretations. Attention could even shift once again, back to speaker A again this time, noting that they've deftly kept several potential interpretations in balance, effectively holding their cards close to their chest as to the precise intended meaning, and keeping everyone guessing.

So, the kind of mastery being displayed here is of a different variety than that previously discussed (Colston, 2015). Earlier discussions of the mastery display pragmatic effect focused much more on master-of-topic and master-of-language underpinnings, as in an apt, double-meaning metaphor that adroitly captures the structure of a target domain, but also does so with linguistic brevity. One example is the following meta-phorical comment overheard by the author in a discussion about people holding public office but who are political outsiders (i.e., invasive species):

4.8   **"Donald Trump is a cane toad."**

The comment is apt in one way at least, pertaining to political outsided-ness (e.g., the invasive species source domain) but also could apply to physical appearances and/or the speaker's negative attitude toward the target domain, all tightly packed in a short, six-word utterance. But the form of mastery on display with the ambiguity involves more of a master-of-social-interaction underpinning, as it involves careful social power engineering.

Vagueness

Speakers can also leverage new meaning of a sort through forms of imprecision-as-vagueness. Consider for instance a man giving a very vague answer to a question from a partner about where the man would like to go out for dinner (presume the interlocutors live in London, UK):

4.9   **"I once really used to like pizza, from that little family place we used to go to in Toronto."**

There doesn't seem to be a way to hone this answer down to a clear set of meanings. On the one hand, you could say the man is either advocating for or against pizza for the dinner. He was, after all, asked to select a cuisine or a restaurant for dinner and he then brought up the topic of pizza. So, the narrow frame of the question seems to limit the possibilities in the answer. The positive advocation could be taken from an interpreta-tion something like, *The man used to like pizza, but hasn't had pizza for a long time, so pizza would be great for tonight's dinner.* The non-advocation for pizza, though, could stem from a different interpretation such as, *The man used to like pizza but doesn't any longer, so pizza would not be a good choice for dinner.*

But these possibilities aren't the only ones. The man could just be reminiscing about past food preferences, having been triggered to think about food by the question. Or the man could be advocating for pizza, but only from a place that makes pizza like the restaurant he remembers. Or he could just be reminiscing about going out for dinner in general. The man could even just be reminiscing about going out only to the very specific place he mentions. It's also possible the man is neither answering nor reminiscing – he could instead be just mentioning a fact about his past.

A few different pragmatic effects could also arise from this vagueness. One could be a similar kind of power play as that produced by ambiguity – the man's partner is put at a modest disadvantage by the vague answer and would thus have to pursue the question further if a clear answer is still sought. Experiences of confusion or frustration could also accompany receiving this answer, as they could have for the earlier ambiguity. But in the particular 4.9 vagueness example, at least, less of a mastery display seems to be going on. It could be that the balancing act achieved by the speaker using ambiguity between just two possible interpretations is more intriguing. The lesser clarity as to even how many meanings are available or even what some of them are, fully, in the case of the vague speaker, however, seems to suggest less relative mastery on display in that example.

But other pragmatic effects could also be at play, which may indicate a bit more subtle skill on the answerer's part, after all. The man may be able to lessen interest in the *very idea of going out for dinner*, with his use of vagueness. If indeed this was his intention and had he succeeded, the man would have accomplished this goal without ever mentioning a disinterest in going out. Putting the partner in the weakened power position, and forcing the concomitant decision to be made (i.e., do I pursue this matter or just drop the idea), seems to be the mechanism through which the disinterest is brought about – the vagueness is a bit exasperating, the partner would have to probe further to get an answer, the partner does not wish to pursue the question because they have already been a bit ill-treated by receiving the vague answer and so are feeling less generous, so they just opt to abandon the idea of going out.[12]

---

[12] A few other pragmatic effects could also be involved (i.e., reduction in intimacy involved with the exasperation, or even possibly an increase in intimacy via admiration at the speaker's ability to wiggle out of this issue without directly criticizing the idea of going out, and/or ingratiation).

Non Sequiturs

Another type of imprecision which can leverage new meaning and/or pragmatic effects is non sequiturs – loosely defined for usage here as seemingly nonsensical utterances which nonetheless can still convey some meaning. For a starter example, consider a brief scene from the American television program, *The Gilmore Girls* (season 7, episode 11, "Santa's Secret Stuff," Sherman-Palladino, Kirshner, & Chemel, 2007). The scene involves a daughter, Rory, talking with her mother, Lorelai, who has been asked to write a letter of recommendation for a friend who is fighting a child custody battle:[13]

4.10

RORY: **Sounds like you're overthinking this. Maybe if you just put pen to paper.**

LORELAI: **I tried that. I thought, "I'll just sit down and write whatever comes – no judgment, no inner critic." Boy, was that a bad idea.**

RORY: **Really? Why?**

LORELAI: **Because my brain is a wild jungle full of scary gibberish. "I'm writing a letter, I can't write a letter, why can't I write a letter? I'm wearing a green dress, I wish I was wearing my blue dress, my blue dress is at the cleaner's. The Germans wore gray, you wore blue. *Casablanca*. *Casablanca* is such a good movie. *Casablanca*, the White House, Bush. Why don't I drive a hybrid car? I should really drive a hybrid car. I should really take my bicycle to work. Bicycle, unicycle, unitard. Hockey puck, rattlesnake, monkey, monkey, underpants!"[14]**

RORY: **"Hockey puck, rattlesnake, monkey, monkey, underpants?"**

LORELAI: **Exactly. That's what I'm saying. It's a big bag of weird in there.**

The line ending Lorelei's long demonstration of linked but chaotic stream-of-consciousness:

4.11   **"Hockey puck, rattlesnake, monkey, monkey, underpants!"**

seems absurd on its surface. But it serves well as a demonstration of Lorelei's point – that she feels her mind is too scattered to enable the writing of a cogent letter for her friend. So, in this case, the non sequitur is

---

[13] This show was well known for the incredibly fast and witty repartee between its characters, especially the mother and daughter, Lorelai and Rory, respectively – a conversational style caricatured, without doubt, but nonetheless demonstrative of many interesting discourse phenomena.

[14] Thanks to Morgan Colston for bringing this non-sequitur example to my attention.

a demonstration of sorts – the non-sensical meaning of the utterance is used to exhibit Lorelei's perceived non-sensical pattern of her thoughts.

But non sequiturs can also be used for wonderful comic effect, in parodies as well as satire. Consider for example some phrases copied from cover matter in the satirical linguistics journal, *Speculative Grammarian*:

4.12   **"In Search of the Mother of all Dad Jokes"** (January 2019)
        "Brought   to   you   by   Occam's   Safety   Razor[TM]**"**
        (December 2018)
        "Friendly Fire? Don't Flatter Yourself" (November 2018)
        "Now with Additional Functional Projections in Every Issue!"
        (October 2018)
        "'Inconceivable' Merely Indicates a Failure of Imagination"
        (September 2018)
        "The Pen *is* Mightier than the Sword – If Launched with
        Sufficient Speed" (August 2018)
        "A Big Fat 'Meh' on the Great Platonic Likert Scale in the Sky"
        (July 2018)
        "Penguins Need Not Apply" (June 2018)

These examples demonstrate a mixture of non sequiturs, references/ mentions of relevant content (i.e., to a Linguistics readership, e.g., "Functional Projections," "Likert Scales"), resemblances to constructions often used for popular magazine cover items (e.g., "Now with more X in every issue!"), as well as a very serious-seeming overall academic publication context (e.g., historic Victorian-esque black-and-white photographs of serious, unsmiling, presumed scholars, adorn each cover, along with a lengthy editorial staff head).

These combinations can leverage interesting meaning. The mixing of relevant content and the overall parodied context of a (seemingly) serious, rigorous, scholarly publication can lend the non sequiturs, along with the extreme cleverness of the writing, a seeming profundity – as if they contain deep intertextual referentiality, multiple-entendre connections, and overall linguistic brilliance. The subtlety of the linguistic jargon as well as the often over-formalized academic language likely amplify this effect – as if the reader can't help but note the writer's intelligence leading to very high expectation of meaningfulness. Of course, some of the non sequiturs reach this plateau. But others are more of the silly-for-silliness-sake variety, with a little jargon thrown in for good measure.

And of course another bit of meaningfulness arises via the pragmatic effect of humor. In part contributing to this humor is the blatant clash of extremely high-brow context, along with writing quality, contrasted with the overall intent of comedic silliness or parody (albeit of an extremely high quality). The *Monty Python's Flying Circus* comic sketches, one of which is discussed next, also achieve this mixture, as do some cartoon captions in magazines with a highly educated readership (e.g., *The New Yorker*).

For a satire example, consider the following opening excerpt from the *Monty Python* skit, "Woody and Tinny Words" (Chapman, Cleese, Gilliam, Idle, Innes, Jones, Palin, & MacNaughton, 1974). The scene opens on the lawn of an English manor house, with a croquet game set up – with hoops, mallets, and balls visible. Credits appear as the camera zooms in toward the house, reading as follows,

4.13   1942
        ~~Egypt~~
        ~~Ecuador~~
        ~~Ethiopia~~
        England

The image then cuts to an interior drawing room where a father, daughter, and mother are seated having tea, with four house-staff members standing behind them – a cook, a maid, a butler, and a chauffeur. The staff members stand at attention throughout the sketch, and they never speak. The following conversation, of sorts, then takes place among the family members:

4.14

FATHER:	**I say!**
DAUGHTER:	**Yes, Daddy?**
FATHER:	**Croquet hoops look damn pretty this afternoon.**
DAUGHTER:	**Frightfully damn pretty.**
MOTHER:	**They're coming along *awfully* well this year.**
FATHER:	**Yes, better than your Aunt Lavinia's croquet hoops.**
DAUGHTER:	**Ugh! Dreadful tin things.**
MOTHER:	**I did tell her to stick to wood.**
FATHER:	**Yes, you can't beat wood. <Pause.> "Gorn."**
MOTHER:	**What's "gorn," dear?**
FATHER:	**Nothing, nothing – just like the word, it gives me confidence. "Gorn." "Gorn." It's got a sort of *woody* quality about it. "Gorn." ... "Go-o-o-o-orn." ... Much better than "newspaper" or "litter bin."**
DAUGHTER:	**Ugh! Frightful words!**
MOTHER:	**Perfectly dreadful!**
FATHER:	**"Newspaper" – "litter bin" – "litter bin" – dreadful *tinny* sort of word.**

<Daughter screams.>
FATHER: **"Tin, tin, tin."**

<Daughter continues screaming.>
MOTHER: **Oh, don't say "tin" to Rebecca, you know how it upsets her.**
FATHER: **Sorry, old horse.**
MOTHER: **"Sausage."**
FATHER: **"Sausage!" There's a good woody sort of word, "sausage."**
          <Laughs.> **"Go-o-o-o-o-rn."**

The scene continues in this vein with family members spewing out wide
varieties of words, testing for their "woody" versus "tinny" quality, and
the daughter continuing to scream at the latter set.

On the surface, the discourse in this sketch maintains a structural normality about it. The morphosyntax is accurate, and turn-taking as well as
other discourse characteristics remain relatively as usual. But the absurdity
of the main topic – seemingly random words and pseudowords being
uttered aloud and tested for their *woodiness* and *tinniness* – has a non-
sequitur overall quality to it. Many of the particular words being spoken
aloud for testing, as well as where they're sometimes placed in the discourse, and how they're said, also have a non-sequitur feel (i.e., the first
introduction of the pseudoword "gorn" by the father and his drawn-out
utterings of it later).

But, taken together, both the sequence of interspersed non-sequitur
words and the overall non-sequitur quality of the entire sketch nonetheless aren't absurd, at least not entirely. They instead leverage
a satirical quality to the sketch and, importantly, a satire which is dependent on that non-sequitur aspect. The sketch appears in this light as
a send-up of a British upper-class, idle-rich family with nothing better
to do than sit and contemplate the "woody" versus "tinny" quality of
English words. All this takes place as they're ensconced comfortably in
a sitting or drawing room having tea, while their house staff stand as
motionless furniture behind them, ignored completely by the family.

It is here that the non-sequitur nature of individual words and the entire
skit performs its work. It adds to the ridiculousness of this family's central,
focused concern – woody and tinny words and the growth of their croquet
loops, taking place in blissful obliviousness to all other matters. Peppering
that concern with the pseudowords (i.e., "gorn"), and otherwise seemingly random words being contemplated (i.e., "newspaper," "litter
bin," "sausage," "antelope," "seemly," "prodding," "vacuum," "leap,"
"bound," "vole," "recidivist," "caribou," "intercourse," etc.), enhances
the feeling of detachment of this family, and by extension their social

class, from the very real and concrete worries of the working-class populace.

Non sequiturs in general also overlap to a degree with at least vagueness and possibly ambiguity in their ability to alter the train of a conversation and/or the interests or concerns of interlocutors. By a fairly blatant demonstration of detachment from or disregard for a conversation's thread, or even of a full-blown separation from all sensibility, for that matter, a speaker can throw interlocutors off balance. This could lead possibly to their ending the conversation or veering it onto another topic. Such disruption can work fairly powerfully to rattle other people, particularly if the user of the non sequitur alternates their inane contributions with more sensible remarks – a sort of mixture of non sequitur and ambiguity. This can keep interlocutors off kilter, not knowing if their conversational vigilance at any point is worth their while or not (i.e., if they'll be rewarded with something meaningful or absurd).[15]

Surprises

Utterances with more sensibility but which nonetheless startle addressees or other interlocutors due to abrupt topic changes, deviances into overly personal or private content areas, or through other means, can also leverage new meaning. Such surprises can also perform the rattling, social-power machinations of non sequiturs, vagueness, and ambiguity, but they do so through some processes of their own. For an illustration, consider the dialog from a 2019 television commercial "Credit Card Envy" (Rietta, 2019) for comparecards.com, a website enabling customers to compare the contract details of different credit cards:

4.15   <Scene in a cocktail lounge, two men and two women seated comfortably around a table, either as heterosexual couples or just friends. One of the men, Gary, holds up his credit card to show the others.>

GARY: **"Just got this. Amazing. Triple points, all restaurants."**

OTHER MAN   <Voice-over, indicating his thinking to himself. >: *Triple points? How did Gary <derisively> figure that one out? I don't even get double points. Is Gary smarter than me? He's definitely not more handsome.*

<One of the women puts her hand on Gary's shoulder.>

---

[15] And as with other processes on the other-side-of-meaning, non sequiturs can also backfire, where interlocutors might just dismiss a speaker and then ignore them afterward.

OTHER MAN   <Continuing to think to himself>: ***Or maybe he is. Triple
             points are <u>pretty sexy</u>*** <underlined segment thought-voiced in
             a breathy, sexy way>.
OTHER MAN   <Aloud and loudly >: < Long pause > "**. . . I hate you Gary!**"

<The three other people are startled; they stop talking and look uncomfortable.>

This scene caricatures how someone might blurt out a surprising remark
to affect the other interlocutors – not so much strategically perhaps, but as
more of an emotional outburst. But the remark's disruptive effect is
apparent since it both misaligns with the direction of the conversation –
the other three interlocutors had continued their friendly, idle chatting as
the man brooded to himself, and it delves into personal matters (i.e., the
one man's jealousy of the other man, Gary).

Surprises can also drive new meaning and pragmatic effects as addres-
sees/hearers react emotionally, as they consider the reason or excuse for
the surprising comment, and as they think about how to respond. In this
particular scene, for instance, the jealous man loses some social status.
His jealousy seems overblown because the Gary character was only calmly
noting the advantages of his card, with little arrogance on display. So, the
interlocutors likely took the jealous man's outburst as revealing one or
more character flaws in him (e.g., over-competitiveness, insecurity,
inability to control his emotions). So, they react negatively (e.g., feeling
embarrassed for the man, feeling some dislike for him in the moment),
and respond accordingly (e.g., frowning at the man to indicate their
disapproval, but not responding verbally, possibly to shame the man –
had they acted more forcefully he might have gotten defensive and not
realized his own overreaction). But had the Gary character been acting
boastfully or smug about his fantastic credit card, then the jealous man's
comment might have lowered Gary's social status as well – calling out
Gary's own character flaws, were he acting arrogantly or
condescendingly.

The shock value itself of surprise utterances can also enhance some of
the pragmatic effects that might arise – if only because surprises can raise
the arousal level of interlocutors. Surprises can also push interlocutors'
search-for-meaning processing into a higher gear. In these ways, surprise
utterances also belong under the category of deviances, discussed in
Chapter 2, given their ability to drive relevance processing. But their
particular form of deviance – fitting imprecisely into an ongoing discourse – also aptly places them under imprecisions. Indeed, such forms
of imprecision take on a special quality when they're not even linguistic,
but are used nevertheless to seize the conversational floor or to emphasize

a point (i.e., the famous incident of Soviet premier Nikita Khrushchev banging his shoe on a speaking podium, a person pounding a table as they speak, etc.).

Noncommittals

An interesting blend between imprecision and another previously discussed area of other-side-of-meaning – omissions (Chapter 3), or more specifically opportunity cost meanings, is also apparent in the case of noncommittals. In these forms of imprecision, a speaker performs an utterance designed usually to explicitly state their full noncommittal to some matter, at least for the present moment. Indeed, these noncommittals play such a large role in discourse that many have become relatively fixed or colloquialized. Consider the following examples from North American English:

4.16   **Duly noted.**
Noted.
We'll see.
I'll take it under consideration/advisement.
Thank you for sharing.
I'll think about it.
I'll see what I can do.
Leave it with me.

Some noncommittals may carry a bit of a euphemistic denial quality to them. They can be taken as if the speaker really wishes to decline to commit or affirm the matter under discussion, but doesn't want to say so at the moment. Or similarly noncommittals could be seen as a delay tactic, used by the speaker perhaps so they won't have to express their views one way or the other – under the presumption that the person seeking the commitment/affirmation may just drop the matter. Or the delay could allow the speaker to render their verdict through a more distal medium (e.g., through an email instead of face to face). This failure to commit/affirm something, coming at the point where a decision is expected or at least desired from interlocutors, especially if a confirmatory reply is desired, may also taint noncommittals to have this *that-just-means-'no'* tendency. But noncommittals may also be just a pure, honest statement of the speaker's current neutrality – the speaker is leaning neither toward denial nor affirmation, hence their noncommittal remark.

Noncommittals can leverage meaning in a few different ways. One is the just mentioned potential indicator of a withheld but eventual denial.

But noncommittals can also be used for power plays, in the ways already described for other kinds of imprecisions (e.g., keeping the hearers guessing or at least waiting). Relatedly, noncommittals can also be a more direct declaration of authority – the speaker, by virtue of delaying their decision through using the noncommittal, would enhance the perception of their authority. By prolonging the time people have to contemplate the speaker making the decision, the more they're reminded that the speaker has that authority. Speakers of noncommittals may even be trying to actively quell interest in the matter at hand in the same way that ambiguity and non sequiturs can do so – by demonstrating the speaker's at least temporary detachment from that matter, in not wanting to make a decision about it at present.[16]

Columbos

This chapter began with a demonstration of a form of imprecision I termed a *double-back*, as it involved a speaker backtracking, as it were, up the garden path taken by interlocutors, and then traversing down a different interpretive path enabled by a previous utterance. This new path, at least in the discussed example, is one the other interlocutors likely overlooked in their haste to go down the original path, resulting in humor and other pragmatic effects as discussed. The humor readily produced by doubling back is thus a commonly used technique in many forms of jokes and other types of humor (Norrick, 2003, 2009; Giora, 1991). But a related conversational change of direction – also an abrupt one, thus justifying its discussion here – has a very different meaningful outcome. I refer to this form of imprecision as a Columbo, after the 1970s American television character, Frank Columbo, for whom this technique was a trademark.[17]

Columbo was a police detective, if an avant-garde one. He came across as a bit disheveled, and seemingly unorganized and/or forgetful (i.e., often patting the pockets of his trademark frumpy raincoat, looking for a pencil and pad to write with, saying he needed to write things down so he wouldn't forget). His persona thus tended to make suspects or interviewees relax their guards a bit, as they didn't attribute much competence to the man. But his signature technique was to approach whatever key information he seemed to be seeking in a particular interview (e.g., the whereabouts of a suspect at the time of a crime) somewhere in the middle

---

[16] And as with other pragmatic effects, this intent could backfire on a speaker – their showing temporary noncommittal could heighten other people's anticipation for a decision.
[17] Played wonderfully by the late Peter Falk.

of his questioning. He'd thus allow the person to face the hard part of the interview (e.g., stating their legitimate, or false, alibi), and then act as if matters were resolved and start to wind up the conversation. Interviewees could often be seen to visibly relax at this point – thinking the detective had believed them and was moving on.

Then Columbo would start to leave the interview scene (i.e., the room or other location), but at the last moment, he'd pause, usually put a hand to his forehead as if in deep thought or puzzlement, and then turn to the person and say there was just one more additional small matter Columbo had forgotten to ask about or that he didn't understand. The interviewees always made for interesting viewing at this point because they'd often go particularly tense – this last question coming just as they thought they'd escaped further suspicion. Then Columbo would ask usually an unexpected question, or even a seemingly trivial one, but one that nonetheless struck to the heart of the crime and often provided the detective with key insights into the crime's plot, if not its full resolution.

Techniques such as this, including both the initial faux incompetence as well as the unexpected lurch at the end, leverage meaning in interlocutors in a few different ways. The techniques also work in cahoots with one another for the purposes of rooting out deception. The initial disarming technique borrows off a Socratic form of instruction. This Socratic technique used for learning leverages an addressee to discover *some new bit of knowledge* on their own, through a speaker feigning ignorance – or, in essence, through the speaker authorizing the addressee to infer that the speaker is ignorant. So, the addressee must then figure things out on their own. Columbo, on the other hand, would marshal an interviewee to infer that they had *duped the detective*, if the interviewee was lying, such that they'd now think they were likely to get away with the crime. If the interviewee indeed was lying and/or was the actual perpetrator, the faux incompetence could also cause additional pragmatic effects in the interviewee, involving relief, relaxation, confidence, or even a sense of superiority over the detective, for seemingly having outsmarted him.

Columbo, by following up this initial set of leveraged pragmatic effects with the final jugular question, would then produce a second wave of pragmatic effects. Whether a caused *reversal* in a pragmatic effect is itself a form of pragmatic effect may be a matter for discussion. But in the present case, as a form of leveraged meaning, such reversals appears to qualify. In any case, a Columbo-esque form of coda question seems to suddenly leverage: loss of confidence, loss of social superiority, loss of relaxation, as well as likely accompanying nervousness, bursts in cognitive activity (i.e., *What am I going to do now?*), and emotional reactions (e.g., fear, worry, anger). All these effects happening at once in a potential crime suspect, especially if they are actually guilty, can afford still other telltale signs which the detective can then observe to further assess the person's status (i.e., innocent or guilty, as revealed with obvious tension, eye-shiftiness, sudden conversational topic changes, perspiration, suspicious subsequent actions or behavior, etc.).[18]

A slight variation on the Columbo method would involve the interjected question at the end of the period of putting an addressee at ease, to return to some bit of seemingly resolved, agreed upon, or abandoned previous conversational content. The method as described thus far had that jugular question go straight to some key issue involved in the crime (e.g., how the addressee ended up with the murder victim's car keys), which hadn't necessarily been discussed before. But if the final jugular question, which also needn't be a question – it could just rehash previously discussed content some other way – revisits older content, it can add some new twists to leveraged meaning. It could, for instance, tip the hand of the questioner, revealing something they find important or of concern – why else would they have returned to it? Of course, the questioner can also be Machiavellian with this technique – throwing off the interviewee as to what the questioner is genuinely interested in. The revisitation of older content can also parallel the other rattle-inducing techniques being used here, working just like the non-revisiting coda question to make the interviewee worry anew over something they thought was settled.

One last imprecision method will be considered here, and it has arisen a bit already in this discussion of Columbos, as well as in the preceding treatment of non sequiturs. It involves not so much the imprecision of a given short piece of discourse – in not precisely fitting the thread of

---

[18] The Columbo character also used a couple of other techniques, sometimes along with the bait-and-switch interviewing mechanism, to root out deception. One was a pattern of repeated and unannounced pesterings of interviewees or suspects. The detective would show up unexpectedly, sometimes at inconvenient times, with his usual bumbling schtick. He'd arrange these visits in ways that would provoke interviewees, who sometimes had difficulty maintaining their patience with Columbo. These constant visits, over time, sometimes using the faux incompetence and then jugular questions, other times just with straightforward questioning, would build up in the interviewees, further breaking down any deceptions they were trying to maintain. Columbo would also at times feign innocent or even naive interest in mundane objects in the environment – sometimes just a random object in a room, other times objects possibly key to the crime being investigated (e.g., a complicated door lock). These would also exasperate interviewees and further test their patience (as well as add intrigue to the scene). The jugular questions, as well as the interest in potentially crime-related objects, would also make interviewees begin to question their initial perceptions of the detective as incompetent – further rattling them (i.e., *Is this guy the doofus I thought he was?*). All these techniques together often rattled interviewees so much that they would eventually confess.

a conversation or something else. But instead the actual pattern of a sequence of pieces of a discourse can itself vary in its level of precision – the pattern can consistently hold to reasonable levels of expected precision or it can wax and wane, varying in precision across the full conversation.

Discourse Pattern Imprecision

The earlier discussion of non sequiturs mentioned that if a speaker varies their discourse contributions between more non-sequitur kinds of utterances versus more sensible ones, they can particularly rattle or distract interlocutors. People participating in the conversation will come to not know at the onset of the odd speaker's next contribution, whether to take it seriously or not. Assuming the interlocutors don't tune out the speaker altogether, they'll have to adopt an extra level of vigilance to their processing, attempting not just to discern what a contribution means, but also having to decide if an utterance is designed to even make sense or not – and if deemed sensible, then how sensible is it?

The Columbo process treated above also can have a wavering pattern of imprecision – a questioner can mix genuine interest in minutia in environmental objects with more implicative such interests, the latter suggesting to the interviewee that the questionnaire is on to them (e.g., *I know you used this dented metal toaster to stun the victim – how does a toaster ever get dented?*). A questioner could also intermix the designed-to-rattle jugular questions at the end of a questioning session with more innocent coda questions – for instance, a simple question to confirm the spelling of a person's name. Alternating or varying Columbo technique versus decoys or foils like this can doubly undermine an interviewee's self-confidence. The interviewee might realize, for instance, that an unwarranted overreaction to a decoy object interest or coda question could itself be telling about the person's level of honesty.[19]

This brief discussion of imprecision in the pattern of content in a discourse, and its concomitant meaning leveraging and pragmatic effect accomplishment, provides a nice segue to the next chapter and its treatment of *indirectness* as an other-side-of-meaning category. This is especially the case for the first subcategory of indirectness to be discussed, that of language structure. As we have seen with several other-side-of-meaning

---

[19] Many other forms of pattern imprecision can also be used by speakers. For instance, a speaker can zigzag back and forth between sensible but separate meaning streams in a conversation to throw interlocutors off balance. A speaker can also rapidly switch between addressing different interlocutors, who may lose track of which of them is the intended addressee at any given turn, etc.

processes, they can belong to more than one of this book's treated categories. Patterns of imprecision can very well be thought of also as a form of language structure. But their employment of imprecision in their functioning separates them a bit from the other to be discussed forms of language structure in Chapter 5, hence their placement here. Many forms of language structure and other means of indirectness demonstrate the next broad category of other-side-of-meaning processes for leveraging additional meaning and pragmatic effects.

5   Indirectness

Faithfully to represent his subject,
adequately to express his own conceptions,
to make plain all that might be obscure;
these are the first essentials for the pantomime.
—Lucian, "Of Pantomime" (Fowler & Fowler, 1905)

Language Structure

Different forms of language structure serve well to introduce this chapter's presentation of indirectness as a category of other-side-of-meaning. These structures leverage new meaning and pragmatic effects often not by deviating greatly (although some might be considered mild deviations). They don't in general omit anything (with one possible exception, which will be discussed shortly). They aren't particularly imprecise (although maybe a little). Nor do they especially belong to different categories of figurative language (although some might get close). And, although some structures can be playful, and occasionally humorous, they differ from the forms of meaning leveraging treated in Chapter 7 ("Language Play") in that they're not predominantly used for the pragmatic effect of humor. Rather, the forms included here leverage meaning and pragmatic effects in subtle, indirect ways, possibly not even noticeable to speakers or hearers who use them (although they are mostly known phenomena, so some knowledge of the processes might be held by users).

As a brief related side note, Chapter 9 undertakes a lengthy discussion of a number of other language structural characteristics and how they can also affect meaning. Those are predominantly treated under the umbrella of metaphor – i.e., what characteristics can reside within metaphorical constructions to affect or leverage meaning, beyond the essential evocation of a connection between the target and source domains? So, the present discussion will only treat a couple of structural characteristics, but apply them more broadly – beyond their potential functioning within metaphorical constructions.[1]

And to refer to the other forms of indirectness, besides language structure, covered by this chapter, they also might overlap in modest ways with other categories of the other-side-of-meaning included in the book. But these forms also predominantly belong among indirect processes of meaning making, due to the mechanisms they employ. Those mechanisms, akin to language structures, seem to leverage meaning and pragmatic effects in indirect ways (e.g., pinpointing, inference authorization, suggestion), which don't match as precisely those processes used in different other-side-of-meaning categories.

The first form of language structure we'll discuss is actually the exception just mentioned, in terms of employing omission to leverage meaning. But the form treated here is slightly different. Rather than purely or directly *omitting* something, it's more apt to describe the form as *minimizing* something – it includes what it needs, but nothing more, to serve as a bare-bones phrase (i.e., in English).

Asyndeton

The form is asyndeton. Asyndeton essentially takes a standard sentence, clause, or phrase from a language, usually a listing of a sequence of things that normally uses conjunctions and other terms, and distills the phrase down into a minimal structure, typically omitting all conjunctions and often everything else not strictly necessary (Harris, 2013). Some North American English colloquial and some English literary and historical examples are as follows:

5.1   **Been there, done that.**
        Garbage in, garbage out.
        I came, I saw, I conquered.[2]
        I stepped into a deserted corridor clogged with too many smells.
        Carnations, old people, rubbing alcohol, bathroom deodorizer,
        red Jell-O. *The Secret Life of Bees* (Kidd, 2003).

---

[1] The treatment in Chapter 9 also considers how those factors residing within metaphorical constructions can interact with one another, as well as with broader factors – i.e., the particular language genres in which the metaphors are embedded.

[2] I was tempted to include "Badda bing, badda boom" in these examples, given its frequency of usage. But the use of pseudowords tipped this example in my mind more toward an instance of colloquialized language play or word play, which also happens to use asyndeton. If anything this is illustrative again of the mixing of the other-side-of-meaning categories and the difficulty of deciding where a given construction or utterance type might best fit.

An empty stream, a great silence, an impenetrable forest. The air was thick, warm, heavy, sluggish. *Heart of Darkness* (Conrad, 1899).
He was a bag of bones, a floppy doll, a broken stick, a maniac. *On the Road* (Kerouac, 1957).
"Duty, honor, country ..." *Douglas MacArthur*[3]
"Of the people, by the people, for the people ..." *Abraham Lincoln*[4]
" ... it could happen anywhere: in the cities, in the courts, in the city councils, in the state legislatures." *Cesar Chavez*[5]

Asyndeton can leverage a variety of different meanings. In the literary examples above, for instance, asyndeton appears to lend emphasis and a bit of seriousness to the lists of mentioned items. For instance, in the Conrad line, "The air was thick, warm, heavy, sluggish," it seems the minimal form removes any possible distractions that might interfere with the punch of the list of modifiers. The narrator's intense focus on those words, evident by their being the only words used in that part of the construction, can also lend the narrator an attitude of seriousness – his not wanting to deviate onto other details. The words also coming in a steady, beating sequence can possibly intensify the embodied simulations taking place – their sequencing not being interspersed and influenced with morphosyntactic filler (c.f., "The air was thick as well as warm, but also heavy and somewhat sluggish too"). So, asyndeton in these cases appears to lend emphasis and seriousness to the mentioned terms, as well as an intensity of embodied-simulation-driven meaning – an interesting mixture of an other-side-of-meaning structural contribution aiding the input of the sem/syn/sym side (i.e., the embodied simulations).

In the historical examples, which were all from public speeches, asyndeton seems to also convey emphasis. The form enables the speaker to state only those words, allowing a rhythm to be developed when saying them, akin to a drum beat. Emphasis can also be aided in both written and spoken genres, although maybe more so in speech, through timing. The speaker can insert steady or lengthening pauses between the stated items, further contributing to the perception of focus on those list items and on only those list items – their standing out amid the silences surrounding them.

Something a bit different, though, might hold for the colloquial examples. These involve a more extreme form of asyndeton as the entire form is

---

[3] Sylvanus Thayer Award acceptance speech at the US Military Academy, West Point, New York (May 12, 1962).
[4] Gettysburg Address at the Soldiers' National Cemetary, Gettysburg, Pennsylvania (November 19, 1863).
[5] Address to the Commonwealth Club of California, San Francisco, California (November 9, 1984).

allowed to stand by itself, as a speaker's or writer's entire contribution, rather than the asyndeton being embedded within larger utterances or writings. This parallels the type of highlighting via pausing between individual words just mentioned for asyndeton list items spoken aloud. And, indeed, when this isolated full form of asyndeton is used by a speaker to express their opinion or attitude about some referent topic, asyndeton appears to express derision or disapproval (Colston, 2015; Colston & Jindrich, 2000; Lusch & Colston, 2000), especially if the referent is a person (Colston & Brooks, 2008; Enfield & Stivers, 2007).

Several processes might underlie this negativity expression. One could be a simple demonstration on the speaker's or writer's part of their reluctance to discuss something. All else held equal, we tend to wish to spend time with things we like, and not spend time with things we dislike. So, a speaker using the most minimal form of commentary to talk about something could be indicating their negative attitude toward that something via the form of their comment itself. They use the most minimal construction they can to talk about something they dislike – effectively to spend as little time talking about that thing as they can.[6]

Another possible explanation for the negativity expression is a type of iconic minimalism, leveraging off a common conceptual metaphor. We often invoke the conceptual metaphor IMPORTANCE is BIGNESS and its corollary UNIMPORTANCE is SMALLNESS when we talk about things.[7] For example, we might use the following phrases to express the relative importance and unimportance we perceive for different topics,

5.2   **"Check out this story, this is really big."**
        "She's a giant in her field."
        "That's small potatoes."
        "Don't phone me with the small stuff."

So, the asyndeton form could in a way be iconizing this metaphor – using nonfiguratively small utterances to talk about figuratively small – i.e., unimportant or otherwise negative – things.

Another bit of negativity might be conveyed as well by the rhythmic, repetitive pattern to asyndetons – their sequences of minimalist words or

---

[6] Of course, speakers can just take this logic to the extreme and not say anything about a referent topic. And in a context where a speaker, for instance, is asked about that topic and makes no response, such a negative attitude on the topic would be a strong contender interpretation. But the speaker could also use the non-response to indicate something else (i.e., the answerer doesn't like the questioner). So, using a response, but indicating the negative attitude toward the topic via the asyndeton form, can express the negativity but also be a bit clearer.
[7] As well as similiarly patterned conceptual metaphors (i.e., GOODNESS is BIGNESS, BADNESS is SMALLNESS, etc.).

repeating similar constructions. Also borrowing off the general knowledge about liked things warranting our time and effort, and unliked things not warranting them, a speaker could use the rhythmic pattern to show a lack of production effort – i.e., just recycle the same initial construction for the subsequent parts of the asyndeton (e.g., "I went, I ate, I left," or "I walked in, I walked around, I walked out"). This repetition structure can also be iconic for a lack of topical variety. Of course, all these explanations are not mutually exclusive, and different mechanisms might contribute more and less to the expressed negativity in a given usage, as dictated by many contextual parameters.

Sophistication and Formality

The next type of language structure which could possibly leverage meaning is the level of sophistication and/or formality in discourse, which can manifest themselves in several different ways. And, of course, the particular factors affecting sophistication/formality will vary considerably across different typologies and languages. But for English examples, the level of lexical and morphological complexity in constructions, or perhaps even the raw amount of lexical and morphological content, can alter the perceived level of construction sophistication/formality. Compare, for instance, the following two constructions:

5.3   **That particular individual is behaving with an excessitivity of unusualness.**
       That one guy is acting very odd.

Invoking loan words or loan-word constructions from languages with certain stereotypical levels of prestige can also alter perceived language sophistication/formality. For example, consider two possible utterances from a speaker expressing a disinterest in some topic, say, watercolor art:

5.4   **"Sorry, watercolor is not my forte."**
       "Sorry, watercolor is not my thing."

"Not my forte" seems to convey an airiness to it, whether the utterance is intended authentically or ironically. The airiness could arise through simple association – the word "forte" having been paired in the past perhaps with a person deemed sophisticated or urbane, or the word simply coming from a language perceived by a hearer to have high prestige (e.g., French). An airiness, or perhaps even haughtiness, could also arise via more phonemic cues – through a pitch-based diminutiveness in the word's second syllabic nucleus with no coda.[8] The same structure also holds for the first syllable of "forte." These pitch contours could suggest a physical lightness and/or high elevation, either metaphorically or non-figuratively. In relation to the alternative word "thing" in the example, any or all of these mechanisms could contribute to greater perceived sophistication in the use of "forte."

Borrowing words or affixations recognizable as coming from particular topical areas with known characteristics is another means of varying sophistication. For example, please consider the following constructions which use content from academic discipline titles, medicine and history, respectively:[9]

5.5   **"He is very much a sportsologist."**
        "She is definitely into horseology."
        "He is a workaphobic."
        "She suffers from acute stage frightitis."
        "I drive a paleoford."
        "Their racist views hail from the bigotazoic era."

Although it seems examples 5.3 through 5.5 could be used to vary sophistication and/or formality in constructions, the exact *means* by which they do so, and especially the particular outcome of that perceived sophistication/formality, appear a bit non-deterministic. For instance, the level of complexity, or the raw quantity, of lexical and morphological content could operate such that the bulkier item in 5.3 would be perceived as more sophisticated/formal. Alternatively the brevity and perhaps concreteness of the slimmer item in 5.3 could make it appear more sophisticated (and perhaps formal) because it seems to punch out the meaning more clearly. So, how perceived sophistication and formality pan out in a hearer's/reader's judgment would likely be highly influenced by many contextual factors. But the point still holds that lexical and morphological levels of complexity can probably affect perceived sophistication/formality, albeit in complex ways.

The same non-determinism may also hold for the loan words and topical affix borrowings. The latter item in 5.4 may seem more sophisticated (and maybe formal) because it drops the pretension potentially residing in the first item in 5.4 – i.e., being sophisticated by not being

---

[8] If taken as haughty, the comment might be heard as ironic, but the phonemic characteristics still apply.

[9] As yet another example of other-side-of-meaning categorization difficulty, these could all also readily fall under language play or word play. But again, as they don't seem constructed exclusively for the purposes of humor, I've included them here.

pretentious. On the other hand, the borrowed French word could lend that item more perceived sophistication just due to potential perceptions about French as a prestige language. The items in 5.5 are perhaps the messiest in this regard. The cleverness in creating some of the mixes (e.g., "... workaphobic," vis-à-vis, *workaholic*) might lend them greater perceived sophistication. But they might also be taken as silly. As was the case for the lexical/morphological complexity, when it comes to conveying sophistication/formality, much seems to depend on the contexts in which the constructions are used. But it still appears as if these structural variations can affect sophistication and formality.

But, however the particular driver of sophistication accomplishes its task, lending a note of sophistication/formality to an utterance can leverage new meaning and pragmatic effects. For instance, saying something is not one's "forte" can enhance a potential ironic hearing of the utterance, as mentioned. The initial bulkier comment in 5.3 could also enhance the level of disdain expressed about the oddly behaving referent person. A bit of a contrast effect could underlie the enhanced disdain – the greater sophistication in the utterance making the odd behavior appear even stranger in comparison. Or the trustworthiness and/or confidence in the speaker's assessment could increase with their using the more sophisticated utterance, making the comprehender attend more significantly to the deviance from normality in the referent person's behavior. Similar mechanisms could be at work in 5.5 – a bit of the mastery display pragmatic effect could drive one's perception of the speaker using the borrowed affixation, possibly increasing the speaker's perceived sophistication (with the concomitant meaningful changes just described – essentially an intensification of the meaning). Or the speaker's perceived sophistication could drop if the pseudowords are taken as silly, perhaps weakening the strength of the expressed meaning.

Diminutivization

The next reviewed form of language structure which can create pragmatic effects and leverage new meaning is diminutivization (Schneider & Strubel-Burgdorf, 2012; Vrabie, 2017; Savickiene & Dressler, 2007; Sicherl, 2018; Sicherl & Zele, 2018). Often appearing in pet names, affectionate names, and nicknames, diminutivization involves affixations or alterations to words or phrases resulting usually in more close front unrounded or high front unrounded vowel sounds and/or higher pitched phonemes. Sometimes shortening of the construction also occurs, along with other similar changes.[10] The label for the phenomenon is apropos because one of the purported mechanisms enabling diminutivization to convey its leveraged meaning is to exhibit the referent as something small in size or stature and/or young in age (i.e., the adjectival form of diminutive as *very small*). The underlying principle being possibly just the simple physics of sound production – small things tend to make high-pitched sounds (i.e., children and piccolos), where larger things make lower-pitched sounds (i.e., adults and tubas). This all corresponds to the sizes of wavelengths that can be produced in differently sized things – the smaller resonance chambers in small objects producing smaller wavelengths (i.e., higher pitch), and the larger chambers in larger objects enabling larger wavelengths (i.e., lower pitch).

Some common North American English examples (these overheard by the author) are people's nicknames, some instances of infant- or child-directed speech, or some terms of affection:

5.6   **Mickey or Mikey (Mike or Michael)**
       Grammy or Granny (Grandmother)
       Ricky (Ray)
       Dipey (Diaper)
       Cuppy (Cup)
       Mingy (Blanket)
       Cutie (Cute)
       Lovski (Love or Lover)
       Morgie (Morgan)

By rendering the referent topic as young or as small, in either a figurative or nonfigurative sense, we can trigger a number of meaningful influences in comprehenders. In many mammals, and especially in humans, young members of a species can trigger affectionate feelings in adult members, who find the youths' appearance pleasing (i.e., cute). First termed the "baby schema" (Lorenz, 1943), the physical appearance of human infants (as well as infants of other species) can make adult humans feel endeared to the infants, experience more tenderness toward them, to exhibit more motivation to protect and care for them, and to overall act less aggressively.

A number of reasons for the existence of this process have been put forth. One is that the reaction in adult humans and the characteristic appearance of infant humans (as well as in other animal infants) coevolved as a means of ensuring infants' health, safety, and well-being. It

---

[10] A related means of diminutivization is more formally morphological – through the use usually in English of suffixation (e.g., adding, "–let" or "–ette" to roots, as in "piglet," "booklet," "diskette," or "dinette").

could also be one of a number of neurally hardwired processes in us that ensure our intricate social connectivity (see Chapter 8 for an extensive review of these processes). Other accounts have argued that our finding infants cute provides a motivation for us to have babies – this, one could argue, is also one of the reasons for the experienced pleasure of sexual activity.[11] Whatever the driving mechanisms, given human infants' significantly greater dependence upon adult and other caregivers at birth, stemming ultimately from our cranial development which forces us to be born much earlier developmentally compared to other primates, the presence of such a process in us is not surprising.

So, rendering a referent topic with characteristics of infancy – i.e., youth, smallness, etc. – with the corresponding feelings that go with it – caring, affection, love, etc. – is a ready means of expressing that one feels those feelings for that referent topic. This explains then why diminutivization is commonly found in pet names, nicknames, and other terms we use for people, animals, or things to which we feel love or affection, or even just a strong friendship or affinity.[12]

Of course, diminutivization isn't always used with positive social intent. Speakers can attempt to engineer a drop in a person's social status by using diminutive terms to refer to that person. For example, in the 2016 US presidential campaign, then candidate Donald Trump infamously referred to US Senator Marco Rubio as "Little Marco" and "Little Rube" (Berenson, 2016; Richter, 2015). Trump used a similar diminutive term along with implied profanity techniques to refer to US Representative Adam Schiff (e.g., "Little/Liddle Adam Schiff/Schitt") (Mervosh, 2018).[13]

Diminutiveness can also be used for many other things than expressing affection or derision. It can be used in labeling, to indicate something is nonthreatening or oriented for children (i.e., "slinky," "Bop-Me," "My Little Pony," "Barbie," "Winnie the Pooh," "Gumby," "TeleTubbies," "Barney," etc.). It can be used to express or hyperbolize actual physical or metaphorical smallness (e.g., "the teeny, tiniest of violins," "an itsy bitsy spider," "just a teeny smidgen of a slice," "it's only a wee bit of a problem"), and it can, of course, be embedded as a characteristic in different other-side-of-meaning processes like hyperbole and metaphor, as just mentioned and illustrated, but also verbal irony (e.g., "Aww, did

[11] Among many other possibilities (e.g., social bonding, building intimacy, expressing devotion, pleasure for its own sake).
[12] A corroborating process to this explanation is the use of terms for loved ones that bear characteristics of infant-directed speech (i.e., reduplication ["my little boo boo"]).
[13] The Representative Schiff example is also discussed briefly in Chapter 9.

you hurt your little pinky," said to a large man who hit his hand with a hammer), idioms ("easy-peasy"), and many others.

Sound Symbolism

The final language structure we'll consider here makes a nice follow-up to the preceding treatment of diminutivization, and may even be considered a broader category to which diminutivization belongs – sound symbolism. Sound symbolism is a somewhat older idea – having been claimed by one account, among other diverse origin suggestions, to have arisen as long ago as in ancient China (Schuessler, 2007). The classic "bouba kiki" research (Kohler, 1929, 1947) revealed that people will reliably associate objects with round and bulbous shapes versus sharp and spiky ones with labels resembling the terms "bouba" and "kiki," respectively.[14] Sound symbolism was further catalyzed as an idea by Dwight Bolinger and others, largely in the 1950s (Bloomfield, 1933; Bolinger, 1950; Brown, 1958; Brown, Black, & Horowitz, 1955; Markel & Hamp, 1960).

In more modern work, the "bouba kiki" effect has been refined to the more specific claim that continuant consonants (those allowing a continuous airflow or vocal cord vibration) are routinely associated by experimental participants with rounded objects or shapers, where stops (phonemes created when airflow or vocal vibrations are stopped) are instead associated regularly with sharp or spikey objects or shapes (Westbury, 2018). This general finding has garnered significant empirical support (Davis, 1961; Holland & Wertheimer, 1964; Maurer, Pathman, & Mondloch, 2006; Nielsen & Rendall, 2011; Parault & Schwanenflugel, 2006; Ramachandran & Hubbard, 2001; Sidhu, Pexman, & Saint-Aubin, 2016; Westbury, 2005; Westbury, Hollis, Sidhu, & Pexman, 2018).

One way to conceptualize these findings is through the embodied experience of either producing or comprehending these corresponding "bouba" and "kiki" phonemes. In the case of pronouncing or hearing "bouba" phonemes, the experienced pattern of an uninterrupted speech stream might better match the perceived shape pattern of smoothly round shapes or objects – which also bear no sudden interruptions in their contours. The opposite holds for the "kiki" phonemes, whose interrupted speech stream patterns, when pronounced or heard, better fit the pattern of angular interruptions perceived in spikey objects or shapes. So, according to this view, "bouba" *means* round, and "kiki" *means* spikey, because patterns in our pronunciation speech streams for those kinds of terms fit

---

[14] Kohler's studies didn't use these exact words, but the effect has come to be widely referred to with the terms "bouba" and "kiki" – or the "bouba kiki" effect.

well with patterns in our motor and sensory experiences when encountering round and spikey things respectively.

A recent series of studies conducted in our lab began to investigate other simple physical characteristics of pronunciation or hearing to determine if they might also give rise to linguistic meaning. Among the characteristics investigated thus far are the speed with which a sequence of phonemes can be produced, the pitch of some sets of phonemes, and alterations in the types of phonemes used in sequences (e.g., stops and vowels versus fricatives and vowels).

In one study, participants were instructed to interpret the meanings of pseudowords which varied in their ease of physical pronounceability (Colston & Kinney, 2015; Colston & Kodet, 2008). In the first task, participants were asked to pronounce aloud the pseudowords presented one at a time in isolation (participants were tested individually, so they didn't hear other speakers saying the words) and to rate the degree of "speech-muscle constriction" the pronunciation of each word required. In a second experiment (with different participants), the pseudowords were used to describe situations designed for being ambiguous with respect to any emotional tension they might normally have. Each situation could be potentially tense or relaxed (e.g., "The mood in a classroom on the first day of class"). Participants in this task rated the perceived tension in the situations. A final study (also new participants) then placed participants into physically tense or physically relaxed bodily states, through instructions on how to position and hold their bodies during the task. Participants then rated the tenseness of the situations from experiment 2, this time when presented with no pseudowords accompanying them.

The first task found that pseudowords designed to require more "speech-muscle constriction" (e.g., "srensh") were rated as being harder to pronounce compared to the lower "speech-muscle constriction" pseudowords (e.g., "sreele").[15] The second task revealed that neutral situations described with the low-constriction pseudowords were rated as less emotionally tense than the same situations described with the high-constriction pseudowords. The third task found that putting people in demonstrably tense physical bodily states (they were instructed to stand, bend all their joints, clench and hold all their muscles, and then complete the rating task holding this posture) produced higher situation tenseness

---

[15] The sets of pseudowords were kept as similar as possible on factors other than the "speech-muscle constriction" difference, and they did not readily resemble other English words.

ratings than putting people in relaxed physical bodily states (participants being instructed to sit, relax fully, and then do the ratings).

A follow-up study addressed the possibility of semantic priming driving the results of the first study. A first task in this study gave all the pseudowords plus some fillers in a random order to a new group of participants. They were asked to generate synonyms for each pseudoword's meaning (they were told the pseudowords were real words from a nearly extinct language – with the words' meanings corresponding to the "physical characteristics of things"). The produced synonyms were then given by themselves to two other different groups of participants. The first group rated the similarity of each synonym's meaning to the meaning of the word "tight." The second group rated how similar each synonym's meaning was to the word "loose."

Comparisons between the average ratings given to the high-constriction synonyms (i.e., synonyms made from the high-constriction pseudowords) versus the low-constriction synonyms did not differ in either group (i.e., in the group making the similar-to-"tight" and in the group giving the similar-to-"loose" ratings). People in the original tasks were thus not being reminded in any systematic way of actual English words such as "tight" or "loose," or words with meanings similar to "tight" and "loose," when working with the pseudowords. The findings thus isolate the explanation for the first study that people were using low-level embodied information (i.e., how much muscle tension is required to pronounce some words) to derive the broader semantic meanings of those words.

So, based on this and other studies investigating sound symbolism, relatively low-level embodied experiences in the actual speaking and perhaps hearing of sounds in a language can leverage meaning fairly directly. If a speaker using an other-side-of-meaning process, such as metaphor, wishes to conjure, convey, or enhance an experience of ease, smoothness, or lack of interruption, for example, she could readily use sound symbolism to accomplish this task (e.g., "We breezed with ease through these meetings"). Where a speaker wishes to do something similar for an experience of difficulty, roughness, or being interrupted, that too can be readily accomplished (e.g., "We stumbled with difficulty across our appointments").

Standard Indirectnesses

A number of standard indirect forms have also been shown to leverage meaning and produce pragmatic effects. One of them also excels at one of the three primary reasons it seems we have indirectness in our repertoire of communication techniques in the first place – for managing face and compliance issues in our dealings with other people. As some of these issues are also discussed in Chapter 8, in the discussion on social motivations and social needs, I'll only discuss briefly here how the form operates. More attention will be paid instead to the background factors that warrant the form's mere existence.

Indirect Requests

One of the simplest ways languages can be divided – a division constituting one of the earliest metalinguistic lessons taught to young children, and indeed something that can show itself in infants' protolanguage before the first-word stage – is the difference between the declarative and the interrogative, or between statements and questions. One gets a period; the other gets a question mark. Although this division between statements and questions is fundamental, it is not balanced. All one need do is count the relative number of question marks versus periods in most written documents and the larger relative quantity of statements over questions in our overall discourse would become apparent. Why might this be the case? Why do we say things to others more often than we ask things of them?

One possibility is that interrogatives – questions or requests – place a greater burden on addressees than do statements, at least en masse and on average.[16] For statements, we place a *modest* burden on addressees – to listen and perhaps respond in kind – a burden addressees can sometimes escape, even without detection, by just not listening or by feigning listening. But listening still isn't always terribly demanding. Questions and requests, however, invoke a larger social imposition – we are placing an onus on someone when requesting or asking to do more than just passively absorb our statements and then perhaps swap roles. When requesting or asking, we want more. And addressees feel the pressure of that want.

So, questions and requests can entail more social risks. We somehow need to place our request/question onus on someone without harming their social motivations or our social relationship. We also need to have our requests met or our questions answered – that's the whole reason we *made* the request or *asked* the question. So, that all this additional social care must be taken could explain part of the relatively lower frequency of interrogatives versus declaratives – interrogatives come with baggage, so we don't move them unless we have to.

But sometimes we must make a request or ask something of another person. And for that we need tools to address the social burdens

---

[16] Another possibility is just that we have more to say than we have to ask (or to ask for). And, of course, context as always matters – i.e., more questions would obviously be found in some settings (e.g., hearings, interviews) than others (e.g., news reports).

imposed. Indirect requests seem to handle these situations fairly well (Gibbs 1981a, 1981b, 1983; Colston, 2015).[17] Indirect requests can enhance addressee compliance and preserve interlocutors' face through a couple of related mechanisms. Indirect requests, at least in English, first often use modal constructions. These extend some flexibility to addressees by indirectly tabling (in the British English sense – of putting out on the table for consideration) an "out" for the addressee. The requestee is provided a means of denying the request if they wish, or if they must, yet still save face (i.e., the person does not *possess* a pen for loaning to the asker who had queried, "*Would* you have a pen I could borrow?"). The consideration implied by providing the "out," as well as the thoughtfulness shown in having constructed the request aptly – i.e., by determining what the most likely obstacle to granting the request would be – can enhance the chances of compliance. And, indeed, in doing all this work in constructing the request carefully, the speaker humbles him- or herself a bit, which might offset the onus they're putting on the requestee, and also add a bit more to marshaling compliance (i.e., the asker has put himself out for the addressee, so the addressee may be more motivated to respond in kind). Altogether, these processes, if used with skill, can enable the compliance – i.e., the requester gets what they need, and everyone saves face.[18]

Indirect requests thus seem to work a bit within the world of a "strategic speaker" (James & Pinker, 2010) as well as in the domain of politeness (Brown & Levinson, 1989), in that speakers are aiming for getting compliance out of addressees but they're doing so by also managing face issues. But other forms of indirect language may not always concern themselves fully with politeness/face issues. We've seen this in the realm of figurative language, where events may have turned out in violation of generally positive expectations, desires, preferences, etc., about the world (i.e., when things go bad). These situations can give rise to forms of figurative language used by speakers to express frustration, to belittle or blame situations or other people, to point out the violation of

---

[17] It should be noted that many designations place indirect requests under the umbrella of figurative language – a categorization I do not necessarily dispute. Their being placed here under "indirect language" is partly due to their label, but also in part because the degree of separation between their surface form and their intended meaning seems a little less than that found in the figurative forms treated in Chapter 6. But either way, different ways of categorizing figurative versus indirect forms of language (i.e., figurative is a subcategory of indirect, they're separate categories, they're indistinguishable, etc.) do not obviate discussing how the different forms and/or subforms function.

[18] But, as with everything, usage of this process can backfire on a speaker unless certain conditions are met (Blankenship & Craig, 2005).

expectations, or for other negative purposes (i.e., to complain). Sometimes, those negative expressions are tempered to varying degrees[19] – i.e., if people express their negativity but simultaneously attempt to massage social issues (i.e., using a verbal irony to register one's dissatisfaction, but also leveraging some humor to, "sugar the pill," as it were), other times speakers let the negativity fly (i.e., "salting the wound," Colston, 1997). The next standard form of indirectness often resides in this realm of *complaining when things go bad*, although they can appear more broadly. These are lateral statements.[20]

Lateral Statements

This form is interesting as it abuts and can morph readily into the figurative form of verbal irony or sarcasm (Gibbs & Mueller, 1988).[21] But it has an important focal difference that warrants it being discussed here as an indirectness form. Lateral statements are indirect via a pretense about the intended addressee's identity. The statements involve a speaker expressing him- or herself, usually aloud, sometimes without a specific *purported* addressee being involved – as if the speaker were merely voicing a thought. But other times lateral statements are performed *as if* a broad audience were the intended addressee (i.e., every person present). Or they can be performed *as if* one person or a small group of people is/are the specific addressee(s). But in each of these cases, a person other than the purported addressee is actually the intended mark of the comment – this indirectness-via-purported-addressee is the signature characteristic of the form. These remarks present a bit of a contrast to indirect requests because they're declarative, and they present a broader range of compliance pressure. But they are also quite social and they use indirectness to negotiate this sociality.

For example, consider the following three statements for possible use by a speaker. Imagine the speaker lives in a house with several other people, one of whom has a habit of opening multiple kitchen cabinets when searching for something, and then leaving those cabinets wide open.

[19] Something certain forms of figurative language accomplish quite well (Colston, 2015).
[20] Indirect as well as figurative language often appears in situations like these where negativity arises. They seem to do so as they provide speakers a toolkit for managing negativity, as do indirect requests, which afford tools for managing compliance (Colston, 2015).
[21] Colston (2000a) investigated similar forms where speakers use ironic statements that are actually true, but don't match the situation at hand (e.g., a car driver fails to signal a turn, nearly causing an accident and the person in the other cars says, "I just love when people use their turn signals"). These remarks differ, though, in that there is no feigning of the intended addressee.

This has been an annoyance to the speaker, who has asked politely in the past for the person to close the cabinets when they're through with them. The speaker now enters the kitchen and all the cabinets are again wide open. So, the speaker says aloud:

5.7a   **"I wish people would close kitchen cabinets around here!"**

5.7b   **"I actually close cabinets when I'm done with them."**

5.7c   **"I close kitchen cabinets, unlike some people I know."**

One can also imagine any of these remarks said in one of three ways. One is saying the remark loudly enough for everyone in the house to hear, but no one is immediately present in the kitchen (although all the housemates are at home). The second would be saying the remark as if directed to one person (or more than one) in the room, but the guilty cabinet culprit is also present. The third would be whispering the comment as if directed to one or more people in the room, again with the cabinet culprit present, but the whisper is delivered loudly enough for all to hear.

In each of the comments, and in all three modes of delivery, the intended addressee is the cabinet culprit. But the comments are delivered as if another person(s) were the addressee. We can first ask why this indirectness is used. We can then consider how this addressee-pretense in its different versions can leverage new meaning and pragmatic effects. It turns out, not surprisingly, that the new meaning and pragmatic effects explain in part why the indirectness is used.

Situations like this are essentially confrontations. A person has politely and not inappropriately requested a change in another person's moderately inconsiderate behavior, but the requestee has not complied.[22] Now the person wishes to confront the requestee on their compliance failure. So, these situations are also ones involving a person seeking compliance from another, as in indirect requests. But here the stakes are raised because that compliance has been refused at least once. These parameters likely explain the nature of the range of remarks in 5.7. They're still attempting to leverage compliance a bit. But they've also pulled off the politeness gloves a bit as well, because the speaker's frustration has increased due to having a previous polite request be rebuffed. The comments are thus indirect for two reasons. Most people generally don't like confrontation but must occasionally face them – indirectness is often the

---

[22] The situation could also change considerably if the cabinet culprit had agreed previously to change their behavior, versus had they not agreed.

compromise people find in these situations.[23] Indirectness, somewhat unusually, can also leverage negativity in different ways, which aids the speaker's motivation to vent some frustration.[24]

By pretending to register the complaint to a different addressee than the cabinet culprit, the speaker might be bending more toward negativity-reducing compliance leveraging – the culprit might hear the comment, note the "out" in that they weren't directly addressed, feel some moderate guilt accordingly, and then intend to comply with the desired cabinet-closing behavior going forward. Comment 5.7a, delivered as if to no particular addressee, might be most successful in this regard.

The comment in 5.7c delivered in the stage-whisper mode, though, might be the least successful at accomplishing compliance because it first pulls two political moves.[25] It draws in one or more other specific people into the speaker's perspective – i.e., their taking the speaker's side in complaining about the culprit. It also positions the culprit's behavior (i.e., not closing cabinets) as being inferior to the speaker's (i.e., closing cabinets) implying perhaps that the culprit is inferior. But 5.7c said in the stage whisper also leverages the feigned bit of privacy – spoken as if privately to the faux addressee(s) but making that pretense transparent.

Conversely, by making the political moves and feigning privacy in 5.7c, the speaker might be leaning more in the direction of venting their frustration and anger – as 5.7c is probably the least likely of the three remarks to produce compliance, especially if said in the stage whisper. Indeed, even if the culprit felt guilty, wished to express an apology, and planned to change their future behavior, the heavy-handedness of 5.7c could make the culprit balk. They might instead stubbornly continue with their inconsiderate behavior – now conducted in retaliation for the slam they felt from the speaker using 5.7c and delivering it in the stage whisper. This new motivation for the behavior and potentially increased

---

[23] This combination of confrontation, negativity enhancement, and indirectness can be volatile. The speaker's opting to leverage more negativity in a confrontation situation but doing so indirectly can backfire on them. The indirectness can be an invitation for the target of the remark to retaliate. In the midst of their getting their back up in registering the negativity, the target person might be motivated to see weakness in the speaker's use of indirectness.

[24] It is not unusual for indirectness or figurativity to be able to accomplish oppositional things, even simultaneously – verbal irony is adept at both diluting and enhancing criticism, for instance (Colston, 2015).

[25] The term "stage whisper" is an interesting metaphorical borrowing of the less figurative use of the term to apply to theater performances where an actor must convey that they're whispering some lines of dialog, yet speak the lines loudly enough to be heard by the audience.

determination on the part of the culprit might make future compliance and social harmony well-nigh impossible.[26]

The way in which the methods of leveraging negativity work – bringing in an accomplice, making the culprit's behavior look especially bad, and feigning secrecy with a faux addressee, is to leverage off people's social needs and motivations (see Chapter 8 for more details on this). Briefly, we're motivated to both get/stay socially connected and to hold/raise our social status. The speaker using any of the 5.7 remarks as if directed to a specific other person(s), relative to having feigned no particular addressee (i.e., in the thinking-aloud delivery), thus pushes social buttons. It threatens the culprit's social *status* (i.e., first, engineering two or more people to be against the culprit, rather than just one, the speaker, and second, making the culprit [who does not close cabinets] look inferior relative to the speaker [who does close cabinets]).[27] The feigned secrecy in the stage whisper delivery then additionally threatens the culprit's social *connection* (i.e., destabilizing the culprit's social connection to the person feigned as the speaker's addressee – through the speaker saying negative things about the culprit behind their back, or feigned as such).

Pushing people's social buttons by threatening to gang up on them, weaken their alliances, turn other people against them, and comparatively make them look bad publicly are powerful influences on people – triggering strong social meanings and social motivations in them to affect their thinking and behavior. But we don't have to necessarily go this far to affect others' behavior. We can use other less pointed methods to give rise to meaning and pragmatic effects in people – perhaps ultimately to affect their thinking and behavior. These methods may not upset people's strong social needs but they can still be a bit distasteful. Accordingly, we've also developed ways of using these methods indirectly, in large part because the indirectness affords a degree of plausible deniability – a speaker can attempt to leverage meaning/thinking/behavior in others with less than saintly methods, but the speaker can deny this intent if they're called out.

Innuendos

Speakers can use a fairly straightforward inference authorization technique when stating innuendos, but the technique comes with a twist. In innuendos, a speaker remains agnostic about that authorization – he/she sets up the inference so the addressee *could* make it, but the speaker can

---

[26] A good lesson in the problems with escalating conflict and confrontation.

[27] Comments 5.7b and 5.7c might vary somewhat on this one point – both making the comparison between the speaker's *good* behavior and the culprit's *bad* behavior, but 5.7c makes that comparison more explicitly.

also claim later that they never *intended* for the addressee to make it, that the surface meaning of the utterance was all that was ever intended. In this way, speakers can get away with some fairly distasteful meaning leveraging.

Consider for instance the following two comments. The first is collo-quialized practically as an English construction used as a veiled threat. The second similarly conveys a veiled bribe. Both are structured to enable plausible deniability:

5.8a   **"Nice car you have here. It would be too bad if something were to happen to it."**

5.8b   **"It would be nice if we could settle things right here, officer, rather than your having to do a lot of paperwork."**

The interesting thing about the plausible deniability in innuendos is that addressees or other hearers likely note, if only subconsciously, this characteristic of the remark. Indeed, a form of back and forth contempla-tion of the likelihood of the remarks being intended as bribes or threats leading to the eventual noting of their plausible deniability might heighten the impact of the comments on the hearers. For instance, a speaker who might be a bit naive in picking up these innuendos might first interpret the remark on its surface form (i.e., *it would be a bummer if my nice car got damaged*). But the hearer might subsequently draw the potential inference of the threat (i.e., *I should do what this person wants because he might be the person to damage my nice car – that's why he brought it up*). Subsequently still the hearer might reject that inference (i.e., *no way, this person couldn't possibly be threatening me*), and then go on to reject the rejection (i.e., *or could he?*). The endpoint of this process might be the hearer realizing that they're in a difficult position – the speaker has in fact, threatened him, but there is no way the hearer can call the person out on the threat. The hearer thus has very little recourse. All of this can lead the hearer to react with much worry or fright – in effect enhancing the impact of the innuendo.[28]

Of course, many other more benign forms of authorized inferences are also indirect. Simple hints and/or indirect suggestions can also lead addressees to infer additional meanings (e.g., "Mallorca is really nice in the autumn" – said when a couple are contemplating vacation locations, leading to the inference that the speaker *would like to go to* Mallorca for the

---

[28] Sadly for anyone who has experienced the victimization of being falsely accused of something, another possible usage of innuendo, the fear and worry displayed at realizing the spot you're in often resembles the reaction to that of an actual guilty person (i.e., people *correctly* accused of doing the misdeed). The worry we have that *people will think we've done something wrong* looks very much like the worry we have when *we've done something wrong.*

vacation). They might also involve a degree of plausible deniability (e.g., a wealthy member of the board of directors of an art museum saying the following about an enormous *anonymous* recent donation [from her] to the museum's operating fund, "It is always wonderful when a person can support the things they love"). But these cases of more positively intended indirectnesses don't come as obviously laden with impact as the negatively intended ones.

This chapter has reviewed a few common means of using indirectness to leverage meaning and pragmatic effects in other people. These means, although variable, nonetheless begin to show patterns of consistency in their forms (i.e., the colloquialized English veiled-threat construction, the use of modals in English indirect requests, etc.). But the next category of other-side-of-meaning processes to be considered takes this form consistency and even fixedness to a much higher level. The next chapter will review figurative language and its encapsulated major processes of leveraging other-side-of-meaning pragmatic effects and meaningful content.

6   Figurativeness

Both Light and Shadow
are the dance of love ...
— Jalal ad-Din Muhammad Rumi, "The Meaning of Love" (Chopra, 1998)

One Big Happy Figurative Family?

In Kim Stanley Robinson's novel *2312* (Robinson, 2012), one of the main characters, Swan, who is mourning the death of her grandmother, maintains an ongoing testy relationship with her head-implanted quantum computer, Pauline – the two often arguing about many things, including rhetorical devices. Consider the following excerpt, where Swan introduces Pauline to another primary character, Wahram (Pauline can communicate with people other than Swan via a speaker and microphone on Swan's neck [pp 52–54]):

6.1

"What kind of artificial intelligence are you?" [Wahram] asked.
"I am a quantum computer, model Ceres 2196a."
 "I see."
"She is one of the first and weakest of the qubes," Swan said. "A feeb."
Wahram pondered this. Asking How smart are you? was probably never a polite thing. Besides, no one was ever very good at making such an assessment. "What do you like to think about?" he asked instead.
Pauline said, "I am designed for informative conversation, but I cannot usually pass a Turing test. Would you like to play chess?"
He laughed. "No."
Swan was looking out the window. Wahram considered her, went back to focusing on his meal. It took a lot of rice to dilute the fiery chilies in the dish.

Swan muttered bitterly to herself, "You insist on interfering, you insist
on talking, you insist on pretending that everything is normal."
The qube voice said, "Anaphora is one of the weakest rhetorical devices,
really nothing more than a redundancy."
"*You* complain to *me* about redundancy? How many times did you parse
that sentence, ten trillion?"
"It did not take that many times."
Silence. Both of them appeared to be done with speech.
"Do you study rhetoric?" Wahram asked.
The qube voice said, "Yes, it is a useful analytic tool."
"Give me an example, please."
"When you say exergasia, synathroesmus, and incrementum together in
a list, it seems to me that you have thereby given an example of all three
devices in that same phrase."
Swan snorted at this. "How so, Socrates?"
"'Exergasia' means 'use of different phrases to express the same idea,'
'synathroesmus' means 'accumulation by enumeration,' and 'incre-
mentum' means 'piling up points to make an argument.' So listing
them does all three, yes?"
"And what argument would you be piling up points to?" Swan asked.
"That I was giving you too much credit in thinking you were using many
different devices, when really you only have the one method, because
these are distinctions without a difference."
"Ha-ha," Swan said sarcastically.
But Wahram had only just kept himself from laughing.
The qube went on: "One could also argue that the classical system of rhetoric
is a false taxonomy, a kind of fetishism –
"Enough!"
The silence stretched on.

What is most interesting about this excerpt is how its contained discussion of "rhetorical devices" is cast more stealthily within a discourse
loaded with other figurative forms – and ones which might even go
unnoticed in casual reading. Indeed, one can identify at least the following figures or their near equivalents, besides the four "rhetorical devices"
explicitly mentioned (emphases added):

Metaphor: "She is one of the ... *weakest* of the qubes, ..." "And what
argument would you be *piling up* points to?" "The qube *went on.*" "The
silence *stretched on.*"
   Understatement and hyperbole: "Asking How smart are you? *was probably
never* a polite thing. Besides, *no one was ever* very good at making such an assessment."
   Metonymy: "It took a lot of rice to dilute the fiery chilies in the *dish.*"
   Rhetorical question and hyperbole: "*How many times did you parse that
sentence, ten trillion?*"
   Verbal irony: "How so, *Socrates?*" "*Ha-ha, ...*"
   Simile: "... the classical system of rhetoric is ... *a kind of* fetishism –..."

One of the richest ways in which the other-side-of-meaning contributes to human meaningful linguistic communication is through the use of figurative language. Although the actual embarkation point from nonfigurative to figurative language is notoriously difficult to pinpoint, and may not even exist (Gibbs & Colston, 2012), there nonetheless does exist extensive territory on the figurative side of this fuzzy line, with a large population of figurative inhabitants living there. By some designations, anything from dozens to hundreds of such residents can be identified.

This chapter will provide a discussion of this range of figures and other rhetorical devices. We'll consider why some figures have been studied more than others and briefly review those figures garnering the most attention. A brief discussion of the constructions that figures can take and how those affect meaning and pragmatic effects will then be provided. A new twist to understanding how figurative language leverages pragmatic effects through embodied simulations follows. The chapter concludes with a delineation of the handful of very generic forms which figurative language families seem to distill into. This satellite view of figurativity reveals some key insights into how figurativity aligns with our cognitive and other functioning, and how figurativity can extend beyond language.

The Figurative Mainstream

A page on Wikipedia labeled "Glossary of rhetorical terms" (accessed November 9, 2018) lists approximately 450 such terms. This list, as do many similar indexes, lumps together what is referred to here as figurative forms of language (e.g., metaphor, verbal irony, idioms) along with "rhetorical devices," à la the Pauline character in example 6.1, as well as many stylistic and structural spoken and written techniques (e.g., "Anadiplosis – repeating the last word of one clause or phrase to begin the next," "Noema – speech that is deliberately subtle or obscure," "Pleonasm – the use of more words than necessary to express an idea").

Many classification systems such as this exist – attempting to organize, group, and define forms such as these. These systems can lead to disagreements, which sometimes can be heated. Indeed, warring camps and cliques of scholars, writers, and others interested in these systems can populate entire castes of proposed relative authority, expertise, rightfulness, and aptness, to vie for command over what gets called what in rhetorical terminology. A great many similar forms, as suggested by the Pauline character, may also not be usefully designative. Different types of "rhetorical devices," for instance, can describe the same specific utterance, but through different means. For instance, *parisosis* is a rhetorical device where sequences of clauses have similar syllabic lengths. But an instance of parisosis could also be a case of *asyndeton* (the deliberate omission of conjunctions), for instance, in "We went, we ate, we danced, we left." Forms can also be nested in complex ways, with one form designated a subset of another, etc., and even vice versa. Even the broad labels applied to the techniques as a set vary considerably (e.g., *rhetorical devices, rhetorical figures, figurative language, persuasive devices, figures of speech, stylistic devices, figures, tropes*).[1]

I will make absolutely no attempt whatsoever to sort this business out. Indeed, in my view, it *cannot* be sorted out, nor does it really need to be. Part of the difficulty lies in the different disciplines that have developed and worked with these sets. Rhetoricians and philosophers have long been busy working with definitions and designations of these forms. Literary scholars have discussed for centuries how such forms are used in writings of many types. Social and cognitive scientists have more recently addressed portions of the forms with empirical methods designed to see what goes on in people cognitively and otherwise when they create or encounter the forms. These disciplines have different foci and agendas and won't necessarily break their disciplinary boundaries to address allied fields' concerns.

Another issue involves the scope of interest in these forms. The scholars just mentioned in psycholinguistics, linguistics, cognitive science, and other experimental disciplines addressing figurative language, for instance, have focused on a smaller handful of prominent figurative forms such as metaphor, idioms, metonymy, hyperbole, verbal irony, proverbs, and a few others. This subset has received by far the greatest attention with empirical and experimental methodologies, trying to answer questions about processing and function (Colston, 2015). But scholars in areas as widely dispersed as philosophy, rhetoric, literary or cultural studies, semiotics, communication, etc., as well as other professionals who work with written and spoken communication (e.g., writers, teachers, journalists) also attend to the wider range of "rhetorical devices" as illustrated in the lengthy Wikipedia list.

Perhaps the newer experimental, behavioral, and neurocognitive approaches just haven't made their way to extensively studying these other rhetorical techniques yet. Or maybe those techniques just aren't

---

[1] The word "trope" interestingly can apply both to types of figurative language and to more banal or trivial language, clichés, chestnuts – as in overused stereotypical arguments, plots, ideas, or sayings. An irony thus holds in this definitional duplicity in that the richness, density, and complexity of the meaning-making process in figurative language is quite the opposite of linguistic or cognitive pedestrian banality.

seen as greatly furthering our attempts to understand human language cognition and behavior, the techniques' purportedly relatively narrow scope seen as not extending beyond a minor morphosyntactic choreography step (i.e., cross one leg in front of the other). The broader mainstream figures may instead be seen as more major socio-cognitive fundamentals (e.g., a full Fred Astaire and Ginger Rogers dance routine).

The focus on the mainstream figures might also be due to the prevalence of those figures out there in human language usage.[2] It could also be because the mainstream forms present some of the strongest cases of surface and intended meaning discrepancy. It could even be due to the relative availability of cognitive, linguistic, social, and psychological processes from which we can select to account for how the mainstream forms are comprehended and used – a case of the tail at least partially wagging the dog. Or this set might just be the forms of which people are most meta-aware, in that many if not most non-academicians probably have at least a sense of what metaphor, verbal irony, idioms, etc., *are*, if not necessarily by those names. Or it could even just be an accident of history – perhaps scholars in the experimental disciplines just happened to take a look at these particular forms before most of the other figures and rhetorical devices, so this popular set had a head start.

But, for whatever reason(s), a very large array of other-side-of-meaning spoken and written techniques exists for leveraging meaning and pragmatic effects in people – techniques which have not undergone extensive and deep empirical testing, at least relative to the mainstream figurative forms. Which puts us in a modest expository dilemma. The mainstream figurative forms attended to by psycholinguists, linguists, etc., have received extensive individual treatments in a number of venues. They have also have been reviewed by several thorough sources, and remain the central topic of ongoing research. In other words, plenty has already been said about them. The relative dearth of experimental research on the wider array of other rhetorical devices, however, also leaves little to report concerning how our cognitive, social, and linguistic skills operate with those forms. Accordingly, we'll next provide only a general overview of the mainstream figurative forms – the rest of the chapter will then consider a few other ideas about figurativity in language, in cognition, its structure and scope.

Whether they exhibit a greater magnitude of deviance between their surface form and their intended meaning, or whether the level of encapsulation around their central set of underlying processes is higher relative to other figurative or rhetorical forms, the main types of figurative

---

[2] Something not always easy to measure (Colston, 2015).

language that have been studied experimentally are *metaphor, verbal irony, metonymy, idioms, proverbs,* and *hyperbole* (Colston, 2015). Other kinds of "rhetorical devices" might have a quite specific characteristic enabling their definition, but they may not have as large a surface form/intended meaning deviance nor a pronounced singular or unitary set of underlying cognitive or other process – at least that have been isolated and evaluated.

Metaphor

Metaphors, for example, have a notable difference between surface form and intended meaning (e.g., talk about general positivity in terms of sweetness, as in, "I have to take this new position, it's such a sweet deal"), where *parataxis*, for instance, has little such difference (e.g., talk about something with sequential phrases or clauses, but with little or no coordination or subordination function words, as in, "Hi, gimme your keys. Work okay? Dinner's done, on the stove. I'm off to pick up Saham"). Metaphors also have a fairly clear underlying process, that of a cross-domain mapping, something like using a usually concrete source domain content (e.g., "bananas" or "crackers" or "bat feces") to talk about usually relatively abstract target domain content (e.g., "mental illness," "insanity," "disordered thinking"),[3] as in the following (see Gibbs, 2017 for a review of metaphor accounts):[4]

6.2   **"I can't talk to him, he's bananas."**
       "She's gone crackers."
       "This guy's ideas are absolute bat shit."

Although parataxis may not cluster as much around a core encapsulated cognitive process, relative to metaphor, parataxis and indeed many of the rhetorical devices can nonetheless leverage pragmatic effects – indeed, this is likely why the devices exist.

Verbal Irony

Verbal irony also exhibits a fairly pronounced surface form/intended meaning difference – one of seeming oppositionality (i.e., using positive

---

[3] I say this well aware of differences in views about these claims – cross-domain mappings versus unidirectional domain mappings, abstractness being the basis of difference between source and target domains versus something else like frequency (Winter & Srinivasan, 2019) or simulatability (Colston, 2018a), etc. But as a general starter course as to how metaphors work, hopefully these broad descriptions suffice.

[4] Some accounts discuss how this underlying mapping changes over time (Bowdle & Gentner, 2005).

commentary in reference to negative referents, as in, "Nice place you've got here," said about someone's slovenly living space). It is also encapsulated around several related cognitive processes, which underlie its comprehension – i.e., pretense, allusional pretense, echo, contrast, negation, suppression, relevant inappropriateness, bi-coherence, and others (see Gibbs & Colston, 2007, for a review). In comparison, *ellipsis* has little surface form/intended meaning deviation (e.g., in gapping ellipsis, "Carmen can play the piano and Juan the drums"), although ellipsis does seem encapsulated around reasonably authorized coherence inferencing and/or priming as cognitive processes.[5]

Metonymy

The surface form/intended meaning separation in metonymy can take on various specific forms (e.g., PART stands for WHOLE, CONTAINER stands for CONTAINED), all arising around its central encapsulated process of substitution (i.e., use X in place of Y, as in, "Get your ass up here now!" [ASS for PERSON] or, "This is really delicious, probably my favorite dish" [DISH for FOOD]). (See Panther & Radden, 1999 for a thorough review of metonymy and its central substitution method.) By comparison, *entallage* – with its characteristic of an intentionally incorrect use of tense, form, or person (i.e., to enable consistency and perhaps demonstrativeness, as in, "Use your brains not your brauns")[6] – seems to have neither a large surface form/intended meaning separation nor an encapsulated underlying cognitive process.

Idioms and Proverbs

Idioms and proverbs are similar in that they're relatively fixed compared to the other mainstream figurative forms, at least in their surface structure. Idioms and proverbs differ from each other though in that idioms often capture a bite-sized chunk of meaning (e.g., "spill the beans" [RELEASE A SECRET], "kick the bucket" [DIE]), where proverbs are more imperative – often adding a level of advocation, extollation, or advisement (e.g., "look before you leap" [BE CAUTIOUS], "Keep your cards close to your chest" [KEEP IMPORTANT INFORMATION PRIVATE], "Get on the trolley" [BECOME FAMILIAR WITH THE LATEST INFORMATION]). So, their surface form/intended meaning separation can range from a structural similarity (i.e., talk or advice about abstract

[5] Which can leverage pragmatic effects (e.g., efficiency) (Colston, 2015).
[6] Which are also pragmatic effects.

human events by discussing more concrete human, physical, or animal events with similar structures) through seeming anomalousness (i.e., the connection between surface form and intended meaning lies in some perhaps lost cultural or historical knowledge). The encapsulated central cognitive processes underlying proverbs and idioms are a bit varied since these types of figures can be made up of many ingredients, including other figures (e.g., metaphor, hyperbole).[7] See Pitzl, 2018; Liu, 2008; Honeck, 1997, for reviews.

In comparison stands *epistrophe* (i.e., repetition of a word at the ends of several sentences, clauses, or phrases, as in, "Who pays for your school, Mom – does your laundry, Mom – coaches your soccer, Mom ..."). Again, also not a wide gap between surface form and intended meaning and perhaps only a mildly encapsulated underlying cognitive process (i.e., something repeated several times in an encountered sequence will become distinctive and might thus be processed more deeply, might be recalled more readily, etc. – effectively, priming and stronger memory encoding via repetition).[8]

Hyperbole

The surface form/intended meaning for hyperbole might be the simplest relative to the other figures discussed here (i.e., talk about something with magnitudes greater or less than the actual referent topics, as in, "It's sub-Saharan in here" [IT'S HOT], "He's gonna blow up the world" [HE WILL DO SOMETHING BAD]). Hyperbole's underlying encapsulated cognitive process seems to involve inflation of an expectation/outcome deviation in order to bring attention to it – often for the purposes of revealing one's negative attitude toward the deviation (Colston, 2015). *Syncope*, by comparison, also shows little difference between surface form and intended meaning nor a deeply encapsulated core cognitive process (i.e., the loss of phonemes within words [or, reduction], as in "gonna," "wouldja," "jeat yet?").[9]

This brief consideration of the mainstream figures, in parallel with some of the relatively understudied rhetorical devices, the latter ones selected effectively at random for comparison, provides an interesting illustration. Although the figures seem to differ from the rhetorical

---

[7] I've likened idioms and proverbs to the "pizzas" of figurative language since they can have so many diverse ingredients in/on them.

[8] Which could be an instance of the pragmatic effect of meaning enhancement, one of the more prevalent of the pragmatic effects performed by figurative language (Colston, 2015).

[9] Which could contribute to a number of pragmatic effects (i.e., identification, tension reduction, social bonding, etc.).

devices in the two main ways mentioned (degree of surface form/intended meaning difference, and level of encapsulation around a core cognitive process or set of cognitive processes), they share something with the rhetorical devices. They all can trigger embodied simulations. As discussed at the start of this book, embodied simulations are activations of neural programs in our sensory and motor cortexes, which take place during language production and comprehension. They are a major source of ingredients of meaning from the sem/sym/syn side of language. But they also can occur in figurative language, also providing part of the fuel for how figures leverage meaning.

Figurative Language and Embodied Simulations

We'll consider embodied simulations in figurative language across three topics: embodied simulations in metaphor comprehension, embodied simulations in verbal irony comprehension, and evidence for embodied simulations enhancing pragmatic effects in metaphor.

Embodied Simulations in Metaphor Processing

The preface of this book cited an enormous body of evidence supporting the idea that embodied simulations underlie concrete language comprehension (i.e., language that specifically talks about things we can process with our senses and/or movements we and other things can make). (See also Bergen, 2012, for a compact background and review of this work.) Jamrozik, McQuire, Cardillo, and Chatterjee (2016) make the specific case that metaphors serve as the bridge between embodied simulations in concrete language comprehension and the comprehension of abstract language. And, indeed, there is an equally large body of work supporting this general idea that embodied simulations taking place during metaphor comprehension are one of the ways we glean more abstract target domain understandings from the metaphors (Boroditsky, 2000; Boroditsky & Ramscar, 2002; Cacciari, Bolognini, Senna, Pellicciari, Miniussi, & Papagno, 2011; Cardillo, Schmidt, Kranjec, & Chatterjee, 2010; Cardillo, Watson, Schmidt, Kranjec, & Chatterjee, 2013; Chen, Widick, & Chatterjee, 2008; Citron & Goldberg, 2014; Desai, Binder, & Conant, 2011; Gibbs, 2006; Gibbs, Costa Lima, & Francozo, 2004; Lacey, Stilla, & Sathian, 2012; Mashal, Faust, Hendler, & Jung-Beeman, 2007; Obert, Gierski, Calmus, Portefaix, Declercq, Pierot, & Caillies, 2014; Ritchie, 2008; Lauro, Mattavelli, Papagno, & Tettamanti, 2013; Thibodeau & Boroditsky, 2011; Wilson & Gibbs, 2007; Zharikov & Gentner, 2002).

A more limited literature has also found evidence for embodied simulations underlying idiom comprehension (Boulenger, Shtyrov, &
Pulvermuller, 2012; Desai, Conant, Binder, Park, & Seidenberg, 2013).
Such a finding is not surprising since many idioms have metaphors
embedded within them or entire idioms themselves can be metaphors
(e.g., "jump ship," "a toss-up," "we're in the same boat," "bite your
tongue," "bed of roses," "off the hook").

The essential finding in the works showing embodied simulations taking place in metaphor (and in idiom) comprehension is that the kinds of
simulations run with metaphors appear very similar, but not identical, to
simulations run on the same or at least similar surface language when
used in nonmetaphorical context (i.e., "Wow, this one is really sharp,"
referring to a smart student or razor-edged knife).[10] What appears to
differ is a sort of wrap-up simulation taking place near the end of the
metaphor comprehension process and its sequence of embodied simulations, where it appears the metaphorical application of the concrete content to the more abstract (usually) target content is resolved (Bergen,
2012). But these simulations can be so rapid that the overall processing
time of contextually supported metaphors need not be reliably longer
than processing of nonmetaphorical language.

Indeed, I've argued in a few places that embodied simulations underlying metaphor comprehension may obviate to a degree the long-standing
debates about stages in metaphor comprehension (i.e., one stage versus
two) (Gibbs, 2017; Colston, 2018a, 2018c; Colston, Sims, Pumphrey,
Kinney, Evangelista, Vandermolen-Pater, & Feeny, in press). Embodied
simulations allow some of the source domain concrete content into
a metaphor's comprehension, but processing can occur and be integrated
so rapidly that it doesn't have to take longer with metaphors. This can
explain nicely the meaning enhancement characteristic of metaphorical
language (e.g., for educational or expository purposes, Cameron, 2003;
Colston, 2018a), as well as its vividness, persuasiveness, memorability,
and the subjective positive affect some people feel when encountering
novel, particularly apt metaphors.

Embodied Simulations in Verbal Irony Processing

Embodied simulations may also underlie at least a portion of the processing of verbal irony as well. A recent study from my lab evaluated

[10] Barbara Kingsolver in her collection of essays, *Small Wonder* (2002), captures this quality
of figurative embodied simulation quite nicely, and quite figuratively: "I rarely think of
poetry as something I make happen; it is more accurate to say that it happens to me. Like
a summer storm, a house afire, or the coincidence of both on the same day."

embodied simulations in verbal irony processing through an action compatibility effect (ACE) task (Colston, 2017a; Colston, Sims, Pumphrey, Kinney, Evangelista, Vandermolen-Pater, & Feeny, in press). Participants were asked to make responses using a desk-mounted joystick which they could move either forward – away from the themselves – or backward – toward themselves – from a resting central position. Participants were presented auditory stories, and were asked to respond as quickly and accurately as possible on whether the comment they heard at the end of each story, made by a character in the story, was a sensible English statement (one of the joystick movement directions was designated "yes" and the other "no"). Some of the comments mentioned participants' attempts to move things (e.g., desks, chairs, desk drawers) either away from themselves (e.g., pushing) or toward them (e.g., pulling).[11]

For a portion of the stories, the direction of participants' "yes" response was *aligned* with the motor movement presumably being simulated from the heard comments (e.g., hearing "Nice shove," said after a description of a successful attempt to move a heavy cabinet forward, and making a forward joystick movement to mean "yes"). These trials were evaluated against stories where the required motor movement response was *nonaligned* with the simulated motions (e.g., hearing "Nice pull," after a description of a successful attempt to open a stuck desk drawer, and making a forward joystick movement meaning "yes"). Both the aligned and nonaligned motor movement responses were directly compared to stories that ended in non-simulation control endings (e.g., "Nice job").

Evaluations of aligned and nonaligned *nonfigurative* versions of the comments like those just described (e.g., when a story character successfully moves something forward and a companion says, "Nice shove") were also made on *sarcastic* comments (e.g., where a character attempts to move something forward but fails and a companion sarcastically says, "Nice shove").

For nonfigurative stories, relative to a non-simulation baseline (e.g., hearing "Nice job"), processing language that was *nonaligned* with response movement (e.g., hearing "Nice shove" and responding by pulling) was slightly inhibited. But, relative to a non-simulation baseline (e.g., "Nice job"), processing language *aligned* with response movement (e.g., hearing "Nice shove" and responding by pushing) is significantly *more* inhibited.

---

[11] Terms for pushing and pulling (e.g., "shove," "yank," "push," "pull") were carefully omitted from the stories proper. They only appeared as the final words in the end comments.

So, for nonfigurative language, it appears as if simulating a movement when hearing language about such a movement, preoccupies the motor cortex enough to produce an inhibition in an actual motor response requiring that movement – if the response is needed at the same time the language comprehension takes place. This inhibition is particularly strong when the movement being simulated (e.g., a pull) *matches* the response required (e.g., a pull). This finding is consistent with other ACE patterns – sometimes results show facilitation where other times they show inhibition, the latter typically occuring if the task being used is relatively difficult. The present task likely falls into that latter more difficult category.[12]

For figurative language, overall processing times are slower compared to nonfigurative, but the pattern just described for nonfigurative language recurs – relative to a non-simulation baseline (e.g., "Nice job"), processing language *nonaligned* with response movement (e.g., hearing "Nice shove" [meant sarcastically] and responding by pulling) is slightly inhibited. But relative to a non-simulation baseline (e.g., "Nice job"), processing language *aligned* with response movement (e.g., hearing "Nice shove" [meant sarcastically] and responding by pushing) is *more* inhibited.

What we thus have is a pattern of results where sarcastic commentary behaves similarly to nonfigurative/non-sarcastic commentary. If a response to indicate one's decision about the language heard (i.e., is the language a sensible English statement or not?) overlaps with the specific embodied simulation being conducted in the comprehension of that language (i.e., a motion of moving one's arm(s) outward or toward oneself), people's responses are slowed. We also have evidence that the overlap doesn't have to be precise. It could be simply along the possible dimension of motion (e.g., pulling or pushing) – recall that inhibition was found for movement in either aligned or nonaligned directions. But the inhibition effect is *stronger* if the precise motion overlaps (e.g., having to move your arm forward to respond to language about moving your arm forward ["Nice push"]), even if the language is sarcastic.

So, as with metaphor, it appears that verbal irony processing also triggers embodied simulations consistent with the nonfigurative surface forms of the language. Our study didn't evaluate whether a "wrap-up" resolution would take place at the end of processing of verbal irony, as is

[12] Participants are having to judge the veracity of the sentences, while at the same time monitoring for whether the comment is used nonfiguratively or sarcastically, which puts a bit of a processing burden on the participants, likely producing the inhibition signature of the underlying embodied simulation.

found with metaphor – likely to accord the sarcastic intent of the comments. But presumably something like that would occur.[13]

Embodied Simulations Enhancing Metaphor Pragmatic Effects

Another recent study of mine also looked at how embodied simulations taking place during metaphor comprehension can enhance pragmatic effects. This study actually looked at metaphors when embedded in proverbs. This was done to use the advocative nature of proverbs as a means to evaluate the strengths of the pragmatic effects of the embedded metaphors (Colston, 2018a)

Many if not most proverbs are advocative. They essentially advise people on how to act, what to be like, how to respond to certain situations, etc. For metaphorical proverbs, they make this advocation using whatever source domain content is contained in the proverbs. But the target domains are actually the contextual situations surrounding the interlocutors. For instance, if a person asks a friend for their advice about an opportunity that has presented itself to the person – i.e., *should I act on this opportunity or not* – the friend could respond with,

6.3   **"Strike while the iron is hot."**

Here, striking or hammering hot things, in a blacksmith or forge sense, is the source domain for the target domain of the person contemplating the opportunity. The key knowledge in the source domain is that hot metal can be worked – i.e., made into the sought-after object – where cold metal cannot. And hot metal somewhat rapidly cools into cold metal – so the window for getting what you want is temporary. Apply this structural information to the target domain and we thus have the effective proverbial meaning of, *take this opportunity to advance your career (life, etc.) while you have the short-lived chance to do so.*

But the same essential advice could also have been given using a nonmetaphorical proverb such as:[14]

6.4   **No time like the present.**

So, the question posed by this study was essentially, which of the two kinds of proverbs are more strongly advocative in a used context (i.e., the situation of the person asking the friend for advice), the metaphorical or nonmetaphorical ones? And, importantly, we posed this questions with

[13] Provided the comments are interpreted correctly.
[14] Of course, the precise meanings of the metaphorical and nonmetaphorical proverbs are a bit different, but in their gist they're very similar (e.g., *act now, take the opportunity*).

sets of metaphorical and nonmetaphorical proverbs *that are equally advocative when measured in isolation.*

The logic behind the question is that, if metaphorical and nonmetaphorical proverbs are equated on a number of important factors (e.g., familiarity, isolated advocacy strength) and are otherwise kept as similar as possible (i.e., in length), then the major contender explanation for any found differences in the advocacy strength of the sets of proverbs when used in contexts enabling that advocacy to be expressed is the presence of metaphor. Moreover, the known activity of embodied simulations underlying the metaphorical proverbs could be the smoking gun if an advocacy difference is found – their being the reason for why metaphorical proverbs are more strongly advocative than the nonmetaphorical ones.

The findings were essentially supportive of this explanation. Metaphorical proverbs, equal in many measured ways to nonmetaphorical proverbs – especially in their advocacy strength when tested in isolation – were more advocative when used in contexts enabling their advocacy to show itself.

We also measured this advocacy in an indirect way (i.e., we didn't have participants just rate how advocative the proverbs were). In a priming paradigm, we assessed the degree to which participants would use advocation descriptive words and phrases (e.g., "[be] cautious," "[be] opportunistic") to describe people in ambiguous situations (e.g., "Emilia sniffs and looks at her glass before she takes a drink"). Participants had been primed, though, prior to seeing the ambiguous sentences like the Emilia one by first reading either a metaphorical or nonmetaphorical proverb related to that sentence (e.g., "Look before you leap," or "Better safe than sorry"). Importantly, we had normed the proverbs and selected the metaphorical and nonmetaphorical sets such that they had produced the advocation descriptive words to the same degree when seen in isolation.[15]

So, in essence, the set of metaphorical proverbs (e.g., "Look before you leap") produced our advocation descriptive words (e.g., "caution") to the same extent as the nonmetaphorical matched proverbs (e.g., "Better safe than sorry"), when those proverbs were presented in isolation. But when paired with the ambiguous sentences (e.g., the Emilia sentence, with the proverb read prior to the sentence), the metaphorical proverbs elicited their specific advocation words and phrases to a greater degree than did

---

[15] In a norming task, the proverbs were presented in isolation (without the ambiguous sentences) to participants who were asked to write what they thought the proverbs were advocating. "Look before you leap" and "Better safe than sorry" produced "caution" and words with the same root (e.g., "cautious") as a response, at the same frequency.

the nonmetaphorical proverbs. So, the greater transfer of those activated concepts (e.g., caution) by the metaphorical proverbs when they were read prior to the ambiguous sentences (i.e., interpreting Emilia *as being cautious*) must be due to something about the metaphors being comprehended right before sentences are encountered.

Our interpretation is that the embodied simulations afforded in the metaphorical proverbs were what drove that increased rate of transfer. Participants ran embodied simulations about looking and leaping, for instance, when reading, "Look before you leap," and could readily conjure meaning from those simulations (e.g., *caution* is warranted when looking and leaping). That conjured meaning could then apply to the ambiguous sentences (e.g., "Emilia sniffs and looks t her glass before she takes a drink" – because she is a *cautious* person). Participants didn't have *as rich an experience* of *caution* when reading the non-metaphorical proverbs (e.g., "Better safe than sorry"), because they hadn't run the simulations. So, even though participants thought of the generic concept *caution* to the same extent when encountering the two metaphors (i.e., evidenced by the norming task), less transfer occurred with the nonmetaphorical proverb.

Given this evidence of embodied simulations' operation in metaphor as well as verbal irony, and especially how embodied simulations seem to assist metaphorical pragmatic effects (i.e., meaning enhancement), it would be useful for researchers going forward to evaluate embodied simulations in figurative language more extensively. Are embodied simulations involved, for instance, in idiom, metonymy, hyperbole, etc., production and comprehension, and if so, how do they leverage meaning and/or affect (or produce) pragmatic effects? Are embodied simulations playing any role in difficulties observed in figurative language comprehension, or its *mis*comprehension? What roles do embodied simulations play in figurative language acquisition (Colston, 2017c; in press)?[16] Might they be particularly involved in the major pragmatic effects of some figures (i.e., persuasion by metaphor), and would widespread knowledge about such an embodied simulation/persuasion connection potentially obviate such persuasion, perhaps even for social good (i.e., disarming the effect of propaganda, political framing, sales rhetoric, etc.)? Whether for basic or more applied research goals, such a line of investigation might be worthy of our efforts.

Returning for a moment to the earlier comparison of the mainstream figures and other rhetorical devices, another similarity between these two

---

[16] The Colston (2017c; in press) works recommended for an investigation of any yoking potentially underlying the acquisition of different forms of figurative language – i.e., do the acquisition points of different figures in children correspond to when certain social or other interactive motivations arise in them?

groups, besides the just discussed embodied simulations, is that both can also come in an essentially infinite array of *constructions*. Metaphors can be declarative (e.g., "Manuel is a tornado"), as can epistrophe (e.g., "You learn things at school, you have fun at school, you meet friends at school"). But both can also be interrogative (e.g., "How goes it flying solo?" [ASKED ABOUT SOMEONE'S POST-DIVORCE LIFE], and, "Did they serve cake, do you like cake, did you eat cake?"). This nature of figures and rhetorical devices, whereupon they can appear in multiple types of constructions, is a very interesting tangent in figurative language research as it shows how the central structural properties of the figurative processes (i.e., source-to-target domain mappings, oppositionality, inflation, etc.) can be greatly affected by the constructions given to the figures. If the core processes deliver the ingredients of meaning in the figures' recipes, then the constructions might provide the preparation instructions.

Constructions and Figurativity

All figurative forms come in constructions. For some figures these constructions are relatively fixed, as in some idioms and proverbs. Other colloquialized figures have relatively fixed forms as well (e.g., some verbal irony and rhetorical questions, as in, "Wise guy," "Isn't that special?"). So, one way to approach constructions and figurativity is to just survey the kinds of constructions found in idioms, proverbs, colloquialized figures, and other fixed figures, and see what is happening. Are the found constructions seemingly built to maximize the figures' impact? Or are their constructions serving other needs (i.e., phonetic or morphosyntactic ease of pronunciation)?

For instance, if we consider the proverb, "If the shoe fits, wear it," what might its construction pattern be doing for a speaker or hearer?[17] The construction is essentially a subordinate followed by an imperative clause. One could easily create a minimal pair by reversing the components of this complex sentence to create, "Wear the shoe, if it fits." One might argue that the original version conveys a stronger proverbial meaning in two related ways, both involving a building of suspense. By putting the subordinate clause first, some suspense can build up for the imperative part which comes later. Since one of the primary uses of proverbs such as this one is to advocate, extol, or suggest some behavior or trait (e.g., do this, don't do that, be this way, don't be that way), the holding of the

---

[17] A tip of the hat goes to my colleague Evangelia Daskalaki for an interesting discussion of this proverb, its minimal pair, and how the proverb leverages its meaning.

imperative clause until the end strengthens the proverb's overall imperative quality. The imperative coming at the end could also enhance the underlying metaphor underlying of the proverb, ACCEPTING/FACING/ACKNOWLEDGING is WEARING. But the reversed order, fronting the imperative part, does not do these things.

Another approach to investigating constructions in figurativity is to look at the range of constructions used in relatively unfixed figures and observe and/or experimentally evaluate what those constructions are doing and how they're interacting with the core figurative processes. For example, the metaphorical constructions,

6.5a   **X is a regular Y.**

6.5b   **Everyone is a Y.**

as in "You're a regular comedian" or "Everyone's a comedian," could bring along predictable other-side-of-meaning content as well as pragmatic effects, due to the interaction of the constructions with the baser metaphorical processes.

For instance, the purported but stealthily weak emphasis imparted by both constructions, through the deadpan modifier "regular" in 6.5a and through the hyperbole "everyone" in 6.5b, might trigger more negative or even ironic interpretations of these metaphors, relative to a slightly different constructions:

6.5c   **You're a comedian.**

6.5d   **You're totally a comedian.**

The semantic flatness of the modifier "regular" might serve to dampen the metaphorical comparison in 6.5a, rendering it a bit weak or even making it ironic (i.e., *the person is not a very good comedian*, or, *the person is not a comedian*). The hyperbolized construction in 6.5b could render the metaphorical comparison unexceptional, also weakening or ironizing it (i.e., *the person is a comedian, but so is everyone else, so this person is not exceptional*, or, *this person is not a comedian*). The comparative constructions 6.5c and 6.5d, however, either don't do these things (6.5c) or they redirect the hyperbolization away from referencing *the size of the category of comedians*, and direct it toward *the likelihood that the referent person belongs to the comedian category* (6.5d), thus removing the negativity expressed, relative to 6.5a and 6.5b.

A great deal of work has been done in this regard, especially for metaphors, borrowing the well-worked-out constructional approach to syntax from Cognitive Grammar and the detailed lexical and phrasal components of constructions from Frame Semantics (Sullivan, 2013,

2016). But other work on constructions has also been applied to all the mainstream figures – verbal irony (Brone, Fayaerts, & Veale, 2006; Veale, Fayaerts, & Brone, 2006; Veale, 2012, 2013; Veale & Alessandro, 2017; Hao & Veale, 2009, 2010; Giora, Givoni, & Fein, 2015; Giora, Drucker, Fein, & Mendelson, 2015), hyperbole (Burgers, Konijn, & Steen, 2016; Colston & O'Brien, 2000a, 2000b; Gibbs & O'Brien, 1991; Gibbs, 1986), idioms and proverbs (Sanford, 2014; Beck & Weber, 2016; Hosinger, 2013; Cain & Towse, 2008; Cain, Towse, & Knight, 2009; Konopka & Bock, 2009), and similes (Hao & Veale, 2010; Veale, 2012, 2013). And one could argue that practically all of the extensive scholarship on metonymy is precisely of this explore-the-construction vein (Sweetser, 2017; Ruiz de Mendoza Ibañez & Mairal Uson, 2007; Attardo, 2005; Panther & Thornburg, 1998, 2003; Perez-Sobrino, 2014; Kovecses, 2013).

Attempts to note how underlying figurative processes interact with the kinds of constructions in which they're embedded are extremely useful for mapping how figurative processes can be corralled, herded, marshalled, and influenced – a marked interaction between the two sides of meaning discussed in this book. But an even broader form of interaction can arise between underlying core figurative processes and something larger than constructions – the language genres in which the figures, and their constructions, are couched.

To foreshadow, Chapter 9 will take up just such a discussion, noting how a figurative form (metaphor), delivered in a particular construction pattern (conjoined antonymy), embedded further within a particular language genre (lyrics from a popular song), can lead to an immensity of meaning-generating interactions and concomitantly erupting pragmatic effects – a veritable stew of other-side-of-meaning content.[18]

This pulling back of the camera, as it were, to briefly gather a broader picture of figurative processes and how they work – taking account of the constructions in which they're placed and the larger genres in which those constructions themselves reside – provides a useful lesson. Aerial photography, although certainly losing some fine grained detail, can reveal patterns not obtainable by cameras on the ground. But this analogy can be taken a major step further. Satellite photography, enabling images of entire hemispheres, can reveal even broader patterns than aerial photography, patterns that can contextualize sub-patterns of constructions' impact on meaning,

---

[18] I've also likened this burst of meaning arising from a tightly interwoven mixture of sem/syn/sym and other-side-of-meaning processes to the jetting action produced by a Venturi tube – the interwoven process bottleneck produces a fountain of meaning on the other side.

and even sub-sub-patterns on figures' contribution to meaning. The final section in this chapter will thus take a look at figurative processes from their broadest, most generic level – the raw handful of patterns of domain structures into which the figures fall.

The Big Figurative Picture

An interesting perspective can be achieved if we attempt to distill the major forms of figurative language into their basest possible pattern – the structure of the domain(s) the figures invoke and what the figures do with those domains. This perspective can give us insights into why we have the particular range of figures we do, how that range matches our cognitive and social capacities, and how some figures can extend beyond language. First, let's do the figural distillation.

What's in a Domain?

Metaphor Metaphor typically invokes two domains, and invites mappings between them. The domains are usually things or actions, even if one domain is usually fairly abstract, and the mappings are often implicit (i.e., implicit in that even in fairly direct nominal [X is a Y] metaphors, the alignments between target and source domains are simply presented as fact, but without drawing attention to their having been presented as such, as is the case for similes [X is *like* Y]). For instance, the simple metaphor "closed-minded" conjures the different domains of *the mind* and *things that are closed*. The metaphor invites mappings between these domains where characteristics salient in one of the domains (i.e., closed things – nothing can enter, nothing can be added, one cannot get inside to move things around, etc.) can highlight similarly patterned but perhaps less salient things in the other domain (i.e., minds – no new ideas can enter, no knowledge can be added, it is difficult to force reconsiderations of held beliefs, etc.).[19]

Verbal Irony Verbal poses a bit of a challenge. Two ways of looking at it seem viable. One is to say it invokes only one domain, which is then nullified. The domain when first invoked is often some expected, desired, preferred, or other similar situation or state of affairs. The speaker then nullifies that domain to illustrate how it is not the current reality. But in this process a sort of second domain is involved – that of the background context which doesn't match up with the invoked

---

[19] Of course, different metaphor theories will differ on some of these details, but most would agree that metaphors invite some sort of correspondence between two domains.

and then nullified domain about expectations/desires/etc. Whether the background context serves more as just the stage on which the domain invocation and nullification takes place, or rather if it's an alternate domain that replaces the invoked and then nullified one, seems a matter of preference. For instance, the simple verbal irony, "nice weather," said about bad weather, conjures the domain of pleasant weather conditions. But through a number of proposed mechanisms, that domain is essentially nullified, in essence as if indicating *it is not the case that we have nice weather*. But we still have the remaining reality of bad weather which is essentially what the figure is commenting upon.

Given how the purpose of invoking and then nullifying an expected/desired/etc. domain is to bring notice to and often cast an attitude about the domain of actual reality, we'll consider verbal irony a two-domain process – one domain is activated and nullified, leaving the other domain to stand and face the commentary.

Hyperbole Hyperbole also invokes usually just one domain. But hyperbole then proceeds to inflate that domain. Moreover, it might often seem with hyperbole that the domain being inflated is some material or other thing such as a person's necktie, as in, "Donald Trump's necktie is eight feet long."[20] But if that were the case then the reason for using the hyperbole isn't clear. What would be the point of saying the necktie is longer than it actually is? I've argued that the domain conjured in hyperbole is actually something more subtle – rather than just a material or some other singular thing, it's instead a *discrepancy* between an expected/desired/preferred state of affairs and the actual reality at hand. These states of affairs *can* be things like the lengths of neckties or essentially anything else. But what the hyperbole is really doing is inflating the discrepancy between expectations/etc. about the invoked thing and the reality of the thing. So, with the Donald Trump example, the user of the hyperbole is inflating the discrepancy between expected necktie lengths and the actual length of Donald Trump's necktie. This is often done for the purposes of drawing attention to those discrepancies, and to express one's disapproval of them, or at least usually – hyperbole can also be used to express pleasure at an expectancy/reality discrepancy (Colston & Keller, 1998; Colston, 2015).

Idioms and Proverbs Idioms and proverbs behave a bit like metaphors if viewed at low resolution – they also usually invoke two

---

[20] Adapted from an actual hyperbole used by American political commentator Chris Matthews on his television program, *Hardball* (January 25, 2019).

domains and invite mappings between them. For instance, if someone "spills the beans," the two activated domains are the concrete action of knocking over or dumping a container of dry beans, and the behavior of humans holding private or secret information but then releasing it. The use of the idiom invites a mapping of characteristics of spilled beans (i.e., their distributing rapidly and uncontrollably, their being difficult or impossible to re-contain, etc.) to that of humans holding and revealing secrets (e.g., revealed secrets being retold repeatedly and distributing rapidly in a group, the secret being impossible to re-hide once told). But idioms and proverbs are more varied. The kinds of mappings between the domains may not be as clearly aligned structurally – they may instead have arisen from some historical or cultural knowledge that could now be lost (e.g., the idiomatic meaning of "bite the bullet," possibly being derived from an historical case of how people once endured pain [i.e., by biting something hard like a bullet]). Idioms and proverbs can also contain other kinds of figures (e.g., "It's always darkest before the dawn" contains metaphor and perhaps hyperbole). And proverbs often differ from idioms, given proverbs' advocative quality. But in a rough sense proverbs and idioms seem to treat their pair of domains a bit like metaphor.

Simile   As already mentioned briefly, simile acts a lot like metaphor – invoking two domains and inviting mappings between them. But simile makes the fact that it is comparing these two domains very explicit with its structure (e.g., often using "like" or "as" in its comparison, as in, "He's like a dog with a bone").

Metonymy   This is another figure that invokes two domains, but metonymy does so less for the purpose of inviting mappings and more for the sake of outright substitution. So, we substitute container for contained (e.g., "I'll have a cup, thanks," *I'll have some tea, thanks*), or a part for the whole in the synecdoche subtype (e.g., "all hands on deck," *All people on deck*), etc.

Rhetorical Questions   Rhetorical questions are a bit of an anomaly in being based on an interrogative rather than a declarative construction (although metaphors and other figures can easily be framed as interrogatives). But rhetorical questions seem to use the interrogative form to invoke just a single domain – that of some bit of knowledge or a knowledge structure like a schema – for the purpose of activating that domain in an addressee. Rhetorical questions get their figurativity (or indirectness, depending on how one wishes to classify them) by not expecting a follow-through on the usual practice of interrogatives (i.e., a questioner asks something, an addressee responds). They instead invoke the knowledge domain just to bring it up in the mind of the addressee. For instance, a person asking, "Who do you think you are?" might wish to make their addressee realize they have an inappropriate self-image or self-attitude – thinking they can do things they should not be doing (i.e., taking something from another person without asking permission). But the speaker is not expecting an answer.

Tautologies   Sometimes also called pleonasms, tautologies are an interesting form of figure in that they also invoke just a single domain, but they do so with a form of circularity. Saying, "A car is a car," for instance, is only invoking the domain of automobiles. But the circular construction can do interesting things, like either forcing an addressee to balk at finding meaning from the utterance or lending the meaning a sense of profundity from the lack-of-closure quality of the figure (Colston, 2015; Gibbs & McCarrell, 1990; Ward & Hirschberg, 1991).

Antonymic Figures   Antonymic figures are an interesting set of figures that behave a bit differently than the ones just discussed. This set typically works also with just one domain, but it also resembles verbal irony, operating a bit differently from irony, though – instead of nullifying the invoked domain and leaving another domain standing, these antonymic figures present their one domain as if it is contradicting itself. *Oxymora, antimony, autoantonyms* and *apophasis* all belong to this set, as might *antithesis* – but the last might be a transitional figure residing somewhere between this set of antonymic figures and the next set of reversal figures.

An oxymoron, as in, "The speech was followed by a deafening silence," conjoins seemingly contradictory elements (silence and something loud enough to be deafening). Sometimes oxymora can be resolved by invoking other figures like metaphor (e.g., the silence was deafening in the *metaphorical* sense of sending an extremely intense message – i.e., that the speech was terrible). Other times, resolution can be had by allowing for extenuating circumstances (e.g., *normally* kindness is a good thing, except in a case where someone brings a speaker a thoughtful bouquet of flowers and in so doing reveals the speaker's whereabouts to her awaiting assassin – with the speaker then saying, "Your kindness is killing me"). But oxymora can also convey the very sense that something is somewhat self-contradictory (i.e., that's just how it is).

Antinomy includes such contradictory examples as paradoxes or self-contradictory phrases – for instance, "All statements are wrong," or "'Never' is a word I never use." Such real or apparent mutual incompatibilities are much harder to resolve than oxymora as they're specifically designed to have and convey this well-contained self-contradictory nature (Katz, 1992; Tsur, 2009).

Autoantonyms   Also called contronyms, autoantonyms are words that can have, or are sometimes mistaken as having, oppositional meanings. Quite a number of these exist (e.g., "cleave," "inflammable," "appropriate," "bound," "cite," "clip," "drop," "downhill," "draw," "dust," "Earthbound," "fast," "left," "original," "peruse," "table," "sanction," "screen," "strike," "weather"). One way in which these might sometimes be resolved is to invoke a higher-level category of meaning that encompasses the oppositional senses. "Dust," for instance, when used as a verb, can mean to put dust onto things (e.g., to dust crops) or to take dust off of things (e.g., to dust a table). But a higher-order action sense, something like *to move dust*, allows those opposites to cohabitate.

Apophasis   Apophasis involves bringing up a topic by essentially stating you won't bring it up (e.g., "Why would Kim Jong-un insult me by calling me 'old', when I would *never* call him 'short and fat'?"[21] or "I won't mention any names ... Jose" – the latter using the pretense of speaking directly to a person, telling him that you won't give away any identities, when you're actually giving out his name via the pretense). These figures can have a cleverness quality to them because of their inherent and irresolvable contradictory nature. Their use of pretense also makes them resemble the nullification process used by verbal irony – but in the present case, they're nullifying only part of the promise to not bring up the topic that is broached.

Reversal Figures   These are a set where one domain is invoked but it's typically shown to be reversible – somewhat like modeling a jacket by wearing it one way, but then removing it, turning it inside out, and then wearing it that way.

Antimetabole   Antimetabole involves a use of word-reversal in adjacent clauses – e.g., "Work to live, don't live to work"; "You stood up

---

[21] Donald J. Trump, tweet, November 12, 2017 (Trump, 2017).

for America, now America must stand up for you";[22] "Ask not what your country can do for you – ask what you can do for your country."[23] It is considered a specialized form of chiasmus – where no reuse of words are found, but the grammatical structures are reversed (e.g., I say "go." "stop" prays you). Antimetoble is used to express or emphasize this reversible or quid pro quo quality of an invoked domain.

Antithesis   This also involves the invocation of a single domain, but some of its internal oppositional qualities are contrasted, typically in adjacent clauses (e.g., "For many are called, but few are chosen" [Matthew 22:14, King James Version]; "It was the best of times, it was the worst of times" [Dickens, 1859]).

Puns   These are the last figure we'll consider.[24] Also occasionally called double or multiple entendres or paronomasia, puns most often invoke two domains, but they can invoke several at a time. The different domains are often unrelated in any essential way, excepting for the coincidental fact that a single surface form of language happens to fit or connect with both or all of the domains. For instance, a classic pun from the late comedian George Carlin stated, "Atheism is a non-prophet organization." This pun invokes the domain or frame of a non-*profit* organization – an institution established for its service only, in which no commercial gain is allowed beyond covering operational costs. But the pun also invokes the idea of atheism, a belief system without any religious *prophets*. The homophonic connection of the profit/prophet lexical items might seem to be the sole link between the domains.

Occasionally, puns can overlap in more extensive ways – often lending to their humorous and playful quality.[25] But a more cognitive phenomenon underlies this playful quality of puns. This is evidenced in the Carlin case. Puns can also trigger other interesting meaningful alignments. Non-profit organizations, for instance, are often admired because they perform some service without seeking material gain – they're thus seen as earnest and honest, not bilking people for personal gain, etc. Carlin's use of the pun could thus have sought to lend some of this aura to atheism – his comedy occasionally made fun of mainstream religions, including Roman

---

[22] Barak Obama, speech, Fort Bragg, North Carolina, December 14, 2011 (New York Times, 2011).
[23] Jack Kennedy, inauguration speech, Washington, DC, January 20, 1960 (Guardian News and Media Ltd., 2008).
[24] They'll be revisited in Chapter 7, "Language Play," as they nicely demonstrate figures being used for playful purposes.
[25] This aspect will be discussed more extensively in Chapter 7.

Catholicism, under which Carlin was raised in his youth but then later rejected (Cline, 2018).

I and others have argued that such a secondary meaningful alignment is an emergent characteristic of some puns – potentially lending them an air of profundity akin to tautologies (Colston, 2015; Solska, 2012). Consider first that by seemingly pure happenstance, two different linguistic term (e.g., the lexical items, *profit* and *prophet*, in the case of the Carlin pun) connect to two separate and unrelated conceptual domains (e.g., income that exceeds expenditures and humans gifted with supposed divine inspiration) via the terms being homophones. Moreover, a common fixed phrase uses one of those lexical terms, *non-profit*, to refer to an institution that has no profit motive. Finally, applying the same phrasal construct to the other lexical item and we happen to also get an apt descriptor for the other domain triggered – atheism being non-*prophet*.

But at the same time, in the context of the usage of the pun, those disparate domains happen to have two other deeper connections. Carlin may be suggesting that the admirability of a *non-profit* is also something deserved by a belief system without established religion – *not having prophets*. By not proposing deities for which we have no hard evidence, atheism might be considered "earnest and honest" in the same way as a non-profit organization.

Another connection concerns the financial sense of profit, but applied to the religion domain. Televangelists, superchurches, and some established religions are well known for the enormous money they sometimes amass, leading to occasional scandal and criticism. Some religions also amass enormous political and other power. Carlin's pun could also be attempting to argue that atheism, in disavowing established religion, is also non-profit in that financial or power sense.

That two words are both accidental homophones but can also bring such a secondary connection seems a mighty coincidence. Speakers like Carlin who also happen to find and use such puns can also be taken as inspired.

The Figurative Photo Finish

What can we now observe about these generic depictions of a variety of figurative forms? The first observation is the fairly limited range of work they do with the domains they invoke. Excepting the relatively rare invocation of more than two domains or frames by puns, each figure I've described invokes only one or two domains. Several of the figures invoke two frames to invite mappings between them, usually for the sake of highlighting something about one domain through the use of the other (e.g., metaphor, metonymy, idioms, proverbs, similes [and possibly exempla, see later this section]). For lack of a better term, we'll refer to this pattern as *domain crossing*.

Another figure invokes two domains to contrast them against one another. Irony nullifies one domain it invokes to leave the other domain standing (*domain nullification*). This process can afford a speaker's expression of an attitude about the domain-that-wasn't-to-be – often a disparaging attitude that things didn't turn out as hoped (Giora, Fein, Ganzi, Levi, & Sabah, 2005).

Several figures invoke only one domain, but they do different things with it. Hyperbole inflates the domain it invokes (*domain inflation*). Rhetorical questions essentially just activate a single domain in the mind of the hearer, without expecting follow-through on the interrogative form (i.e., a response) – *domain activation*. Tautologies invoke a single domain to give it a circular quality – *domain circularity*. Antimetabole and antithesis invoke a single domain to point out some of its reversibility – *domain reversal*. Puns seem a bit like rhetorical questions in that they mainly serve to just activate domains, but puns can occasionally reveal mappings, similarities, or shared characteristics between or among domains. But puns do this for two or more domains simultaneously – *domain multiplicity*.

Finally, several other figures also serve to activate only one domain, but they convey a sense of contradiction about that domain – *domain contradiction*. This set includes oxymoron, antimony, autoantonyms, and apophasis. Antithesis might belong here as well if the degree of its reversal quality is strong enough to reach a form of self-contradiction. One could also possibly add irony and its nullification process here – the nullification achieved by a contradiction between the purported state of affairs mentioned in irony's surface form versus reality. But irony can also stand alone because the other contradiction figures seem to present contradiction largely just for its own sake rather than for nullification of one of the pair of domains invoked for the contradiction.[26]

These actions performed on domains, listed in an imperfect but rough order of increasing complexity (going from top to bottom) are presented in Table 6.1.

A second observation we can take from the above discussion is how the generic domain structures seem to fit our capacities in both cognitive and

---

[26] Another way to think about irony versus the antonymic figures is that the latter point out or highlight a contradiction *within* a domain. Irony, on the other hand, points out or highlights, *or creates*, a contradiction *between* two domains – the referenced, hypothetical, ideal case versus what actually obtained. In irony, the ironist pretends the former is in place to actually show how the latter is in place instead.

Table 6.1 *Actions performed on domain(s) invoked by primary figurative forms*

One Domain	Two Domains
domain activation*	domain multiplicity*
domain inflation	domain nullification
domain reversal	domain crossing
domain circularity	
domain contradiction	

* Puns fall into both of these categories because they often perform
   mere domain activation but they do so for two or more domains.

social functioning. Humans have processing limits, especially when deal-
ing with the kinds of "domains" we've been discussing, which are really
potentially complex schemas or other knowledge structures – they're not
just simple unitary things. They thus have a lot of internal content and
possibly intricate internal structures. It is no surprise then that nearly all
figures invoke only one or two domains at most in their functioning.

Most of the figures discussed also invoke only a single domain in their
workings. Of course, we didn't review every figure or rhetorical device
known to humankind, but we did cover the major ones. Of these nearly
twice as many invoke just one domain rather than two. And it is also true
that we did not include a very large set of exempla (e.g., fables, parables,
morals, apologues, allegory), all of which at least weakly invoke two
domains – the surface story being told (e.g., "The Town Mouse and the
Country Mouse," "The Boy Who Cried Wolf"; see Clayton, 2008) and
the broader array of ongoing human affairs to which the tales might
apply.

But exempla don't provide quite as tight a linkage between two
domains relative to a proverb or a metaphor, for instance, due to exempla's lack of density. For instance, a lengthy tale about an animal that
behaves selfishly and accordingly gets into trouble can convey the idea
that it is good to not act selfishly in the real world of humans. But exempla
are more aptly described as residing in the realm of two domains that just
happen to be similar, rather than a tight element-to-element and struc-
ture-to-structure mapping found between two domains such as in proverbs or metaphors.

If we then look at what actually gets done to the domains invoked by
figures, a nice fit with the basic affordances of domains and simple human
cognitive, behavioral, and social functioning is also found. For example, if

you don't have something, you can go and get it (domain activation). If you have something, you can get rid of it (domain nullification). If you have something you can also alter it, making it bigger or smaller than it is (domain inflation), or you can move it back and forth between two states (domain reversal). If you have *two* things you can grab them both at the same time (domain multiplicity) and you can try to put them together somehow (domain crossing). About the only things you can't seem to do readily in a physically simple way to a domain, but which you can do with a figure, is to somehow contradict the domain (domain contradiction) or to somehow invoke its circularity (domain circularity). All the other actions seem to be basic things we can do with the simple ability to manipulate objects.

So, figurative language domain invocations and actions tightly mirror what we can actually do with simple physical objects. We can easily handle one and sometimes two objects when juggling. But handling three or more doesn't come as easily. So, the cognitive processes in figurative language align neatly alongside our motor-material abilities. But another layer also holds to this patterning. When we manipulate objects or perform isolated cognition, we typically do those things by or for ourselves. But when we do figurative language, we're inherently seeking to trigger those cognitive domain invocations and actions *in other people*. So, the existence and operation of figurative language are also inherently social, and they reveal our social connection, knowledge, awareness, and skill – we seek to trigger in others no more than what can happen in ourselves.

But the biggest observation taken from the analysis above is that the two domain actions with the highest number and most varied sets of figures doing them are domain crossing (i.e., *metaphor, metonymy, idioms, proverbs, similes,* and perhaps many forms of *exempla*) and domain contradiction (*oxymora, antimony, autoantonyms, apophasis, antithesis,* and possibly *verbal irony*).[27] And if we put these domain functions side by side, they seem to reveal two of the most fundamental human cognitive abilities we have – and these abilities are oppositional. We see things that are apart as if they are together (we combine), and we see things that are together as if they are apart (we dissect). So, the autoantonym "cleave," with its oppositional meanings of splitting, severing, etc., as well as its meanings of adhering, attaching, etc., seems quite appropriately invoked here. Much like how

---

[27] We've already mentioned that antithesis would only belong to domain contradiction under certain circumstances (i.e., the reversal antithesis displays is pronounced). Irony was listed separately as using domain nullification, but the broader purpose for doing domain nullification is to show that what should have been is not what is – which can be interpreted as exhibiting a form of contradiction.

figurative language seems to operate at its basest level, the contranym "cleave" is also a conjoined antonymy, but one in concentrate.

Figurativity Beyond Language

One last point is worth making about this exploration of the generic structure of domains and the actions we do to them with figurative language. Of all the actions performed on domains listed in Table 6.1, including the different figures underlying those actions, nearly all of them can be extended into domains beyond language.

We can easily identify and create, for instance, visual, and other kinds of nonlinguistic metaphors – *domain crossing* (Forceville & Urios-Aparisi, 2009; Cienki, 2016; Cienki & Muller, 2008a, 2008b; Muller & Cienki, 2009). Irony is readily depicted in images and we perceive it in situations in the form of situational irony – *domain nullification* or *contradiction* (Luciarello, 1994; Shelley, 2001; Colston, 2017b; Gibbs & Colston, 2007; Utsumi, 2000; Burgers, van Mulken, & Schellens, 2013). Metonymy is as easily obtainable in images as almost anything – *domain crossing*.[28] Antonymic figures can be readily depicted in images (e.g., the yin/yang symbol), and even as antonymic visual perspectives (i.e., the filming technique called a "dolly zoom," where a film camera's lens zooms in at the same time that the camera itself is pulled back from the shot on a wheeled dolly) – *domain contradiction*. Hyperbole is easily found in images such as caricatures – *domain inflation*. Antimetabole can be readily seen even in simple events in the natural world (e.g., water freezing and thawing, a pendulum swinging back and forth, the sun rising and setting) – *domain reversal*. Even tautology can be depicted easily in images as beautifully demonstrated by some surrealist artworks, notably images by the Dutch graphic artist Maurits Cornelis Escher (Escher, 2001). And the very simple concepts of domain activation and domain multiplicity underlie all of these nonlinguistic extensions – the mere seeing of an image or event or situation and it triggering meaning in us.[29]

---

[28] I say this because at the very moment I first wrote that sentence I saw an Internet advertisement for a cold medicine out of the corner of my eye on an adjacent computer screen – depicting a man with a cold as a large walking red nose (the exact source of the ad was not recoverable – it was observed as a rotating ad on a mainstream news site and could not be relocated).

[29] Even figures we didn't discuss here can extend into nonlinguistic domains. Euphemism (i.e., putting something taboo or disgusting in politer-than-actual language, e.g., "she's not quite herself today"), for instance, is seen outside of language when video recordings pixilate nudity or gore, or when we build vision-blocking fencing around unsightly things (e.g., landfills or junkyards).

One of the funniest of these nonlinguistic extensions of figurative forms is with domain multiplicity coming in the form of visual puns.[30] Examples of these are abundant, so just a single example will be discussed briefly here. I recently tried a California Cabernet Sauvignon label known as Dark Horse. The winery's logo, shown on the bottles and printed on the cork, depicts the face of a horse with its blaze – the pattern of differently colored fur on many horse's foreheads – in the shape of a wine stemware glass. At first I didn't notice the pun. I was either too distracted just by noticing the horse face overall – something a bit unusual for an image on a wine cork. Or I missed the stemware because it very closely matches the actual common shape of a horse's blaze. So, I was amused when I first noticed the double depiction – the one simple shape depicting both a wine glass and a horse's blaze – two things not normally associated. But the connection with the wine's name, Dark Horse, bridged things nicely.

Many of the figurative forms reviewed here, perhaps especially puns, as in the visual one just described but also linguistic ones, can have a very playful and humorous quality to them. This explains in part why they're ubiquitous in advertisements and other genres seeking to get our attention and to gain a foothold in our memory – humor and punning are good at doing those things. But language play can go significantly beyond puns, metaphors, irony, and other figures – rising both above and below them in terms of complexity, sophistication, and functioning. Language play, after all, by virtue of the term need not be a serious thing – it can invoke fun simply for its own sake. But language play can also perform a number of other functions similar to and yet different from other processes from the other-side-of-meaning. It is this that we happily skip to next.

---

[30] An interesting mixture of linguistic and visual puns can be found with orthographic puns (Takanashi, 2007).

7   Language Play

It rained all night the day I left, the weather it was dry.
The sun so hot, I froze to death – Susanna, don't you cry.
—Stephen Foster, "Oh Susanna"(1848)

All the Crossword That's Fit to Solve

The brief discussion of the George Carlin pun, "Atheism is a non-prophet organization," at the end of the last chapter sets up the current chapter's treatment of language play very nicely – with puns being a major way in which language can be playful. But language play is a much broader category of other-side-of-meaning content, and indeed language play also resides on the sem/syn/sym side of language, or it can bridge the two sides. Or language play can even extend beyond language to encompass nonverbal and even nonlinguistic content as well. Language play need not even be a social thing between interlocutors, nor need it always be engaged in for pleasurable purposes. Language play can arise in an individual without communication even or ever taking place with other people, and language play can be used for serious and even socially aggressive or otherwise negative purposes. To illustrate some of these possibilities, please consider, for instance, the following anecdote.

I've been a subscriber to *The New York Times* newspaper for most of my adult life. Since I moved to Canada, this subscription has converted to an electronic one, except for the Sunday issue, which I still receive in print – mainly for the Sunday crossword puzzle, which I attempt religiously to complete every Monday morning when I receive the paper.[1] This famous crossword puzzle is an interesting mixture of language play content from both sides of meaning. The bulk of the crossword's material is essentially

---

[1] It necessarily arriving a day late due to the international delivery system I must use to get the print version.

clue and answer sem/syn/sym puzzles – some of which are quite difficult. The puzzle-solver attempts to derive lexical items, short phrases, or even just letter strings as answers from clues such as,

7.1 **CLUE:**   **ANSWER:**
     Google Calendar   w e b a p p
     In addition   a t t h a t
     "Foundation" author   A s i m o v[2]

But many of the crossword's clue/answer pairs are also wordplays themselves – wordplay being one form of language play (Onysko, 2016):

7.2 **CLUE:**   **ANSWER:**
     One out?   p a r o l e e
     Locker-room shower?   e s p n

And at least the Sunday version of *The New York Times* daily crossword is also usually built on a larger thematic word or language play, where multiple answers in the puzzle fit a clever pattern which the solver must discern beyond deriving just the individual answers – and, indeed, deciphering that thematic pattern can help with completing individual clue/answer pairs. For instance, under the theme title, "Unemployment Lines" (note the pun), several clue/answer pairs in a recent crossword involved very playful multiple-entendre content:[3]

7.3 **CLUE:**   **ANSWER:**
     Unemployed salon worker?   d i s t r e s s e d h a i r d r e s s e r
     Unemployed men's clothier? d i s p a t c h e d t a i l o r
     Unemployed educator?   d e g r a d e d t e a c h e r
     Unemployed loan officer?   d i s t r u s t e d b a n k e r
     Unemployed rancher?   d e r a n g e d c a t t l e m a n
     Unemployed   d i s i l l u s i o n e d m a g i c i a n
     prestidigitator?

So, *The New York Times* crossword puzzle is a form of language play on many levels. It's a challenging mind-puzzler game based on language. But it also contains many instances of different kinds of word and language play within itself.[4] It thus nicely illustrates a dichotomy between language play where language is the *object* of play versus being the *medium* of play

---

[2] Having answers to crossing words adds to the fun of crosswords, as would having the crossing word to supply the "v" in this answer – suggesting, for example, that this author has a Russian surname.

[3] All of the examples provided in this discussion come from one puzzle, January 27, 2019.

[4] These are usually indicated in the crossword with question marks at the end of the word play and sometimes thematic item clues.

(Norrick, 2017). And, of course, these categories can be blended – the crossword embeds a little of the latter into the former. The multiple players in another language play game, charades, also work with language as an object of play (i.e., fixed phrases, as in, "I shall return," which a player/actor must attempt to get other players to guess, without the actor speaking). But charades also uses language as the medium of some of the play – part of the fun of this game goes beyond just trying to guess the fixed phrase being portrayed by the current actor. Other players can also have fun with their attempted answers, sometimes trying to be funny with them or doing other things like exasperating the player/actor or other players.[5]

The New York Times crossword also shows how language play needn't be social. Although, of course, the puzzle *is* social in that an author/ builder created the puzzle and I and other solvers work on it. And both builders and solvers likely do a bit of generic mind reading in the process (i.e., *this is clever, solvers will enjoy this,* and, *... Oh, for God's sake, this clue is lame! The author/builder must have known this clue was too cringeworthy*). But part of the solving can be amusement experienced purely by the solver themselves. For example, at one point in solving the *Times* puzzle in question, I glanced at a clue I hadn't strategically selected – it just caught my eye. The clue was: "A special gift." I immediately suspected the answer was "e s p" (extrasensory perception), given how many puzzle author/builders will clue for answers that aren't words. When I found the location for the answer in the puzzle and saw it required three spaces, I broke into a smile. I then had the innocent thought to myself of, *How did I know?* And then only after completing this thought did I notice the completely accidental and unintended joke quality of my self-directed rhetorical question – itself demonstrating a pun. All of this, admittedly perhaps sadly pathetic fun, was enjoyed by myself alone, without involving communication – of course, until this writing.

This chapter will first provide a brief review of some of the content under the rubric of language play in its various forms. But then the chapter will pull back and widen its viewing angle to consider what *play* itself actually *is*, in both humans and other animals. This broadened perspective helps reveal the major theme of this chapter: that language play exists for a number of reasons but perhaps most prominently *to help prepare people for practicing the art of leveraging pragmatic effects in interlocutors and language witnesses*. The chapter will then discuss how different

---

[5] Immortalized by the Igor character portrayed by Marty Feldman in Mel Brooks' classic 1974 American horror movie spoof, *Young Frankenstein* (i.e., "Said – a – give ... Give him a sedagive!") (Gruskoff & Brooks, 1974).

genres of language play train people for performing which particular pragmatic effects, in individual utterances as well as in language play, occurring during talk-in-interaction.

The Playground

On the occasional driving road trip I've taken with my family, we would often play a simple game we invented called *fixed phrases* to help pass the time. While in the car, one person would just say aloud two letters, often picked at random, for instance, "T" and "C," and then everyone was challenged to come up with and say aloud reasonably fixed terms or phrases that matched those letters (e.g., Tom Collins, toy car, trash can, tin can, the Clash, tea cup, terracotta, ten count, taxicab). We weren't terribly picky about quality of match (e.g., tender [loving] care), and if an offering seemed not terribly fixed (e.g., trading company) we'd then debate whether it was fixed enough to warrant acceptance.

This and many other games like it illustrate one part of language play mentioned briefly in the previous section and discussed by Neal Norrick (2017) in the Nancy Bell–edited book *Multiple Perspectives on Language Play* – that of language games or puzzles, or essentially play that has language as its object. Examples of such games and puzzles are innumerable. They can be customized ones invented by players like *fixed phrases* or one called *alphabet* I used to play as a kindergartener with my mother as we waited for my school bus.[6] They can also be generic types of games, puzzles, or challenges like crossword puzzles, anagrams, hangman, palindromes, charades, tongue twisters, etc. Many have become manufactured board and related games like Scrabble, Boggle, Mad Libs, etc. Others have formed the basis for broadcast game shows like the American television programs, *Password, Wheel of Fortune,* or *Jeopardy.*[7] Many print media sources like magazines and newspapers regularly printed (and still do) language games like crosswords as already mentioned but many other types as well.[8]

Many forms of formula jokes also have structures or constructions that, although told or written usually for the sake of bringing laughter to

---

[6] I'd go through the alphabet trying to think of and say the longest word I could starting with each letter.

[7] *Jeopardy* is mostly a general knowledge quiz show, but each answer a contestant provides to the clues given must be phrased in the form of a question, and many forms of word play are involved in categories of clues (e.g., a clue category might be "get your FiX," in which each answer will contain the letters F and X).

[8] The Sunday *New York Times* magazine has a puzzle section with several recurring word and language puzzles (Spelling Bee, the Acrostic, Winding Down, Puns and Anagrams, Switchbacks, etc.).

hearers/readers, along with other purposes (i.e., belittling a person or group, either playfully or less so, honoring someone, humanizing someone, etc.), still largely involve language as the object of the play.[9] Jokes with patterned storylines (i.e., "a man, a woman, and a priest walk into a bar ...," mother jokes, etc.), structured discourse patterns with embedded word play (e.g., "knock-knock" jokes), and others illustrate this category.

Other kinds of language play fall *more* on the side of language being the medium of people playing together, even if the ways in which the language is used are constricted by different parameters. For instance, rap, poetry, and other language-based live competitions along with some cheers, taunts, trash-talk, etc., either formalized or more informal, can restrict the produced language in different ways (i.e., adhering to rhyming or rhythm schemes). But within those parameters poets, emcees, etc., can make their topic essentially anything, thus making the constrained language form mostly the medium of the play, but also a bit of the object of the play as well.

Still other examples of language play seem to reside fully on the side of using language as the medium of play. Among these are imitation or impersonation, punning, teasing, cases of intertextual reference, and layered meanings where, for instance, adults may realize some humor leveraged in language play yet younger hearers may not. And the techniques for doing all this playfulness are essentially limitless. Many of the techniques discussed in this book are tools for language play (i.e., the huge range of rhetorical devices [e.g., alliteration], figurative language, indirectness, imprecision, deviation, etc.).

Perhaps most interesting is how language play can meld into other forms of playfulness, in images, behavior, etc., and work together with the affordances of the different media for a very rich communicative experience. And, indeed, even in very simple forms of language play/other play combinations, we can see very sophisticated things going on. To illustrate, please consider the short animated film, or cartoon, from the Warner Brothers studio near the end of its famous production run in the mid-twentieth century. The cartoon in question is titled, *Transylvania 6–5000*.[10]

A Play Bunny

The overall plot is fairly simple and involves only three characters: Bugs Bunny – a smart aleck rabbit; Count Bloodcount – a bumbling vampire;

---

[9] Humanizing people in the cases of, say, joking anecdotes told in wedding toasts.

[10] Produced in 1963 and one of the last Warner Brother's cartoons directed by Chuck Jones (DePatie, Jones, & Noble, 1963).

and Emily/Agatha – a two-headed female vulture. Bugs Bunny thinks he's traveling (by digging an underground tunnel) to Pennsylvania, but has instead arrived in Transylvania. He first meets the Emily/Agatha character, who unbeknownst to Bugs is/are sizing him up for a meal. Bugs then goes to a scary-looking castle, which he thinks is a hotel, to ask for directions. Here he meets Count Bloodcount, who invites Bugs to stay for the night.

Bugs then finds a book on magic words and phrases in his bedroom which he reads aloud since he cannot sleep. He uses these words through the rest of the film, accidentally at first and then purposefully, to switch Count Bloodcount back and forth between being a vampire and a bat, to physically beat up the Count, and eventually to wear him down (the Count had been trying to attack Bugs ever since meeting him). In the final sequence, Bugs starts mixing up the magic words that had been used thus far (e.g., "abracadabra" and "hocus pocus," changing them to "abraca-pocus" and "hocus-cadabra") to eventually turn the Count into a male two-headed vulture, which Emily/Agatha then chase(s) out of the castle in loving pursuit. The end has Bugs Bunny using magic words to turn his own ears into bat wings, so he can finally leave and get back on his intended path.

This cartoon is just over six and a half minutes long, and my best count has it containing fifty-seven instances of word play, language play, sight gags or combinations of these. This comes to an average of almost nine instances per minute, or about one instance every seven seconds. Some of these are very simple, using stock Warner Brother's cartoon techniques applicable to a child audience, like mispronunciations or "funny" words (e.g., Bugs pronounces the French word for waiter, *garçon*, as "gar-kon," and the word, *fatigued*, as "fat-ee-gyood," and he mentions at one point that he's hungry because he hasn't eaten since "Cucamonga"). But other instances of language play are fairly clever. Near the end of the cartoon when Bugs wishes to bring Count Bloodcount's new two-headed vulture status to the attention of Emily/Agatha, Bugs leans out a castle window to call to Emily/Agatha, saying, "Oh goyles" – a pun playing on a New Yorkesque accented pronunciation of "girls," as well as the fragment "goyle" from the word "gargoyle," many of which are commonly found on castles like Count Bloodcount's, and which Emily/Agatha visually resemble. "Gargoyle" also has the vaguely scary connotation of much of the film's imagery.[11]

---

[11] The scenes are filled with rope nooses, skulls, gallows, execution axes, and other stock Halloween paraphernalia.

The title of the film itself is also a multiple-meaning pun with inter-textual references. It plays off the resemblance of the place names Pennsylvania and Transylvania, and refers to a Glen Miller song from 1940, "Pennsylvania 6–5000." Terms like this were commonly used at the time in the United States as ways of saying telephone numbers – using two letters and then five digits, the letters being the first two of the pronounced word. "P" and "E," the first two letters of Pennsylvania, correspond to the numbers 7 and 3 on a phone dial. So, in the modern American seven-digit format, this phone number today would be 736–5000. Part of the reason for using the telephone nomenclature in the cartoon's title is the link with a portion of the backstory – Bugs enters the castle (hotel) in search of a telephone, to call his travel agency to get him back on track. And telephones come up throughout the film as Bugs asks the Count early in the story where the phones are located. The end scene has Bugs finally finding a phone booth, where he begins a call before turning his ears into wings and then hanging up. A related sight gag involves this telephone booth, which is shaped like an upright coffin.[12]

Another intertextual reference is found in a song Bugs hums aloud in the middle of the film. Just as Count Bloodcount is about to attack him, Bugs hums the "abracadabra" magic word aloud to the tune of the song, unknowingly turning the Count into a bat, which Bugs mistakes for a big mosquito and sprays with insecticide. This causes the Count as bat to alight over a doorway as he endures a coughing fit from the spray. Bugs then continues humming the song and this time sings aloud the "hocus pocus" magic phrase. The Count accordingly turns back into the vampire, and subsequently falls from the doorframe onto his head on the floor. The song turns out to be a popular hit by the late Doris Day from the late 1950s, "It's Magic" (Styne, 1947).

A number of other language play and visual gags are interspersed throughout. A place sign at the beginning of the film reads, "Pittsburghe Transylvania." A sign on a portrait shows children with one adult, all wearing execution hoods and gloves, carrying maces, broad axes, and bombs. The adult's hood also resembles a scout cap, and a sign beneath the portrait reads, "Ghouls scout camp, 1832." A sign on another portrait of a lady wearing a ring reads, "Aunt Lucretia," referring to the historical Lucretia Borgia who was rumored to have a ring in which she kept poison to put in people's drinks.

A number of instances of figurative language are also found. Bugs uses a sarcastic comment after reading that "abracadabra" is among the most powerful magic words, saying, "Huh, yeah, oh, sure it is!" Emily/Agatha

---

[12] Many things in the film are shaped like coffins: doors, doorways, a television, etc.

also use(s) several puns when they/she first meet(s) Bugs Bunny (e.g., "Who is that delicious young creature, Emily?" and "Doesn't he look sweet and crunchy, Agatha?"). One of these meanings could be metaphorical terms for "adorable," "cute," etc., and Emily/Agatha have/has certain appearance details (e.g., wearing bonnets, speaking with a vague British accent) to give them/her a look of a British nanny, who might stereotypically use such metaphors. But the other meaning is the nonfigural one, matching what vultures do – eat other creatures – sometimes decaying ones. Count Bloodcount uses his own pun when putting Bugs to bed, saying, "Sleep is good for the blood" – meaning both a general term of saying something is good for you as well as the specifically intended goodness for the *blood* that a vampire would seek.[13]

Still other sight gags play off linguistic terms. For instance, a television shown in one scene has actual rabbit ears on top instead of the kind of antennae found on televisions of the era, which were referred to as, "rabbit ears," due to their shape – this also foreshadows the film's end. The doorknob to Bugs Bunny's bedroom is in the shape of a skeleton head. Keys used on old doorknobs like this were often called skeleton keys. And the board between the bedposts near Bugs Bunny's head has a skeleton carved onto it. This part of a bed is referred to as a headboard.

So, we can see that language play, even in very simple venues like this cartoon, can afford quite a bit of sophistication – through using language as a medium, possibly coupled with parallel media, a user can leverage an awful lot of meaning and pragmatic effects. We'll also see later that language play is used to convey this meaning and these pragmatic effects because it is good at it. But for now, given alternative and less playful ways are available to communicate, we can ask why we even have language play as something we do, or for that matter why do we even have play of any kind? The next section will address this.

Do You Play?

When we move into the realm of language play where language is clearly and obviously the medium through which people conduct play, whether or not being mixed with nonlinguistic content as in the Warner Brothers cartoon, it immediately gets difficult to come up with a definition or set of defining principles to clarify what language play *is* or *is not*. On the one hand, language play seems to involve fun, amusement, enjoyment, etc. But it can also be used for heated competition and for negative social goals. Indeed, we see both of these even in the Warner Brother's cartoon

---

[13] And of course Count Bloodcount's name is also a cleverish pun.

Table 7.1 *Five criteria for identifying play (Berghardt, 2006)*

1.	Activity is nonessential for the moment.
2.	Behavior is spontaneous, voluntary, intentional, pleasurable, reinforcing, autotelic.*
3.	Play is incomplete, exaggerated, awkward, or precocious with modified forms, sequencing, and targets.
4.	Behavior is repeatedly performed in similar but not rigidly stereotyped form.
5.	Actor needs adequate food, health, and low enough stress, or a "relaxed field," for play to occur.

* Performed for its own sake.

reviewed above. Moving back to the world of real-world language play, much of it might also seem unserious, yet it is frequently used for very serious matters like heady medical discussions and ethnic battling (Zayts & Schnurr, 2017; Holt, 2017; Haugh, 2017; Sinkevicinte, 2017; Otsuji & Pennycook, 2017). Language play might also be thought of as creative language usage. Yet non-playful language can also be creative and not all language play is all that creative (e.g., lame "dad" jokes). This section accordingly broadens out the discussion of what play overall actually *is*, in both humans and other animals, to help us get a better sense of what language play is and why we have and do it.

Gordon Burghardt in his book, *The Genesis of Animal Play: Testing the Limits* (2006), lists five criteria for identifying play in this more general animal behavior sense. These criteria are listed in Table 7.1.

Much of the content of this table might help define language play. For instance, that it is nonessential *in the moment of use*, etc. But as mentioned, language play may not always be done for pleasurable, reinforcing, or autotelic purposes. Perhaps a better approach might be to consider what play in general is *for*. According to Burghardt, play in animals serves a number of related functions. It is first and perhaps foremost a form of practice, rehearsal, or training for things necessary in life. Carnivores, for instance, will play at stalking, pouncing, or hunting. Herd animals will play at grouping and moving together. Many animals play at different means of locomotion or other movement. Many animals also play at intraspecies combat or fighting. Some animals play at child care. Many animals play at object manipulation. And social animals in particular play at socializing.

As a corollary to all these forms of play, several parallel or sub-forms of development occur. Playing animals form and strengthen social bonds within their species and even across species. They work out their and other animals' position in social networks and hierarchies, and how to move within these social systems. They learn means of social display (i.e., *Look at me!*). They practice at several subtypes of sexual activity. They do a great deal of learning, about themselves, their group mates, other species, prey, the physical environment, the practices of their rudimentary cultures, etc.

And as part of all of this, a number of baser functions get performed and develop. These range from the physiological (i.e., calorie burning, cardiovascular and cardiopulmonary capacity improvement, muscular coordination and strengthening, speed and agility increases, etc.), through the sensory (i.e., fine tuning of sensory processes, vestibular development, integrating behavioral practices into sensory uptake [e.g., ear and head movements to improve hearing and seeing]), to the neurocognitive (i.e., neuronal connection density increases as a function of learning, emotional regulation, association formulation, neural network training, etc.).

But animal play also serves other functions. It can be a form of self-stimulation to learn and to overcome boredom. It can be a form of individual or group tension reduction. It enables exploration and selection from amid a predispositional behavioral subset (i.e., learning what *not* to do, what *not* to eat, where *not* to go, etc.). And importantly it might be done purely for its own sake – doing it is good for animals, for all the above reasons. So, animals have evolved processes that make play feel good to make the animals do it. So, animals may sometimes play for that reason alone – because it's fun.

Transfer all these reasons for play to the human animal and we have a solid "all of the above" answer to the question of why humans play. But with humans, at least three of these developmental enhancements of play are much more pronounced – cognitive development, social development, and communicative development. In humans, these three interrelated abilities are on steroids, so we require more play at them to bring them up to their necessary adult-functional levels.

For cognitive development, we play with all sorts of objects and in many kinds of environments. We play at all sorts of pretend situations, pretend relationships, pretend adventures. We mimic other people's actions, acts, mannerisms, behavioral patterns, and contexts as part of this play. Social development is very much intertwined into all of this as shown when we play with other people (i.e., learning to share and to take turns, etc.) and when we play with other people *as other people* (i.e., playing house or school or doctor, etc., with the different roles involved). And, of course, language play is interwoven among the cognitive and social play as we explore, discover, learn, rehearse, and refine ways of making meaning happen in the minds of others.

So, this puts the notion of language play in perspective. It is essentially training for leveraging meaning and pragmatic effects in other people. We learn how to influence other people via all the other-side-of-meaning processes discussed in this book, along with the sem/syn/sym side, by doing language play. We continue to practice it creatively as adults, in part to continue that meaning and pragmatic effect leveraging. And we do it in part because we are rewarded on occasion for it – it's fun.

Works and Plays Well with Others: "A Big Phish Story"

Coincidentally, early in the morning on the very day I started writing this chapter I'd received an email message, purportedly from a head administrator at my university, with a very odd, short single sentence in all caps at the top, "ARE YOU AVAILABLE?" I immediately found this message suspect as it was extremely out of character – the person who'd supposedly written it would never be so curt, would not use scare caps, and most likely wouldn't have written me very early in the morning. So, I scrolled down below the sentence to unsurprisingly find a large warning label affixed to the message – likely posted as an automatic function of my email program – warning that the message might be fake. So, I closed the message and wrote the administrator in question – who later confirmed the message was not from her. I then forwarded the whole email conversation to our primary IT person who handles our university computers, cc-ing the administrator, with the following short note (emphasis added):

7.4   **Dear Daniel:**
FYI (*a big phish story* – please see email stream below).
Should I forward the original email to you?
Herb

I'd engaged in this bit of language play quite innocently, and without putting much thought or effort into it. And, most interestingly, I hadn't even fully registered that I had played with language play on the very day I'd intended to start work on this chapter devoted to the topic. Only later in the day (a few minutes ago as of the time of this writing) did I note this coincidence.

Why had I used this bit of language play? At the time I'd written the email, I'd not really registered my intentions. But later when I took an honest look back on the moment of composition I could see at least a bit of what I was probably doing. On the one hand, the IT addressee is a very clever person, who I'd interacted with many times before. I suspected he'd have a little smile over the pun in this message, which I was happy to induce – just for its own sake. I'd also cc'd the administrator, mainly to alert her that I'd reported the phishing episode in case she'd want or need to know that. But I was also happy if the message produced a smile in her as well, as I suspect it did – she having a very wry sense of humor.

I'd also been a bit annoyed at receiving the message – it coming as it did as a misrepresentation, likely designed to draw in unsuspecting recipients to gather some information or attempt to sell something, or some other ill-intended motive. So, I was happy to invoke the idea of a "big *fish* story" – an obviously fabricated and hyperbolized tall tale, a bit of lame fakery by some boastful and clueless speaker, about fish or something else – to impart its characteristics onto the email message and its sender.

And, finally, I was also probably showing off a bit, using whatever little cleverness it might have taken to construct the comment to make me and my actions appear superior to the unknown email sender and their behavior – rising above their act of deception as it were. I was essentially highlighting that I'd not only been wise to the deception but that I could also now distance myself from it, and include two colleagues with me in that bit of minor social engineering – placing all of us as if superior to the mystery person who would send the fake email (or who would program a bot to do the deed).

But *how* had my short message done these things (or attempted them, at least)? How had the use of essentially one word, "phish," in my message attempted all these pragmatic effects of mastery display, humor leveraging, social bonding, identification, distancing, social engineering, and perhaps others (Colston, 2015)?[14] The short answer is that it did so through the myriad of processes underlying pun (or *double-, multiple-entendre*) usage. It had used a type of language from the other-side-of-meaning to leverage a package of extra meaning and pragmatic effects.[15]

The longer answer to the question is essentially the content of this section – how do different types of language play, puns, and others, accomplish other-side-of-meaning content in interlocutors, and how does that content match speakers', writers', and signers' motivations in

---

[14] Or, if not just one word, then the short phrase, "a big phish story."

[15] It bears noting that the use of the phrase from the email message, "A big phish story," as part of the header to this section of the chapter gives the phrase at least a third meaning. The original two meanings invoked were (1) the idea of a "big fish story," or an obviously fictitious tall tale, as described in the section, and (2) the homophone "phish," corresponding to a fake email or the verb "phishing," the process of using fake emails to gather information from unsuspecting users. The *telling* of this story in this section of the chapter is then a third meaning: my slightly lengthy telling of the story about my receiving a "phishing" email message, which itself can be described essentially nonfiguratively as a "big phish story."

discourse? In the case of this one pun I'd used, my message to the IT person simultaneously carried the "big *fish* story" sense of the received email – that email being something misrepresented or fake like a tall fish tale. But my email also carried the sense of *phish* or *phishing* as these terms apply to a fake email message, and the process of sending fake emails to glean people's personal information, respectively. So, two separate meanings resided in the same base construction – the meanings were coincidentally connected via the homophones, *fish* and *phish*.

It is this coincidence of two separate meanings residing in one utterance, and with both those meanings being quite apt in the context, that enabled me to do what I did. And my doing what I did reveals my underlying motivations. Here is how it all fits together. Recall that I probably triggered a brief bit of positive affect in my two addressees. I had also belittled the fake email sender, and attempted to make myself and my addressees seem superior to such a person. These two basic actions were also motivated very likely by an internal desire to connect with other people and to maintain and/or increase social status (more on these to come; see also Chapter 8). The cleverness of the pun is the key to all of this. By finding and uttering the pun, I revealed a bit of cleverness on my part (i.e., the pragmatic effect of mastery display). This likely impressed my addressees at least a little bit, their getting a little pleasure out of the pun itself and their also likely admiring me a bit for delivering it (i.e., humor, ingratiation).[16] This, in contrast to the more slimy machinations of the fake email sender, makes us look good, and the sender look bad in relative comparison (i.e., social engineering, belittlement, identification).

Indeed, if we look across examples of language play, we repeatedly see these and related pragmatic effects in operation – likely driven by those same root social motivations. For instance, consider the following news story about a response to a tweet from Donald Trump:

7.5   **In response to a tweet posted by Donald Trump (November 18, 2018) with a misspelling of Senator Adam B. Schiff's name as "Schitt," Walter M. Shaub Jr., former US federal government ethics watchdog who had recently resigned after battling the Trump administration, tweeted the following (Mervosh, 2018):**

---

[16] Of course, puns don't *always* impress, and my pun may not have done so in this circumstance. Occasionally, people groan inwardly (or outwardly) at hearing puns. I may have had a little insulation from groaning in this example, though, both interlocutors knowing I am a psycholinguist who studies figurative language, including irony. Had they felt the need to groan at my pun, they might have given me the benefit of an ironic reading of the pun (i.e., my pretending to find the pun hilarious through using it, but my actually rolling my eyes at it as well – which could have also mirrored my attitude toward the fake email I'd received).

"The Office of the President was made for better things than an infantile tweet misspelling a congressman's name like a curse word."[17]

Here, Donald Trump's original tweet with the likely intentional misspelling and profanity is probably trying to demean Senator Schiff in order to win favor with Trump's political base (e.g., mastery display [albeit of a fairly low-hurdle sort], ingratiation, belittlement, social engineering, identification). Shaub's response achieves his own range of pragmatic effects in its punning usage of "infantile tweet," which could refer to the juvenile-esque original tweet sent by Donald Trump, or it could be a tit-for-tat return faux misspelling of "twit" – effectively calling Donald Trump an infantile twit. The relative sophistication of the second tweet aids in its attempt to demean Trump as well as to appeal to Shaub's constituency. So, again we have mastery display (of a more sophisticated sort), ingratiation, belittlement, social engineering, identification, etc., taking place.[18]

Nancy Bell (2017) in her introduction to the already-mentioned *Multiple Perspectives on Language Play*, also talks in more generic terms about what benefits people can glean when engaging in language play. These "cognitive" (Bell, 2012; Feingold and Mazzella, 1991), "social" (Baynham, 1996, Fraley & Aron, 2004; Holmes, 2000; Holmes & Marra, 2002; Pomerantz & Bell, 2007), and "emotional" (Martin, 2007; Pogrebin & Poole, 1988) benefits nicely correspond to the pragmatic effects being discussed here.

For instance, interlocutors who engage in humorous language play report greater feelings of closeness with their play partner (Fraley & Aron, 2004). Employees whose supervisors use language play in the work environment view their supervisors as more effective and approve of them more (Mesmer-Magnus, Glew, & Miswesvaran, 2012). People also use language play with interlocutors to disparage tedious tasks they're doing, and interlocutors who participate in this play are also more engaged in those tasks (Dunbar, Banas, Rodriguez, Liu, & Abra, 2012). Language play among police officers also serves to maintain "organizational relationships" (Pogrebin & Poole, 1988). Co-engagement in language play even among strangers is also argued to serve an affiliative function (Holt, 2017) and to reinforce norms, behaviors, and values (Bell, 2015).

---

[17] The Representative Schiff example is also discussed briefly in Chapter 5.
[18] We also have a degree of imprecision of the sort described in Chapter 4. Shaub's creation of a clever pun, which just won't settle into one meaning or the other, keeping both meanings simultaneously active, can impress the reader beyond just the double meaning itself.

But other pragmatic effects can also arise from our core motivations in using language play. In second language (L2) or lingua franca contexts, for instance, speakers are often motivated to show proficiency and/or to belong to the L2 or lingua franca language group or culture (Bell, 2017; Firth, 1996; Huth, 2017; Kecskes, 2007; Kecskes & Horn, 2007; Kecskes & Papp, 2003; Kescskes & Mey, 2008; Seidlhofer, 2009). Speakers in these situations might use language play to leverage the kinds of socially affiliative pragmatic effects we've been discussing (i.e., building social connections, social engineering etc.), and indeed L2/lingua franca situations might enhance those social motivations as people might feel a stronger need to belong (Hann, 2017; Van Dam & Bannink, 2017). But speakers might also wish to leverage the pragmatic effect of *identification* to assist their goal to belong to the L2 or lingua franca culture (Eskildsen, 2017), or even to *resist* the appearance of belonging to a particular group, as in the case of anti-language (Lefkowitz & Hedgcock, 2017).

Instant Replay

As noted earlier, word and language play can be a solitary experience, not involving interlocutors. But in cases like the ones just described, language play occurs between people, with varieties of mind-reading and audience design taking place, whether in some time-delayed back-and-forth dialog occurring with language play interwoven, or in live interaction. But language play arising during live talk-in-interaction can be particularly interesting because time pressure and lack of revisability gives the language play an ad-libbed or improvisational quality. Interlocutors must craft their language play spontaneously and on the fly. Of course, scripted dialogs of interactive live language play can thus be very entertaining, tricking us into being awed at the seeming intelligence and pragmatic pliability of the conversers.[19] But when language play actually happens live in interaction, it is particularly interesting – overhearers or even participants knowing this discourse is being crafted right before their eyes.

One very brief example of language play in talk-in-interaction is an exchange between myself and a university colleague. At the time the exchange occurred, I had been reading a book about the American presidents John F. Kennedy, Lyndon B. Johnson, and Richard M. Nixon, in which the importance of the year 1948 in the formation of each of these figures' political careers was discussed centrally (Morrow, 2005). In

[19] See Colston (2015, pp 115–118) for a discussion of a scripted discourse involving clever trumping.

mentioning the title of the book to the colleague, the following quick verbatim exchange ensued:

7.6A   HC: <First talking about the book and then introducing its title> "... it's *The Best Year of Their Lives: Kennedy, Johnson, and Nixon in 1948.*"

7.6B   GM: **"1948 ... isn't that the year Dewey defeated Truman?"**

7.6C   HC: <Pause ... smiling> **"Yes!"**

This brief example demonstrates language play in interaction in several ways. But first some background details are needed. The two interlocutors were long-standing friends, who had a great deal of knowledge about one another, including that both are knowledgeable about US presidential history, that I study figurative language including verbal irony, that we both are frequent users of verbal irony, and that I had previously published a paper with a title containing a word play on the famous American newspaper headline, "Dewey Defeats Truman."[20] The published paper was about ironic restatement – repeating back a speaker's or writer's erroneous statement in an ironic fashion to highlight the error and to suggest the speaker should not have made the error (Colston, 2000a).

The headline was mentioned in the published paper's title because of a famous incidence of ironic restatement by US President-elect (at the time) Harry S. Truman. Truman had actually won the 1948 US presidential election, but a Chicago newspaper had called the election for Dewey, and then run the erroneous headline in large print on the front page of their issue the day after the election. Truman had great fun showing that headline to photographers – this act itself illustrating a complex form of language play (i.e., the ironic restatement conveyed by displaying someone else's bit of erroneous printed language, and a very important "someone else" at that – the news writers of a major metropolitan newspaper, who are normally expected to get their facts right).

My colleague's response to my telling him the title of the book began the language play. His question about whether 1948 was the year that "Dewey defeated Truman" was partly rhetorical, but also partly not. Although a number of senses of his question are available (see discussion of Table 7.2, below), any of them, whether ironically intended or not,

---

[20] The *Chicago Daily Tribune*, November 3, 1948.

Table 7.2 *Possible factual underpinnings of example comment 7.6b,*
"1948 . . . isn't that the year Dewey defeated Truman?"

Speaker has election outcome wrong	Speaker is not sure of the year
Speaker has election outcome correct (i.e., is ironic)	Speaker is not sure of the year
Speaker has election outcome wrong	Speaker is sure of the year (i.e., is ironic)
Speaker has election outcome correct (i.e., is ironic)	Speaker is sure of the year (i.e., is ironic)

could have just been rhetorical. If my colleague wasn't being playful, he may have just been wondering aloud if 1948 was the year Dewey won the election. Or my colleague may have genuinely sought confirmation of the date. More likely, though, is that the colleague *was* being playful with his question. But even here the question could have been rhetorical or not. If intended rhetorically, yet still also intended playfully, my colleague may have just been being funny – not expecting a response. But again, it's more likely that his question wasn't meant rhetorically and that my colleague was instead inviting me, or perhaps even challenging me, in a good-natured way, to join in his play. So, on the rhetorical issue alone, the 7.6b comment is already quite complex.

But 7.6b is even more complicated in its punning technique. Two essential propositions are contained in the comment: that Dewey defeated Truman (i.e., in a US presidential election), and that this defeat occurred in 1948. Neither, either, or both of these propositions could be intended and/or taken ironically, making for no fewer than four possible readings of the comment. These possibilities are presented in Table 7.2.

In the first row of Table 7.2, nothing is ironized and the question stands on its surface form – the speaker genuinely thinking Dewey defeated Truman, an erroneous belief but nonetheless what the speaker thinks, and the speaker is genuinely unsure if the defeat was in the year 1948, hence the question. In the second row, we have the speaker also being genuinely unsure of the year, but the "Dewey defeated Truman" part of the comment is a playful, ironized referent to the actual event of the erroneous newspaper headline. In the third row of the table, the speaker is again genuinely holding the incorrect belief that Dewey won, but here the speaker is ironizing the question about the year, as if the speaker knew that Dewey won *in 1948*, but is pretending to wonder about this date, perhaps just to be flippant. This third possibility seems least likely given the colleague's personality – being both incredibly smart but also sophisticatedly clever. The most likely possibility is the fourth one in Table 7.2, where both propositions are ironized – the speaker is well aware that Truman actually won the election, so the "Dewey defeated Truman" part is ironical. The speaker also knows fully that Truman won the election and the Chicago newspaper made its famous error in the year 1948 – so, the date inquiry part is also used ironically.

The reason my colleague was almost assuredly ironizing the whole 7.6b comment is the degree of common ground held by the two interlocutors. My colleague knew without doubt that I was aware of his extensive knowledge of US history, presidential and otherwise. He also was familiar with my abilities with irony. So, his comment was both completely and intentionally ironic (i.e., pretending to be wrong about who won the election and pretending to be unsure of the year) and was also fully transparent in all of this pretense.

So, what were the pragmatic effects then leveraged by all this rhetoricalness, punning, and irony? One straightforward pragmatic effect taking place is a bit of social engineering. Regardless of my participation, my colleague was likely at least partially belittling people with poor knowledge of US history. My colleague might also have been playfully (or perhaps not so playfully) testing me to see if I belonged to the group he was making fun of. That I demonstrably did not belong to this group, evidenced by my 7.6 c ironic answer to the colleague's ironic question, also possibly engineered me a bit – my gaining or at least maintaining a bit of social status by passing my colleague's test.

In a few related ways, my colleague was also possibly expressing some affinity toward me. His alluding to the "Dewey Defeats Truman" headline could in part be a nod toward my earlier-published paper which also used that headline. Through this mentioning my colleague could be demonstrating his admiration of my work by revealing that he'd read it or at least knew of it and could now recall it at the time of our 7.6 exchange. Ingratiation was also likely involved in expressing affinity – enhanced perhaps by a bit of mastery display. My colleague was clearly showing his knowledge and witty language skills with his sophisticated comment. And by virtue of his demonstrating his expectation, presuming he wasn't genuinely testing me, that I would cleanly field his comment, evidenced in his opting to use the comment, he was effectively complimenting me (i.e., as if thinking, *This is pretty clever, but I believe you can handle it*). And the use of playful language itself, with its implicit invitation to join the play, is also complimentary. We tend to invite participatory and amusing play only among people we like.[21]

---

[21] Unless the play itself is used ironically.

I fortunately had my wits about me at the time of the exchange so I was indeed able to handle my colleague's opening play salvo. I was also able to return in kind some of the compliments I'd received. By noting the ironies in my colleague's 7.6b comment, I was able to sustain and return both of them with my brief 7.6 c reply, "Yes!" With this brief affirmation I pretended to go along with the pretense that Dewey had defeated Truman, and the pretense that my colleague wasn't sure of the year. That these tit-for-tat ironies neatly fit in the brief one-word response was also to my benefit. It afforded a tiny bit of mastery display of my own, which I was happy to leverage into a returned compliment to my colleague.

This brief look under the hood of the short 7.6 exchange reveals some of *how* my colleague and I were able to leverage pragmatic effects (i.e., social engineering, meaning enhancement, mastery display, affinity expression, identification, ingratiation, etc.) in one another via a bit of language play. But it doesn't really address *why* we did this. Returning to the earlier similar question about play in general, why had we engaged in language play in the first place? As we've seen with similar questions asked in this book, both short and longer answers can be provided. For this question, I'll provide the short answer here, but I'll refer to the upcoming Chapter 8 for the larger answer, as nearly that entire chapter discusses our fundamental and intense social motivations and needs, which drive much of our thought and behavior, including our leveraging of interlocutor pragmatic effects with other-side-of-meaning processes like language play.

My colleague and I had engaged in this instance of language play predominantly to further forge our social relationship and to maintain and/or elevate our positions in social networks and hierarchies. We also might have done it purely for the sake of fun, and maybe also for convenience. But let's first consider the social motivations.

The rich development of shared ironic situations is a highly prevalent activity among social intimates (Gibbs, 2000; Pexman & Zvaigzne, 2004). Indeed, our social goals regarding connection and status are evident in the particular pragmatic effects my colleague and I had leveraged in our 7.6 exchange. The various exercises in co-compliments served the first goal of building or reinforcing our social connection. My colleague and I were already friends. We'd also engaged in playful exchanges like the 7.6 one before. So, the 7.6 episode was likely in service of affirming that social connection. The exchanged instances of mastery display with their implicit acknowledgments of one another's abilities also helped to co-affirm our social statuses. And the bit of belittlement expressed toward people with poor knowledge of US history probably massaged our collective egos for a little while, making us feel rewarded a bit for this one particular knowledge ability we are able to muster.[22]

Of course, the language play between my colleague and me was also mostly positive in that we were bolstering one another without any direct victimization.[23] But there can be negative sides to our species' social tendencies. Goals to get and stay connected and to maintain/increase social status can take the form of preventing other people from fulfilling those same goals in themselves (i.e., preventing others from nosing in on *our* social connections and destabilizing others' social statuses). It remains a challenge to humankind to preserve the positive incarnations of our social milieu and motivations, and to minimize the negative ones.

My colleague and I also had probably engaged in the language play for the pure amusement of it. As discussed earlier, play purely for the sake of amusement is one reason people and some animals engage in it. That this amusement is also reinforcing our practicing the execution of pragmatic effects is part of the process – serving to perpetuate language play in our culture. The American professional baseball player Yogi Berra was well known for his usage of language play purely for the fun of it. Indeed, he was so well known for such language play that many famous quips were attributed to him even though he hadn't originated them. He even published a book discussing this entitled, *The Yogi Book: I Really Didn't Say Everything I Said!* (Berra, 1998). Among the comments attributed to Berra but with other presumed originations are those listed in Table 7.3. Table 7.4 contains "Yogi-isms" confirmed as Berra's (Mather & Rogers, 2015):

But another reason for language play speaks to the issue of why my colleague and I hadn't tried to fulfill our social motivations through some other means – the indirectness inherent in the act of playing (i.e., not really doing/expressing something but merely playing at or pretending to do/express it) *more readily* accomplishes some pragmatic effects than other

---

[22] Let me rapidly pinprick any inflating balloon of perceived self-arrogance surrounding this on my part. I am proud to know something about US presidential history and I feel fortunate for the opportunity to follow this one particular odd side interest of mine. But there are uncounted numbers of experts out there on everything from air conditioners and beta-blockers to yam farming and zooplankton to whom I humbly tip my hat.

[23] Excepting the brief mild derision of the generic category of people who don't care about their history. But this is more of a critique of some aspects of our species and our cultures whereby occasionally unnecessary ignorance is rewarded. It is not meant to deride individuals. Moreover, I would defend this perspective. It bears repeating that history comes round to blindside those who've lost track of it. So, some people being willfully ignorant about history can bring harm to others.

Table 7.3 *Famous "Yogi-isms" Yogi Berra may not have originated*

"It ain't over until the fat lady sings."
"When you come to a fork in the road, take it."
"It's déjà vu all over again!"
"Nobody goes there anymore. It's too crowded."
"Always go to other people's funerals. Otherwise they won't go to yours."

Table 7.4 *Famous "Yogi-isms" Yogi Berra originated*

"I want to thank everybody for making this day necessary."
"Baseball is 90 percent mental. The other half is physical."
"If you can't imitate him, don't copy him."
"It ain't over till it's over."

more direct ways of expression. This is especially the case for some of the pragmatic effects involved in language play (i.e., social engineering, affinity expression, mastery display, etc.).

Mastery display, for instance, requires that one shows what one is good at, rather than just perhaps saying one is good at it. Now, of course, under the present circumstances, what a person is displaying mastery over is in part how they talk (or write, or sign). But mastery display is also about a person's displayed command over understanding some situation, and their ability to communicate that understanding. So, the more detail the person can show about their understanding, the more other people will admire the sophistication of that understanding. Moreover, the more concise a person can be in their display, the better the communication will be. So, a person is faced with a situation where they need to pack as much information into as little a package as possible. This is why other-side-of-meaning processes like deviance, imprecision, omission, indirectness, figurative language, and language play – the last of which can employ all of these other processes – are so good at mastery display. Meaning in concentrate, just add brain.

Affinity expression, which as argued can ride the coattails of mastery display, is also well accomplished by language play – again we tend to invite for play people we like. But as with the demonstrativeness of mastery display, affinity can often be conveyed best if we show we like someone perhaps more than just saying it.[24] The greater effort required of the demonstration, over mere utterance, can show more strength in one's feelings. Also, the indirectness underlying some forms of affinity expression in language play might lead to better acceptance of that expression in addressees. A bolder more direct expression of affinity can occasionally backfire on speaker, potentially embarrassing or overwhelming the target of the affinity.

And social engineering, of both the more positive and more negative sorts, is well served by language play. The positive affect and amusement accompanying positive language play can be a powerful tool to bolster our and others' social connections and standing. And even for more negatively oriented social purposes, language play is useful. It can be used to "outdo" others in status competition. It can leverage humor to camouflage or ameliorate more negative pragmatic effect parries conducted in parallel. And it can soften people's resistance to social engineering, directed toward them or other people, perhaps if they're enticed to join in on the fun.[25]

This chapter has considered instances of language play as individual isolated experiences, as communicative experiences but with senders and receivers far removed from one another across space and/or time, as brief individual remarks/performances with interlocutors closer together, and as full-blown talk-in-interaction. All but the first of these are exercises in social interaction.[26] We've touched briefly on the social underpinnings of pragmatic effect leveraging in language play – as part of explaining how language play is good for some types of pragmatic effects and how language play seems itself to be the means by which we practice and refine our pragmatic effect leveraging skills. But we didn't delve very deeply into these social motivations within us. The next chapter will make that exploration, showing that we're not just social by choice, but instead we are social by hardwired socio-neural evolution. As we'll see, evolution has in as fashion booby-trapped us in ways that force us to be social.

---

[24] Of course, there can be exceptions where a person shows their love by what they say (e.g., admitting to a misdeed one didn't commit to protect the actual perpetrator who one happens to love). And at times a person just telling someone they love them, something not always easy to do, is a very powerful act.

[25] Which, if people *do* join in (i.e., laughing at a joke that engineered a person or group downward), can trigger the powerful cognitive dissonance mechanism.

[26] And even the first instance of solo play can *practice* social interaction.

For one thing, there was no great original connexion (sic) or friendship between Dialogue and Comedy; the former was a stay-at-home, spending his time in solitude, or at most taking a stroll with a few intimates; whereas Comedy put herself in the hands of Dionysus, haunted the theatre, frolicked in company, laughed and mocked and tripped it to the flute when she saw good; nay, she would mount her anapaests (sic), as likely as not, and pelt the friends of Dialogue with nicknames – doctrinaires, airy metaphysicians, and the like. The thing she loved of all else was to chaff them and drench them in holiday impertinence, exhibit them treading on air and arguing with the clouds, or measuring the jump of a flea, as a type of their ethereal refinements. But Dialogue continued his deep speculations upon Nature and Virtue, till, as the musicians say, the interval between them was two full octaves, from the highest to the lowest note. This ill-assorted pair it is that we have dared to unite and harmonize – reluctant and ill-disposed for reconciliation.
—Lucian, "A Literary Prometheus" (Fowler & Fowler, 1905)

We've now had a thorough look at several examples from each of six major sources of other-side-of-meaning: deviance, omission, imprecision, indirectness, figurativeness, and language play. Stepping back now for a broader view, what can we say about these processes and the other-side-of-meaning as a whole? Three standout observations are worth making. The first two comprise the content of the present chapter. The larger third point is discussed in Chapter 9.

These three findings, in order, are: Other-side-of-meaning processes enable an enriched idea of the sense to which *language is social*; second, the review of other-side-of-meaning processes gives us a better understanding of why there's been an *imbalance of attention* in thinking about and studying these two major sides of meaning – with the sem/syn/sym side garnering the greater scrutiny; finally, understanding fully how the array of other-side-of-meaning processes work together at *making and affecting meaning is a much more complicated business* arguably than it is for the sem/syn/sym side. It requires a deep analysis of every other-side-of-meaning process at work in a given comment, conversation, or discourse, as well as all of their interactions – a combination whose complexity and extent can be vast.

Language Is Social, Revisited: "Poetry and Romance Are Connected for a Reason"

One of the important themes to be conveyed by this chapter was also a major theme of my most recent authored book (Colston, 2015) – the inherently social quality of language, especially figurative language. Upon completion of that book, the publisher asked me to contribute a blog post to their venue, Cambridge Express, which they'd recently set up for their authors. The venue allows authors to discuss new works and readers to follow with commentary. I was pleased at this opportunity to put into a page-length or so summary all that I'd attempted to express in the entire book. But one line in particular from this post was a thought I'd actually not explicitly stated in the book, although it was a background theme throughout the work. The thought came very naturally, though, when contemplating the book's entire content from the satellite-view perspective provided by the blog's summary format – trees can apparently obscure forests after all. The entire post is copied below with the relevant passage curly-bracketed and bolded and the section containing it separated from the main text:

8.1   Blog post written by Herb Colston, author of *Using Figurative Language*.

Many people think figurative language is special or unusual somehow, used only or mostly in poetry, song lyrics or other creative outlets, or just when a speaker/writer is being flamboyant. Some people even think it's a bad form of language, used to baffle or mislead people, or to be uncooperative in some way, or that it's incomprehensible (or just *hard* to comprehend) and thus not how we ought to communicate. Even if people are more appreciative of figurative language they still often acknowledge its presumed higher potential for being misunderstood.

A common question thus posed about figurative language is why it even exists. Why do people speak (write) figuratively when more direct ways are available? Or, put most pointedly, *why don't people just say what they mean?*

Using Figurative Language attempts to address this question. It reviews and discusses several decades' worth of interdisciplinary research and theorizing which show first that the question itself is a bit odd. Many people don't realize that speakers have been using figurative language as long as we've had *language*, and that on some level, there isn't even a principled way to distinguish figurative from other supposedly nonfigurative language. Figurative language is also way more prevalent in normal everyday talk and writing than most people recognize. Although many of its instances *can* be creative and colorful as in song lyrics etc., most of it shows up right under our noses in ways we may not notice as figurative. By way of example, although Linguists and Psycholinguists would certainly argue over this specific quantity, one could readily claim the text I've used thus far in this blog post has well over three dozen figures in it, far more than the perhaps more obvious "colorful" and "under our noses." Figurative language is *stealthy*.

As for the misinterpretation likelihood, true, figurative language can be and is misunderstood occasionally, but so is purported nonfigurative language in all the ways it can be unclear. Figurative language can also provide incredibly rich meaning (meaning in concentrate – just add brain). So the above question presumes we have the option of just omitting figurative language from talk and text to improve communication, when doing so would be effectively impossible.

Despite the oddity of the question, though, the book also gives us the general answer to it – we use figurative language because *it does things for us*, things not as easily done with other kinds of language. These "things" include meaning enhancement (for instance, by **metaphor** – "That job interview was a root canal"), negativity management (by **rhetorical questions** – "Are those your dirty dishes?" or **verbal irony** – "Yeah, right, just hysterical"), persuasion (by **hyperbole** – "Doing it that way will take forever," or **idioms** – "That's a tough row to hoe"), compliance improvement (by **indirect requests** – "Could I ask you a question?"), as well as social engineering, humor, bonding, tantalization and many, many others. The book not only documents *that* figurative language does these things, it also explores *how* it does so. For this the book gathers explanations from psychology, linguistics, evolutionary biology, anatomy, neuroscience, the history and variety of communication methods, semiotics, philosophy and other fields interested in figurative language.

The book also goes beyond the general usage answer, though, to show that understanding what figurative language accomplishes requires thinking about more than just *language* or *communication*. Figurative language is intertwined with our senses (seeing, hearing, touching, etc.) how we move physically (walking, jumping, reaching, etc.), our emotions, our broader concepts, our mind-reading and memory abilities, the actual physiology of pronunciation and many other diverse aspects of human life.

> Figurative language is perhaps especially intermingled in our social interactions with other people. It can function as social honey, glue, lubricant, a lever, a ladder, a weapon, a pedestal, a pillow, a trap, a Trojan Horse, territory marking, handcuffs, a Band-Aid and perfume, among many other things. As just one brief concrete example, speakers use more figurative language when interacting with people they like, admire or wish to impress in some contexts, and using figurative language for this succeeds generally for speakers – other people like you back or *are* impressed if you use it right. {**Poetry and romance are connected for a reason!**}

The book also deals with many other questions one can ask about figurative language. How should we study it? How has it changed over time? Have we exhausted its potential? How might we best explain it? How does it arise in children? Why is there occasional resistance to it? How prevalent is it out there in the world?

Finally, the book treats all these issues concerning figurative language with many examples taken from authentic recorded talk and text by speakers as well as from diverse instances in popular culture (e.g., movies, television, advertisements, news sources, cartoons, novels, commercials, the Internet and others). It thus provides a treatment scholarly readers can appreciate, but also might be enjoyed by broader audiences as well.

Thanks to Cambridge for publishing it and future thanks to everyone who reads it. I hope you find it enlightening and enjoyable.

I wanted to highlight this comment about the connectedness of poetry and romance because it accomplishes an important point for the current chapter. It helps illustrate the crucial and necessary braiding that exists between language (especially figurative language but also other processes from the other-side-of-meaning and even from the sem/syn/sym side to an extent) and social interaction (e.g., love and romance) (Kovecses, 1986). It also assists in highlighting differences in the social interaction processes in the two different sides of meaning – differences between embodied simulations and other processes in the sem/syn/sym side of meaning versus all the other-side-of-meaning components discussed in this book.[1] That poetry and romance are so interconnected indicates the special way that the other-side-of-meaning processes enable and even catalyze our social interaction by means which might exceed the sem/syn/sym side.

But to *fully* appreciate the extent to which language is ultimately and deeply social, and especially how other-side-of-meaning processes support this social function perhaps differently than the sem/syn/sym side, we need to first discuss how language has been considered a social phenomenon thus far. How has language historically been considered social? How has the social view of language changed over time? And how might these past and current views have underestimated the overall degree to which language is social?

Social History

In a number of ways, it is essentially obvious that language is social. Language, after all, takes place most often between a speaker and a

---

[1] The comment also explains why many of the epigraphs in the current work involve poetry and love.

hearer(s), or between a signer and a seer(s), or with a writer and a reader(s). Each of these activities by definition occurs between two (or more) people. The activities are not just taking place within one person – never crossing the interpersonal boundary.[2] Or, put more inclusively, language often involves a complex interaction between two (or more) people as they take *turns* talking, across broader conversations and discourses. So language can involve two (or more) people who are both acting as speaker *and* hearer (signer/seer, etc.), comprehending and producing language back and forth, and sometimes simultaneously when people both talk at once. Conversers will also often present a continuous stream of complex two-way linguistic and metalinguistic interaction behaviors in the form of reactions, facial expressions, gestures, nods, headshakes, other back-channel responses, overt responses, completing one another's comments, etc.

Of course, there can conversely be long delays between productions and comprehensions, and even open-ended productions of language, where conversers may never even meet. In the former case, many instances of language are crafted, either in written form or in recorded spoken or signed forms, with a specific plan that they'll be comprehended later.[3] For instance, when our recipient receives and reads our text message, when the writings of the forgotten medieval scholar or ancient hieroglyphographer are discovered and read for the first time today, etc. In the latter case of open-ended productions, we on occasion craft language without a recipient in mind or even without confidence one will ever exist.[4] Sometimes we also operate in a hybrid space where we write something perhaps for pure expressive pleasure, for catharsis, or just to pass the time – not writing specifically for an expected reader but open to the possibility that one might exist someday.

But in all these instances, the language being created still serves or at least can serve the purposes of getting two or more separate human beings to synchronize their states of consciousness even if just for a moment (and

---

[2] Of course, they *can* reside within just one person, in the form of thinking aloud when no one else is around, of leaving notes for oneself, or of talking to or with oneself, etc. But even in these cases we still act at least partially as both producer and receiver of the language – we hear what we say aloud and read what we've written. So in that sense language used even in these limited solo contexts is still social in a way. As I've learned in leaving notes for myself that I later can make absolutely no sense of whatsoever, these forms of self-communication can even fail.

[3] We even have the added twist when written forms are read synchronously with their composition as in certain live chat boxes or in the case of writing out a message for someone as they watch you write (imagine a lawyer and client conferring this way to communicate live but silently in a courtroom).

[4] Any reader who has also been a writer is likely familiar with the feeling of wondering if anyone will ever read your work.

even if those moments are actually separated in time). This is inherently social. Conversers might achieve that synchronization in real time and even see it occur in one another. Or, as said, conversers may never meet.[5] Even in the case of a person leaving notes for herself, she is in a sense synchronizing her current consciousness with another consciousness – that of herself at a later time. One could even push this argument far enough to say a person talking aloud with themselves is also synchronizing such consciousnesses – but in this case between their speaking self and their hearing self.[6]

And further, the extent of this synchronizing of separate human consciousnesses can be profound. Beginning with the advent of writing forms (or arguably even when early humans or proto-humans first started making large-audience public speeches, or even when telling stories around campfires to small groups), individuals have had the ability to synchronize with many other people – potentially millions of other people in the case of early writing. Today, with our instantaneous, hyperlinked, recordable, botable, multimodal, cc-able, list-servable, fiber-optic, global maelstrom of communication technologies, we are fast approaching the state where any one person, a speaker, signer, or writer, can synchronize consciousnesses with *any other person*, or even with *every other person*, and through essentially any medium. We even face the possibility that every single one of the multiple billions of us now living can all synchronize consciousnesses, even at the same point in time.[7]

Language can also be social, though, in ways beyond aligning consciousnesses. It can also contain social content and it can perform social acts. One speaker, for instance, can tell another that a new mustard-pistachio flavored gelato is disgusting and that the person should avoid it. This is an alignment of consciousnesses or transfer of information between people, but it is also a favor done by one person for another – both social processes. And the informational or semantic content of language itself can also be directly social. A woman can, for example, tell her brother that the woman's daughter is due to have a second baby.

---

[5] It is interesting to contemplate the difference between a reader, for instance, gleaning a writer's intended meaning from a text and feeling a sort of communion or bond with the writer, relative to two people talking with one another also feeling that sense of communion at achieving shared meaning but additionally noticing one another noticing it. Both forms of bonding can be profound, but the second can be more intimate.

[6] A form of "communication" not to be made light of. Self-talking in this manner, or even doing inner speech, can lead to self-insights and clearer thinking – even serving as the core of many therapeutic, meditative, stress-reducing, and self-help practices.

[7] Reality being what it is to limit these possibilities. Our attentional capacities are one obvious limitation, as are time zones and hemispheres and the sheer bulk of communicated content. But the modern potential of interconnectedness for enabling consciousness synchronization is still unprecedented.

Such transfer of, or alignment in holding, social information can also take on more social-act qualities itself, as in the nasty ice cream flavor advice. For instance, a person describing a job applicant's extreme talents to a potential hirer is both passing along social information (i.e., information about another person) and doing the recipient a favor (i.e., enabling her to hire this high-quality applicant).

However, even in this expansive view of language as a social thing – people exchanging meaning, sometimes social meaning, and people doing things with other people via language (e.g., doing favors, dropping insults, lauding with praise), we may still be underestimating the nature and extent of the sociality of language. We often, for instance, get distracted by the amazing capacity of language to comment essentially about anything (i.e., from ice cream flavors to physics, to tire treads, to sex, to reverse mortgages, to language itself, etc.). As both lay users of language and scholars, we frequently become fixated on the *informational* component of language – or it's semantics (as well as some semantics coming from schematics, i.e., information coming from schema activations).

Of course, language does have this crucial semantic/schematic component, and one could argue the other levels of language from phonology through morphosyntax (and, again, partially schematics) are really at the service of semantics – to get the *meaning* across as it were. But we often don't appreciate the degree to which this semantics component of language is arguably also at the service of the *social* component.

There is still a widespread focus on language functioning, which is distracted by this powerful capacity of semantics – for language to supposedly have some type of holistic, self-contained, semantic meaning completely freestanding by itself irrespective of its usage by or between people. By way of illustration, consider the following snarky, admittedly, comment submitted by the author back in 2006 in response to a *New York Times* news item about former US Supreme Court Justice Antonin Scalia's understanding of semantics and language as a whole:[8]

8.2   Re "Public Comments by Justices Veer Toward the Political," National Section, *New York Times*, March 19, 2006.
       Antonin Scalia defeated his own argument in his classical demonstration of the recently oft-used "framing" tactic by "right" thinkers of rebuttal analogy (essentially, belittling a viewpoint by embedding it in a ridiculous-seeming framework or analogy). In response to the "living document" view of the US Constitution, Scalia said, "You would have to be an idiot to believe

[8] To my knowledge *The New York Times* did not publish this comment.

that ... The Constitution is not a living organism, it is a legal document. It says some things and doesn't say others."

Scalia attempts to make the "living document" view look untenable by portraying (unfairly) its proponents as confused about the difference between inanimate and living matter. Scalia misses the point, though, that the correct comprehension of *any* language, written or spoken, even his own comment (indeed, that comment in particular), requires speaker-authorized or author-authorized inferences of a great deal of knowledge, as well as the operation of a variety of processes outside the supposed raw semantics of the particular statements (which themselves are always necessarily ambiguous). To understand his comment as intended, for instance, one must make the inference that a "living document" is alive in the sense of a carbon life-form, instead of alive in the sense of being *dynamic* (or being a number of other relevant senses of "living" – being *flexible* or *open to interpretation, active*, etc.).

It would behoove some legal scholars to become familiar with the modern sciences of language comprehension which lay bare many arcane myths such as Scalia's. Indeed, perhaps the wool of this tactic is finally wearing thin, one need only use it in reverse to see its operation: "... [The Constitution] says some things and doesn't say others" – the Constitution isn't an orator with a pair of vocal chords vibrating out speech sounds with warm breath or holding its tongue. It is a dead piece of animal skin with faded ink on it. It must be read or heard by a living mind to have meaning – a process which interpretation never escapes.

This kind of view, believing in the existence of holistic, free-standing, self-contained, core, or kernel language meaning independent of the *use* of that language, residing in fixed forms of language, either written or spoken, is simply untenable. All one need do is consider how some ways of "replaying" that fixed language, occurring when a person reads the written form (aloud or silently) or speaks the fixed language aloud from memory, for instance, can introduce great variability in the meaning. Different meaning arises, for instance, if we prosodically emphasize different portions of a fixed phrase (i.e., "WE the people," "we THE people," "we the PEOPLE"). The emphasis given to any given word, or even to a sub-lexical morpheme or combinations of these, increases that particular bit of sub-phrasal semantics' contribution to the broader phrasal meaning, among a number of other things (e.g., contemplating *why* the speaker emphasized that part), which renders the phrase's comprehension different. And, importantly, even if skeptics acknowledge this meaning variability introduced at the point of reading, they might hold to the idea that these different readings are just alterations to the *original* form. The problem with this view is that *any* reading must commit itself to a number of possible branchings on a decision tree. For instance, decisions must be made in a given reading about what parts to emphasize. And, moreover, there simply isn't a pure, original, central, one true reading from which to deviate or alternate *from*. There can be similarities across readings. But meaning depends upon how the fixed form is read in any given instance.[9]

Perhaps the closest we get to a generally objective freestanding meaning is when we have an enriched recording of a person speaking with great prosodic, gestural, emotive, and other embellishment a fairly concrete and simple bit of language. But even here, any given hearer/watcher of this speech will bring their own suite of embodied simulation through cultural knowledge and belief differences to bear on the comprehension, making the speech have different meaning in different people. And the contexts both of the local replaying situation through the larger cultural or historical framework will also alter the interpretation – and will do so differently for different people. So, in essence, we never escape the import of usage and contextual influence in language meaning.

And one final important point is worth emphasizing regarding the just-argued potential difference in approaching, albeit never reaching, objectivity. The rich recording of a passionately delivered speech of some language demonstrates the influence of other-side-of-meaning processes. The rich recording captures many of those other-side-of-meaning processes which can help narrow the variability in the later semantic meaning which occurs in comprehenders. Without those other-side-of-meaning processes, the language's meaning is left more adrift. Whatever Shrodinger's Cat kind of meaning potentiality that resides in yet-to-be-spoken or yet-to-be-read language, the level of other-side-of-meaning available will greatly matter. The less other-side-of-meaning that we have at our disposal to steady the language, the more variability the language's meaning will have.

But, overzealous literal-mindedness aside, we have, nonetheless, noted *some* of the more advanced social capacities taking place to enable language. For one example, language production often involves varying levels of audience design. Speakers usually make cognitive efforts to ascertain what their addressees know and don't know when producing

---

[9] Of course, the *degree* of variability across different possible readings is itself variable – some texts can be more ambiguous than others. And it remains possible that a large number of people cohere on a relatively stable meaning of a fixed text. Consistency can arise from frequent repetition in a standard context, from simplicity of structure, and from other sources. But it remains the case that meaning inherently varies according to characteristics of individual instances of usage.

utterances (Clark, 1996). Speakers will also often select their register and craft the level of their utterances' complexities and other things to fit their addressees. Again, these are by no means universal or perfect processes. Sometimes people behave quite egocentrically and speakers undoubtedly make mistakes in audience design (Keysar, Barr, & Horton, 1998; Barr & Keysar, 2002, 2005; Epley, Keysar, Van Voven, & Gilovich, 2004; Horton & Keysar, 1996; Kerns, Cohen, MacDonald, Cho, Stenger, & Carter, 2004; Keysar, 1994, 2007, 2008; Keysar & Henley, 2002; Keysar, Barr, Balin, & Brauner, 2000; Keysar, Barr, Balin, & Paek, 1998). And speakers often make mistakes in adopting appropriate registers with addressees. And, furthermore, we often can still manage to deal with such mistakes as hearers, if only by factoring the fact of the mistake into the comprehension product (Colston, 2015). But, by and large, audience design and register adjustment are nonetheless practices that take place, working to some extent to make language operate more efficiently. And, at times, they are absolutely crucial tasks facing speakers, as in situations where speakers must "choose their words carefully" (i.e., think, court-room testimony under oath, high stakes). To do audience design success-fully and to maneuver among registers we must perform the social process of thinking about other people's thoughts.[10]

Other socio-cognitive processes such as building common ground, using common ground in comprehension or production, using a variety of social cognition skills (i.e., assessing another person's temperament) for socio-strategic language production and comprehension, Theory of Mind, etc., have also been proposed and empirically established (Clark, 1996). And, returning briefly to the notion of social content being con-veyed, studies have shown that an enormous percentage of the normal, everyday talk taking place between people is of this social content kind (Dunbar, 1996). Something on the order of 70 percent of our talk is social, "gossip."[11] So let's not give short shrift to the social-processing activity and the social content enabling meaning making on the sem/syn/sym side of meaning.

But as we'll see next, we don't *just* use socio-cognitive assessment processes to make our utterances adhere to other people and to better comprehend language we receive from others. Nor do we *just* exchange loads of social content between one another. Nor do we even just perform social acts with other people via language. We additionally live extremely socially *motivated* lives. Indeed, *necessarily* socially motivated lives. We've

---

[10] Even a hearer's ability to overcome mind-reading mistakes by a speaker is evidence itself of mind reading, in this case operating in that hearer.

[11] Robin Dunbar uses the term "gossip" a bit loosely in this regard, referring to all talk concerning social content, not just juicy social tidbits or "the dirt."

evolved specific neurally hardwired systems to drive us to become and remain highly social, on which we are dependent for our very survival. So, essentially there is a demand on us to be social, a demand that cannot be fully met by sem/syn/sym meaning processes due to their nature. These social motivations are thus intricately intertwined with the other-side-of-meaning language processes, which serve to fill this gap.

Social Needs and Motivations

Socially *motivated* activity in us isn't just something we happen to do. We are instead neurally hardwired to do it. We can't not do it.[12] It orients and motivates much of what we do throughout our lives. We depend on it as much as we do on food, air, shelter, and water. Our societies are built around this central nature of our being.[13] In his 2013 book, *Social: Why Our Brains Are Wired to Connect*, Matthew Lieberman details the neuroscientific evidence arguing for how we operate *fundamentally* according to social processes.

Perhaps the simplest such process in us is pair-bonding, probably arising out of the necessity for care-givers and infants to become connected to enable infants' survival. But pair-bonding stays with us our entire lives as the basis of friendship formations and friendship-group bondings.[14] It is driven by a usurpation of neural centers for managing pain and pleasure experiences – yoking them to social interaction to create pressures in us to get and stay socially connected as well as socially positioned (i.e., feel pleasure when achieving social connection/status, feel pain when failing at social connection/status).[15]

---

[12] Excepting in the case of certain psychological or neurological disorders.

[13] It is interesting to contemplate which activities we do socially in our cultures versus which ones we do in private or isolation. The 1974 French film, *The Phantom of Liberty*, depicts such a contemplation – embedded in a broader political statement (Picard, Silberman, & Buñuel, 1974). In a scene midway through the film, a group of bourgeois friends gather for a party at a professor's home. But rather than sitting around a table to share a meal, they instead gather around a table that has toilets for chairs and proceed to do their bodily business accordingly. The table is nicely appointed with magazines for reading materials and ashtrays for smoking. They exchange idle chitchat as if at a dinner party. But if one of the guests becomes hungry, they politely excuse themselves and go into a small bathroom-sized room where they eat some food – entirely in privacy and isolation. At one point in this scene, a young girl says aloud at the table, "I'm hungry," earning herself a scolding from her mother for speaking of such things in public.

[14] And note that such powerful friendship bonds are not due to just selfish genetics, by definition, as one could argue is the case for blood-family bonds. Friends are evolutionarily beneficial for us for reasons that are social.

[15] A nearly perfect corollary to this social need to get and stay connected socially is the oppositional motivation to avoid social isolation. Ostracism, argued to extend far beyond a mere cultural practice, rising to a force of nature (Williams, 2001), acts as the stick to the social pleasure carrot.

The next most sophisticated social connection principle or process in us is mind reading. This process, referred to by Lieberman as the Default or Mentalizing Network, is nothing short of remarkable. Most of the brain activity we expend is due to this process. We can focus on other kinds of mental tasks for short periods of time, but just as an automobile engine idles after temporarily racing, after exerting effort to concentrate on some other mental activity, the Default Network kicks back in and resumes its background work. Its main task is to analyze and compute our way through the complex social environments and situations we inhabit – effectively allowing us to interact with other people as successfully as possible, and to communicate with one another via language. As Lieberman puts it:

The mentalizing network does something incredibly special to facilitate our dealings with other people. It allows us to peer inside the minds of those around us, take into account their hopes, fears, goals, and intentions, and as a result interact with them much more effectively. It allows us to figure out the psychological characteristics of people we see every day so we can better predict their reactions to novel situations and avoid unnecessary feather ruffling. We use these abilities to achieve cooperatively things that we never could to on our own, as well as to strategically compete with those around us. The mentalizing system allows us to filter our experience to figure out the best information to share with others and how to do it. We would be absolutely lost without our all-purpose mindreading machine. (Lieberman, 2013: p. 126)

The third and most recently evolved system, residing in the medial prefrontal cortex (MPFC) of humans, Lieberman refers to as harmonizing. He uses the metaphor of the "Trojan Horse self" to explain this system, whereby the notion we each have of who we are, and what our "self" is like, is actually an internalized construction crafted for us by the social beings around us. It is as if the generic collection of what everyone around us thinks we should be like is indeed what we become. Such a form of external remote control makes us behave in ways that align with what others prefer, wish, and expect out of peoples' behavior in general, and of our behavior in particular – hence the harmonizing. But we operate on the illusion that we are actually fully choosing, building, and guiding this "self" of ours.

Of these three major neural social interaction systems the first is not unique to humans. Many animals form pair and group bonds of many different sorts. It is an old evolutionary solution that there is safety, power, greater sensory vigilance, and a number of other benefits to group life. But foraging, migrating, and nesting together, along with other relatively simple group activities (e.g., fending off predation, corralling young), are not quite the same thing as navigating more complex and advanced social networks and hierarchies, as many mammals and especially primates must do. As Lieberman put it, "Creating ways to keep us connected is therefore the central problem of mammalian evolution" (p. 99). This connection requires some of the capacities of the mentalizing system, or something like it, to negotiate the more complex problems of not just group life, but group life in highly dynamic hierarchies and networks, with continuously changing leadership, memberships, statuses, opportunities, competition, advancement, even maintenance challenges, etc.

So, the mentalizing system is also not completely unique to humans. Carnivores, for instance, have to be pretty good at predicting the behavior of prey animals and can even at times display Machiavellian sorts of behavior within their own species, all enabled by mind reading. But we humans likely advanced mind reading in significant ways, molding it for our more complex levels of interaction and for use with our language (i.e., think again, mind reading, Theory of Mind, audience design, comprehension monitoring, etc.). Just as any preexisting system is significantly impacted by new systems that come to be used with it (i.e., imagine how roads, which already existed, were changed with the advent of the automobile), the mentalizing or default system became more sophisticated in humans in part due to its service to language. And, indeed, these two abilities of ours, language and mind reading, essentially put us on the road to becoming the modern humans we are. And that the socio-cognitive processes we have noted and documented in language functioning thus far reside in this system is not a surprise – they seem necessary for many parts of language to work.

But similarly to how advancements in transportation created needs for greater traffic coordination (i.e., traffic rules, signage, driver training, legal systems to handle mishaps, maps, signaling systems, GPS, self-driving hard- and software, etc.), so did socio-language advancement create a need for the third neurally driven social interaction process in us, the one termed harmonizing by Lieberman. We also needed a system where we can internalize and automatize rules or guidelines for our behavior and beliefs in the world and with respect to other people – rules that mostly reflect the preferences of the masses so that we can all get along. But as with many things, we are more apt to internalize, formulate, and follow these rules if we believe they're of our own making.

There are two intertwined parts to this latter system, culture and our sense of self. Culture is the set of material and social interaction practices forged into "beliefs," "morals," "understandings" about the social and material worlds and the unknown beyond them that we hold and follow. Our sense of self is the particular collection of personality and interaction characteristics that we are capable of pulling together and indeed do construct, as the set that is both achievable by us and that fits our perception of our place in society (i.e., I am: a nurse/musician/mother/ dependable friend/kind/a bad cook/great joke teller/I like karate, etc., because I have skills or interests or talents in those capacities *and* because there is a place for me in society in being those things).

But note the crucial part concerning *fit in society*. The ingredients going into who we become are a little bit fixed, but certainly not entirely – we may not be able to make ourselves taller, but we can absolutely train ourselves, learn new knowledge and abilities, get better at things with practice, etc., effectively overriding some possible restrictions. And, of course, many people do not experience the luxury of crafting who they get to be based on their ideal choosing of abilities and fit with the external world. But if our self is forced upon us in these situations, and even if we have more flexibility to choose and craft our self more to our liking and preference, we still receive those self-building instructions or affordances largely *from the social world around us*. The self thus appears as a bit of an illusion to us, making us think we have more control than we likely do, but it appears we are largely what the society around us wants us to be, or at least lets us be. We just trick ourselves into thinking these preferences of others are instead what we internally wanted all along.[16] So, at core, even this highest form of neurally driven social interaction of harmonizing, molding us (our "selves") to fit in among our social environment, is deeply and centrally social. So to an extent, then, "culture" and the "self" overlap to a great degree.

If we distill these three neurologically hardwired social connection systems down into what they mean for us in our everyday lives, we can begin to see how the other-side-of-meaning language processes do more for us socially than what might first meet the eye. These three systems mean essentially that we are strongly motivated to do the three following things (Lieberman, 2013):

1. Become and remain socially connected with other people. These connections are occasionally within families, but family relationships are

[16] Of course, such a system can and indeed does go overboard and impose unwanted and unfair expectations and restrictions on us (i.e., a person is physically tall, so many people expect them to play basketball even though they dislike the sport) – injustices many people strive to correct and happily succeed at so doing sometimes. And some human injustice is likely perpetuated due to this system's potential to go too far (e.g., "A woman's place is ..."). But according to Lieberman, we also likely align many of our pro-social behaviors to conform to group norms (i.e., use your inside voice, don't shove, work and play well with others, the golden rule, etc.) – and group norms to which we also contribute our expectations and preferences, aiding us in feeling they're our own. So, the system has some positive consequences for interactive success as well, positive enough at least to have become established in our neural functioning. The system also can explain why people sometimes fall in line with many cultural practices, despite their disbelieving in them through rational thinking.

usually outnumbered by our friendship connections and networks, and our more intimate close friends and lovers. We even project these friendships onto fictional people, as when we feel we've come to know and love people who don't even really exist.[17] These connections provide a direct sense of social/physical pleasure to us and an avoidance of direct social/physical pain (Anderson, Kraus, Galinsky, & Keltner, 2012; Kasser & Ryan, 1993).

2. Attempt to maintain or elevate our positions in social networks and/or hierarchies.[18] These provide social status for us which is a *far* stronger motivator to us than material wealth.[19] This status can also come not just from our receiving social acclaim but from our giving it as well. Indeed, often we receive an especially strong dose of pleasure/reward for doing positive things for others, even if such acts are detrimental to us in other ways.

3. Determine the nature of, and then construct, a sense of self (i.e., how people might describe what you are and what you are like), which seeks the best possible match between what you are capable of being, and what society/culture expects of someone with your self "ingredients." For some people, the societal/cultural expectations will outweigh the individual's preferences, interests, and capacities. But for everyone at least a portion, if not a majority, of those "internal" preferences, etc., have been internalized from external societal/cultural expectations. We just have a tendency to be blind to this.[20]

These three social motivations can now be used as a framework through which to assess the social functioning brought by the other-side-of-meaning processes, relative to the sem/syn/sym ones.

Being Social: The Indirect Capacities of the Other-Side-of-Meaning

So how do the other-side-of-meaning processes discussed in Chapters 2 through 7 serve the above three primary social motivations? The most

---

[17] Not to mention pets, imaginary friends, inanimate objects, etc.

[18] It is unclear if this social motivation manifests itself more often as a strive-to-climb versus a fight against downward pressure – probably a varying little-bit-of-both, interacting with an individual's personality and the particulars of given situations.

[19] Lieberman makes a sobering and convincing case that many of our societal motivations, reward systems, beliefs, and practices are designed to almost perfectly mismatch this key human characteristic – contributing in his view to many of our most pressing modern problems.

[20] Chapters 9 and 10 talk at various points about cognitive dissonance and how it permeates many aspects of language and other human behavior. Cognitive dissonance seems intricately intertwined with this neuro-social system.

general answer is analogous to the one I and others have given when asked, "What's the point of figurative language? Why don't we just say what we mean?" (see also the Cambridge Express blog post at the beginning of this chapter). We use figurative language for a wide variety of expressive goals precisely because it is good at expressing such content – much of the content cannot be as readily expressed by nonfigurative language. It appears similarly that the other-side-of-meaning processes help us better achieve these primary social motivations than do the sem/syn/sym ones – they're also just "good at it." The sem/syn/sym side is *capable* of meeting *some* of the motivations, or at least being squeezed into service for the attempt, in the same way that nonfigurative language can attempt to convey figurative meaning (i.e., paraphrasing metaphors; saying aloud, "That's ridiculous," to an addressee's absurd idea, instead of pausing a significant beat before pointedly ignoring the idea and the addressee). But the sem/syn/sym side just isn't as well equipped to perform many of the delicate social tasks required of us to meet our social motivations. Of course, sem/syn/sym can do things like compliment or lavish praise on an addressee. It can also, as noted earlier, perform pro-social acts (e.g., helping by giving needed information). It can also soothe, calm, etc., possibly in its own subtle ways (e.g., if a person is tense or afraid, sometimes just hearing another person's voice can be comforting). And, of course, it can also be directly negative. But all these social interactions are essentially direct, or at least conducted "in public," as it were. Many much more powerful and subtle social things can be done with the other-side-of-meaning processes.

The biggest cause for this difference is that the processes on the other-side-of-meaning operate a bit under the radar. They're indirect. They're in camera. They're off record. They largely don't reside in the mainstage semantics of the sem/syn/sym side, or at least in the semantics directly. As is aptly captured in the idiom, *Actions speak louder than words*, other-side-of-meaning processes serve to *perform* social activity like making others feel positively, or delivering to them wayward compliments or negotiating potentially hazardous social territory (e.g., handling negativity), or marshaling desired action from people, etc., without explicitly putting those things into the open declarative sem/syn/sym system in the language.

Relatedly, the kinds of social motivations the other-side-of-meaning processes are trying to fulfill must operate amid other people who also have and are trying to meet those same social motivations for themselves. Off-loading some of the social interaction onto the other-side-of-meaning processes might thus help avoid collisions. For instance, residing in social hierarchies often means that one person has some degree of authority over another. But having authority over others can cause resentment in some people – due to their wanting to rise in the hierarchies themselves. It can lead those people to find other people positioned over them in the hierarchy to be obstacles in the way of their advancement. So, how might the authority person behave in this situation?

Consider for an analogy a common practice I've often observed when flying on airplanes. At times when a flight crew calls for passengers to "bring their seat backs to the full, upright, and locked position," not everyone always complies. Whether due to headphones, sleeping, distraction, or something else, some passengers simply miss the directive. When flight attendants then speak to such passengers, I've noticed that nearly every time they'll first ask the passenger to straighten their seat, but then they'll immediately walk away. It is as if they've been trained (and I suspect they have been) to allow passengers in these situations the fullest opportunity to comply. Were the attendant to stand there and wait for the passenger to move their seat back, the passenger might feel a bit resentful or even belittled by the vigilance as if the passenger weren't being trusted to comply, or were being scolded for their error. These attitudes, if directed toward the passenger, would probably clash strongly with the passenger's genuine feelings (i.e., of actually being trustworthy but just having made a mistake, of wishing to comply and being sorry for their error).

But with the attendant leaving, most passengers won't feel those conflicts and, indeed, often seem eager and even overzealous to demonstrate their feelings (i.e., of trustworthiness, cooperativeness, etc.) and correct their error almost as if they're grateful for being given the room to demonstrate their trustworthiness, etc. This practice thus seems to maximize compliance, while keeping everyone in a good mood. Everyone's social motivations are met – everyone saves face. Other-side-of-meaning practices such as indirect requests, the negativity management marshaled by well-crafted verbal irony, the overall ingratiation process by many forms of figurative, indirect, and playful language, etc., seem to follow this same general principle.

For instance, in indirect requests, as discussed in Chapter 5, speakers can enable better compliance by not directly saying what they're requesting. They instead ask in a way that usually demonstrates an effort on the speaker's part to pinpoint the likely obstacle that would be in the way of the addressee granting the request (i.e., "Could I borrow a pen?" or "Would you have a pen I could use?", etc.) (Gibbs, 1981a, 1981b, 1983, 1986; Gibbs & Mueller, 1988). The granter might note this effort and appreciate the consideration demonstrated on the speaker's part, raising the likelihood of compliance – even if compliance is an inconvenience for the granter.

But the request's structure also uses the general kind of indirectness found in the airline example – giving the granter ample room to comply through the affordance of an "out" – the granter can always deny the request and save face (i.e., "Sorry, I don't have a spare pen"), even if the granter could actually provide what was asked. The mere presence of having an "out" prepared for them might additionally enhance the likelihood of compliance beyond the demonstrated consideration of a potential obstacle – much like the flight attendant's walking away helps compliance in that situation.

In the case of verbal irony, many times speakers are faced with needing to deal with forms of expressed negativity. For example, another person has committed a disservice to you with witnesses observing the deed. So, you feel you need to let this person know of your displeasure at the disservice, to prevent continued misdeeds or for just pure retaliation. You also wish to preserve your status among the witnesses by not letting someone publicly push you around. At the same time, you don't wish to escalate negative interactions between you and the other person, which would be costly to everyone. Nor do you wish to lose your cool in front of the witnesses. So, you need a means to navigate this potentially delicate social gauntlet.

Verbal irony can serve situations like this very well. It can enable your expression of displeasure. But it can also couch the disapproval in humor, or demonstrate your cleverness at language, or your deftness at social navigation. Or it can even put down your addressee, perhaps without their even noticing it – all depending on the addressee's cleverness, your level of desired retaliation, the vigilance of the witnesses, etc. It can even demonstrate your calm-headedness in the face of an insult or disservice done to you – showing maturity and composure (Colston, 2015). So, a pretty simple comment of an ironic rhetorical question such as, "Well, well, Victor, who knew you were so clever?" accompanied with perhaps a sly, Mona Lisa smile, or, of course, a comment and delivery more aptly suited to the given particulars of the actual situation, can meet all the speaker's social needs.

Verbal irony also follows the indirectness airline example because it manages these social delicacies without your being on record as having directly said anything negative about the other person. On the surface, you've seemed to express your admiration of their abilities. So, by burying your retaliation into the other-side-of-meaning process of verbal irony, you're also affording compliance on the part of the addressee. They might see, for instance, that you opted for an indirect response rather than directly retaliating (i.e., saying something directly negative about them, e.g., "Bite me, you jerk"). This might lead them to let the retaliation sit, without further response, effectively quelling the situation. The verbal irony might also act as a deterrent for future disservice from this person, who might contemplate your cleverness before setting out at you again.

For the more general cases of figurative, indirect, and playful language as a whole, they can bring their performance of wayward complimentation through the process of ingratiation. By opting to use figurative, indirect, or playful language, when more direct options are available, the speaker effectively delivers a compliment to their addressee(s) – demonstrating through action an appreciation of the addressee's abilities to successfully comprehend the language. If addressees notice this compliment, they might feel warmly in return toward the speaker. All of this takes place essentially behind the scenes of any sem/syn/sym processes doing their work to convey semantic meaning. The compliment comes in the form of a subtext.

So, again, this pattern in figurative, indirect, and playful language as a whole matches that in the airline example. You give a person plenty of room to comply in this context – essentially room to take note of your wayward compliment or to ignore it. They essentially aren't beholden to respond in any way. But were a similar compliment to be set directly in the sem/syn/sym portion of the language (i.e., "I think you are very clever"), then the addressee is put a bit more on the spot. They may feel more pressure to either respond some way (i.e., with an acknowledgment, with a return compliment in kind, or by just ignoring your statement – any of these bringing subtextual meanings of their own). So, the compliment may be stronger in the indirect case in the same way that the flight attendant's walking away leads to compliance. Your allowing the person to take or leave your compliment, without putting any additional pressure on them, might make them more likely to accept it.

These specific processes just described for indirect and figurative language, such as indirect requests and verbal irony, as well as the general operation of figurative, indirect, and playful language, are really in the realm of specific and general pragmatic effects (Colston, 2015). Pragmatic effects themselves provide another way to demonstrate how other-side-of-meaning processes are particularly well suited for helping us meet our social motivations. They not only have this specific and general capacity of indirectness akin to the airline example, allowing social interactions to occur back channel, lessening the possibilities of social conflict, and perhaps enhancing compliance and ingratiation; but the categories that pragmatic effects themselves seem to fall into also seem to particularly align well with the three specific social motivations discussed earlier.

Being Social: The Contribution of Pragmatic Effects

Although pragmatic effects utilize the same kinds of social processes used by the sem/syn/sym side of meaning, such as comprehension and state monitoring (i.e., this person doesn't know the answer and feels nervous accordingly), they nonetheless also tap directly into the kinds of social motivations that drive much of our behavior, like deriving social relationship and/or social hierarchy goals (i.e., I like this person and would like to become friends with her) and using apt other-side-of-meaning processes to achieve those goals (i.e., whispering a side-mouthed, "She croaked" – giving the person the answer to the teacher's question, "What was the outcome of Marie Curie having handled radium?"). But such a comment also successfully shrouds the illicit delivery, etc., allowing the person to save face, making her laugh, indirectly partaking with her using a socially bonding private key, and impressing her in the process – both with the knowledge displayed and through the effective metaphor usage.

Many of these latter meaningful accomplishments, like impressing people, ingratiating them, etc., belong to the larger set of pragmatic effects people perform (Colston, 2015). A quick perusal of a list and organization of such pragmatic effects provided in my previous book demonstrates their high degree of social motivation alignment and their tendency to direct positivity toward others. For example, in one table (reprinted here, see Table 8.1), an array of pragmatic effects were organized into three sets according to variance in how they operate socially (Colston, 2015, p. 141).

The largest set contained pragmatic effects designated as (emphasis added) "… mostly hav[ing] an impact on other people or operat[ing] through other people and, either solely or additionally, often *serv[ing] to improve those people's perception of the speaker's status.*" This set essentially contains ways to maintain or improve one's social connection or social status, usually through marshaling positive experiences indirectly in others, for instance, through mastery display. Mastery display demonstrates to others your quick and deep understanding of some situation, and your mastery at conveying the understanding efficiently. At the same time, you demonstrate your expectation that the hearer will also see and share this understanding. Indeed, the ability of an other-side-of-meaning process to leverage these two pragmatic effects simultaneously (i.e., mastery display and ingratiation) can lead to a very strong social bond – the hearer first notices the brilliance in your comment, and then realizes they're being included in it. And even without the latter realization, the hearer noticing that another person "gets it," with "it" being some subtle observation demonstrated by the person, itself can perform a strong bonding (i.e., as if the hearer were thinking, "How amazing, someone else actually sees this too!").

The second set in the table provided effects that (emphasis added) "seek to affect others and/or improve the speaker's status, but they do so more *through a mediation of negativity* rather than a gain in positivity." This set thus also seeks to work with one's social connection and status motivations, but it does so through the management of negativity (e.g., modulating negativity – as in being able to express a necessary bit of negativity, but doing so in a way that is as constructive as possible and which might be recognized and appreciated for adroitly doing so).

The final set listed pragmatic effects that (emphasis added) "... *are possibly more internal to the speaker*. They include things a speaker may seek for personal enjoyment, whether or not they operate in or on other people." This final set might be things we do predominantly for our own internal social needs, for instance, identification – aligning ourselves with a particular social or cultural group, as in quoting aloud a line from *Monty Python*, "Nudge, nudge, wink, wink, know what I mean, know what I mean," (Casey, Lownes, Gil, & MacNaughton, 1971). This can make you feel part of a particular social or cultural group (i.e., the cool, smart, arty kids who like *Monty Python*). But such internal workings can also clearly have social effects – others might note how you've identified yourself with this cultural subset and appreciate you for doing so or for bringing the subset to their attention.

I should note briefly a few background items related to the social motivation alignments shown in Table 8.1. The pragmatic effects discussed in the book from which the table comes were mostly limited to those arising from figurative language, which was the focus of the book. Also, when attempting the broadest possible summary categorization of figurative pragmatic effects at another place in the book, it was determined that they fell into three most general categories: *enhancing meaning, managing negativity,* and *improving compliance* (Colston, 2015; Roberts & Kreuz, 1994). So, that two of the columns in Table 8.1 relate to expressing positivity and managing negativity is probably not an accident – these just seem to be two prominent things figurative language does. As a major part of managing one's social status is building oneself up and perhaps doing so under competition with others, it is clear that the positivity expression and negativity management are key to social motivation achievement. The third function of figurative language identified in the book, improving compliance, belonged mostly to the category of indirect requests or other indirect expressions (e.g., "Would you have a pen?"). The compliance management is perhaps

Table 8.1 *Pragmatic effects arising from figurative language (adapted from Colston, 2015)*

Improve Speaker's Status	Reduce Negative Appearance	Speaker-Internal Benefits
Ingratiation	Modulating negativity	Catalyzation
Persuasion	Objectification	Efficiency
Social engineering	Humor	Impoliteness
Catalyzation	Politeness	Humor
Efficiency	Tension reduction	Identification
Mastery display	Machiavellianism	Guiding others' actions
Enhancing meaning	Guiding others' actions	Tension reduction
Highlighting discrepancies		Meaning enhancement
Identification		Highlighting discrepancies
Humor		Emotion expression
Emotion elicitation		Mastery display
Extollation		
Impoliteness		
Tension reduction		
Machiavellianism		
Guiding others' actions		

Note: Some effects appear in more than one category.

adhering most obviously to a social motivation – existing to get others to do what you want them to do with all parties saving face. But, it is important to note, pragmatic effects can arise from other processes on the other-side-of-meaning, and even from the sem/syn/sym side. So quite a range of pragmatic effects are available to accomplish social motivations.

So, the take-home message is that pragmatic effects – a paramount product of the other-side-of-meaning processes, by both figurative language but also all the other processes discussed in the current book – are at core a form of social activity, which very closely aligns with the three main social motivations: get and stay socially connected; maintain or raise one's status in social networks and hierarchies; and form a sense of self which aligns with social and cultural expectations, but that ideally also accommodates a person's interests and skills.

But we have one remaining additional source of evidence that the other-side-of-meaning processes are highly suited to helping us meet our social motivations. And this source is gotten at quite a bit differently from our discussions so far of pragmatic effects and indirectness and how they align with social motivations. Those treatments were effectively looking at the *functioning* of other-side-of-meaning processes. What if we simply take a look at the diversity of language genres out there in the world, in written and spoken form, and see what those tell us about the social motivations we seek to meet with language.

Being Social: The Nature of Language Genres

This discussion will necessitate a foreshadowing of the content of Chapter 9, as I wish to borrow a table prepared for that chapter and discuss it here. I'll save the reasons for creating the table for that chapter, though, as they don't pertain particularly to the current topic. And it isn't even necessary to view the table for the point being made here. Suffice it for now to say that a table was created for Chapter 9 (Table 9.4) that lists a very wide variety of basic level language genres. By basic level, I mean it includes concrete names for spoken or written language genres (i.e., graduation speeches, wedding toasts, bedtime prayers, Dear John letters, office memos, short stories, etc.) rather than more specific level genres (e.g., the Lord's Prayer, Barak Obama's 2016 Howard University commencement address, "The Whore's Child" [Russo, 2002]) or broader ones (e.g., fiction, motivational talk). In the interest of space, the table is not copied here.

I encountered something interesting when compiling the list of language genres for Table 9.4. Most of the items I just thought of myself. But to flesh the list out I also turned to Internet searches for assistance. Aside from a few fairly short but useful listings found here and there with search strings such as "types of talk," "types of speech," "types of written documents," most often what turned up were more abstract categories of talk, speech, writing, etc. centered on the *purposes* or *functions* of concrete types of talk, speech, etc.[21] Many such listings also repeated a fairly finite set of functional categories pertaining to talk or speech or writing, such as *informative, expository, persuasive, special-occasion, confrontational, dialogical, exploratory, Socratic, playful* or *entertaining, and deliberative.* Indeed, I encountered these types of terms so often I kept pushing the results aside in frustration as I was seeking more concrete, basic level categories for the table. I only realized their import for social motivations later.

---

[21] A few listings also produced narrower categories or more physically derived categories than the basic-level set in Table 9.4 (i.e., murmur, whisper, handwritten, machine printed, etc.).

This informal internet research exercise interestingly parallels more scholarly and rigorous products which have also attempted to categorize language at an analogously broad but functionally basic level. One could even argue this endeavor was a primary motivating purpose of at least part of Speech Act Theory (Austin, 1961; Searle, 1969, 1975, 1979; Colston, 2015), and it also serves to guide many of the products in conversation analysis and meaning negotiation as well as sociolinguistics (i.e., turn taking, comprehension monitoring, repair, grounding, etc.) (Cameron, 2001; Sacks, Schegloff, & Jefferson, 1974; Clark, 1996; Schegloff, Jefferson, & Sacks, 1977; Pomerantz, 1978, 1984).

The crucial common denominator of these two very general categorization schemes for language at a reasonably basic, functional level – the one coming from my informal search and the other from related scholarly work – is that they're all *social*. But, in particular, they are also social in a way that aligns very closely with the three social motivations I've already discussed. "Expository" or "informational" language is for the purposes of *a person giving other people* some information they do not already possess. "Persuasive" language involves *a person's attempt to change other people's* attitudes or beliefs, usually to bring them in line with or *together with the speaker's* beliefs.[22] Confrontational language involves *a person challenging or combating other people* and their beliefs. Deliberative language involves *people attempting to strategically work out* some problem or issue. Dialogical language occurs when *people are working cooperatively together* at something for some purpose. When *people are mutually curious* about something they'll use exploratory language to approach it. Socratic language is particularly social, feigning – itself a complex social process – ignorance about something *to enable someone else to learn* about it. And, of course, playful or entertaining language is purposefully used toward the goal of *making people happy*.

We could also perhaps add a few more categories. Inquisitive language is where *a person seeks information from someone else*. Antisocial language is where *people are not necessarily being nice* to other people but are nonetheless acting in a socially driven manner (i.e., to insult another person, to make another person look bad, etc.).[23] Self-display language could be used *to impress other people*, etc.

This is not, of course, to argue that each and every instance of a person using language, either talking or writing, or signing, is inherently social.

---

[22] Not in all cases, of course, as when a person attempts to persuade someone else to purchase something the seller knows is worthless.
[23] Anyone who has been involved with manipulative, backstabbing, bullying, or other "antisocial" acquaintances, relatives, coworkers, etc., can easily attest to the cunning social skills sadly inherent in acting these ways.

Table 8.2 *Social actions underlying functional descriptions of language genres: organized by primary social motivations*

Get and Stay Socially Connected	Maintain or Raise Status	Create a Sense of Self-Internalizing Social Norms and Ideally Affording Individual Abilities/ Interests
Giving people things	Giving people things	
Align beliefs with others	Align beliefs with others	Align beliefs with others
Strategically work things out with others	Strategically work things out with others	
Work cooperatively with other people	Work cooperatively with other people	Work cooperatively with other people
Be mutually curious with other people	Be mutually curious with other people	Be mutually curious with other people
Enable others' learning	Enable others' learning	
Make others happy	Make others happy	
Seek information from other people	Seek information from other people	Seek information from other people
Impress others	Impress others	

Note: Some social actions appear in more than one category.

Nor does it mean that all uses of language are providing for our social motivations. If a person counts aloud as they're taking inventory of something while all alone, or similarly just states the names of items being inventoried, that language might just serve as an internal memory anchoring process for that person (i.e., dually encoding the count or content so that it is less easily forgotten). But just as many very basic human functions probably evolved in service of a core need (e.g., bipedalism evolving to perhaps enable locomotion with free hands), they can provide double duty and serve corollary functions because of what they can do (e.g., improved vision across a landscape, useful technique for memory encoding). But all the functional descriptions of language I've given nonetheless pattern neatly with our social motivations. This correspondence is presented in Table 8.2. The arrangement in the table is not offered as a fixed or rigid set of designations – certainly some other arrangement could also be reasonable. But the table does show how the social actions underlying the functional descriptions of language genres readily fit our primary social motivations.

Social Conclusion

So, returning to the main theme of the chapter so far: Language is inherently a social activity, it can contain social content, it can perform social acts, and language functioning requires social processes like mind reading. But perhaps overlooked in past treatments of its sociality, language, and especially its components from the other-side-of-meaning, exists also and perhaps predominantly for the purposes of enabling us to meet our social motivations – bond with people, establish/maintain/raise status and align one's sense of self with sociocultural expectations. And these motivations are hardwired in us neurally.

So it isn't as if we just happen to do social things, nor that language might require the operation of some of those social things (e.g., mind reading). But much more extensively, we are neurologically *compelled* to do certain social things. We must do them as our essential well-being as individuals and our existence as a species depends on our doing them. So we need interaction systems in our language that particularly suit the three major social motivations distilled from Lieberman's work (2013).

So, we have cobbled together a complex consciousness alignment system, language, to serve these social needs. And, indeed, the most advanced social processes appear to have coevolved with language (Lieberman, 2013). Much of the operation of this system enables powerful alignment on semantic content (a mechanic can describe the inner workings of a fuel pump to her apprentice, a bully athlete can describe how she has injured competing teammates to a rookie, a twelve-year-old boy can talk about something disgusting with his friends, a man can describe his charity work with his new boyfriend, etc.). And this complex content alignment can additionally perform social acts (e.g., helping, intimidating, bonding through grossing out, wooing).

But this system, in excelling at the semantic component, with the obvious corollary of being able to do some social work, may not excel at *all* social work. Being able to do some things socially (e.g., impressing, demonstrating alignment, delivering a stealthy compliment, diffusing tension, transporting an insult that only the victim sees or that everyone except the victim sees, making people feel they belong, demonstrating one's loyalty, persuading people to agree with you, leveraging compliance, building rapport, establishing trust, proving one's worth, saving face and enabling face saving, and many many others) may be better performed in some instances by back channel, subtextual, off the record, in camera, suites of processes – those espoused by all the means of leveraging other-side-of-meaning meaning.

"Mom Always Liked You Best": Imbalanced Attention toward the Two Sides of Meaning

The header quote for this section comes from a running joke on the Smothers Brothers American television program from the late 1960s, *The Smothers Brothers Comedy Hour* (Kiley, Harris, Pasetta, Gary, & Davis, 1967–1970), and was the title of one of the Smothers Brothers' comedy albums (Smothers & Smothers, 1965). The line was often spoken by Tom to his younger and only brother Dick, complaining about an imbalance in maternal affection. The line is apt for the present discussion as it corresponds to a parallel imbalance of attention between two entities, in the present case between the two sides of language meaning.

The brothers' screen personae were also interesting as Tom acted as if he were cognitively slow, where Dick acted as if he had superior intellect. This pattern matches some attitudes toward figurative language, as one example of an other-side-of-meaning process, reflected in the blog post copied at the beginning of the chapter – where some people find some figurative language forms misleading, crude, or in some other way inferior than non-figurative forms. Such attitudes are also revealed in a process labeled "figurative outing" (Colston, 2015, p. 69), where a person attempts to belittle not just figurative language, but also a speaker using it – by acting as if such usage is imprecise, flakey, or otherwise inferior. The aptness also applies to the Smothers Brothers show's cutting edge political satire, which was bold for the time,[24] as well as to the roster of other extremely talented comic writers, many of whom also became famous for their comedy based largely on leveraging other-side-of-meaning processes.[25]

So, why do we have this imbalance of attention toward the two sides of meaning? Why has most attention, by lay language users and scholars alike, focused on the sem/syn/sym side of meaning, with embodied simulations as one of its more recent developments? As discussed back in Chapter 1, work *has* addressed other-side-of-meaning components, as we've clearly seen in multiple separate literatures addressing the components from this side. And a few accounts have attempted to grapple with big portions of the other-side-of-meaning collectively and its relationship with the sem/syn/sym side. And among lay users, they're probably aware of other-side-of-meaning processes and could likely talk about a number of them, perhaps with some terminology varying from that of the scholars

---

[24] Bold enough for the two brothers to be fired by the CBS television network before their series had been completed (Bianculli, 2017).

[25] Among many others, writing credit is given to Steve Martin and Rob Reiner (Internet Movie Database Search, January 10, 2019).

but with keen insight notwithstanding (i.e., hinting, implying, saying one thing but meaning another, the subtext, it's what she's *not* saying that has meaning, being two-faced, talking out the side of your face, that has a double meaning, being sarcastic, there's what you say and *then* what you mean, there's what you say but then *how* you say it, etc.). But such lay users would probably also argue, as might many scholars, that this content is the minority of language – most of language instead being words and phrases and their infinitely generative meanings, all accessible in a dictionary.

Potential answers to the imbalance question are varied, and some may overlap with others a bit. But they're worth delineating as they reveal some assumptions about language and its functioning that may not always be apparent, even among some scholars who think deeply about language much of the time. Some of these assumptions may also arise from most of us having lived in a world where we have writing as well as talk as means of doing language, something that's only been in place for a tiny relative sliver of modern human history.[26] And lastly, these "answers" must be delivered honestly as the speculations that they are. Although some answers might seem probable, definitiveness would require derivation of hypotheses and thorough empirical evaluation of some sort.

One possible answer is the presence of writing as a means of doing language, just alluded to. If we think about how different kinds of writing systems work, they often do a very good job of capturing the content of the sem/syn/sym side of meaning. The nouny, verby, modifier-y stuff mostly, along with the necessary morphosyntax-y choreography stuff. This is quite apparent if we contemplate the continuum of prose as written in the paragraphs here, to dialog as written in a novel or other fiction work, to actors' lines as written in stage plays or screenplays, to light transcripts of actual spoken discourse through the most highly annotated transcription techniques we have available for visually documenting actual talk. And even the latter tools fall *far* short of capturing all that goes into

---

[26] As a classroom exercise in my Linguistics and Psychology of Language courses, I often have students imagine a four-year window of their lives. Perhaps the time they spent attending high school. Or for seniors (some of them anyway), the rough amount time they've spent attending college. I'll then ask them to imagine just a single month. How long is that? How much time does that seem in relation to the four years (one-forty-eighth)? I then tell them, with many caveats about the inexact nature of the upcoming numbers, that the ratio they just imagined is roughly equivalent to how long we've had writing as a language system (perhaps 5,000 years) relative to having talk (perhaps 200,000 years). And this presupposes just having writing as something some smart people invented somewhere. Widespread writing/reading ability is barely 100 or 200 years old, and we still haven't reached the point where all humans are literate.

meaning making between conversers in genuine talk settings (e.g., where people are looking at all points in time, nuances of prosodic information, their full facial expressions, body stances, their complete range of gestural and other nonverbal behavior interactions among all of these).[27]

This range shows that even our most pointed attempts to capture more than just the sem/syn/sym side of language in written forms does very little actually to capture other-side-of-meaning content. And, moreover, even with what advanced transcription techniques *do* capture, what it takes to capture them makes the transcripts very difficult to read. You have to have advanced linguistic or related training to make sense of them. So trying to capture all of the other-side-of-meaning going on from a conversation in a transcript may be damningly unwieldy at the least. And even were many aspects of other-side-of-meaning capturable, people would likely balk at reading it. Consider the difficulty many people have with learning to read and write as it is, without having to learn the complex transcription techniques, which again don't remotely capture all of the other-side-of-meaning nuance, or some other even more complex system.

So, that the written form of language corresponds so closely to the sem/syn/sym side of meaning, and that most modern people in at least the wealthier parts of the world are literate – a literacy forced upon them barely on the heels of their having acquired spoken language(s) – could be a large source of the attention imbalance. Moreover, multiple corresponding effects on our understanding of how language works and our language performance are traceable to our having writing. The very notion of a relatively fixed range of meanings for lexemes, the idea of agreed-upon definitions, the idea of a mental lexicon, even perhaps the notion of viable, pure, stand-alone, divorced-of-usage meaning discussed earlier, etc., all arise in part at least from having writing as a medium. We just can't help but forefront the parts of language that are readily written in our thinking about how language works. But we have more difficulty seeing the relevance and prevalence of the parts that are hard or perhaps impossible to write down.

And it is important to note that this bias in writing systems is not due to some failure on the systems' parts to capture other-side-of-meaning functioning and content. Those other-side-of-meaning products would likely be incredibly difficult to capture somehow in a visual symbolic form. Many of them arise out of the interaction of language with many other perceptual, cognitive, social, and other mental processes *in the experience of doing language,* such that they cannot be externalized to

---

[27] Even where a person is located, and how (i.e., sitting, standing, etc.), within a physical space or within/among other interlocutors can affect meaning (Colston, 2015).

visible marks as can uttered sounds in a phonetically based writing system. Non phonetically based writing systems may have more to work with here,[28] and people have proposed some forms of punctuation for other-side-of-meaning content conveyed in writing (i.e., the percontation point for rhetorical questions, the irony mark for written irony, and others [Houston, 2013; Kunneman, Liebrecht, van Mulken, & van den Bosch, 2015]), but writing systems may only be able to capture so much.

Consider, for instance, how one might represent in a written form the meaningful richness (the gravity, empathy, sympathy, fear, shock, even perhaps some humor, the conveyed insight, ingratiation, etc.) put into and likely gotten out of the following authentic short conversation overheard by the author, especially the underlined metaphor, relative perhaps to a nonfigurative usage of the same underlined term:

8.3   **[A son and his brother-in-law were discussing the colonoscopy procedure the son's father had just undergone.]**

SON: **Did you _see_ that apparatus?!**
BROTHER-IN-LAW: **Yeah. It's a <u>garden hose</u>.**

To do so at least with what current writing can do, we'd have to somehow incorporate all those modifiers and the pragmatic effects in the utterance:

8.4

SON: **Did you _see_ that apparatus?!**
BROTHER-IN-LAW: **Yeah, it's an apparatus that gives one a sense of gravity at its length, that triggers empathic feelings and indeed sympathy for your Dad, to which I experienced much shock and even fear at first seeing, along with a little dark humor – it also is described cleverly here by me and I'm insightful for noting all these details.**

which still fails utterly to capture all the meaning nuance and is obviously ridiculously wordy and long. So we often think of all the other-side-of-meaning content as being peripheral to the core, central sem/syn/sym

---

[28] Non phonetically based written forms of languages work differently in that more definitional content is contained in the written system itself – a bit as if written English sentences were strings of compact definitions we would read.

part. We don't often think that this perspective may be due to only the sem/sym/syn portion of language lending itself to a written form.[29]

Two related but briefer answers to the imbalance question concern the auditory or visual, spoken or signed versions of produced language. The written form of English, as for many languages, is phonemically based – attempting to capture, to some extent at least, the spoken sounds of the language. This is a useful way to translate language into a written form as we can have base symbols in writing which correspond roughly to the thirty or so basic phonemic units in speech. So, the number of atomic writing units one must learn is manageable and might align well with internal processing, given the similar structure to speech (i.e., combinations of those thirty building blocks). But this fact highlights another difference between the two sides of meaning, implied in the first answer but not explicitly stated: Much of the sem/syn/sym side is contained fairly directly in those uttered or signed units. The other-side-of-meaning content is maybe *partly* contained in the uttered/signed units, but resides also in *interactions* of those units with other perceptual, cognitive, social, and related processes. So, they don't make as much of a mark in the world that can be detected by our senses. It is far easier to attend to an idea (e.g., the idea that it is okay to proceed walking across a street) when one of our sensory systems receives an explicit signal of that idea (e.g., a green light) than if we just cognitively form the idea (e.g., seeing no moving cars crossing our path). The explicit signal hitting our sensory detectors and being processed by our sensory systems makes the represented idea stand out.

Relatedly, sem/syn/sym meaning content in being carried by the spoken or signed parts of performed language can leave strong sensory or memory echoes in us since they traversed through our sensory systems. We can thus replay what was said or signed in auditory or visual loops. Meaning processes on the other-side-of-meaning might have their own impacts on us, perhaps emotional ones, especially socio-emotive ones. But the sem/syn/sym side can also convey strong emotions directly through the

---

[29] A similarly patterned hidden bias often comes up when people in Judeo-Christian regions, countries, or cultures grapple with accommodating people with other religious practices wishing to have their work schedules and responsibilities accommodate their religious beliefs and practices. This is especially the case when such people hold jobs where deviations from established day or week schedules can be disruptive (i.e., school teachers). What people who are resistant to such accommodations often fail to realize is that the widely used standard five-day work week, or five business days, followed by a two-day weekend, is already designed to accommodate Judeo-Christian beliefs, with Sabbath days falling on Saturdays and Sundays. That that purportedly "standard" work week/weekend pattern is already biased to accommodate some people but not others often goes unnoticed.

embodied simulation triggered or other means. So, the experiences in us coming from the other-side-of-meaning processes might just be more ephemeral overall, leading us to attend less to them.

Another potential answer to the imbalance question could be the poignancy of embodied simulation content in our experience of language. Embodied simulations reach deeply into our evolutionarily older and fundamental processes of sensing and moving. They thump those processes to get them to drum up highly vivid and rich meaningful experiential gestalts to use for meaning construction (when describing this process, I sometimes use the analogy of someone poking another person in the side to get their attention). As we come equipped with the extremely well-developed eye–hand coordination of primates, crafted for honed acrobatic movement in arboreal environments but adapted to our modern built worlds, triggering motor simulations in us can produce very rich meaning (i.e., "The crashing airplane cartwheeled over the ground"). The same can be said for our rich, stereoscopic, color visual ability. Simulations that tap this process also provide vivid meaningful content (e.g., "The fallen leaves moved across the lawn like crabs on a beach"). So, it could just be this sheer power of embodied simulations that steals the show when we contemplate meaningfulness. The simulations drive us to think that they and the bits of language that trigger and direct them – the combined sem/syn/sym portion of language – are primary.

Still another possibility is the very nature of the social interaction processes carried out by the other-side-of-meaning. As said in the initial discussion of this chapter on language's social functioning, many of those other-side-of-meaning social processes work because they're conducted in camera or under the radar, as it were. This might contribute to the attention imbalance – those social interaction processes are just less noticeable because they can operate so stealthily. Indeed, at times people are baffled at why they've responded in the way they have to some other-side-of-meaning operation occurring (e.g., not knowing why you're smiling and liking a person who used a witty metaphor or hyperbole when you thought you didn't like the person). They're overshadowed by the brighter, shinier, and more obvious sem/syn/sym processes like embodied simulations.[30]

A somewhat related possibility is not just that we *tend* to see the background social processes less than the more foreground embodied

---

[30] And, of course, *both* the boldness of embodied simulations and the quiet operation of the other-side-of-meaning social interaction processes could be at play – not being mutually exclusive. The same point also holds for other pairs or groups of answers to the imbalance question.

simulations, but rather we *must* see those social processes less. Recall in the discussion of Lieberman's three social interaction systems the third system that tends to make us all align our senses of self with socially received instructions – for at least some of our beliefs, actions, self-characteristics, etc. And recall that we seem to be largely blinded to this major source of who we are. It likely would not sit well within many of us to know that our selves are actually largely built and honed by other people – what others collectively and generically want is what we tend to become.[31]

Now, what might make this realization perhaps more palatable is that most of those socially derived rules or guidelines for our behavior generally make us all work and play well together – they are, after all, what we *all* expect, of all of us. So, we even contribute to the rules. But to the extent that the rules are restrictive, or that they apply more to one group over another (e.g., as in differential expectations about social roles for males versus females [or for other genders or any groups]), and to the extent that the expectations might genuinely not fit our subjective wishes (e.g., a daughter does not want to take on her mother's family business), we don't like the idea of them. So, in an odd kind of circular self-delusion, we may not readily see the third social neural process operating in us, because if we did see it, it couldn't work in us. And for us to be us, it must work in us. So we don't see it. This could then contribute to our seeing more of the fronted sem/syn/sym part of language operating.

Another slight alteration on the above answer might also apply to *all* the social interaction neural processes in us, besides just the third social sense-of-self one. Overall, some people may dislike the idea of our being so socially influenced – driven to connect, to gain/maintain status, and to align with other people. This might also particularly be the case in some human cultures compared to others. Some people or cultures may place high value on human independence, freedom, being unfettered from unnecessary human or social tethers, etc. Whether such attitudes strive against our basic human social natures, and whether this is a good or bad thing, is up to people to decide on their own. But this mindset could result in a lesser emphasis or lower level of attentiveness being given to other-side-of-meaning processes, especially the mainly social ones.

Perhaps a corollary answer to the above one involves less an under-valuing of social connectedness than a heightened value being placed on the supposed concreteness or logic of sem/syn/sym meaning products. Indeed, such a value could underlie at least in part the "figurative outing" phenomenon mentioned earlier in this chapter. It also could drive a wide

---

[31] There, of course, being many possible cultural variations on this acceptance level.

variety of cultural memes ranging from *Star Trek*'s Mr. Spock, through the difficulties in getting computers to understand metaphors, through the character Sheldon Cooper – a genius physicist who cannot understand sarcasm – on the American television program, *The Big Bang Theory*, to sexist attitudes about relative gender differences involving a supposed dichotomy between maleness and logic versus femaleness and emotion or sociality. A core driver of these memes and misconceptions could be simply an emphasis being placed on the supposedly more advanced, concrete, sem/syn/sym side of meaning.

Yet another answer might be wrought by returning to the Robin Dunbar book mentioned previously, concerning the amount of our everyday talk that contains social content. The larger idea offered by Dunbar's book (*Grooming, Gossip and the Evolution of Language*, 1996) is that language effectively replaced grooming as the primary means of social interaction among the members of primate species. According to Dunbar, all primates groom, except humans. Primates also groom extensively – for large amounts of time and promiscuously between different members of the primate group (i.e., all members groom all other members). This grooming does serve utilitarian functions. Often living in arboreal and/or warm, lush environments, many primates attract parasites and can have bits of plant matter stuck to their fur, or their fur itself can get matted. So grooming has a very concrete health-serving function.

But grooming's primary purpose seems to be as a form of social interaction. Dunbar discusses extensively how increases in group size, especially in highly active, emotional, socially driven primates can lead to increased conflict, which already exists in primate groups due to competition over food, mates, social position, etc. Some form of countermeasure must therefore be in place to enable group life to continue: a form of peacemaking, if you will, to offset the squabbling, or worse. Group sizes even seem to be limited by the amount of grooming a group can perform. If the level of conflict driven by the group's size overrides the ability of grooming to patch things up, the group must become smaller or divide.[32]

Dunbar further argues that as early humans or pre-humans developed language, although it too serves obvious utilitarian purposes (e.g., conveying semantic meaning), we did so mainly as a means of replacing the social interaction enabled by grooming. This was where Dunbar's 70 percent measure, mentioned earlier, came in, of the amount of our everyday talk that contains social information – to demonstrate just how much social interacting we do with talk. Given how live language can also take

---

[32] Some primates, particularly bonobos, also use promiscuous sex for a similar peacemaking purpose.

place among small groups of people, instead of strictly being one-on-one, as is necessarily the case for grooming, language seems to have also effectively allowed us to live in larger groups – our bearing the same increase in squabbling as group sizes increase.

The point of all this for present purposes is that language having replaced grooming for social interaction purposes brought other changes with it – big ones. Language, by virtue of its *aboutness* quality – its ability to conjure meaning in us through embodied simulations and other processes, meaning which can relate to *things in the world* – added a huge component to language's social interaction repertoire. It added the semantic component referred to throughout this book as the sem/syn/ sym side.

So language was able to continue and even enhance greatly our degree and type of social interaction. Language even likely coevolved with enhancements to the first two neuro-social processes discussed by Lieberman and almost certainly coevolved with the third one. But language also came with this huge other capacity of conveying semantic content – and highly complex, indeed infinitely complex, semantic content, at that. So, one other reason for the attention imbalance toward the two sides of meaning could be the distracting quality of this major upgrade – language bringing with it an enormous power of semantic content, rendering its parallel and crucial function to enable us to meet our social motivations as smaller by comparison.[33]

And finally, another mechanism may exist in part to perpetuate this imbalance of attention, if not create it. For whatever the mixture of possible answers, or others not discussed here, an imbalance may simply have gotten in place at some point in our thinking about how language works. Once such a framework then exists, people subsequently have difficulty thinking differently.

An unusual but apt analogy might illustrate this idea. I'm often taken aback somewhat when I am presented with a change in perspective on well-entrenched physical aspects of my environment. For example, in holding a driver's license as well as using public transit, and in having lived in many places involving long commutes or errand trips, I've gotten used to being on roads, whether in a vehicle or walking alongside roads on

---

[33] We can see similar upgrades and expansions in functionality as media formats have changed. The advent of cable and satellite systems for television transmission, which replaced broadcast television in many parts of the globe beginning en masse in the later twentieth century, allowed for simultaneous Internet, movie, phone, and other communication and entertainment services to take place in parallel, alongside enabling much improvement in the television itself – improved picture quality and number of channels.

foot. My general perspective in using roads is that they seem to loom rather large to me, at least relative to other things.

Even now, as I look out my second-story study window onto the street in front of my house, the street seems in a way rather large to me, at least in relation to the other area spaces in my neighborhood (i.e., the houses' and other buildings' footprints, the gardens and yards, the alleyways and parking pads, etc.). And this is the case even though my street is not a large one by comparative road standards (i.e., a small residential street in a somewhat compact, prewar, urban neighborhood). Perhaps this is due to streets necessarily having to be open and clear to enable traffic, so we can see long stretches of them. Or it could be due to the high level of attention one must pay to the street areas when walking, riding, or driving on them (especially driving in Canada where pedestrian rights-of-way are honored and when driving near large universities with much foot traffic). Or it could even arise by pure frequency of attentiveness – I simply attend visually to roads, their extents, what is on them, the signage around them, etc., far more often than I see the other neighborhood area spaces just mentioned.

This perspective is then upended, though, whenever I see the amount of space roads actually take up in relation to the other spaces between them. When viewing aerial photographs, satellite imagery à la Google Earth or other systems, or even when flying overhead, I'm often struck at how thin and insignificant roads actually are in relation to their surrounding areas. I've had this same feeling of modest perceptual shock also when I traverse some bit of land area differently from my normal routes, usually on roads and sidewalks (e.g., when walking cross-country).

So, we may simply have gotten used to thinking of language as being entirely or exclusively made up of the sem/syn/sym side, from whatever mixture of origin sources. And now we just perpetuate that perspective by not having experiences of perceptually altering different exposures (e.g., going cross-country, as it were, in thinking about how language works).

A few of these possible answers to the imbalance question might also contribute to this perpetuating function, as they serve to frequently remind us of the showier side of the sem/syn/sym side of meaning. So, for instance, that the sem/syn/sym side is often the content of spoken words where the other-side-of-meaning processes are stealthier can perpetuate our initial perception that the sem/syn/sym side is primary. It's akin to how ongoing exposure to streets and roadways serves to perpetuate our perception of their large size, even when we've been reminded on occasion that roads are actually very small in comparison to areas between them.

One last perpetuating mechanisms is also worth noting. And it relates to the cognitive dissonance process discussed at a few points in this book. We tend to place value on things whose existence indicates effortful human behavior. The value is imparted to justify the effort. For instance, one mechanism in aesthetics argues that created things which obviously took enormous time, effort, and skill to produce (e.g., ornate architecture) are perceived as better, more valuable, more aesthetically pleasing, etc., relative to more easily produced things (e.g., plain architecture). We also tend to place value on things we've had to endure, even if the endurance was a negative experience, and indeed *especially* if the endurance was negative. Again, the value is imparted to justify the suffering experienced. This mechanism is used often to get people to form affinities to different things (e.g., the military service to which they belong, the sorority or fraternity to which they're pledging), by making them suffer through an initial period of negativity (e.g., basic training, hazing rituals).

This cognitive dissonance mechanism could help preserve the imbalance of attention toward the two sides of language through a process of **semantic consolidation**. That some bit of language merely exists, as something spoken or written, can tend to make people encountering that language place value on it. The creation of the language artifact, after all, took effort, thought, and time – so it must be worth something. This value can, indeed, take the form of believing the meaning of the language to be true. Many unscrupulous leaders, political and otherwise, know this well – just saying something will make some people believe it.[34] But semantic consolidation can also strengthen people's attention to the sem/syn/sym side of meaning. Since most of what is captured by spoken or written words is sem/syn/sym content, people will end up placing relatively more value on that content. Since other-side-of-meaning processes largely don't result in "preserved" artifacts we can see, hear, and value – in the sense of a recalled utterance said by a speaker or some bit of writing existing in the world – those processes don't benefit as much from semantic consolidation.

This chapter began with an introduction of three standout observations gleaned from the previous chapters' consideration of different segments of the other-side-of-meaning. It proceeded then to discuss the new perspective leant to social interaction when considering other-side-of-

---

[34] And repeating the falsehood over and over just strengthens the misconception – people find it hard to believe that a public figure would have the audacity to repeat a falsehood multiple times, knowing they're likely to be called out. So a repeated falsehood would therefore have to be true to justify the person's repeated statements. Cognitive dissonance again at work on a broader scale.

meaning processes. It also discussed more briefly some possible reasons for these other-side-of-meaning processes receiving relatively less attention than the sem/syn/sym side of meaning. The third of these observations suggested that the ways in which the other-side-of-meaning processes make and affect meaning is a much more complicated business arguably than it is for the sym/syn/sym side of meaning. The next chapter will take up this discussion.

9   The Art of Language

Love is the way messengers
from the mystery tell us things.
—Jalal ad-Din Muhammad Rumi (Chopra, 1998)

The last chapter made an argument that we often don't appreciate the degree to which the sem/syn/sym component of language is arguably at the service of the social component. The very reason we evolved a system of conveying semantic information between people is to convey that semantic information *between people* – serving the ultimate purpose of meeting our social motivations and functions. Moreover, as complex primates we were already ridiculously social even before evolving language. So, all the social practices and processes primates exhibit (i.e., motivations to make and maintain social connections [as well as to break them and maintain those breaks – forming in-groups and out-groups], as well as motivations to solidify and elevate our positions in social hierarchies and networks) are still going on in humans. We've also enhanced these social motivations relative to other primates and even added a new one involving aligning our senses of self with common social and cultural expectations – internalizing what society expects us to be like, as it were. This is the harmonizing neuro-social system discussed by Lieberman (2013).

But this dual increase of adding the semantic power of language to our functioning, while also amping up our needs and motivations for being social, may have resulted in some gaps. The sem/syn/sym side of language may not be able to service all those social motivations, which themselves are often best served via back channel, often non-semantic ways.

But we now have the high bandwidth medium of language within which to work on some of these social motivations (along with the multiple remaining older ways of handling social interaction, i.e., gesture, vocalization, emotion, facial expressions, touch, behavior, etc.). So, we were able to find multiple very creative ways of using the newfound complexity of language to achieve some of those social goals – we essentially created the other-side-of-meaning – mixing it with those older ways of handling socializing just mentioned.

But, to more fully understand *how* this myriad of other-side-of-meaning processes supports this social function of language, we need to look more closely at all the different other-side-of-meaning components and especially how they all can intricately interact, doing so ultimately for the purposes of enabling our social interaction needs. We must also look at larger structures in which other-side-of-meaning processes can reside and operate. We essentially now need to look both inside and outside the other-side-of-meaning processes – or to look at what kinds of processes can exist within, alongside, and external to other processes, to see how they all can work together.

Gotta Mingle

This book thus far has explored a variety of ways in which meaning is leveraged outside of the standard semantics of words and phrases marshaled through their morphosyntax – or the sem/syn/sym meaning as first discussed in Chapter 1. Although this sem/syn/sym central source of meaning is very powerful, arising in part from embodied simulations and their sequencing, it only constitutes a portion of how the mind makes meaning. In this exploration, we've considered deviations, omissions, imprecision, indirectness, figurativeness, and broader language play, all as means of achieving other-side-of-meaning meaning. At points, this discussion has noted overlaps between these processes. For instance, many forms of indirectness are inherently deviant. Figurative language by definition also omits certain aspects of potentially uttered nonfigurative language, etc. But most of the discussion has treated these processes as if separable, perhaps isolated phenomena for meaning making.

But a lesson can be borrowed from looking back at that core sem/syn/sym meaning, and applying a principle from that source to the other-side-of meaning – that of the blending, sequencing, and other forms of interactive *choreography* that morphosyntax supplies for embodied simulations and semantic meaning. If embodied simulation and semantic meaning are the construction materials for meaning qua meaning from the sem/syn/sym side, then morphosyntax is the blueprint.[1] Applying this idea to the other-side-of-meaning reveals a level of complexity in meaning

---

[1] A bit of a simplification, perhaps. Semantic meaning can also arise somewhat directly from morphosyntax itself.

Or, to rehash another metaphor, if embodied simulations and semantic meaning are raw foodstuff ingredients, or what is usually listed in the first half of a food recipe, then the morphosyntax is the preparation instructions found in the second half of the recipe.

making mostly overlooked by the various literatures addressing the other-side-of-meaning processes in isolation (e.g., figurative language, omission, deviance). It turns out that as morphosyntax choreographs how embodied simulations and semantic meaning arise and interact to create new meaning on the sem/syn/sym side, so does construction formation as well as the particular mixture and configuration of other-side-of-meaning processes work to choreograph how *those* processes interact to produce new meaning.

One straightforward way of illustrating this lesson is to consider one particular process of meaning making from the other-side-of-meaning. But rather than looking at that particular process per se, alone and in isolation, we instead zoom both inwardly and outwardly to detail how that process interacts with and melds into other processes. To do this, we'll first consider probably the most widely studied process from the other-side-of-meaning, that of metaphor.

At core, metaphors perform the function of connecting source domains to target domains. But metaphors (at least linguistic ones) are also flexible, multi-word phrases, or even larger structures. So, they can accordingly accomplish many other things as well. Metaphors can be crafted to perform pragmatic effects and other meaningful changes in hearers based on structural components of the metaphor's construction which go beyond the achieved connections between source and target domains.

Interestingly for purposes of this book, as one such possibility, consider the primary thematic proposition the book offers – the idea of conjoined antonymies – but imagine those conjoined antonymies as embedded within metaphors. This additional structural characteristic to the metaphor's construction can amplify and add to the suite of pragmatic functions performed. Other external structural characteristics that can leverage other-side-of-meaning meaning, such as the genre in which the metaphors appear, can also be invoked at the same time.

To illustrate all of this, please consider the following lyrics from Howard Jones's 1980s popular song, "No One Is To Blame" (Jones, 1985):

9.1   **You can look at the menu, but you just can't eat.**
You can feel the cushion, but you can't have a seat.
You can dip your foot in the pool, but you can't have a swim.
You can feel the punishment, but you can't commit the sin.
And you want her, and she wants you.
We want everyone.
And you want her and she wants you.
No one, no one, no one ever is to blame

You can build a mansion, but you just can't live in it.
You're the fastest runner but you're not allowed to win.

Some break the rules, and let you count the cost.
The insecurity is the thing that won't get lost.
<Chorus>

You can see the summit but you can't reach it.
It's the last piece of the puzzle but you just can't make it fit.
Doctor says you're cured but you still feel the pain.
Aspirations in the clouds but your hopes go down the drain.
<Chorus>
No one ever is to blame.
No one ever is to blame.

Two interesting characteristics of the sequence of metaphors in this song may be highlighted, one internal and the other external.

The internal component, as stated earlier, illustrates how structures given to metaphors can afford additional other-side-of-meaning expressional content – beyond that invoked by the source/target domain linkage. Each of the metaphors in the lyrics in 9.1 accordingly creates a unique conjoined antonymy. But nearly all of those antonymies are conjoined in a similar way by their particular metaphor. These metaphors first invoke a certain conceptual structure via their nonfigurative source domains (e.g., a person perusing a list of potential food items to order in a restaurant, a person constructing a home for themselves, a person sampling a swimming pool's water temperature, a person being cured of a disease or affliction by a physician). But the metaphors then negate, obviate, or nullify those conceptual structures with a subsequent clause contradicting the structure, again still within the nonfigurative source domain (e.g., the person *being denied* the opportunity to eat, the person *being forbidden from* living in their constructed home, the person *being disallowed from* swimming in the pool whose temperature they sampled, the person *still exhibiting symptoms from* the disease they've supposedly been cured of).[2]

The external component to the metaphors is the framework of the language genre in which the metaphors reside – lyrics from a popular cultural song. This song structure allows groupings of the metaphors to be presented in sequences within verses (four metaphors together in each verse), with each grouping separated by a repeating chorus. So, the song begins with a string of four different but similarly structured conjoined antonymies, each serving as a source domain for the common target domain of LOVE THAT IS FORBIDDEN. At first, this target domain

---

[2] A couple of the metaphors structure their conjoined antonymies in a slightly different way – the addressee being forced to endure negative consequences for something they didn't do (e.g., "You can feel the punishment, but you can't commit the sin," "Some break the rules, and let you count the cost").

may not be apparent to a new hearer (reader) of the song's lyrics. But the repeating pattern of the source domains, as well as the first appearance of, and then repetition of, the chorus, likely helps clarify matters (e.g., "... you want her and she wants you ..."). A second sequence of four new conjoined antonymies then follows, each again couched within metaphorical source domains all linking again with the common FORBIDDEN LOVE target domain. This pattern of four metaphors/conjoined antonymies in a verse followed by the repeated chorus then recurs one additional time, followed by an ending which repeats the songs title twice.

So, the song's lyrics are essentially a sequence of twelve metaphors, each with the target domain of FORBIDDEN LOVE but each also with a unique source domain. These metaphors are divided into verses by a repeating chorus which serves to clarify that those lyrical lines are indeed metaphors. Moreover, each of those source domains is structured as a conjoined antonymy – conjoined via the juxtaposed contradicting clauses, but antonymic because those clauses contradict (e.g., A person CAN do what leads to X, but the person CANNOT do X, or, in the case of a couple of the metaphors, A person experiences negative consequences for something he or she didn't do). These source domains all serve to highlight, over and over, the primary characteristic of the target domain of forbidden love – *its inherent conjoined antonymy*.

Love is arguably the most powerful social bond that exists between and among human beings. People sacrifice their lives for it. We are utterly miserable if it is unrequited or forbidden to us. It is even neurologically hardwired into our species through a number of embodied-simulation-esque usurpations of more primal brain functions (i.e., pleasure and pain) driving us to attempt to have and maintain it and making us profoundly unhappy, and even physically ill, if we are denied it (Lieberman, 2013). Having something as powerful as love being forbidden to a person is thus one of the most powerful conjoined antonymies we can experience. It resides in the general semantics of forbidden love (i.e., a desperate want and need of something coupled with an absolute denial of that something), but also powerfully and even ruinously in the emotions involved (i.e., feeling ecstatically overjoyed about mutual love with another person, coupled with the abject misery of having that love forbidden).[3]

So we really might consider this particular song's lyrics as having a third major meaning-creating, influencing, and enhancing component. In addition to the internal conjoined antonymy structure of the

---

[3] It points out the obvious by saying this idea is ubiquitous in human culture, especially popular music, evidenced from the multiple recordings of the song 1960 Boudleaux Bryant song, "Love Hurts," by the Everly Brothers, Cher, Roy Orbison, Nazareth, and Jim Capaldi (Bryant, 1960).

metaphorical constructions as well as the external standard framework of songs and their lyrics, we have the particular target domain activated repeatedly by the metaphors – love and its being forbidden. Indeed, the importance and human-existential immensity of this target domain makes it one of the primary components of the very human condition itself.

So what does this internal, external, and human-central triad of characteristics of this bit of human-created language add to the meaning involved? We'll first consider each characteristic in isolation, and then discuss how they interact.

Internal Features: Conjoined Antonymy

Taking the conjoined antonymy internal aspect of the metaphors first, we might begin by noting the sequencing of the clauses in each of the metaphors, and the effect that has on the conceptual domain (the source domain) being manipulated. Each of the metaphors having the *X followed by NOT X* pattern, upon close inspection don't really contain the conjoined antonymy in their surface forms. They rather conjure the conjoined antonymies in their invocation of the schemas of the particular conceptual domains (source domains) being called up. For instance, the very first clause of the song,

9.2   **You can look at the menu**

could invoke a number of possible schemas including looking at a pull-down menu on a computer screen (e.g., the list of commands or options under some category like page formatting), or some other generic detailed list of things (e.g., a listing of television programs, a list of activities at a resort of some kind). But the most frequent usage of *menu*, corresponding to a list of food items available for ordering at a restaurant, is probably the one most people would derive initially.

Moreover, hearers/readers will likely conjure some portion or the entirety of the actual schema of *ordering food at a restaurant* rather than just the bare minimum semantic meaning possible (i.e., *a person being allowed to cast their eyes at a list of food items*). This particular schema is well known in cognitive science. It is certainly variable but nonetheless usually contains a few typical components (e.g., a server/wait-person of some sort giving you the menu [or your reading it on a wall or screen], your selecting food or drink items from the menu and telling them to the server, the server then bringing you those items). Importantly for present purposes, these varying ingredients in a menu/food-ordering/etc. schema essentially all culminate in your *receiving the food/drink and then devouring it*. This final act is indeed the raison d'être for the entire schema. So, to have this schema and its culmination activated but then be reneged by an adjacent, second clause in the song,

9.3   **but you just can't eat**

creates the conjoined antonymy.

Similar invocations followed immediately by their oppositional revocations also hold for most of the other metaphors. People typically feel cushions as a prelude to sitting on them ("but you can't have a seat").[4] People frequently test the water temperature of a swimming pool before then swimming in it ("but you can't have a swim"). People typically build houses to then live in them ("but you just can't live in it").[5] People normally climb mountains to reach their summits ("but you can't reach it"), etc.

The metaphors in the song that have different structures than the explicit *X followed by NOT X* pattern also create conjoined antonymies. Moreover, they also do this through a similar invocation and immediately subsequent revocation of a conjured schema. For instance, receiving and experiencing punishment usually invokes a schema of the experiencer having first committed some form of wrongdoing to warrant the punishment,

9.4   **You can feel the punishment**

which is then contradicted in the clause immediately following,

9.5   **but you can't commit the sin.**

Similarly, a person violating some laws or rules governing human behavior usually invokes the schema of those persons eventually (and/or hopefully) being punished for the violations, which is contradicted by the second clause in that metaphor from the song,

9.6   **Some break the rules, and let you count the cost.**

These metaphors tapping into senses of unfairness or injustice may also have deeply embodied bases, residing in key neural structures hardwired in us, acting as hair triggers in identifying unfairness (Lieberman, 2013).

---

[4] This source domain in particular seems quite strongly embodied. Were we to compare it to an alternative of, say, "*You can pull out a chair,* but you can't have a seat," which seems a reasonable semantic equivalent to the original, "*You can feel the cushion,* but you can't have a seat," the effect seems weaker. Something about feeling cushions relative to pulling out a chair seems a stronger and more vivid elicitation of someone seeking to sit down – perhaps because feeling a cushion conveys a stronger sense of a person seeking or needing comfort, or perhaps it's just rarer than the more generic pulling out a chair.

[5] Home construction as an occupation and/or house flipping being obvious exceptions.

This repeating pattern across all the metaphors, nicely captured in the *bait-and-switch* idiom, is a common one in human experience. Indeed, the pattern itself also has a schematic structure probably held by most people mature enough to have experienced it, evidenced by the very existence of the idiom itself. It also has a quality of cynicism to it, in that baiting but then switching is a negative thing we've all mostly likely encountered in our lives, perhaps repeatedly, and accordingly have been frustrated over. But baiting and switching also nonetheless seems to persevere and even perpetuate in our culture, rather than fading away. So the broad elicitation of this *bait-and-switch* idea might help convey a powerful sense of deep frustration at something known to be bad that just won't go away.

But, the *individual* instantiations of these *bait-and-switch* conjoined antonymies can also convey specific nuances of the resulting frustration. For instance, the opening conjoined antonymy expressed in 9.2 and 9.3 speaks to one of our most absolutely basic physiological needs – food. Having food denied to us is not merely frustrating, it can be fatal. So to have food dangled in front of us first but then have it be denied taps into a deeply seated physiological necessity in us, as well as all its accompanying aspects (i.e., the many ways in which we make this physiological need not only enticing, but also useful for a wide variety of cultural practices such as gifting, wooing, apologizing, etc., and also our evolved physiological caloric hoarding process which is one major contribution to obesity). Also, the second conjoined antonymy in the lyrics involving cushions (i.e., being allowed to feel them but then being denied sitting on them) is a deeply embodied form of denial, conjuring up past experiences of the misery inherent in having been on one's feet for prolonged periods and the intense comfort and satisfaction of then sitting comfortably.

Moreover, despite the likely ongoing occurrences of embodied simulations when these lyrics are comprehended, they might also trigger outright explicit memories of full instantiations of these conjoined antonymies. For instance, we might consciously recall experiences of smelling great food but it being denied to us, or our building something but then being denied use of it, or our nearing a destination but then failing to reach it. Also, the multiple recurring triggerings of these similar conjoined antonymies might increase the likelihood that any individual lyric would produce a vivid concrete memory. A general sort of priming might arise whereupon the instance of a given conjoined antonymy coming later in the lyrics might be more likely to produce strong memories relative to a conjoined antonymy nearer the beginning of the song, all due to the collective priming coming from the repeating similar source domains/conjoined antonymies.

Since the slightly differing invocations of this bait-and-switch kind of conjoined antonymy are also separated yet sequenced in a package, they might serve well to build up the full enriched picture of the target domain in question – forbidden love. Were only a single source domain to be used once, or the same source domain to be used repeatedly, we may not have as fully developed and fleshed out an experience with forbidden love in all its uncomfortable through ruinous detail.

Related to this point, by also including the at least couple of conjoined antonymy source domains involving unjust punishment for deeds not committed, the unfairness aspect of forbidden love is included. Whether explicit in an actual experience of forbidden love (i.e., you as a kind person are denied love but another horrible person you know finds it), or just as a generic characteristic of such a deeply experienced pain (i.e., your finally meeting someone, after a long time of loneliness; a person you find the best ever, once-in-a-lifetime, perfect match to your picture of the ideal partner, who might even love you back, is denied to you for some reason), the feeling of unfairness is often an additional insult to the emotional injury of forbidden love.

Finally, at least one of the conjoined antonymy source domains can trigger strong social motivations in comprehenders. As mentioned earlier, a primary drive in much of our behavior is to maintain or elevate our and others' positions in social hierarchies and networks. So, if we happen to be in a position to rise higher in such a hierarchy, or especially to reside at least for a while at the top of one – with the inherent recognition, admiration, etc., of other people, all of which is deserved – this is a very strong enticement to us. To then have that status denied to us somehow or for some reason is a particularly social twist on the bait-and-switch disservice to us. The lyric concerning the hearer being the fastest runner but not being allowed to win seems almost perfectly crafted to tap into this social conjoined antonymy. It also parallels the functioning of the other conjoined antonymies based on unfairness.

A number of other processes can also be invoked by the different conjoined antonymy source domains listed in the lyrics, which can bring additional components to meaning. A bit of clever nestedness and perhaps double entendre, for instance, seems present in the particular lyric:

9.7   **The insecurity is the thing that won't get lost.**

Normally, *secure* things stay fast to wherever they're mounted, where *insecure* things might become loosened and break free, perhaps going away. So, for the lyric to say that "insecurity" is the thing that won't become loosened or go away, or to "get lost," seems a conjoined antonymy embedded within another broader one paralleling some of the other

source domains – a negative thing forced upon you unfairly or undeserv-
edly, adjoined with a teaser for something more positive. This also
matches the pattern of the forbidden love target domain. So the word
insecurity seems to carry double meaning here, referring to the concrete
sense of how well something is physically fastened to something else –
a sense not unrelated to the topic at hand. But it also refers to the more
emotional sense of insecurity often accompanying the emotions one feels
when love is forbidden to us.

The source domain/conjoined antonymy referring to the unreachable
summit, occurring presumably during a mountain climb:

9.8   **You can see the summit but you can't reach it.**

might also invoke a number of powerful and related cognitive mechanisms. Being able to physically see the summit of a mountain might imply
a significant portion of the mountain has been climbed already. Mountain
summits are often visible from a distance, but while on the slope of
a mountain, often the summit cannot be seen until the climber is relatively
close to it. So being unable to complete the climb, after a great effort has
presumably already been expended toward that goal, can bring a number
of relevant phenomena to the fore.

Cognitive dissonance, for instance, which seems a frequent player in
many forms of figurative processing (Colston, 2015), could be one. By
having already expended much time and effort on the climb, a person
would inherently tend to more greatly value that climb – in order to justify
the effort expended/time taken. So to have the completion of such a task
denied to us is particularly frustrating when cognitive dissonance is in
operation.[6]

The denial of the conceptual domain initially invoked, in this case
climbing a mountain, being so particularly strong in this situation,
where it appears as if the task has been quite nearly accomplished,
approaches that found in ironic situations. In these cases, what one
expects, prefers, or desires is strongly violated (e.g., as in a person who
won a Nobel Prize in Chemistry [i.e., is expected to be good at chemistry],
who then causes an explosion when mixing household cleaners). Not that
nearly reaching a mountain summit but being unable to complete the
climb is necessarily ironic. But the stronger the contrast gets between

[6] A related process is that of sunk costs, which in some ways are driven by cognitive
dissonance. The idea that we *must* follow a course of behavior, even a very negative and
unpleasant one, merely and only to justify the effort/expense having already taken place
(i.e., enduring the last few days of a miserable resort vacation, instead of aborting, because
the room has been paid for), is also a highly memorable and distinctive experience possibly
conjured by reminders like the song lyrics.

expectations and reality, the closer we approach irony (Colston, 2002). This could potentially bring in meaning components associated with irony (e.g., triggering the schema of irony, producing contrast effects that render the outcome even more negative, conjuring feelings of negativity [i.e., unmet expectations are often frustrating]).

As just noted, ironic contradictions between expectations and reality usually go beyond just a mere deviance from expectations. They instead usually include a full-blown contradiction – the very most improbable thing to occur in a situation, the very thing that absolutely cannot be, is in fact the very thing found in the situation, and its existence is obvious and beyond question. Such a quality seems the case in the one conjoined antonymy/source domain involving the jigsaw:

9.9   **It's the last piece of the puzzle but you just can't make it fit.**

If a jigsaw puzzle piece is the only one remaining detached from its puzzle, it must, by definition, be the one that fits into the last hole in the puzzle. For it to not then fit into the jigsaw is just the sort of blatant contradiction discussed above. This also doesn't make this particular conjoined antonymy ironic – a couple of other things might still need to be in place (see Colston, 2000b). But it at least demonstrates another way in which one can enhance the oppositionality in source domain conjoined antonymies, helping to further highlight the conjoined antonymy, and its unpleasant oppositionality, in the forbidden love target domain (i.e., want/need love – can't have love).

At least one of the source domains/conjoined antonymies also taps into another metaphor beyond the *forbidden love is X* one,

9.10   **Aspirations in the clouds but your hopes go down the drain.**

additionally calls up the ubiquitous GOOD is UP/BAD is DOWN conceptual metaphor (Lakoff & Johnson, 1980). So, one might argue this line provides a double dose of conjoined antonymy: that between the figurative pair of meanings in the lyric (i.e., hopefulness versus despondency) as well as that of the concrete nonfigurative vehicles (i.e., up [GOOD] versus down [BAD]). Indeed, the potentially added strength of this multiple entendre may be the reason for its placement at the apex point of the song – being the final one of the string of a dozen source domains.

At points it has been mentioned that the use of concrete source domains/conjoined antonymies in these song lyrics can conjure the running of embodied simulations during the comprehension of these metaphors. It is worth noting here that these embodied simulations are likely a key aspect of the song's conveyance of meaning. It is known that embodied simulations take place during metaphor comprehension in ways not identical to but nonetheless similar to comprehension of similar nonmetaphorical language (Bergen, 2012, see also Chapter 6, "Figurative Language and Embodied Simulation"). It is also known that these embodied simulations in metaphor comprehension can enhance certain aspects of meaning, such as the strength of proverbial advocations (Colston, 2018a). It seems very likely, then, that embodied simulations would also be present and magnify the meaning potency when comprehended in lyrics like those in the Jones song.

Indeed, the yoked presence of metaphor and conjoined antonymy could result in a multiple feedback process where each component enhances the other. For instance, the concrete content in the lyrics (e.g., reading food menus, not being allowed to eat; climbing mountains, not reaching summits; dipping toes into pools, not swimming) very likely enhances the metaphorical meaning being conveyed (e.g., love being forbidden). This content also very likely sharpens the contrasts presented by the conjoined antonymies – the various forms of *X but then not X*. It then follows that these enhanced and sharpened metaphors and conjoined antonymies would also intensify one another, all again contributing to the fleshing out and enhanced poignancy of the comprehension experience of the pain of forbidden love.

One source domain/conjoined antonymy in particular might benefit from the spiking arguably taking place from the embodied simulations involved in the metaphors and conjoined antonymies. The lyric referring to the physician's apparent misdiagnosis,

9.11   **Doctor says you're cured but you still feel the pain.**

relates quite directly to schemas involving health and sickness, and even life and death. It's already been stated that love being forbidden is one of the most powerful conjoined antonymies we can experience. But another perhaps even more powerful one is our struggle with the love of life coupled with the knowledge of inevitable death. This metaphor could access a bit of that conjoined antonymy, enhancing its poignancy. The invoking of social power structures may also reside in this metaphor – triggering potential feelings of frustration and resentment at elevated social figures (e.g., physicians) with power and authority over us, who end up failing at their job and status.

This discussion of the power of underlying embodied simulations parallels another one concerning the centrality of conjoined antonymies not only in our language but also in our very ability to think about the world. Foreshadowing a bit toward Chapter 10, the nature of conjoined antonymies may not be just an innocent and arbitrary pairing of oppositional components in some linguistic or propositional structure (i.e., like the song lyrics or in concepts [love of life and knowledge of death]). It might instead be a very fundamental aspect of how we think and communicate, and indeed of how nature and the world around us are structured. That conjoined antonymy then resides in bits of language like the Jones song lyrics may be a more fundamental thing than just one songwriter's clever creation.

External Features: Popular Song Structure

Turning now to the external part of the meaningful influences, we can observe a number of characteristics of popular songs, their lyrics, and the usual structure of these, and how all this can affect meaning. But one might first note overall how the mere presence of a bunch of conjoined antonymies, embedded in the source domains of metaphors in a popular song, is itself telling. It was previously foreshadowed that conjoined antonymies might be a larger component of thought and language, and even nature, than we typically realize (see Chapter 10 for this full discussion). That conjoined antonymies make their way even into old popular metaphorical song lyrics about the intense pain of forbidden love might thus suggest how common and communal they are. If they can successfully enhance communication in this venue, which by nature is designed for mass consumption by a broad and diverse listenership, they might be tapping into something very core to human experience.

A standout characteristic of popular songs and their lyrics is the patterns of rhythm and rhyme found in the music and words respectively.[7] Whatever the time signature used by a popular song, it usually involves at least two recurring patterns of rhythm, one in the verses and another in the chorus. The lyrics in the verses and sometimes the chorus also typically follow a particular rhyme scheme. The Jones song lyrics I have discussed, for instance, follow generally an AABB rhyme scheme in each verse, with the last words in lines 1 and 2 rhyming with each other, and the same pattern for the end words in lines 3 and 4 (no rhyme scheme is found in the chorus). These recurring patterns can afford a scaffold of sorts, for the meaning-making processes coming from the words, voice sound characteristics, music sound characteristics, and all the other bits than can contribute to the meaningful experience of the listener. Similar to how the recurring pattern of the conjoined antonymies in the source domains can serve to prime one another (i.e., as the hearer registers this

---

[7] People who share the author's propensity for earworms (also referred to as brainworms, sticky music, stuck song syndrome, or Involuntary Musical Imagery [IMI] by Wikipedia) can attest readily to this characteristic of popular music.

recurring pattern in the conjoined antonymies, she might come to predict them, resulting in their facilitated processing as the song progresses), the recurring patterns in the rhythm and rhyme can prime analogously the processing fluency of many meaning contributors.

The recurrence and reduplication found in popular songs' music and lyrics, along with some slight variations to these, also serve to build up the breadth and complexity of the single target domain that all the songs' content is contributing toward, the concept and experience of, the emotional reactions toward, forbidden love. All the slight alterations to these patterns, found in the slightly varying conjoined antonymies in the source domains, the slightly varying pitch contours in the verses, etc., all nonetheless housed within patterns of regularly recurring rhyme and rhythm found in songs, work toward this goal. It is essentially a pattern of allowable variation contained within a pattern of regularity that achieves this building process. It's a bit like the way hearing a number of differing voices, but all singing the same song, as in a choral performance, gives richness to the listeners' experience.

We also have large and complex schemas concerning popular songs from which we can automatically access knowledge and information to bring to bear on our meaning construction in hearing the song. Popular songs are often about the topics of love, lost love, the angst of unrequited love, the joy of mutual love, the pain of forbidden love, etc. So it isn't as if we must build up the concept of forbidden love purely and solely from the bottom-up information coming from the song. Once we realize we're listening to a popular song, and not even a conscious realization is necessary, we can predict more readily that the content might be about forbidden love, with all its accompanying corollary content.

That songs come typically with the structure of recurring verses and choruses, and in the present example, given those verses hold sequences of similar metaphors (containing the conjoined antonymies) and the chorus provides a clue as to how those metaphors should be interpreted (i.e., the "you want her, and she wants you" line in particular), we have yet another means of clarifying the referent of the source domains. It was argued earlier that some form of cross-priming might arise across the repeating source domains – aiding and perhaps facilitating their comprehension. But a similar mechanism might be had through ellipsis. Perhaps even before a cross-priming pattern could emerge, people might project either the conjoined antonymy structure onto subsequent verse lines or the referred to target domain of forbidden love, after just having encountered as few as two of the initial source domains.

One interesting emergent characteristic of this particular popular song might be had from a collection of sources pertaining to the usual characteristics of popular songs – that of an emergent form of *consolation*. Popular songs usually have titles. As already pointed out, they also typically have a recurring chorus. Songs also have obviously other words, the singer's voice, the music itself, etc. Each of these components in the present song seems to contribute a bit to an emerging feeling of consolation for the pain of forbidden love, expressed cumulatively across the song. Indeed, the very title of the song suggests this, "No One Is To Blame." Those words also recur repeatedly in the chorus and at the end of the song. A subtle hyperbolic line in the verse also applies here, "We want everyone." The tone of the singer's voice at times also takes on a soothing quality, as does the music – particularly at the song's coda where the music softens and slows in a comforting manner.

It is as if a prominent goal of the song is to bring up this painful experience of forbidden love, with all the hurt and frustration typically accompanying it. But the song then attempts to give comfort to the hearer by noting the ubiquity of romantic and social yearning ("We want everyone"). That failure of love to happen, via its being forbidden or for some other reason, is pointed out as a fact of living ("No One Is To Blame"). That this fact of life is as old as humanity itself and will not go away in the future is also expressed (emphasis added): "No One *Ever* Is To Blame." Also, the soothing quality of the singer's voice and the music at the end all culminate in a manner as if to say that forbidden love is a horrible experience, but we're stronger for knowing about it and facing it. In the end, it is something that cannot be avoided and the pain from it will eventually fade and even pass. Indeed, this emergent quality of the song, providing comfort in the face of pain, is also a common characteristic of popular music.

One final point pertains to this comforting quality of the song. One particular lyric in the verse of the song, the line argued previously to possibly aid in the clarification of the target domain for the repeated source domains, "... you want her, and she wants you," is particularly interesting. The notion of forbidden love aside for the moment, this lyric by itself can serve as a poignant positive emotional hook for the listener as it describes the essential core of requited love – its mutuality. Requited love is itself a very special experience. Many if not most instances of love go unrequited. So when love is mutual it has a very powerful emotional hold on us – not many things feel better than the first moment of mutually realized, fully requited love. So to have this lyric embedded in the song which is repeatedly reminding us of the pain of forbidden love, is making essentially the harshest demonstration of the pain of forbidden love possible – contrasting the two against one another. But it can also contribute to the comforting process. To remind the listener of this degree of forbidden love pain, but to then add in the recurring comforting reminders of requited love, might actually enhance the overall level of consolation. If a song has taken a person to the most painful extent of suffering possible – reminding them of how good it feels to have requited love alongside showing them the miserable pain of forbidden love, then the only way to go subsequently is to feel better.

We have thus far looked deeply into how internal characteristics of metaphors, including the kinds of constructions they can take, and how external characteristics of popular songs, the language genre in which the Jones's lyrics are found, can effect meaning. We'll now look at the particular target domain elicited by the metaphors in the Jones song lyrics, forbidden love, and discuss how this topic in particular enables meaning components of its own, additional to those brought by things internal and external to metaphors in the song.

The Human Centrality of Love: Love Hurts

William Shakespeare once wrote, "The course of true love never did run smooth" (1596). He was definitely on to something important. Romantic love is a feeling people may encounter throughout their lives. But for younger people in particular, where feelings of romantic love may be novel or at least relatively new to their experience, it might be particularly salient. Younger people, also by virtue of perhaps not having felt romantic love before and, of course, for perhaps emerging hormonal or other related factors, may thus feel romantic love more powerfully, or desire it more particularly, than other people. At least for *some* younger people and *some* other people. Moreover, that popular music, particularly when involving topics related to love, is often directed at youthful audiences, coupled with the just argued relative importance of romantic love to younger people, might overall act to enhance all the various processes for meaning making regarding romantic love, and especially its being denied, in this song.[8]

Forbidden love may also have a kind of double level of rarity to it. Consider as mentioned that requited love is already relatively rare compared to just feeling love for someone else. Such love is not always returned. So, to have requited love end up forbidden for some reason (e.g., by parents keeping couples apart, due to prejudices against different

---

[8] Of course, one can also make the opposing argument, encapsulated in the saying, "Youth is wasted on the young," that younger people fail to appreciate the experience of love. Older individuals, perhaps less capable of the energy levels useful for building romantic relationships but greatly valuing romantic love due to their experience, might actually yearn for it more strongly – especially if it has been denied to them for a long period of time.

kinds of love, due to various societal mores or taboos or something, due to age, class, or ethnicity differences) can be particularly devastating to people experiencing it.[9]

Related to this point, if those reasons for requited love being denied between two (or more) lovers are taken as ridiculous by the lovers involved, the experience of forbidden love can be particularly galling and destructive. For instance, if the forbiddance arises from some of the more negative and restrictive tendencies in human belief and culture (i.e., ignorance, closed-mindedness, phobias, jealousy, sour grapes, fear, prejudicial belief systems [e.g., love between different ethnicities or within a single gender being viewed as wrong]), the parties experiencing the ban on exercising their feelings can feel especially resentful.

Deeply negative feelings when experiencing forbidden love are also driven by deep-seated biological and neurological forces. Among the several neurologically hardwired systems within us, motivating us to get and stay socially connected, are ones connected to evolutionary ancient neurological systems governing pain and pleasure. Put as simply as possible, the experience of social pain, arising when we don't have or lose social connection, is effectively the same experience as physical pain. The same holds for physiological pleasure. Indeed, as these social connection systems were evolving in mammals, primates, and humans, they usurped some of the most fundamentally basic and powerful motivation systems in us, those driving us to avoid life-threatening things (i.e., pain) and to approach life-benefiting ones (i.e., pleasure), (Lieberman, 2013).

As noted earlier, this experience of forbidden love is one of the most prevalent tropes in the human condition.[10] We have strong schematic structures for understanding it, built up from authentic experience as well as second-hand exposure. Indeed, forbidden love is one of the most frequently used themes in literatures written throughout history in most if not all cultures.[11] As just an absolute scratching of the surface of this body of written fiction works, consider the list of novels from Western and Chinese literature presented in Table 9.1, all with forbidden love as one of their

---

[9] It should be noted that the particular type of love discussed in the Jones song appears to be either heterosexual or lesbian, evidenced in the chorus lines pertaining to the partners involved ("... you want her, and she wants you"). Obviously, many other kinds of love could be involved with varying levels of prejudices directed against them by certain parties.

[10] Trope in the sense of a widespread common occurrence, not in the sense of a form of figurative language. The prevalence of forbidden love is evidenced in the oft used English idiom of "forbidden fruit."

[11] Not to mention movies, television, theater, art, music obviously, and many other forms of expression.

Table 9.1 *Western and Chinese literary and folklore works pertaining to forbidden love*

Romeo and Juliet	*Doctor Zhivago*	*Wuthering Heights*	*Girl with a Pearl Earring*
Lolita	*Jane Eyre*	*The Thorn Birds*	*Phantom of the Opera*
Gone with the Wind	*The English Patient*	*Memoirs of a Geisha*	*Love in the Time of Cholera*
Death in Venice	*The Reader*	*Atonement*	*Hunchback of Notre Dame*
Maurice	*The Scarlet Letter*	*Rubyfruit Jungle*	*Lady Chatterley's Lover*

The Butterfly Lovers	*Song of the Everlasting Regret*
Legend of the White Snake	*Niulang and Zhinu*
Romance of the West Chamber	*The Peacocks Fly to the Southeast*
Dream of the Red Chamber	*The Legend of Dong Yong and the Seventh Fairy*

central themes.[12] It is abundantly apparent that forbidden love is a central and crucial part of the human experience (Brontë, 1847a, 1847b; Brown, 1973; Forster, 1971; Chevalier, 1999; García Márquez, 1985; Golden, 1997; Hawthorne, 1850; Hugo, 1831; Idema, 2009, 2012; Koshoibekova, 2015; Lawrence, 1928; Leroux, 1911; Mann, 1912; Mark, 2016; McCullough, 1977; McEwan, 2001; Mitchell, 1936; Nabakov, 1955; Ondaatje, 1992; Pasternak, 1957; Schlink, 1995; Schomp, 2010; Shakespeare, 1993; Wang, 1995; Yu, 2001; Yuan & Chunde, 2008).

Interactions

We may next discuss ways in which these three factors – embedding conjoined antonymies in metaphor source domains, the popular song structure, and the centrality to us of the target domain topic, forbidden love – each interact with the others. Considering first the interaction between conjoined antonymies in metaphor and the song structure, recall that many of the meaningful processes produced by the song structure arise from its repeating sequences of things (i.e., the verses, rhythms, tonal patterns, etc.). Especially important are the repetitions of the metaphorical content – the source domains and their shared target domain. In normal face-to-face conversation or even written correspondence, a speaker using such repetitions would seem extremely odd. Were someone to actually attempt to converse or write this way, many of those meaningful processes would most likely fail – the listener would likely

---

[12] Not being a literary scholar, I'll be forthright in admitting the lack of representativeness of the works listed in this table. I picked the Western titles just from ones I happened to know about. I conducted a brief informal Internet search to find the Chinese works.

be so taken aback at the bizarreness of their converser that the mechanisms would not leverage their meanings. But the popular song structure is so very well known to us, including its standard patterns of repetition, that it normalizes those repetition processes. This in turn enables the repeating sequence of metaphors with their embedded conjoined antonymies, and all the other repeating factors, to accomplish their meaningful contributions.

It is this normal pattern of repetition, expected in popular songs, that also enables the cross-priming among the metaphors discussed previously. The recurring rhythm and rhyme structure can contribute to this as well. Put more precisely, hearing the first source domain and accessing its corresponding target domain make likely that the processing of the second source domain, and the target domain again in a subtly different manner corresponding to that second source domain, will be more fluent. Concomitantly, picking up on the AABB rhyme structure and the rhythm of the music and sung lyrics can also facilitate downstream language processing. Retroactive embellishment processes taking place downstream but harkening back to earlier encountered source domains can also be enabled as the source domains build up.

The song structure also enables a particular sequencing of the sets of conjoined antonymy source domains, ramping them up interestingly in a pattern resembling something like Abraham Maslow's famous hierarchy of needs (Maslow, 1943). Note how the first verse talks about the denials of physiological functioning and physical movement (e.g., eating, sitting, swimming), along with an unfairness metaphor. The second verse discusses denials of wealth or property and social status (e.g., one's house and winning a competition), also with unfairness and illogic metaphors. The final verse then climaxes on denials of hopes, dreams, goals, life, and faith.

This building up in the level of needs being denied in the lyrics might be working with the previously mentioned processes of enhancing the perception of negativity of forbidden love, and then comforting the hearer about this negative fact of life. By having the song's structure alternate between allusions to forbidden love from the source domains, and the "hook" as described previously of the mentioning of requited love in the chorus (". . . you want her and she wants you"), the devastating pain of forbidden love can be thoroughly depicted. But the concurrent processes of comfort leveraged by several components of the song – particularly the soothing voice and music at the end – might serve to counterbalance the negativity being pointed out. The same could hold for the buildup in denied content. It might be easier to comfort someone experiencing a major denial (i.e., of their hopes, dreams, etc.) if they've recently been successfully comforted from loss of lesser things (e.g., property or physical needs).

Indeed, this comforting process might particularly benefit by the interaction between the song structure and the conjoined antonymies embedded in the metaphors. The alternation of the verses, which show the pain of forbidden love, and the chorus, which reminds the hearer of the joy of requited love, is essentially a demonstration of the healing process (i.e., you get hurt, but you then heal and feel better). It is shown several times, thus suggesting emotional healthiness always falls on the heels of emotional pain.

Interactions between the internal conjoined antonymy structure within the metaphors and the importance of forbidden love as an experience of ours is particularly interesting. The combination of conjoined antonymy and metaphor almost could not better fit the topic of forbidden love. Love is an abstract concept. It is extremely complex. It is rich, embodied, and central to our lives. All these characteristics are almost perfectly gotten at with metaphors. Forbidden love is a peak form of conjoined antonymy, as previously mentioned. So, a sequence of varied conjoined antonymies embedded in metaphors pointing to forbidden love is an extremely apt way to convey the bigger forbidden love conjoined antonymy.

The subtly differing source domains also serve collectively to highlight many of the nuanced aspects of the forbidden love target domain. For instance, the frustration it brings (i.e., "You're the fastest runner ..."), its pain ("Doctor says you're cured ..."), its unfairness ("You can feel the punishment ...," and "Some break the rules ..."), its illogic ("The insecurity ..."), its sense of withheld sustenance ("You can look at the menu ..."), its sexual denial ("You can dip your foot in the pool ..."), and its sense of extreme value, lost to us ("You can build a mansion ...").

This collective group of subtly varied differing components of the forbidden love target domain, being conveyed by all the metaphors, without their overlapping too much (i.e., each source domain is slightly different from the others), serves to convey the rich complexity of love, by itself and when it is denied to us. The level of richness of forbidden love almost demands this range of source domains – any single one of the source domains would not do justice to the forbidden love concept.

Lastly, we can look at interactions between the song frame and the power of the notion of forbidden love. Here, we can also look at more of the musical characteristics of the song frame and how they connect with aspects of forbidden love – to give rise to new meaning. First, emotions carried in the singers' voices and triggered by the music serve to highlight aspects of forbidden love being conveyed. For instance, the ramping up of emotional intensity, discussed earlier with the increasingly deep forms of denial being discussed, and the role of all this in the ultimate comforting function of the song, are paralleled by the voices and music (i.e., the drums do not kick in until the start of the second verse, the male background singer [who happens to be Phil Collins] only joins in during key parts of the chorus and a group of female background singers do not appear until the third verse, who then join a call-and-response exchange in the final chorus). The intense hurt of forbidden love is acutely portrayed by Howard Jones himself when singing the line, "... but you still feel the pain," especially on the final word, which he extends with a drawn out falling pitch, as if the singer were actually crying out in despondency or physical pain. And, also as mentioned previously, the coda sequence in the song, through both voice and music, serves to give resolution to these emotional peaks by offering a comforting finish.

The broader patterns of rising and falling pitch contours to Jones's voice also contribute to the emotional expression. In the first verse, lines 1 and 3 end in rising pitch with lines 2 and 4 falling. In the second verse, lines 1 through 3 rise at the end, with line 4 falling. The final verse has lines 1 and 4 rising or remaining essentially flat, with lines 2 and 3 falling in pitch. So, paralleling the subtle pattern in the source domains – each tapping into the forbidden love target domain but with slight alterations each time – the pitch contours also repeatedly mirror the pain of forbidden love, conveyed by falling pitch, but also alter that pattern in each verse.

The consolation factor is also conveyed by the broad musical contours of the song. The song actually begins with an interesting percussion riff resembling a heartbeat. Interspersed with this is a piano tonal sequence first ending on a minor key but then on a major one, conveying first a sad feeling followed by a happier one. Then the song sequences through the three versus and choruses – ending with a pattern similar to the song's beginning. This pattern seems to suggest that the pain gone through when falling out of an initial normality into a state of forbidden love will be followed by a return to that initial normality.

Given this degree of comforting leveraged by the song through the different interactions and individual processes discussed, it might be warranted to include comforting as a fourth major meaningful component of this song. Together with the conjoined antonymies embedded in the metaphors, the complexities inherent in the song frame and the overwhelming weight of the topic of forbidden love, the package serves to adroitly give hearers a powerful experience of a profound human emotional tragedy, but to then feel comfort at having gone through it – much resembling the peace people often find after having wept.[13]

What is perhaps most remarkable about this package is, indeed, its surface level of unremarkability. Howard Jones is an extremely talented songwriter, musician, and artist, and his work is worthy of much acclaim. But this song in particular does not come across as particularly bold, brash, loud, or essentially using any of the anthem-seeking or attention-grasping prowess of many forms of popular music. That it nonetheless contains such an extreme degree of complexity and finely crafted mean-ing-making processes, working neatly together in a balanced but stealthy manner, is testimony to what can be accomplished with meaning making occurring directly but perhaps unnoticeably under our noses.[14]

The Guest List and Type of Party

We've seen through this close reading of the Howard Jones lyrics and the other meaningful components of the song that considerations of an other-side-of-meaning process, such as metaphor, can reveal intricate and power-ful interactions among internal factors such as the construction form taken by the metaphor (e.g., *X, but not X*) and other characteristics of the meta-phor (e.g., its repetition). As mentioned, in addition to leveraging a target domain through a source domain, metaphors can do many other things internally, such as containing a conjoined antonymy, as the metaphors in the Jones lyrics do. We've also seen just how elaborate these interactions can be.

But, the presence/absence of conjoined antonymies in metaphor is but one of a huge variety of other internal components to metaphor which can all produce accompanying independent and interacting meaningful effects

---

[13] Quite a number of covers of this song by other artists are available for viewing on the Internet – some of them bringing enough emotional intensity, in effect amplifying this experience.

[14] Full disclosure: As an author of a certain age, I was quite aware of Howard Jones's music at the time of its release – Jones's work being ubiquitous in and even iconic for the mid-1980s. But I must admit I was not a follower – notwithstanding my tastes even then indicating an interest in conjoined antonymies (Led Zeppelin). But I'm very happy now to much better appreciate Jones's lyrical and musical artistry in all its subtle and sage complexity.

It is also worth noting that, despite the artistry of the braided forms of meaning making crafted into this song, it is unlikely that Jones predesigned every miniscule bit of leveraged meaning the song contains. Rather, the major ones, likely on the mind of any talented songwriter, were probably deliberately wrestled with, but the others came along with the mix. This makes a telling point about meaning making – any effective use of language, particularly language embedded in an art form (i.e., songs), dredges up many tendrils of interacting processes, whether intentionally or not. It's a process akin to pulling one or a few things across a lake bottom. Only a few things are being actively manipulated yet many strains of silt are stirred and lifted.

Table 9.2 *Internal characteristics of metaphors*

Characteristics	Examples	
Diminutivization:	"Don't worry, it's just an itsy bitsy scratch."	"Don't worry, it's just a tiny little scratch."
Reduplication:	"This market is just going boing, boing, boing."	"This market is just going boing."
Pluralization:	"Her brains are popping."	"Her brain is popping."
Modification:	"He's a boy scout."	"He's a heart-crossing boy scout."
Tense:	"We will be toast."	"We are toast."
Specificity:	"His houseplant personality."	"His variegated philodendron personality."
Homophily:	"This class was a piste."	"This class was a ski run."
Formality:	"Her elocution is odiferous."	"Her speaking skill stinks."

of their own. Among many, many others, metaphors can also include or take the characteristics or constructional forms shown here in Tables 9.2 and 9.3 (Goldberg, 1995, 2003; Culicover & Jackendoff, 1999; Culicover & Nowak, 2002; Culicover & Winkler, 2008).

We may also consider how any of these characteristics or construction forms might enable different meaning processes. For instance, note the tense characteristic listed in Table 9.2 and the example provided with it, "We will be toast" versus "We are toast." Could the present tense in the latter possibility, in inherently suggesting a state is now in place relative to the former, future tense case, suggesting the state will come to be at a later time, somehow affect metaphorical meaning? One might speculate that the present tense perhaps enhances the metaphorical meaning. By suggesting that the target domain state triggered by "toast" (i.e., being defeated or in a similar dire state of affairs) is already in place and therefore will be lengthier overall – relative to the future tense which puts the state's onset into the future, therefore producing a shorter overall duration – the present tense strengthens the metaphor.[15]

---

[15] Of course, the contextual information might be crucial for these processes – present tense may not enhance metaphors in all situations.

Not all of these processes may result in systematic changes in meaning, although they might result in idiosyncratic ones. In a not remotely scientific examination (I asked my daughter), it appears that pluralization, for instance, sometimes (i.e., in positive contexts – "Her brains are humming") seems to enhance metaphorical meaning (e.g., there is more of something?) relative to the singular form (e.g., "Her brain is humming"). But the reverse was the case for negative contexts (e.g., "Her brain[s] are/is exploding"). This might warrant attention by future research.

Table 9.3 *Constructional forms metaphors can take*

Constructional Forms	Examples	
Covaritional conditional:	"The more you toot your own horn, the less music you make."	"Tooting your own horn too much reduces the music you make."
Nominal extraposition:	"It's amazing the splash news makes."	"The splash news makes is amazing."
Ditransitive:	"The rookie gave Coach a choke."	"The rookie gave a choke to Coach."
Resultative:	"The prosecutor carved the alibi open."	"The prosecutor carved open the alibi."
Caused motion:	"The voters booted the politician out of DC."	"The voters gave the DC politician the boot."
Locative inversion:	"Into his heart slithered the gold digger."	"The gold digger slithered into his heart."
Way:	"He elbowed his way into office."	"He got into office by elbowing."

For the construction forms, could the *way construction* in Table 9.3, for instance (i.e., "He elbowed his way into office" versus "He got into office by elbowing"), in its entirety affect meaning somehow, or would we need to look at some subcomponents of the construction? For example, the way construction is likely a familiar one to at least North American native English speakers – it has a sort of idiomatic or at least recognizably fixed structure to it. Such recognized fixed language forms which convey meaning (i.e., idioms, proverbs, aphorisms, etc.) can provide a degree of objectification – offloading the source of the meaning to the fixed, known structure rather than the speaker, who is merely ushering the meaning when uttering the fixed forms (Colston, 2015). Objectification can thus in some ways aid in effecting persuasion. The way construction is also more concise – demanding less from working memory. The resulting more likely more fluent processing might enhance meaning. The way construction also fronts the expression of manner, switching effectively to a verb-framing typology from a normally satellite-framing one. Fronting is a known mechanism of emphasis – drawing on cognitive principles of attention and memory (i.e., things encountered at the onset of a sequence are more easily attended to and remembered) (Colston, 2018b; Escandell-Vidal & Leonetti, 2014). This particular construction also through "verbing" the manner of the action might enable a more vivid embodied simulation – shortening the proximity to the actor and thus enabling the actor and action to more readily be simulated together. That enriched embodied simulation might also afford greater inclusion of the negativity involved (i.e., the rudeness, crassness, or simple dirtiness of one person elbowing another to get past them).

Any or all of these submechanisms might work to enhance the meaning conveyed by the construction. And, of course, they can always and likely would intersect with one another. But it could also be the case that the construction has more or less encapsulated all these subprocesses into its form. Accordingly once a hearer notes the presence of the construction (again, not necessarily consciously), any enhancements or other changes of meaning happen somewhat automatically – perhaps akin to subcomponent activation that accompanies schema triggering. Or it could be the case that both explanations hold to a degree – the construction does what it does (and is what it is) because it affords all those subprocesses.

We have also seen that considerations of primary other-side-of-meaning processes (i.e., metaphor) are greatly affected by the language genre, or the general container or packaging housing the metaphor and its characteristics and construction forms. Popular songs and their lyrics for instance, bring many characteristics, schemata, patterns, and other components. Many of these are also pseudo- or metalinguistic, and most of them can interact with metaphor and its contained characteristics to produce and affect meaning.

But as with the internal characteristics and constructional forms, the external language genre is also extremely variable and can be exceptionally complex – each particular genre potentially bringing in scores of other influences to meaning. Among just some of these very numerous possible genres are those listed in Table 9.4.

We can also, as we did for the internal characteristics and construction forms for a metaphor, have a look at a couple of these external language genres and consider how they might affect an other-side-of-meaning process like metaphor. In this case, though, since all the external constructs involve genre, we'll offer this consideration in the form of a comparison, at least in part.

Accordingly, please consider epigraphs and listicles. To begin, one might first ask if metaphor might be reasonably more or less prevalent across those two genres. To answer this question let's first consider the nature of these genres.

Epigraphs, in the sense considered here, are quotations frequently found at the beginning of fictional or other works – for instance, novels and chapters. Their purpose varies. But generally they exist to foreshadow, analogize, give honor, recognize a person's accurate previous prediction, suggest a theme, or to parallel or otherwise inform or comment

Table 9.4 *Language genres: written or spoken forms*

small talk	troubles talk	sales pitches	political speech
songs	chants	storytelling	fables
jokes	poetry	flirtation	roasts
news reporting	science reporting	other reporting	sermons
lectures	rebukes	cheers	comic skits
prayer	tributes	eulogies	obituaries
memos	love letters	emails	texts
tweets	online posts	advertisements	notices
arguments	insults	phatic language	heckles
complaints	letters to editors	legal documents	business communications
legal testimony	proclamations	reporter questioning	opening/closing arguments
police questioning	autopsy reports	locker room talk	smack/trash talk
testimonials	briefs	contracts	pledges
press releases	instructions	recipes	technical documents
proposals	op-eds	critiques	essays
reviews	memoirs	manifestos	theses
profiles	white papers	blogs	cover letters
pledges	rebuttals	free verse	comic strips
personal ads	posters	allegories	commandments
pillow talk	listicles	diaries	vignettes
scripts	plays	screenplays	banter
short stories	novels	negotiations	bartering
mission statements	opening monologues	pep talks	toasts
introductions	acceptance speeches	artist statements	work songs
sweet talk	leaflets	(auto)biographies	movie trailers
exegeses	proverbs	idioms	commencement addresses
keynotes	plenaries	commendations	commemorative speeches
after-dinner speeches	rants	scholarly articles	lay articles
books	podcasts	movies	television episodes
websites	warning labels	packaging labels	public service announcements
language art	running commentary	epigraphs	guidelines
encyclopedias	wikis	interviews	writs
profanity	hate speech	signage	abstracts
exemplums	legends	satires	parodies
anecdotes	improvisations	filibusters	captions
slogans	headlines	titles	names
labels	nicknames	auctioneering	animation language
debates	dictionaries	fortunes	shop talk
back talk	smooth talk	fast talk	straight talk
villanelle	soliloquy	limerick	summons

Table 9.4 *(cont.)*

ballad	colloquialism	sonnet	elegy
big talk	slang	graffiti	gossip
idle talk	dirty talk	hearsay	reported speech
foul talk	empty talk	lies	double talk
heart-to-heart talk	sweet talk	table talk	tough talk

upon the work they accompany.[16] Indeed, their very name reflects this role, *epi-* (Greek "on") and *–graph* ("write") (Barnhart, 1972).

Listicles, which have flowered in recent decades in parallel with Internet growth, are articles of sorts, found in print or electronic form, organized around lists of items, appearing typically in news or popular cultural venues.[17] They'll typically involve the "top" N of something, as in the top ten grossing international films for a given calendar year. Their purpose is usually to provide bits of trivia for light reading, often on pop-cultural or unusual content.[18] Their name is also telling as it combines informatively the roots *list* and *article*. But the name also achieves a multiple-entendre bit of word play. It suggests the word *popsicle*, with its triarity of semantics involving foodstuffs (i.e., a quick and perhaps refreshing treat but lacking in nutrition), the root *pop* (i.e., something quick but short-lasting, popular, pop cultural, etc.), and the occasional *pop-up* appearance of listicles on Internet sites.

As to the relative presence of metaphor in epigraphs and listicles, given their divergent purposes one might suppose reasonably that epigraphs would involve more metaphor usage than listicles. The nature of that involvement, though, is unclear. The specific metaphorical content

---

[16] As an interesting corroborative side note, Cambridge University Press, publisher of the current work, institutionalizes this function of epigraphs in their copyright permission policies. Copyrighted works not yet in the public domain may be copied, cited, and discussed in academic works under the doctrine of fair use – academic work being conducted for the betterment of humankind rather than for an authorial profit motive – but only if these works appear in the main text of the publication. Quotations or other material in epigraphs are an exception as they're considered artistic or other commentary being made *upon* the academic work proper, which appears in the main text. So their usage requires copyright holder permission, again excepting in the case of works in the public domain.

[17] In many instances, they're more marketing or sales tools *disguised* as articles or reports, but they can on occasion also be informative.

[18] Their popularity explains partly their prevalence – they're often used to hook readers, enabling tracking of reader interests in online venues, as well as to present and also track reader interest in accompanying advertisements.

residing *within* epigraphs and listicles may not necessarily differ – depending, of course, on length, composition of any lengthier work of prose is difficult without using metaphor, at least of an everyday, unnovel variety. Metaphors might also appear in both forms as they aid usefulness in discussing particular specific topics. But epigraphs in their *totality* can often be used as metaphorical devices in and of themselves, serving as source domains for the thematic target domain to which they apply (e.g., the theme of finding love after experiencing tragedy found in the main work).

To illustrate this difference, an extremely unscientific comparison was made between a sampling of both epigraphs and listicles. This demonstration is offered merely to reveal the potential difference in these two genres with respect to how and how much they might use metaphor. Of course, a true scientific comparison on this question would require much larger samples, random selections, and resolution of the multiple quantification and operational definition issues raised in such a comparison (see Colston, 2015 for a discussion of such issues in corpus research).

Six recently published, fairly well-known American English novels were selected with a meager attempt made at establishing diversity in terms of author gender.[19] The epigraphs from these works are as follows:

9.12a   **Epigraph to Jonathan Franzen's 2010 novel,** *Freedom*
        Go together,
        You precious winners all; your exultation
        Partake to everyone. I, an old turtle,
        Will wing me to some withered bough, and there
        My mate, that's never to be found again,
        Lament till I am lost.   — *The Winter's Tale*

9.12b   **Epigraph to Anthony Doerr's 2014 novel,** *All the Light We Cannot See*
        In August 1944 the historic walled city of Saint-Malo the brightest jewel of the Emerald Coast of Brittany, France, was almost totally destroyed by fire ... Of the 865 buildings within the walls, only 182 remained standing and all were damaged to some degree.   — Philip Beck

        It would not have been possible for us to take power or to use it in the ways we have without the radio.   — Joseph Goebbels

---

[19] As these were selected from the author's personal fiction library they'll certainly be biased according to the author's tastes – I essentially tried to think of novels I had enjoyed reading in the preceding fifteen years and picked the first six that came to mind (which happened to also contain an epigraph).

9.12c   **Epigraph to Dave Eggers' 2012 novel, *A Hologram for the King***
It is not every day that we are needed.   — Samuel Becket

9.12d   **Epigraph to Jane Hamilton's 2006 novel, *When Madeline Was Young***
Fabrizio thought of Clara. When he thought of her thighs and breasts he sighed; weakness swept him; he grew almost ill. So he thought of her face instead. Gentle, beautiful, it rose before him. He saw it everywhere, that face. No lonely villa on a country hillside, yellow in the sun, oleanders on the terrace, but might have inside a chapel, closed off, unused for years, on the wall a fresco, work of some ancient name known in all the world, a lost work – Clara.
                           — Elizabeth Spencer, *The Light in the Piazza*

9.12e   **Epigraph of Viet Thanh Nguyen's 2015 novel, *The Sympathizer***
Let us not become gloomy as soon as we hear the word "torture": in this particular case there is plenty to offset and mitigate that word – even something to laugh at.
                           — Friedrich Nietzsche, *On the Genealogy of Morals*

9.12f   **Epigraph of Annie Proulx's 1993 novel, *The Shipping News***
In a knot of eight crossings, which is about the average-size knot, there are 256 different "over-and-under" arrangements possible ... Make only one change in this "over and under" sequence and either an entirely different knot is made or no knot at all may result.
                                       — *The Ashley Book of Knots*

Even a casual reading of these epigraphs reveals a peppering of standard and perhaps more colorful metaphors in text (e.g., "... the brightest jewel of the Emerald Coast of Brittany," "... weakness swept him"). But the standout observation is the metaphorical quality of the entirety of epigraphs 9.12a, d, and f.

The Jonathan Franzen novel's main character is a man who laments a failed marriage (the relationship is later restored), a subsequent new young love who then dies tragically, and advanced environmental damage (the character is an avid environmental advocate). This serves nicely as a target domain for the "old turtle" sitting on a "withered bough" ruing a lost love until he himself is "lost."

Jane Hamilton's main character is also a man, whose wife suffers an horrific brain-damaging accident – affecting her memories and rendering her permanently frozen at the developmental status of a young girl. The man and one of his wife's nurses then fall in love mutually. The nurse, his new love, then dies in an extremely emotion-inducing segment of the book, but only after she and the man had constructed an unusual but successful, loving and long-lasting family situation, benefitting all the parties involved. The epigraph's description of a beautiful face on a fresco in a chapel, "lonely" and "unused," but at the same time "yellow in the sun, oleanders on the terrace," metaphorically captures some of the mixed but poignant feelings of love salvaged from loss and tragedy in the novel.

Finally, the description of how one change in the sequence of "over-and-under" crossings in a nautical knot can create either "an entirely different knot" or "no knot at all" serves keenly to silhouette the main characters in this novel – a widowed man, his young daughter, and his aunt, who also patch together happy and supportive lives after overcoming many personal tragedies, including an incestual family heritage.

To offer a comparison with these epigraphs, a perusal of standard Internet news sites was conducted (on December 29, 2018), searching for the first six listicles encountered. The only imposed restriction was that the lists selected had to be reasonably small.[20] The listicles obtained were the following:

9.13a   **"12 Best and Worst Movies of 2018: All the Films You Need to See and Avoid"**   (Williams, 2018)

9.13b   **"4 Can't Miss Trips for 2019"**   (Brown, 2018)

9.13c   **"Google's Top Trending Health Questions of 2018"**
                                                            (Welch, 2018)

9.13d   **"The 10 Best Films of 2018"**   (Morgan, 2018)

9.13e   **"The Biggest Unsolved Mysteries of 2018"**
                                                        (Silverstein, 2018)

9.13f   **"Top 10 Weird Gifts for Christmas 2018"**
                                                          (Martins, 2018)

---

[20] Four encountered lists were accordingly skipped, including "The 100 Most-Read Stories of 2018," the "Top 20 NFL Stories" of the year, "Notable Deaths of 2018," and "Highest Grossing Films of 2018" (all from CBSnews.com).

As this informal search was conducted near the end of the calendar year when such listicles proliferate, the search took only a matter of minutes to obtain the desired number of six.

Although, as is germane to listicles, their lengths were not enormous, space constraints prevent reposting all of them here. Only the 9.13c and 9.13f listicles are provided for brevity (see the end of this chapter). But a casual reading of all the listicles confirmed the suspicion that essentially the only metaphors present were standard, non-novel forms arguably necessary for expository writing in any format, or ones useful and commonly used to convey the particular topics at hand. So, the copied listicles are essentially representative of the other listicles on this matter.

Two observations are nonetheless worth noting. The first is that a couple of the listicles (the ones copied at the end of the chapter) seem to demonstrate the range in sophistication commonly found in this language genre. The second is that a relationship might hold between this range of listicle sophistication and the level and type of metaphor present.

The two listicles copied at the end of the chapter provide a feel for the range of content density found in many listicles. Most of the listicles involve rather mundane pop-cultural content (i.e., movies, vacation destinations, unsolved mysteries and unusual holiday gifts [the latter being the content of 9.13f]). A minority of listicles, such as the 9.13c example concerning health questions, are more in-depth.

The 9.13c listicle reviewed a list of the ten most increased (relative to the previous calendar year) medically related search topics on Google. This article provided more in-depth descriptions of the diets, diseases, and physiological processes, symptoms, and disorders that held people's interest in the year in question, making it notably more educational than the other listicles.

This listicle nonetheless contained essentially nothing beyond the standard type of everyday, expositional prose metaphors, or those metaphors germane to discussing medical matters (Sontag, 1979, 1989; Hanne & Hawken, 2007), (e.g., emphases added, "... *into* a state of ketosis," "... *burn* fat," "... *calls* for its *followers*," "... disorder that *attacks and kills*," "... curiosity about it *spiked*," "... doctors have been *moving away*," "... people also *turned* to Google," "... *weed*," "... *sticking to* a sleep schedule," "... *high* in fat," "... *high* blood pressure," "... the *silent* killer").

The 9.13f listicle covered the ten most bizarre (according to the author) Christmas gifts for 2018. This listicle also used only standard expository metaphors and a few pertaining to the topic of toys and their operation (e.g., emphases added, "... *comes* to mind," "... *come across*," "... comes with an *angry* cloud," "... sensor that *triggers*"), with the possible exception of "... white elephant gift," which is a stock metaphor for unusual gifts or items.

A couple of the uncopied listicles, 9.13e and 9.13d, involving unsolved mysteries and the top movies of the previous year, reside somewhere in between the 9.13c and 9.13f listicles in terms of their content depth and density. One might also note a corresponding level of metaphor usage in these listicles relative to the others – showing a bit more than the barest expository and topic-related metaphoricity found in the simplest of listicles, but not up to the frequency of metaphoricity observed in the most sophisticated listicle. This might be a topic worth exploring by future research – more sophistication in language genre might require more metaphoricity to achieve that sophistication.

These cursory observations aside, it nonetheless holds that some other reasons might exist to predict variance in metaphor usage across the genres. As mentioned, listicles are purposefully designed for broad audiences seeking light reading where epigraphs might arguably pertain to narrower audiences and more sophisticated reading. But the types of editorial practices that would follow from these differences could also play a role – perhaps caricaturizing each genre more stereotypically into their different audience niches (i.e., urging relatively simple metaphors for broad audiences and more sophisticated metaphors for narrower readerships).

Readers of epigraphs might also be seeking more metaphoricity relative to readers of listicles, with authors and editors might comply accordingly. Indeed, the very *aboutness* inherent in epigraphs and their purposes seems to beg metaphorical, allegorical, iconic, idiomatic, or other similar structures. Relatedly, epigraphs, by virtue of standing apart from the main text in fiction works, sort of require a reason for being. A metaphorical or other similar quality to them provides aptly for this need. Moreover, by accompanying fiction works, epigraphs are already in the realm of a readership being invited to imagine the unreal. Listicles, although often light and/or whimsical, are instead typically lists of factual, albeit often trite, information or at least infotainment. A propensity for metaphor might accordingly reside in the readers of epigraphs relative to listicles.

But the central observation regarding metaphor confirms the primary difference expected in that listicles, in their entireties, do not act as metaphors themselves as some epigraphs do. Their light-reading through educational expository functions seem to obviate this meta-function, relative to the more sophisticated thematic highlighting and/or commentative functions of epigraphs.

But putting aside overall usage *as* metaphor as well as internal frequency and type *of* metaphor in epigraphs and listicles, many other genre differences could also affect metaphoricity.[21] Any selection of pairings or groups from the list of genres above or from other genres could lead to predictions about differences for metaphor, in turn leading to possible empirical comparisons, some of which have been performed (Gibbs, 2017). The same can be said of possible genre differences affecting any of the other-side-of-meaning processes. If one contemplates all the possible combinations of language genres with other-side-of-meaning processes, the resulting landscape looms enormous. A full accounting of all of these possibilities is simply far beyond this book's capacity. But consideration of the extent of such an analysis is sobering. Any possible pairing of a single other-side-of-meaning process with a single language genre could produce a unique set of meaning-making interactions.

For just a brief demonstration, selecting essentially at random *hyperbole* from the other-side-of-meaning set of processes and *toasts* from the language genres, we can already see interesting possible interactions. Toasts usually have a target topic – a person, some milestone or event, some new creation, etc. Toasts are also usually performed or lead by one person, with some number of participants following along. So, attention is focused for a moment on one speaker, who is usually lauding or praising some referent thing. This attitude of praise is also usually held by the other participants. But the person making the toast is also a bit in the position of a leader – the other participants are looking to this person to say something inspirational about the topic at hand. So the social stakes can be high for a speaker making a toast, especially if the target is a person or persons. They can involve the speaker's status – does he or she live up to the inspirational expectations? They can also involve multiple social connections – between the toaster and toastee if the latter is a person, between the toaster and each of the participants or onlookers, between the toastee and the participants, etc.

Hyperbole, as a form of figurative language, often is used to point out a deviance between expectations and reality (Colston & Keller, 1998; Colston 2015). Hyperbole usually succeeds at such a demonstration by

---

[21] No specific reason governed the decision to select epigraphs and listicles for comparison here. Indeed, the selection motivation *was* quite trivial. I picked epigraphs because discussions with the publisher about including epigraphs in the present work had elevated their intrigue to me. I selected listicles because I had not previously heard of that term for them until researching potential items for the list of language genres (despite their ubiquity). That this pseudorandom pair produced such a fruitful discussion likely speaks to the enormity of complexity among all the various genres, all the meaning-making ingredients that can reside within them, and the level of potential interaction among all of it.

following a simple principle of psychological perception – if you wish to draw attention to something, make it bigger than it actually is. So hyperbole *inflates* the discrepancy between expectations and reality to draw people's attention toward it. And often, but not always, such a highlighting is done for the purposes of complaining – the person doesn't like that the reality has deviated from expectations, often because the deviation is in a less desirable direction. So the person uses the hyperbole to bring attention to, and express a negative attitude about, the deviance from expectations. So, hyperbole coupled with a toast could be interesting.

As hyperbole, whose frequent usage for complaint is being applied in a genre usually performed for praise, a couple of outcomes might go up in their probability. Either the hyperbole might be taken as disingenuous, even tipping the toast toward the ironic perhaps, or the hyperbole could be seen as performing its rarer function to proclaim that things are *better* than expected. The latter could also work to greatly enhance the level of praise taken from the toast – given hyperbole's relative rarity and thus distinctiveness in serving this function. The former could also be a simple irony (e.g., pretend to praise, actually belittle), or even an ironic irony, in which the toaster is seen as only pretending to ironically put down the toastee, perhaps as an innocent form of banter or teasing intended, in fact, to be positive (e.g., "Let me tell you about this guy here, he is absolutely the most generous tipper who has ever entered a restaurant. Never have I seen so many pennies put to good use" . . .).[22]

Conclusion

This chapter has taken a look inside and outside other-side-of-meaning processes and shown the almost ridiculous level of interactions possible between and among these levels. The myriad ways in which different other-side-of-meaning processes can influence meaning within different language genres approaches the levels of complexity attainable by the generative quality of combining and sequencing embodied simulations. Language can be about essentially anything, both through an infinite combination of embodied-simulation, experiential, and other embodied content and semantic meaning, but also through a seemingly infinite combination of other-side-of-meaning nuance processes interacting with different language genres and their characteristics.

---

[22] Roasts and wedding toasts sometimes work this way. And, of course, with social stakes so high, the hyperbole could also simply backfire on a toaster.

Lest one get overwhelmed by this level of complexity, we do seem to handle quite readily language like this in our everyday lives. Martha Nussbaum, in her book *Love's Knowledge* (1990), puts this in apt perspective:

> For stories cultivate our ability to see and care for particulars, not as representatives of a law, but as what they themselves are: to respond vigorously with senses and emotions before the new; to care deeply about chance happenings in the world, rather than to fortify ourselves against them; to wait for the outcome and to be bewildered – to wait and to float and be actively passive.[23] (Nussbaum, 1995)

The next and final chapter will now take the two sides of meaning discussed throughout the book and present them perhaps in a novel way – as a conjoined antonymic structure which melds together somewhat oppositional meaning-making forces. On one side, we have the power of embodied simulations, semantic meaning, and their infinite levels of combination leveraged through morphosyntax to relate to an infinite number of semantic topics. On the other side, we have processes serving both the core reason for why we evolved that first side of meaning in the first place – to meet the social needs wrought for us by our complex neuro-social interconnection motivations. But the other-side-of-meaning processes also serve the shortcomings of that first side of meaning, and bring in new meaning on their own – leveraging through a myriad of interwoven processes many complex subtleties of meaning difficult to achieve on the sem/syn/sym side. As we'll see, the social connectedness enabled by the other-side-of-meaning might also be the biggest gap-filling process of them all – giving us the illusion that we've perfectly aligned our consciousnesses with interlocutors on a singular semantic message, when, in fact, we maybe only have met them partway.

Listicles

9.13c   (in full)
"Google's Top Trending Health Questions of 2018"
(Welch, 2018)
While it's not always a good idea to Google your symptoms to diagnose an illness or source of pain, the Internet can be a useful tool for learning about health. This year, people turned to "Dr. Google" to answer their questions on health questions ranging from the keto diet to ALS to endometriosis and much more.

Google has compiled data on the top trending health-related questions searched in the United States in 2018. While these were not necessarily the most frequently asked health questions,

---

[23] Thanks to Carina Rasse for bringing this quote to my attention. See Rasse (2016).

they were the topics that showed the greatest increase in searches over the previous year.

Here's a closer look at the health questions at the top of Americans' minds.

1. What is the keto diet?

Google says the top trending health question of 2018 was people looking for information on the ketogenic, or keto, diet. The diet involves drastically reducing your intake of carbohydrates and replacing them with fats, forcing the body into a state of ketosis – when you burn fat instead of carbohydrates for energy. The notoriously restrictive diet calls for its followers not only to reduce intake of unhealthy carbs like sugar but also those that are normally considered healthy, like most fruits and certain vegetables. Research has shown that a ketogenic diet can help control seizures in children with epilepsy and may be beneficial to people with type 2 diabetes, but in 2018 it garnered particular interest for its potential weight loss benefits. However, because it is so restrictive and difficult to adhere to, dietitians generally do not recommend the diet for weight loss.

2. What is ALS disease?

This year, people were also interested in amyotrophic lateral sclerosis, or ALS. Also known as Lou Gehrig's disease, it is a neurodegenerative disorder that attacks and kills the nerve cells that control muscle movement. Over time, patients with ALS have difficulty chewing, walking, breathing, and talking. Most die from respiratory failure within three to five years. ALS is rare, with a little more than 5,000 Americans diagnosed each year, according to the ALS Association. World-famous physicist Stephen Hawking died of ALS in March 2018 at the age of 76. Hawking was diagnosed with ALS as a 21-year-old Ph.D. student and told he had only one or two years to live. Instead, he became a rare longtime survivor, though he spent much of the rest of his life in a wheelchair and largely unable to speak except through a voice synthesizer. There is currently no cure for ALS.

3. What is endometriosis?

Endometriosis is an often painful disorder in women in which the endometrium, or the tissue that normally lines the inside of the uterus, grows outside of the uterus. Curiosity about it spiked in February 2018, when writer and actress Lena Dunham wrote a personal essay for *Vogue* in which she talked about her decision to undergo a hysterectomy due to complications with endometriosis. The disease affects roughly 1 in 10 women during their reproductive years. There is no cure but symptoms can be treated with pain medication or hormone therapy. Surgery can also be performed to remove the endometriosis tissue. Surgery to remove the uterus and ovaries was once considered the most effective treatment for endometriosis but doctors have been moving away from that approach in recent years.

4. How long does weed stay in your urine?
With more states legalizing medical and recreational marijuana in 2018, Google saw an increase in questions about the drug. There is no standard answer on how long marijuana is detectable in urine since it varies according to dose. According to a 2017 study looking at the effectiveness of drug testing, marijuana can be detectable in urine for anywhere between 1 to 30 days after the last use.

5. How long does the flu last?
The 2017–18 flu season was the worst in nearly a decade and prompted plenty of Googling by people concerned about the illness. According to the Centers for Disease Control and Prevention, adults typically develop flu symptoms one to four days after becoming infected with the influenza virus. The majority of people get better after about three to seven days, though some symptoms like coughing and fatigue can persist for two weeks or more. However, young children, older adults, and people with weakened immune systems are more susceptible to complications like pneumonia and additional infections, which can last much longer and lead to hospitalization and even death.

6. How long is the flu contagious?
People also turned to Google to find out how long the flu is contagious. According to the CDC, people with the flu are most contagious in the first three to four days of the illness. Healthy adults may be able to pass the flu virus to others beginning one day before symptoms emerge and up to five to seven days after getting sick. That means it's possible to infect others even before you know you are sick. Children and people with weakened immune systems may be able to pass the virus for longer than a week. Generally, kids should be kept home from school for at least 24 hours after their fever is gone.

7. When does implantation bleeding occur?
Women who are pregnant or trying to become pregnant may have questions about when implantation bleeding – typically defined as a small amount of light spotting or bleeding after conception – occurs. The bleeding is thought to happen when the fertilized egg attaches to the lining of the uterus. According to the Mayo Clinic, this happens about 10 to 14 days after conception.

8. Why am I always tired?
It's no secret millions of Americans are overworked and sleep-deprived, and many turned to Google this year with questions about their fatigue. Unfortunately, there is no easy answer. According to the National Sleep Foundation (NSF), most adults should be getting seven to 10 hours of sleep per night. The foundation also recommends making sleep a priority by following simple habits like sticking to a sleep schedule,

practicing a relaxing bedtime ritual, exercising daily, sleeping on a comfortable mattress and pillow, avoiding electronics before bed, and avoiding alcohol and caffeine. The foundation says to talk to your doctor if you're experiencing daytime sleepiness when you'd normally expect to feel awake or alert; if you snore or have difficulty breathing while asleep; or have prolonged insomnia or other symptoms that are preventing you from sleeping well.

9. What does heartburn feel like?
Many people turned to Google this year to learn about the symptoms of heartburn. According to the American College of Gastroenterology, more than 60 million Americans report having heartburn at least once a month. The telltale sign of heartburn is a burning sensation in the chest just behind the breastbone that occurs after eating and lasts anywhere from a few minutes to several hours. Other symptoms include chest pain (especially after lying down or bending over), a burning feeling in the throat, difficulty swallowing, and hot, sour, or acidic taste in the back of the throat. It occurs when stomach acid flows back into the esophagus. Certain eating habits can lead to heartburn, including eating large portions or foods like onions, garlic, tomatoes, chocolate, foods high in fat, citrus fruits and spicy foods. Drinking alcohol, smoking, stress, and eating shortly before bedtime can also bring on heartburn. Heartburn can often be controlled with changes to lifestyle and eating habits. Medication is also available to relieve symptoms.

10. What causes high blood pressure?
High blood pressure is one of the most common chronic health conditions in the United States, affecting more than 100 million Americans, according to the American Heart Association. Many turned to Google in 2018 to find out its cause. High blood pressure, also called hypertension, is when a person's blood pressure, or the force of blood flowing through blood vessels, is consistently too high. Known as "the silent killer," it raises the risk of stroke, heart attacks, and early death. High blood pressure can be caused by a number of factors, including an unhealthy diet high in salt, fat, and/or cholesterol, lack of exercise, being overweight or obese, tobacco use, drinking too much alcohol, stress, chronic conditions such as diabetes and kidney and hormone problems, and a family history of the condition. Some medications, including certain forms of birth control, may also lead to high blood pressure. Treatment for the condition includes lifestyle changes and medications to lower blood pressure.

9.13f   (in full)
"Top 10 Weird Gifts for Christmas 2018"
(Martins, 2018)

While editing almost 80 gift guides this holiday season, we've come across all kinds of gifts. Some are endearing – like the long-distance friendship lamps from our best friends gift guide. Some are genius: The pancake art kit from our gift guide for dads comes to mind. And, some ... well ... are just odd. From a slime-pooping unicorn kids are completely obsessed with to a cat toilet brush, here are some of the weirdest gifts we've seen in our 2018 gift guides.

1. Poopsie the Slime-Pooping Unicorn
One of the must-have toys of the holidays, this unicorn comes with a little frappé, an angry cloud (?!?), a key chain in the shape of rainbow poop, and "unicorn food." Kids mix the slime inside the unicorn, then press the belly button for the concoction to come out of its rear end. This has got to be the weirdest toy of the year.

2. Bob Ross Chia Pet
The original king of ASMR and painting tutorials, Bob Ross takes the form of a chia pet to bring you a truly odd novelty gift. The chia makes up his iconic afro and the packaging features this quote: "There's nothing wrong with having a tree as a friend." The Bob Ross Chia Pet is truly weird, but I also feel like I need one for my desk ... to accompany my Stranger Things Chia Pet.

3. Yodeling Pickle
I get it: The Christmas pickle tradition is widely practiced. But, this one features a motion sensor that triggers a yodeling alarm whenever some-one reaches within 3 feet of your Christmas tree. It certainly makes for an amazing white elephant gift if you want to get something unique. This ornament is as unique as it gets.

4. Llama Duster
Is a duster handy? Yes. Is this one cute? Yes. But, we've got to admit: It's one of the weirdest gifts on our gift guide for coworkers.

5. DishFish
I have this sponge and I like it. But, it was chosen as one of the best gifts for your in-laws, which is simply hilarious.

6. Motion Sensor Toilet Bowl Light
Stocking stuffers, anyone? Perfect for people who don't turn on the lights when they make their way to the loo in the middle of the night, this motion sensor toilet bowl light is an oddly popular gift.

7. Cat Toilet Brush
Speaking of toilets: You can now make the process of cleaning your toilet cuter than you ever imagined. From our cat lover gift guide, this cat toilet brush is really something.

8. Sausage Gift Basket
I feel like your giftee has to really love sausage for this gift basket to work. To each his own!

9. Star Wars Cookbook
I'm no "Star Wars" expert but I'll hazard a guess that the galactic movie franchise is not known for its recipes. The scenes that stand out don't really take place in a kitchen, do they? Yet, someone felt compelled to create a cookbook featuring "Wookie cookies," and it's one of our top Secret Santa gifts of the year. Astonishing.

10. Shakespeare Insult Bandages
If you're buying a gift for a college student without much room in a carry-on, why not get Shakespeare insult bandages? The bandages will surely prove useful in a dorm full of college students, and Shakespeare insults make for great party conversation. Not that your college student is partying. Straight A's, everybody!

10   The End Game

I'm drenched
in the flood
which has yet to come
I'm tied up
in the prison
which has yet to exist
Not having played
the game of chess
I'm already the checkmate
Not having tasted
a single cup of your wine
I'm already drunk
Not having entered
the battlefield
I'm already wounded and slain
I no longer
know the difference
between image and reality
Like the shadow
I am
and
I am not

—Jalal ad-Din Muhammad Rumi, "I Am and I Am Not"
(Chopra, 1998)

I've written relatively little fiction in my life. I did, though, have an idea years ago for a novel set in the near future. Not science fiction exactly, but with a sort of sci-fi theme at its core. The story would be set in the Silicon Valley or Bay Area in California at a technology company working at the forward edge of consumer electronics. I have some real-life experience in this regard – getting dated now but still more or less relevant. I worked for several years during and after graduate school, in the 1990s, at Interval Research in Palo Alto, CA. Interval was a Paul Allen–funded think tank, pondering the longer-term future of consumer electronics for personal entertainment.[1]

The Halo Interface

The company in my envisioned story was aggressively striving to stay at the precipice of new technology. So much so, it was willing to gamble all of its non-trivial investment capital developing a new form of human/ gizmo connection: an interface that's been much bandied about and pined for, for decades and perhaps centuries – direct *gizmo-to-brain* and *brain-to-gizmo* communication. The interface would bypass all human peripheral sensory and motor ports and parts. The user just thinks, and the machine responds. The machine then sends output directly to the user's brain.

What the *medium* of this interface would actually be, I wasn't sure. Technologies used for brain scanning like magnetic resonance but made bidirectional somehow could have been used. Or some other type of ultrahigh resolution electromagnetic linkage, of a to be determined sort, could also possibly work (e.g., signature radio, heat or magnetic waves emitted by the firing patterns of selected small groups of neurons being scanned, compiled, and transmitted, with a neural excitation/suppression process working somehow in reverse). I was also unsure if the connection would be via transcranial contact – a cap or other wearable of some sort – or by wireless – a Bluetooth for your brain, with or without some sort of implant. But I had put these technical concerns off for later research. The main point was that the gizmo's connection, affording both human control over, and reception from, the machine, would be *directly with the brain* – no sensory input or motor output would be needed.

The hinge pin of the novel was to be an antagonist character, plotted somehow as central to the company's plan, who throws a spanner/wrench into the works at a key point in the plot, perhaps a Machiavellian ploy to destroy the company from within. This character would be a lead scientist employee perhaps (disenchanted founder? mole competitor? psychopathic Luddite?), who hypes and evangelizes in favor of the interface at first – her advocacy resulting directly in the company's irreversible commitment to the new technology. But the person then abruptly changes tune and shows her cards at the later climactic point of no return (e.g., economic ruin) – "Ha, such an interface is *impossible!*"[2]

---

[1] Paul Allen was the cofounder of Microsoft with Bill Gates. Interval was a place where people thought a lot about high-tech, future-fun gizmos.

[2] This is probably why I don't write fiction.

The main point for purposes here, though, is the rationale given by the character to explain the interface's ultimate failure. A machine giving input to a person, so the argument goes, cannot bypass the person's senses, nor circumvent the person's motor-behavioral functions to receive output, in an attempt at direct access to the so-called core cognitive essence of a person's mind. Those presumed peripheral systems, instead, *are* that mind. The way in which the mind functions is embedded in and intertwined with those peripheral systems. The systems are part and parcel of what the mind does. To try and *reach* cognition without accessing peripheral systems would thus be folly. That would be like thinking you could skip an elaborate manufacturing process and just create a finished product in one step – like 3-D printing a car. Although 3-D printing is a powerful new technology that shows much promise – with more potential possibly coming – making an automobile in one shot with 3-D printing would simply not work.[3] All the intricate component parts of a car, made from a huge variety of materials, could not be fashioned in a one-step, raw-material-to-finished-product process.

Consider, for example, one simple car part, the gear shift (or gear shifter). At core, a gear shift is a rod, made of a metal alloy most likely – part steel perhaps for strength and part something else for lightness.[4] One end is usually covered by a plastic and/or leather grip material for the knob handle – leather preparation itself being a hugely complex process traceable back to agriculture and industrial chemistry (e.g., cattle production and however truckloads of tannic acid are made). The rod's shank might be treated with an elaborate chemical-primer, rust-inhibitor, scratch-resistant, etc., layer of coatings, whose application and drying (e.g., baking) environments require time and specialized application tools and processes. What lies below the gear shift boot I have no clear idea.[5] But that end could consist of mechanical couplers made from a different blend of metals designed for their specific in situ characteristics (e.g., lateral torque strength) to connect the gear shift to the automobile's transmission.

If one then expands all this complexity to the myriad component parts and their customized materials (e.g., metals, glasses, multiple plastics, resins, glues, coatings, fabrics, woods, foams, lubricants, rubbers,

---

[3] At least in terms of how 3-D printing currently works.

[4] I'll confess I'm no expert on car-part manufacturing, so some of this example may be correctable. But the main point holds – these parts and their construction are incredibly complex, multistep processes, even just to refine the raw materials used, much less crafting them for their final configuration.

[5] The skirt of material around the base of the rod, to seal the hole enabling the shift to exit the floor of the vehicle cabin to connect with the transmission or gear box.

ceramics, fluids, organics, carbon fibers, plexiglass), and what it takes to refine, distill, rarefy, etc., all of them, the complexity revealed is astounding.[6] Putting the materials together into parts, and then putting all these parts together, is another huge layer of complexity itself. Assembly can sometimes involve *The Wolf, the Goat and the Cabbage* types of solutions just to hook things up.[7]

So the functional end product cannot be had directly by skipping all the processes that go into that product. Analogously, so too is it impossible – again, according to the fictional antagonist character's argument – to directly access the *mind*, as a kind of end product, by circumventing the processes that enable that mind to function, its peripheral motor and sensory systems.

In writing the present book, this old idea for a novel came back to me, but in a way I hadn't considered before. I don't remember exactly when I first had the idea for the novel. But it preceded the bulk of the recent research on embodied simulations. As I now think of the novel in light of that research, I realize language has in a way achieved what my fictional "Halo" interface could not.[8] Language reaches inside your brain, as it were, to directly activate primary brain regions. It forces those systems to give up their goods, without your eyes or arms (sensory or motor peripheral systems) doing anything. It then takes those "goods," cobbles them together in elaborate choreographed sequences, and essentially makes meaning happen inside you (recall my earlier "under the table," "direct deposit," and other metaphors for this process). Language stealthily gets past the gate security, and then works things from the inside.

Of course language does use a sensory medium to *get* "inside." But then it triggers meaning by poking multiple brain systems directly once it has gotten inside. It's not as if language has to send additional stuff through your sensory systems or has to make you move somehow to achieve meaning (e.g., moving your ear close to a drum-set high hat to hear the

---

[6] Barbara Kingsolver, in her classic novel, *The Poisonwood Bible* (1998), describes a fictional young woman with special savant-like cognitive skills who is incapable of *not* seeing such chained physical connections in the material world. Her ability is so powerful that she is partially debilitated when returning to a complex industrialized nation after having spent time in more agrarian and hunter-gatherer cultures.

[7] *The Wolf, the Goat and the Cabbage* puzzles typically involve a farmer needing to transport all three of these things across a river in a small boat that can only carry the farmer and one of the other things. The problem is the wolf and goat cannot be left together and the goat cannot be left alone with the cabbage. The solution involves a complex series of back-and-forth, take-one-thing-over, return, take-another-thing-over, bring-one-of-the-things-back steps that eventually gets all three things to the other side but never violates the restrictions.

[8] "Halo" was my working title for the interface and/or company – since adopted for a very popular computer game.

backbeat, *tse – tse – tsip, tse – tse – tsip, tse – tse – tsip* ... to comprehend, "cymbal").[9] Language comprehension instead works because a speech signal sneaks in through an audio (predominantly, but by no means exclusively) channel, and then activates all your core sensory and motor brain regions, and possibly others,[10] to give you meaning. The peripheral sensory and motor parts are left largely alone.

The same violation of my novel character's constraint-on-bypassing principle also holds for language production. Relatively less research has addressed the role of embodied simulations on language production. This is partly due to the old reason that comprehension is simply easier to study than production. But embodied simulations also seem to play a central role in language production, as they do for comprehension (Glenberg & Gallese, 2012; Pickering & Garrod, 2013). Indeed, embodied simulations can *leak out* of people a bit during production in the form of co-speech gesture and other prosody through metalinguistic behaviors. These leakages can also help communication. But we can nonetheless produce readily the primary content of our messages without overt peripheral sensory or motor function – except, of course, that needed to produce the actual speech, signs, or text.

Put differently, when we simulate T*H*R*O*W in saying, "Throw me one of those apples wouldja?", our arms can easily stay mostly at our sides.[11] So language also sends meaning outward from the brain effectively by, again, largely skirting the peripheral sensory and motor systems whose core brain regions enable that language production. Language thus evolved long ago to give early humans or pre-humans a direct, hands-free, as it were,[12] system of communication that today we dream of developing for computers. Evolution essentially accomplished long ago what Silicon Valley wants to do now.

Starting to End

The result of this inside-job meaning making is the phenomenon described in Chapter 1 as an *as-if-I-just-sorta-experienced* experience.

---

[9] Or turning your eyes to look at the shiny brass disc resting atop a stand.

[10] Less attention to-date has been given to how embodied simulations of non-sensory or non-motor components might work, such as emotional simulations, simulations of other forms of arousal, internal sensory simulations (e.g., nausea, dizziness), etc.

[11] Except again in the case of leakage – if a person holds up their forearm slightly and flicks their wrist forward when uttering, "Throw." And, as mentioned, leakage can be communicative and thus relatively common – given its boost to comprehended meaning.

[12] With the obvious exception of sign language. Note also that several theories propose that language evolution depended on some form of signed or both signed and spoken language (Arbib & Rizzolatti, 1999; Rizzolatti & Arbib, 1999; Jackendoff, 1999).

This language experience has aspects of genuine sensory- or motor-driven mini-experiences (e.g., *actually* seeing, grabbing, biting, and tasting an apple), which can be fairly vivid. But language experience isn't equivalent to those full mini-experiences because the peripheral systems normally involved in real mini-experiences are temporarily and largely cut off during language-driven brain activation. This lends those simulation activations a more ghostlike quality. The meaning the activations build up is thus usually something substantially less than a full hallucination or authentic experience. It is also less than the final product "meaning" at which a hearer ultimately arrives. This ephemeral quality of sem/syn/sym meaning thus sets the stage for "the other half of meaning," which acts to solidify, clarify, and motivate those ghostlier, bottom-up, incomplete embodied simulation building blocks.[13]

Chapters 2 to 7 took us on a tour of this "other half of meaning." Analogous to how both dark and light areas on a photographic negative are necessary to achieve the final image, both embodied simulations and semantic meaning with their contribution organized by morphosyntax, as well as the collection of other sources of meaning from the other side, are necessary for a language to function, somewhat like bricks and mortar. That these two categories of contributors are malleable also enables them to ably fit together to create in situ meanings on the fly that are customizable to different situations.

Chapter 2 started the tour by looking at how deviations from discourse expectations can leverage the other-side-of-meaning. Contributions coming from varieties of utterance senses encoded or partly encoded in deviant utterances were considered. These were accompanied by additional and interacting sources coming in the form of pragmatic effects. A third source of meaning, involving schematized knowledge about standard conversation types or categories, was also introduced.

Among the other relatively concrete meaning sources discussed in Chapter 3 were *omissions* (expected sem/syn/sym meanings that are not contributed by a speaker) and opportunity cost meanings – sem/syn/sym contributions that could have happened but did not. A brief discussion of how intentionality interacts with omission was also provided.

Chapter 4 then discussed forms of imprecision including *ambiguity, vagueness, surprises* (unexpected turns of sem/syn/sym meanings), *nonsequiturs* (*highly* unexpected turns of sem/syn/sym meanings due to their seeming non-sensicality), *non-committals* (where speakers allow a discourse contribution to remain on the conversational floor while providing neither affirmation nor denial of its veracity), *"Columbos"* (last-

---

[13] As well as supporting our social needs and motivations detailed in Chapter 8.

minute interjections of new conversational content and/or re-visitations of previously stated or indicated meanings after roundabout deviations to other meanings), and *discourse pattern imprecision* (imprecise patterns in what a speaker is doing broadly in their discourse contributions, such as their zigzagging back and forth among meaning streams or between sensicality and non-sensicality to keep hearers off balance).

Chapter 5 then looked at both language structure and explicit types of indirectness and what these forms achieve. *Innuendoes, hints, suggestions, inferences,* and many other processes where speakers intentionally (usually) leverage their indirect actions to achieve some meaning in hearers (readers) were discussed. The necessity of mind reading, although also present in the softer forms of indirectness discussed in earlier chapters, was introduced here as necessary for successful execution of indirect exchanges.[14]

We then explored more encapsulated instances of indirectness that come packaged in standard forms of figurativeness (Chapter 6). A wide variety of figures were discussed, including *metaphor, irony, metonymy, hyperbole, idioms, proverbs,* and some relatively unexplored items under a category labeled rhetorical devices. That these figures have relative degrees of fixedness, either on their verbatim wordings or in their general figurative structures, affords them a set of meaning contributions that exceed or at least differ from those of other forms of indirectness or even relatively direct contributions. The range and detail of these contributions, packaged under the term "pragmatic effects" (Colston, 2015), and how these interact with sem/syn/sym meaning, were also briefly discussed.

Other contributions to meaning in the form of language play were treated separately from the contributions discussed in other chapters, allowing that those other sources can also be treated playfully (Chapter 7). Among the processes treated here were the large array of possibilities afforded under the loose category of *puns* or *multiple entendres,* where more than one meaning or pseudo-meaning are afforded under the same surface form used in a particular context. How language play can interact with play in other forms of media (e.g., images, music) was also discussed.

Chapter 8 then took a look back over the previous six chapter and discerned three take-home observations about how the other-side-of-meaning works. The first two of these were discussed at length – how other-side-of-meaning processes may teach us something new about the extent to which we use language to meet our powerful, neuro-social

---

[14] Mind reading is taken up more extensively in Chapter 8.

motivations. The chapter also presented some possible ideas as to why we've historically seen much greater attention paid to the sem/syn/sym side of meaning of the other side.

How these different sources from the other-side-of-meaning come together and interact, mutually and with both the sem/syn/sem side and some metalinguistic meaning influences, was then discussed in Chapter 9. This discussion was motived by the observation that the level of complexity in ways that the other-side-of-meaning creates meaning seems greater than the more core meaning-making processes (e.g., embodied simulations) on the sem/syn/sym side. This was done by focusing on one particular and prevalent kind of other-side-of-meaning source, metaphor.

We took a close look inside metaphors and at some of their structural and constructional characteristics that can affect their meaning. A parallel look at many of the various language genres in which metaphors can be embedded also indicated an astounding array of features of different genres that can affect the meaning making provided by metaphors. How all the potential interactions among internal and external meaning-making processes are at core serving the needs of our neurologically driven social needs provided a framework for this discussion.

One oft repeated reminder in all these discussions was that an intricately intertwined package of meanings can be engineered and delivered by a speaker or writer, through parallel, cascading, emergent, and symbiotic paths. But, equally, a more random chaos pattern of meanings can also occur where interlocutors lose the thread of control and meanings arise and interact in a kind of Brownian free-flowing pattern. Akin to the dynamism of physical movements in social animals (e.g., birds in flocks, mammals in herds), both coordinated and chaotic motion are possible, depending on the complex interaction of group-internal and -external factors (Gibbs & Colston, 2012).

So what can we now observe and report about the major meaning contribution categories in language – the sem/syn/sym, embodied, "bottom-up" half, and the structural, indirect, figurative, schematic, cognitive, psychological, social, playful, cultural,[15] etc., "top-down" remainder? At least four observations are apparent. The first is that this dichotomy of contribution is reflective of a common pattern in nature. The second is that this "dichotomy" in language is in fact something far more intricate than simply the juxtaposed opposition observed under

---

[15] Although culture was not the foremost topic of interest in the present work, it is treated occasionally. It is worth noting that culture is also a major component of both of the contributing halves of meaning in language.

conjoined antonymy. It is something motivated ultimately by a compromise between complexity and simplicity. The third observation is that when scrutinized closely, the conjoined antonymy of language is at best an illusion, perhaps oppositional but also something not actually fully dichotomous. The fourth is that the supposed "dichotomy" structure of language has led to some misconceptions about how language works among academics and non-scholars alike. These misconceptions involve both underestimations and overestimations of issues ranging from inter-activity to embodiment.

A Common Rarity

The majority of my research career has been spent studying irony of one sort or another. It turns out irony provides a poignantly apt example of something we think is unusual, but is actually commonplace and pre-valent and may reflect the core structure of language being revealed here. One of the amazing characteristics of irony is how it encapsulates opposition. In *situational irony,* for instance, some situation, thing, or turn of events involves opposition in the form of contradiction. The exact nature of this contradiction has been a slippery thing to pin down (Colston, 2015), but it involves the general sense of things explicitly not possibly belonging together actually residing together perfectly in reality.

As one simple example, consider a personal story involving a time-keeping device I refer to as my *irony clock*. A university colleague of mine, who gave me this unique clock, was shopping for bargains at a resale store when she came upon the retro-styled, bedside, wind-up alarm clock. It possibly was originally used as an advertising prop, because it had the name, logo, and address of a clock repair service on its face. Ironically, though, this particular clock, normally supported by four short but sturdy metal legs, had only three legs remaining, the fourth leg having been broken off at its base. The clock thus rested at a very cockeyed slant, half sideways and half leaning backward onto its broken stub, with one of the front legs sticking out prominently into thin air, obviously portraying a thing broken. Given that the clock's original purpose was to convey to people the ready availability of clock repairing, it thus exhibits a classic ironic contradiction – something espousing clock repair is itself blatantly eschewing clock repair.

Other types of irony involve similar kinds of contradictions, but the things which are contradicted vary in different ways. In *verbal irony,* for instance, the contradiction lies between a surface expression made by a speaker and the actual attitude they hold.[16] An example of such a verbal irony would be, for instance, a speaker saying, "Gee whiz!" as an American English colloquial statement of amazement, when the speaker's actual opinion is that the referent topic is trite or uninteresting (i.e., a speaker exclaiming amazement is actually experiencing boredom).

A third family of irony types lies somewhere in between situational and verbal irony and involves several kinds of portrayed irony (e.g., tragic, dramatic, irony crafted or captured for presentation in images). A classic cartoon image from *The Far Side* comic strip illustrates this nicely. It depicts a student pushing hard on a door to a school for gifted children. Above the child a sign reads, "Pull."[17]

The kinds of contradictions irony displays also have a quality of exceptionality. *Most* things in the world seem to align according to patterns we predict and expect. Occasionally, though, predictions, expectations, preferences, desires, and the like go unmet, a deviance on which we often take notice given the departure from expectations, etc. Ironic situations, portrayals, or statements are particularly exceptional in that they exceed mere *deviance* from expectations and instead usually portray *contradiction* of expectation(s). This exceptionality is not due to rarity of occurrence – spoken or verbal irony is frequent in some regions, cultures, and social groups (Dress, Kreuz, Link, & Caucci, 2008; Gibbs, 2000). It instead involves a particular exceptionality from expected norms, expectations, desires, etc. – *their* **contradiction** *with actual reality*.

For instance, one might readily expect that a clock advertising clock repair would itself be in good repair. One would also predict that things expected or desired to be exciting (e.g., some tidbit of late-breaking news) would fulfill those expectations and indeed cause intrigue or arousal in people encountering them. Hence the feigned excitement, "Gee whiz!" when that arousal expectation fails (a breaking news story is dull, trite, or trivial), or the ironic situation presented when a clock endorsing good timepiece repair is itself broken.

But one doesn't have to look to irony to see these kinds of contradictions. If instead of ironic contradiction we look for simpler cases of mere juxtaposed oppositions, the high frequency of this pattern can be seen (e.g., hot and cold faucets, sweet and sour flavors, yin and yang

---

[16] Another way to describe this is as a contradiction between the statement and actual reality. For instance, imagine a person saying, "Nice weather," in reference to bad weather. The two definitions align because whatever is internally felt (e.g., CRITICISM, COMPLAINT) matches external reality (e.g., BAD WEATHER), and both of these are contradicted by the actual statement made by the speaker (e.g., "Nice weather" as a statement of praise).

[17] Gary Larson was the cartoonist. *The Far Side* ran in newspapers from 1980 to 1995.

symbolism, on and off switches, and even in the claimed nature of language structure itself) (Danesi, 2009). I should hasten to note that not all of these oppositions can be objectively confirmed as truly *oppositional*, as if we even know or agree upon what that is. But they nevertheless are often taken as opposites or at least oppositional by peoples' common perceptions.[18]

Moreover, the nature of many of these juxtapositions is keen. On occasion, juxtaposed opposites are mutually dependent or at least mutually defining, a relationship I've been referring to **conjoined antonymy**.[19] Many times, conjoined antonymy is even necessary to enable broader functioning of natural and man-made systems. As we'll discuss shortly, conjoined antonymy may even reflect a fundamental pattern in the natural world or at least in humanity's cognitive and social constructions of it. First, though, please consider a few common examples from biology, ethics, political science, and other widely arrayed domains.

Many if not most instances of biological reproduction are sexual, with two sexes mating to produce offspring. These male and female sexes are also often considered oppositional in some capacities with male/masculine/man having, or perhaps more accurately being *believed* to have, characteristics opposed in some ways to those of female/feminine/woman.[20] For instance, in many bird and other species one of the sexes is frequently large and brightly colored relative to the other which is small and dull-hued. In other species one sex is often responsible for the predominance of offspring care while the other sex is not. Other sexual differences can involve things such as levels of overt aggressiveness, level of subtle aggressiveness, roles in reproduction (pursuer versus pursued, wooer versus wooed, offspring-bearing versus not), work roles (nest/den/etc. builder versus not, food hunter/gatherer versus not), roles in social hierarchies (competing for alpha position in the group versus not), and many others.

Morality also is frequently divided into oppositional good and evil. This dichotomy is embodied in many religious, spiritual, mystical, and other

---

[18] For other extensive treatments of oppositionality or antonymy, please see among other works, Panther & Thornberg (2012), and Jones (2002).

[19] Or complementary antonyms, according to Lyons (1995). See also the "unity of opposites" (McGill & Parry, 1948), yin and yang (Ames, 2002). See also Danesi (2009) for a review of the history of this concept in language and philosophy, as well as Ogden (1932) for an early treatment of opposition as a theory of mind.

[20] The genuineness of these instances of opposition is very difficult to objectively verify, and in biological systems a wide array of patterns are found, ranging from gender similarity to great division of labor/activity/structure/appearance, etc. Yet the perception or belief of relatively simple oppositions between male and female is probably widespread.

belief systems (e.g., heaven versus hell, dark forces versus light forces, naughty and nice, the id and the superego, black versus white, the conceptual metaphors GOOD is UP and BAD is DOWN, right and wrong, yin and yang, angels versus demons, gods and devils, sinner and saint, le Père Fouettard et le Père Noël, good guys versus bad guys). This dichotomy is so pronounced that violations of it, as in portrayals in fiction depicting antiheroes, moral ambiguity, and related character and plot complexities, which might indeed more accurately reflect reality, are occasionally considered avant-garde and are accordingly not always well accepted by mainstream or generally conservative audiences.

The political spectrum, despite many different national and other political party and governmental structures, is often expressed in terms of conjoined antonymy. Left wing versus right wing, conservative versus liberal, Tory versus Labour, Democrat versus Republican as in the context of the United States, etc., are common dichotomies observed in political affiliation, thought, and discussion.

This list of emergent conjoined antonymies goes steadily on, appearing in domains as diverse as social psychology and song lyrics – in-groups versus out-groups, friends and enemies, wanted – dead or alive, part of the solution versus part of the problem, do or die, sink or swim, make or break, "east is east and west is west . . .," "The North and the South," feast or famine, black versus white, with us or against us, ". . . should I stay or should I go now?" etc.[21]

The point for present purposes is that, despite the common categorization tenet of *alike things go together*, this basis on similarity often just isn't the case – oppositional or opposed things instead frequently go together as dichotomous pairs.

Returning now to language for a moment, the "two sides of meaning" described in this book may share this pattern. A pseudo-symbolic half (my sem/syn/sym portion) that strives toward alignment in individuals' comprehension largely via embodied simulations corralled by shared morpho-syntactical structuring and function is mutually dependent on an oppositional pseudo-pragmatic half (my other-side-of-meaning portion), driven by an array of distinctly nonsymbolic meaning influencers. The latter half may also strive toward alignment but additionally can provide an *illusion of alignment* through mechanisms such as cognitive dissonance when genuine shared meaning is not readily attainable (Colston, 2015).

---

[21] It could well be that the very concept of opposition or opposites itself is fully embodied – emerging from the source pattern of our bisymmetrical bodies.

A Short Distance: The Point(s) of Lines

The second observation outlined earlier about language, that this supposed conjoined antonymy is really much more than it appears to be, can be shown by noting how complex patterns of things in the real world often get collapsed in human thinking, if not in objective reality, into *twos*. This pattern may also reflect a fundamental aspect of our bodies – their general bilateral symmetry. Similar to how our dominant base-ten math system might be the way it is because we have ten figures (toes), our categories may frequently become dichotomous and oppositional because we have bi-symmetrical bodies which are also arranged that way.

For some examples, let's first return to the earlier case of sexual reproduction as an instance of a conjoined antonymy. That so many life forms have evolved into having two biological sexes is possibly the result of a grand compromise. Indeed, underlying this compromise is another embedded example of a more-than-meets-the-eye conjoined antonymy. Taking the internally nested example first, in order for species to successfully function in their environmental and social niches, they must simultaneously do two somewhat oppositional things – be consistent and change. Consistency is required for all the physical and behavioral adaptations of the species to glean the advantages for which those adaptations were evolutionarily selected. Change is needed for adaptability.

For instance, let's say a particular bird species evolved a long narrow beak to gain access to a particular food source (e.g., worms) that lives deep in mud. Were that species, either within one generation's lifetime or across one or even a few generations, to simply lose that beak and develop instead a short wide one, the species would immediately be at a survival disadvantage (all else held reasonably equal). The species has adapted to a particular ecological niche and is advantaged to the degree it keeps consistent the tools it developed to succeed in that niche. Lose the tools suddenly and you lose the niche.

Or for a behavioral example, imagine a new generation of animal species simply lost the widespread fight-or-flight response to danger. This species would immediately risk extinction because this particular response has proven a very successful adaptation in many species. The response prepares individuals to combat or avert contact with some form of threat to life.

For a social/behavioral example, say a particular species of grazing mammal evolved a process of changing group behavior in response to predator threats. If a predator is detected by an individual member of this species, for example, imagine the member elicits a signal via an audible call or visible posture or movement. Other members of the herd have learned (or have ingrained in them, or even have a mixture of the two mechanisms) to close ranks when this warning signal is displayed. As long as the species follows this system it bears the advantage of strength in massed numbers. But if an individual of the species (or a generation) again within one lifespan or as a new individual or generation somehow doesn't produce or comprehend that warning call, it could be at a serious and life-threatening disadvantage. It will no longer function in coordination with the group and will miss the protection enclosed ranks provide should a predator appear.

So, species must maintain a degree of consistency in their structure and function. Consistency allows alignment among fellow members of the species and with the surrounding physical environment, enabling interactions that befit the ecological niche. Misalign somehow, and coordination with others as well as physical fit with the environment will diminish and survival risk will increase. So, there is evolutionary pressure on species to be consistent.

On the other hand, species also need to change. At any particular time, the idealness of fit of any species to its ecological niche will be imperfect. Species might improve existing advantages or develop new ones if they change to improve their interactions among fellow members or within their environmental niche. Environments themselves are also frequently changing, altering the quality of fit of any given species. So, species must adapt to cohere with those changing environments. Species are also not alone in their ecological niches. Other species may be in competition over scarce resources. Species must thus adapt to maintain or gain a competitive edge over rivals. So, all species are also under evolutionary pressure to change. All told, every species experiences continuous and oppositional evolutionary pressures – stay consistent but also change.

The way species master this seemingly contradictory set of pressures is also an example of a (seemingly, at least) conjoined antonymy. Due to the pressure to maintain consistency, species would be best suited if they reproduced asexually – so the genetic content of any individual generation wouldn't drastically change from its parent's. Only mutations or genetic miscopying between generations could produce species change. But in response to pressure to change, species would benefit by maximizing the input of new genetic material during reproduction. So, it might behoove species to have many different sexes, all necessarily contributing to the conception and development of new generations. For instance, a species might have five different sexes, all of which must mate together at one time and combine genetic material to produce the next generation.

One possible reason for the predominance of sexual reproduction is its compromise between these opposing pressures. Always have more than one parent participating in reproduction to bring genetic diversity. But hold the number of parents to only two to maximize ease of coordination in the mating and rearing processes and to keep the rate of change reasonable for the sake of consistency.

One consequence of this grand compromise is that, as with any diverse category which becomes regularly represented by only two individuals, any potential or slight continua lying within that category will emerge, elongate, and often settle into a divided bimodal distribution. The two representing exemplars of the category might begin, for instance, as slightly different depictions of a tendency toward a continuum in the population. But they'll eventually move to represent a full dichotomous opposition in the category and end up caricaturizing the X and Y extremes. So, for the purposes of compromising between the oppositional pressures on species to be consistent and to change, most species have developed two biological sexes, male and female. These can diverge in ways we end up perceiving as oppositional (e.g., masculine versus feminine).

Again, to stress, these so-called oppositions are a complex matter of genuine biological tendencies (e.g., physical size), along with perceptual tendencies in observers (e.g., people also *like* the simplicity of seeing things as oppositional so they tend to categorize things that way even if they're objectively more complex), and self-serving belief systems (e.g., if the current state of perceived opposition between male and female produces an advantage for one of the genders, that gender will tend to wish to perpetuate that advantage).

So, for reproduction at least, it appears that a conjoined antonymy is an emergent characteristic of the system. Whether this outcome is due broadly to human embodied projection or something more objective, however, remains to be determined.

The Dolly Zoom

One other way in which the conjoined antonymy pattern, at least when applied to language, is more complex than it might first seem is that the two sides into which language divides each espouse characteristics seemingly residing in the other side. The categories are thus not as discernably "antonymic" as they might first appear. This can be observed by simultaneously expanding the view as well as zeroing in on a key surrogate example. Consider the classic *nature versus nurture* conjoined antonymy oft discussed in Introductory

Psychology and related university courses as espousing the two main contributors to human and other behavior. Also consider the role DNA plays in this.

On the one hand, we have nature, or the genetic predispositions toward structure and behavior which are built into a life-form's DNA. On the other hand, we have structures and behaviors acquired during the lifespan, themselves not specifically encoded into DNA but instead learned or acquired through exposure to and experience within an external environment, or nurture.[22]

One simple way to think of this conjoined antonymy is that most plant species, or any life-forms without a nervous system, have essentially most if not all of their structure and behavior hardwired into their DNA. Not much in this arrangement allows structure and behavior to adapt according to what the plant encounters within its lifespan (i.e., as would be the case with a nervous system). True, the environment can influence *how* that DNA-dictated structure and behavior are manifest – too little nutrients, water, or sunlight will produce less growth than that enabled by DNA. But the environment cannot generally exceed what DNA allows. A plant receiving excess nutrients, moisture, or sunlight will not grow much taller than what the plant's DNA enables (e.g., a genetically unaltered daisy will not grow 100 meters tall in a 1 g environment). And the plant cannot change its structure/behavior in response to lifespan experience in ways not prescribed by the DNA blueprint.[23]

But for animals with nervous systems an additional guidance system is in place – that of neural-based learning. Animals can encode experiences occurring amid their environments into their nervous systems which can in turn alter the animals' current and future behavior and structure in ways somewhat independent of DNA's instructions (e.g., a primate can learn to not eat a certain red fruit after a negative gastrointestinal experience of doing so, no matter what their DNA prods them to eat).[24] This learned influence on behavior is a way of offloading from DNA, in part at least, some of the means of managing a life cycle. Learning is thus in

---

[22] The learning *ability* is provided by DNA, but not the learning *content* (although see below).

[23] This is admittedly a bit of an oversimplification. Some non-neural-based "learning" of a sort can take place in plants' biological systems (e.g., change in rate of growth as a result of previous rates of growth). But these appear to lack the sophistication and versatility of neural-based learning.

[24] People, albeit without universal success, can limit their food intake because they've learned of the associated health benefits of avoiding obesity, even if their DNA pushes them to eat more as a survival adaptation.

essence a hardwired short-term form of additional flexibility to adapt to environments within an animal's lifetime.[25]

But if we look closely, DNA hardwired structures and behaviors also implicitly take account of and enable adaptation to within-lifespan environmental influences at least to a degree without resorting to neural learning mechanisms. Concomitantly despite the presumed open-endedness of learning mechanisms, learned behaviors can also be fairly constricted according to limits imposed by the animal's genetic makeup and related factors connected to DNA. Consider two brief examples, daisies and pandas.

Daisies have DNA instructions to grow to a certain height (provided adequate nutrients, sunlight, etc.). No matter how favorable an environment is for a particular daisy plant, the plant will not exceed generally the maximum height prescribed by its DNA, barring mutations. Interestingly, though, that particular prescribed height implicitly takes account of the within-life-cycle environment of the plant. Wild daisies typically grow amid a predictable suite of surrounding plants. The prescribed ideal height of daisies will thus have become encoded in DNA due to previous natural selection. DNA is thus accounting for this environmental or contextual parameter. The plant will not invest nutrients and energy in growing enormously tall because it need only grow tall enough to get enough light relative to the plants around it, and DNA provides for this. In a fashion, then, DNA is doing the learning, albeit over multiple generations, rather than a nervous system doing the learning within one lifetime.

Non-learning DNA-prescribed structures/behaviors can also enable the plant to adapt to within-life-cycle local conditions. If a daisy is partly shaded to its left, for example, it will tend to grow to the right to absorb more sunlight. This adaptation isn't driven by learning. It instead is controlled by elaborate biomechanical mechanisms, which give the plant flexibility to adjust its structure and behavior in response to environmental factors the plant senses. So, the DNA blueprint *is* in essence taking account of within-life-cycle environmental conditions to a degree – having adapted daisies to similar situations in the past.

Even animals that have nervous systems and thus can learn within one lifetime still have this DNA-prescribed adaptability. Pandas, for example, have encoded into their DNA one particular behavior that best suits their

---

[25] Learning can also affect structure in addition to behavior – for instance, consider health and medical science where humans have learned how to confront and combat DNA tendencies.

Extending this idea, one could argue that culture is then a means of carrying that learned-within-lifetime knowledge across to new generations.

environment. Unlike most bear species, pandas live in and on a protein-depleted environment (bamboo forests). This environment can only support a relatively few number of pandas in a given area, relative to that of other bear species who live where more protein is available. Accordingly, pandas have a very weak sex drive, and reproduce at very slow rates, again relative to other bear species.[26] This keeps populations small enough to survive in their environment. So, again, we have encoded into a life-form's DNA an implicit consideration of the environmental factors that will be encountered by that animal.

Indeed, the picture gets even more complicated than this. DNA-prescribed structures/behavior and learning mechanisms are not the only ways in which animals can adjust to their environments within their lifespan. Some animal species will adjust their birth rates and litter sizes biomechanically – for instance, according to the amounts of food in their environment – on a birthing cycle to birthing cycle basis. Of course, these adaptabilities as well as neural learning mechanisms are ultimately themselves prescribed by DNA. But they bring flexibilities of their own in that exactly what size litter or what is learned by a given animal is *not* fully DNA-dictated. Only *that* the animal will adjust according to experiences encountered within its lifespan is prescribed by DNA.

Conversely, we also have constraints imposed upon the supposedly open-ended learning potential of life-forms that have nervous systems and are thus capable of lifespan-adjusted lifestyles. As just argued, DNA provides for learning and enables behavior, but *what* an animal learns and accordingly much of *how* it specifically behaves are not written in its DNA.

For instance, imagine a particular gazelle learns that a spikey grass it has never seen before is toxic (perhaps an invasive species, its seeds carried to the gazelle's range by a freak storm). This learning took place as a result of an unpleasant gastrointestinal aftermath some minutes post-meal that the animal cannot forget.[27] This particular knowledge about purple spiky grass is not coded into DNA. Rather, DNA enables a fast learning system that encodes avoidance of *whatever* food substance was consumed prior to disingestion.

But what gets learned by animals and the behavior that ensues are nonetheless corralled and funneled in genetically prescribed ways. For instance, that a baboon hurls a stick into a watering hole, making a big noticeable splash, also isn't encoded into DNA. The baboon just engages

---

[26] One of the contributing factors to the difficulty often found in breeding pandas in captivity.

[27] Taste aversions being a very primitive, primary, and powerful learning mechanism found even in relatively simple animals.

in this behavior because it's performed it or seen it done before and subsequently experienced/observed the attention-getting consequence in its peers. But this and other behaviors and what is learned from them may nonetheless be guided in a way by DNA. That the animal *can* grab a stick (having opposable thumbs), *can* throw things (having appropriate shoulder anatomy and well-developed hand–eye coordination, etc.), *can* see and hear the resulting splash (has the appropriate sensory systems), *can* have particular emotional responses (due to a functional limbic system), and *can* care about the social ramifications of all this (has hard-wired socio-cognitive motivations) might lead the animal toward some and away from other behaviors (i.e., the animal may throw branches into a pond to make both a literal and figurative splash, but the animal may *not* attempt to fly from a small cliff onto a tree, try to hear things outside of its hearing range, respond with anger to a rock on the ground, throw the branch into the pond when no other baboons are around as witnesses, etc.).

If we now transfer all these characteristics of the supposed two contributors to life-forms' structure and behavior – DNA and learning (i.e., nature and nurture) – over to language, we can see a similar complexity. The bottom-up(-ish), sem/syn/sym, embodied-simulation-driven half is akin to the structural/behavioral instructions provided by DNA. The more top-down(-esque) suite of processes affecting meaning are then similar to the array of learning mechanisms enabled by nervous systems (e.g., habituation, taste aversions, operant conditioning, classical conditioning, observational learning, deduction). Together these two halves of meaning afford the same flexibility as that seen in animal structure and behavior – enabling the same complex interactions between sem/syn/sym and "top-down" other-side-of-meaning processes as we see between DNA-prescribed structure/behavior and within-lifespan learning. This flexibility comes in part because, as with the less-than-perfectly-dichotomous DNA/learning division, the division between the two halves of meaning derivation is also messy.

To make this a bit more concrete, please entertain for consideration an equivalence between a life-form and an utterance. Also please consider the *structure and behavior* of even a very brief example of the making of an utterance: a speaker saying a single word. We know that the structure and behavior of this simple utterance (e.g., its form/how it is said, and its meaningful impact on a hearer) are influenced by the bottom-up(-ish) sem/syn/sym half of meaning. A speaker produces a speech signal that corresponds to and thus triggers an embodied simulation(s) in a hearer. So, a speaker saying "school" will likely trigger sensory- and motor-encoded neural programs associated with SCHOOL in the hearer's mind – in other words, the embodied simulation(s) S*C*H*O*O*L.

But even in this DNA-esque bottom-up(-ish) system we still have a built-in consideration of the environment (context) in which that utterance will reside. This consideration also appears in levels ranging from phonetics through pragmatics. Coarticulation clearly shows that phoneme production is influenced by the broader word or utterance context in which the phoneme is embedded (e.g., consider the physical production of "school" versus "skill"). Prosodic and many other production parameters can also readily guide how a hearer should run their embodied simulations and even which ones to run. Consider the different ramifications in a hearer of a speaker (both hearer and speaker knowing English) saying, "school," with falling versus rising intonation in response to the question, "What is your favorite thing to do?" Falling intonation would likely convey the propositional content along with, perhaps, *confidence* and *certainty*. Rising intonation on the other hand could indicate less certainty along with possibly *worry over the answers' acceptability, sought fulfillment regarding the answer's social desirability,* and other possible pragmatic aspects. So, even at the "DNA level" of language, built-in consideration of embedded context is present.

We also know that the structure and behavior (again, form, how said, and meaningful outcome) of an utterance are influenced by the broader top-down(-esque) pragmatic effect half of meaning. A speaker hones their language to produce a desired array of pragmatic effects in hearers. So, a speaker would likely make concerted choices between word and even phoneme alternatives (among many other things at the speaker's command) in an attempt to shepherd the structural, semantic, and pragmatic inferences in a hearer.[28] A speaker using the word "skill," for instance, would result in a different array of pragmatic effects than that same speaker saying "forte" in the same situation (e.g., as in saying, "painting with watercolors is not my _____" in the context of being invited to paint with watercolors). The latter word, "forte," connotes more of the sense of preference rather than just mere ability in this context. "Forte" can also convey an airier attitude concerning the ability in question, among many other things (see also Chapter 5).

Here again, though, we can also see constraints on what a speaker can marshal with these pragmatic effect mechanisms. What a hearer will experience as the suite of pragmatic effects is constrained by a number

---

[28] "Inferences" for lack of a better term. See Colston (2015) for a discussion of how pragmatic effects are both similar to and different from inferences, as well as other similar constructs.

of factors. The pragmatic effects that were computed previously, the social relationship between the interlocutors, the agenda(s), personality(s), physiological state(s), among many other hearer and contextual characteristics, will all corral, segment, sequentialize, prioritize, strengthen, weaken, etc., the resulting pragmatic effects the hearer experiences from a speaker's utterance.

To briefly summarize, DNA is essentially a set of instructions for how *life* gets built and for how it functions. Collectively, embodied simulations and semantic meaning guided by morphosyntax is an instruction system for how *meaning* gets built and functions. Just as DNA guides construction of life structures (e.g., plant and animal tissue), it also guides the establishment of intricate forms of plant and animal *flexibility* (e.g., plant stems, branches, and limbs that can bend in the wind without breaking; roots and branches that can grow toward water and sunlight; and life forms' behavioral patterns catered to survive within "known" environments).[29] But much of life-forms' flexible behavior is not fixed directly by DNA. Rather, behavior is off-loaded onto dynamic brain–body–world learning systems, typically nervous systems, to afford maximal flexibility. This heightened flexibility itself has the advantage of enabling a creature or species to adapt far more successfully than would be possible were behavior only hardwired by DNA, even if hardwired as flexible. Higher-level adaptive behavior in animals is thus a lot like open source code software – it is way more flexible and responsive to external challenges. Language bears this same mixture of fixed-from-DNA as well as adaptive open-sourced-ness. Through the complex processes which enable pragmatic effects to occur in language comprehension amid more guided embodied simulations, language appears to resemble biology in being driven by two general sources.

Understanding Misunderstandings

The model of language presented here, whether a projection on humans' part due to our bilaterally symmetrical bodies or something more fundamentally objective somehow in nature (or a combination), has been described as that of a **conjoined antonymy** (see the section, "It Takes Two to Tango," for a discussion of possible sources of this structure). Two opposing parts – (1) sem/syn/sym embodied simulations and semantic meaning honed by morphosyntax, and (2) the array of processes producing additional meaning and pragmatic and similar effects – are

---

[29] "Known" not in the sense of conscious awareness or control, but merely encoded in DNA through natural selection from similar past environments.

mutually dependent and work together to construct meaning in our minds from received linguistic input. However, despite this structure, a number of misconceptions or misunderstandings about how language functions seem prevalent in both lay and scholarly accounts of how language works. These involve both overestimations and underestimations of key processes in language functioning.

Overestimating: Determinedness of Influences

In Chapter 8 we discussed the relative attention given previously to the two sides of meaning. We argued that multiple factors have contributed to the sem/syn/sym side receiving far greater consideration by language scholars (and everyone else), including the powerful *semantic consolidation* effect brought about by a given piece of linguistic input merely existing (as spoken, written, or otherwise performed by someone). That we have this attentional imbalance likely contributes, then, to an overestimation of language determinedness.

Perceiving the sem/syn/sym side as isolated and separate or possibly the sole component of language creates an overestimation of determinedness because it overlooks the cognitive work taking place by the mechanisms on the other-side-of-meaning. Without an appreciation of the framing, orienting, solidifying, and perhaps even fudging influence of these other mechanisms, one must turn to some different solution for language to appear workable. The solution involves heightening the credit given to the so-called "objectivity" of meaning, which deludes us into thinking meaning is fully or at least partially determined by lexical and syntactic input alone. Were there a more widespread understanding of the complex intertwining and interdependency of the two sides of meaning, and of the contributions of the other-side-of-meaning, the attentional imbalance and overestimation of determinedness would likely diminish.

Overestimating: Sequentiality of Influences

Perhaps the most stealthy of the overestimations about language functioning is of the sequentiality of the purported autonomous halves. Again, by misappreciating the intertwinedness of the two halves of meaning, an illusion that the sides are separate can create the need to see them as sequential. How can a hearer know which pragmatic effects to compute, so one version of the sequential argument often goes, unless she first has a sense of the semantic content of an utterance? If the two sides of meaning do not talk to one another, as goes another version, then why should we presume they happen simultaneously or in tandem? That would seem to have a high processing cost. It seems more parsimonious to sequence them – the latter building upon the products of the former. Finally, what would pragmatic factors involving, say, the interlocutors' social relationship have to do with presumed encapsulated and lower-level language processes like lexical access or its modern equivalent, embodied simulations?

As the treatment presented in this book has hopefully demonstrated, all levels of language from phonology through pragmatics are mutually influential in deriving information at any one of those purportedly separate levels. If we consider a very simple act by a person, say the biting of an apple, *multiple* motor, sensory, and other physiological processes are intertwined to enable such an event to happen (e.g., seeing the apple, reaching for it, visual feedback steering the arm toward the apple, visible feedback involved in grasping the apple, muscle and tactile sensory feedback enabling the apple to be lifted, visual feedback again steering the apple's approach to the person's mouth). Yes, one *can* dissect the different processes (either in biting an apple or in comprehending or producing language) for consideration and discussion as a scholar or person contemplating the process. But this does not entail their separable nor sequential functioning in situ.

Underestimating: Embeddedness and Parallelism of Influences

Even if someone were to give full appreciation to the existence of the other-side-of-meaning, an underestimation usually remains of the level of interaction between the two sides of meaning in normal everyday instances of language comprehension and usage. This was alluded to also in Chapter 8 to be an epiphenomenon of the imbalance of attention toward the two sides.

But this underestimation may be due additionally to an underappreciation of the embeddedness of language processing amid all the other things going on in a human language comprehender. My recent book, *Using Figurative Language* (Colston, 2015) detailed the range of these other processes, ranging from physiological through socio-cognitive to cultural, and how they "leak in" to language processing proper in ways both independent and interactional:

Psychology and Pragmatics – An enormous amount of work in cognitive and social psychology has demonstrated that no instance of cognition occurs as an island, completely independent and isolated from other bits of cognition (Amit, Algom, & Trope, 2009; Trope & Liberman, 2010; Bar-Anan, Liberman, & Trope, 2006; Maglio & Trope, 2012; Caruso, Waytz, & Epley, 2010; Burns,

Caruso, & Bartels, 2012; Caruso, Gilbert, & Wilson, 2008; Caruso & Shafir, 2006; Cokely & Feltz, 2009; Epley, Caruso, & Bazerman, 2006; Fausey & Boroditsky, 2010; Fausey & Matlock, 2011; Helzer, Connor-Smity, & Reed, 2009; Uttich & Lombrozo, 2010). People's on-the-fly cognition is influenced by other recent cognition(s), things the person is worrying about, even people's physiological state. Indeed, a great deal of recent and older work has shown just how powerful these influences are. People can be influenced in their person perception by the temperature of a cup they're holding (Williams & Bargh, 2008). People's interpretations of metaphors can be affected by the nature and direction of movement their body is experiencing (Boroditsky & Ramscar, 2002; Wilson & Gibbs, 2007). People's memories of past events can be altered by the descriptions of those events in the present (Loftus, 1975; Loftus, Miller & Burns, 1978; Loftus, 1993, 2003).

None of this is necessarily a new observation. What is potentially new, how-ever, is the growing recognition that processes that underlie the above influences, and many, many others, can be very fast, automatic to a degree, can be triggered in parallel by online language comprehension or things that accompany or even precede it, and indeed can *leak in* to affect that processing, even at very early stages. This may be the case particularly for figurative language processing where one could argue the invoking of rich comprehension mechanisms through an enhanced search-for-meaning can and would readily absorb automatic and fast cognitive operations. (Colston, 2015, p. 194)

The bottom line of this argument is that no human internal processes (e.g., cognitive but also others) are completely separate and isolated from fellow processes. Rather they all can play roles in all human functioning, sometimes as just additional ingredients in the stew of functioning, other times in highly interactive and influential capacities with other functions.

Underestimating: Interaction of Influences

Further to this argument, many human processes, cognitive linguistic and otherwise, do not exhibit switch-throwing swiftness and completeness. Rather they unfold in time unevenly and have asymptotic and other messy endgames, where they're open to the influences already described in this chapter and elsewhere at all stages toward completion, which itself is not even always a fixed event. Indeed, processes can self- or re-arise in intensity as an outcome of cascading contributor interactions in much the same way a woodfire can spark pseudo-spontaneously and re-intensify after having calmed down in its level of activity. A wood fire's level of activity does not decrease as a simple linear function of amount of fuel remaining to burn. Rather, buildup of ash, altering physical structure (i.e., as the pile of logs collapses and/or rearranges), changed exposure to oxygen, internal air and smoke flow, all have complex interacting effects. So can it be said of language subprocesses.

Underestimating: Chaotic-ness of Influences

Although at least a degree of predictability does hold for the unfolding of pragmatic effect and sem/syn/sym meaning contributions, they nonetheless can be somewhat chaotic. Colston (2015) also discusses the applicability of dynamical system behavior to explaining *figurative* language comprehension, at both relatively immediate and longer-term time courses (see also Gibbs & Colston, 2012). The same argument holds presently for the broader treatment of the two sides of all language – the contributions of both sides can be predicted with reasonable accuracy but a modicum of randomness remains.

Underestimating: Embodiment of Influences

Finally one might argue for an underestimation of embodiment's role in overall language functioning as an outcome of our seeing mostly or only the sem/syn/sym side of meaning contribution, or our overstating the separation in the sides of meaning. Interestingly, this underestimation holds despite the recent discovery of the inherently embodied processes in sem/syn/sym functioning through embodied simulations. Too little attention being given to the other-side-of-meaning and an underappreciation of just how embodied many of the other side's processes are lead to this overall embodiment underestimation.

One need look only at the level of social influences in top-down meaning processing to illustrate this point. People produce and understand language through the social lens of their relationship(s) with other interlocutors, their relative position in social hierarchies, their met and unmet social needs (Colston, 2015), and their level of empathy toward others, all of which wax and wane (Rasse, 2016; Nezlek, Feist, Wilson, & Plesko, 2001; Nezlek, Schultz, Lopes, & Smith, 2007). Indeed the level to which people are wired to function as social beings has been greatly missed even by some of the most recent broad interdisciplinary scholarship on human functioning (see Lieberman, 2013). These social influences are directly traceable to embodied neurological underpinnings in much the same way as the sem/syn/sym side of meaning (see Chapter 8).

For instance, the discomfort people feel when becoming disconnected socially involves a very similar usurpation of more primitive brain functions as that accomplished by language via sensory and motor embodied simulations. Put very simply, social pain *is* physical pain. Social removal, rejection, or isolation borrows the same brain mechanisms as those underlying physical pain (Lieberman, 2013). Social pain thus provides a powerful motivator for people to get and remain socially connected.

This social connection is necessary for us on multiple levels. For instance, general social animal advantages are wrought when individuals live in groups. Among these are advantages from having multiplied sensory inputs, from being able to communicate information obtained by those sensory inputs, from having a larger learning repository, and from sheer numbers. For example, an individual member of a herd (pack, troop, flock, etc.) really has as many eyes, ears, noses, etc., as there are members in the group – if one animal detects a predator it can communicate that knowledge to the other animals. These sensors are also spread out over the full area occupied by the herd, increasing the swath and resolution of vigilance of any individual. A larger learning repository is also gained in group settings, not just because multiple brains and nervous systems are present to hold information, but because this information can also become more specialized (e.g., individuals or small groups can specify their knowledge about important tasks, such as rearing young, finding food, maintaining social cohesion) and can be passed through generations. And, of course, the sheer larger numbers of individuals can have advantages for defense against predation and other threats.

Social connections are also needed, though, for purposes germane to being human. For example, our large brains force infants to be born before the preponderance of later-stage cognitive and other development has occurred – necessitating a powerful child-caregiver(s) social bond – while newborns finish this crucial stage of development. This also enables that latter development to take place in a social world rather than in utero. Our built cultures also depend upon distributed, shared knowledge about the world we inhabit which is only obtainable and maintainable via powerful mind-reading, empathic, imitative, and cooperative mind functions, which are hardwired in the human brain (Leiberman, 2013).

The underestimation of the degree to which overall language functioning is embodied provides a nice segue to the penultimate and final sections of this book. Consideration of the embodied nature of human language, and cognition more broadly construed, enables us to discuss, finally, just why it appears that language, our bodies, and a host of other phenomenon are or appear to be structured as conjoined antonymies. Considering embodiment's prevalence is also a bit of a Pandora's box, though – once we acknowledge embodiment's role in all language functioning, it becomes difficult to keep it out of everything else.

It Takes Two to Tango

Before addressing the full issue of the nature and prevalence of conjoined antonymies in nature, let's first consider a more basic question, or rather a related pair of basic questions. These questions query the two most fundamental characteristics of conjoined antonymies – that they're composed of two parts or halves and that those halves appear in opposition. Why is this the case? Or, asked most basically, *why two?* and *why an oppositional two?*

The quantity of *two* might be simply where we end up when, put in cosmological terms, we take the simplest possible step away from a state of pure entropy. Consider that, if everything in the universe were uniform, it would be as if nothing existed at all. No means would be available to discern any one thing from everything else. No structure or complexity would be discernable. Whether such a state describes what presumably existed at the moment of the Big Bang, or what purportedly will exist when/if things cool down enough to exhaust all atomic and other activity into a state of entropy, I'm by no means qualified to answer. But it seems reasonable that having *two* possible types of matter or energy or some other primary mode of existence is one step more complex than having just one or having none.

Couple this idea with the partner notion of parsimony in that systems tend to devolve to their simplest possible state, and we have a similar compromise to what we had for biological (i.e., sexual) reproduction (see earlier this chapter). Much like how a single geometrical point is free-floating in space, but a line is immediately demarked when a second point is added, something fundamental seems to happen at *two* – we gain a toehold onto subsequently ratchet-able complexity.[30]

Or perhaps rather than appealing to the nature of entropy, the universe, definability, and complexity – cascading through everything in existence – it could simply be that the kind of compromise resulting in sexual reproduction, the political spectrum, language, and many other things is just a handy one that gets used a lot. This possibility also begins to address the question of *why an oppositional two?*

Species need to both stay consistent and to change. Political processes need to represent both the haves and the have-nots. Languages need to align consciousness between people but also deal with all the difficulties in achieving that alignment. Oppositionality may just be the structure that emerges as systems attempt to grapple with these dichotomous challenges.

To illustrate, consider bilateral symmetry. Views differ as to the original reason(s) for why most animals' bodies are bilaterally symmetrical, or are

---

[30] I'll admit to the temptation here to apply this general notion to the conjoined antonymy of space/time. The limited understanding I have from a brief stint as a university major in Physics, along with an ongoing spectator's interest in all things stringy and beyond, give me a sense the application is apt.

essentially so at low resolution. A number of interesting and not always mutually incompatible competing accounts have been put forth. These range from specific to broad and pertain to the origin as well as the maintenance of bilateral symmetry in animal bodies.

One account involves the efficiency of genetic coding for bodybuilding – an easy way to double the size of a body is to just reuse the code or blueprint for constructing what is already present, and then just keep the two halves connected.[31] Another account involves the need for physical balance in a gravity environment. To resist gravity and achieve mobility, bodies need a means of balancing. The simple physics of equivalent masses on either side of a fulcrum provides a very easy solution to this challenge. A third explanation could be related to neurological management efficiency – it is much easier for a nervous system to manage two halves of a body that are essentially identical than it would be if the halves were very different, or if there were multiple parts to the fraction instead of just two (e.g., thirds, quarters, ninths).

Some lower-level accounts point to simple extensions of the process of cell division, the ease of growth for multicellular organisms and simple organizational geometry (e.g., expansion into sheet structures and then folding). Some very broad accounts put the origin of bilateral symmetry on the more abstract idea of stability – for organisms to survive changing environments they need a degree of stability across varying circumstances. For the same reason a bicycle is more stable than a unicycle, bilateral symmetry evolved for this general function of increasing stability, in both abstract and concrete senses. Another manifestation of stability is the inherent redundancy obtained with bilateral symmetry. If you lose one hand, claw, eye, etc., you still have another. Perhaps such an injured state is non-ideal for functioning in a harsh environment. But it is also likely enough to aid survivability and subsequent gene pool contribution.

Still other accounts speak more to the *perpetuation* of bilateral symmetry rather than its origin. Within the range of symmetricity in animals, those individuals which are or appear to be more symmetrical than others are often selected over less symmetrical ones. Even human attractiveness demonstrates this – people with more symmetrical faces are rated as more attractive, prettier, handsomer, etc., than those with less symmetrical ones (Smith, 2018). So, whatever the origin, we have built-in mechanisms for maintaining and enhancing symmetricity.

---

[31] Many housing developments in different parts of the world have discovered this principle, where many of the individual houses are built from the same architectural designs, with maybe only some cosmetic surface tweaks. Car and many other types of manufacturers also use this principle, with engine and other drive platforms being duplicated across models.

Further still are accounts addressing the collateral benefits of having bilateral symmetry in a body design. These may not have been original causes of bilateral symmetry. Nor are they external mechanisms directly acting to perpetuate symmetry (i.e., the aesthetic we hold for things that are symmetrical). But they might end up serving to perpetuate symmetry since they come with benefits that are adaptive, and thus selected for by evolution. For example, having auditory sensors on opposite sides of a head enables precise echolocation of sources of environmental sounds. The same principle can hold for other similar sensory systems (e.g., sonar, magnetism sensing). Having visual sensory systems on opposite sides of the head also maximizes coverage of an individual's environment. These eyes evolving into parallel, forward-facing positions, as they did for primates, then serve the ability of precise distance judgment and hand–eye coordination. Also for primates, having *pairs* of manipulator and locomotion limbs enables two things to be done at the same time (e.g., a lemur can hold on with one hand while picking a piece of fruit with the other).

But perhaps the most widely accepted account of bilateral symmetry concerns the principles involved in early locomotion. Certainly some animals can move without such symmetry (i.e., floating plankton and pulsing jellyfish; even cephalopods and arthropods are bilaterally symmetrical). But a certain efficiency is availed by having opposing body parts which can alternatively or simultaneously push against water (and later mud, land, trees, air, and space station walls). If you've experienced both single paddle canoe propulsion and dual-oar boat rowing, you likely have the embodied simulations to help illustrate this.[32]

It could thus be simply that this general principle of conjoined antonymy in nature, found pointedly in bilateral symmetry and sexual reproduction in animals, is oft repeated, giving us inhaling and exhaling, life and death, an infinity of concepts in opposition (e.g., up and down, good and evil, this or that), and, most important for our consideration here, the nature of language.

One last possibility is the intriguing idea that conjoined antonymies are epiphenomenal of something very much weirder. One might, for instance, consider the cycle of night and day as found on astral satellites not yet tidally locked in their astral orbits. Standing on the surface of such a satellite, such as the Earth, one could easily think the circadian cycle is a conjoined antonymy which, in a sense, it is – periods of lightness and

---

[32] This account is supported by the fact that our greatest levels of bilateral symmetry are found in our body parts devoted to locomotion and sensation. Less symmetry is found on some internal structures (e.g., digestion).

darkness juxtaposed and oppositional and mutually defining. But the origin of this particular conjoined antonymy is not exactly among the kinds of fundamental compromises discussed thus far (e.g., animal species needing to both stay consistent and to change, resulting in sexual reproduction; animals needing to balance and move in a gravity environment producing bilateral symmetry; or language needing to trigger aligned resonances in conversers' cognition but then also needing to fill in for those resonances' limitations and deal with other social and communication systems). It isn't the case, for instance, that the Earth somehow *needs* to be both light and dark, so it settled into a circadian rhythm as a compromise between these forces. It is rather an *epiphenomenon* of rotational and orbital mechanics. Interestingly, though, even those rules of physics arise from conjoined antonymies themselves – a perfect balance between gravitation and momentum allowing both a satellite to orbit a celestial body and celestial bodies to spin. So, these balanced oppositional processes produce the circadian cycle through a fairly tangential route. We see patterns of opposing lightness and darkness alternating in our days. But this is really just a short-lived phenomenon, existing only temporarily before an orbiting body becomes tidally locked. Things involving reproduction, bilateral symmetry, and language could be thus way more complex, epiphenomenal, and maybe even temporary than we realize.

Eve's Apple

Bringing things back down to Earth, for the moment at least, we're now poised to ask one additional question about the nature of language. We know that one part of language is relatively concretely embodied in the form of embodied simulations. "Lamp" means LAMP because you've interacted with LAMP(S) many times both sensorily and motorily (e.g., turning them on and off, reading under them, dusting them, selecting them during purchase, changing their bulbs, knocking them over, and possibly wearing their shades at raucous parties) such that you have L$\star$A$\star$M$\star$P recorded neurologically within you, as something both generic and in many ways quite specific.

We also know many parts of the other side of language are also embodied in multiple ways – being moored in baser processes. Sarcasm can make its target topic look particularly bad by invoking a contrast effect rooted in sensation and perception. Noncommittal conversational turns can cast a shadow on a preceding topic and/or its contributor by withholding a much sought after social bond in the form of an acknowledgment. "Not my forte" can carry an airiness to it, authentically or ironically, through (1) the fundamentally neural process of association – the word *forte* being associated with airiness or snobbery; (2) pitch-based diminutiveness in *forte*'s second syllabic nucleus with no coda (and possibly the same structure in the first syllable), suggesting something lighter and higher, both metaphorically and nonfiguratively; (3) invocations of social alignments and ostracism, with the speaker partnering with the hearer to belittle another speaker using that word authentically – classic in-group/out-group social engineering, etc.

But are these the only ways in which language is embodied? Moreover, is it fair to stop at *the body* when we consider the nature of something being *embodied*? Thirdly, given how our very cognition is embodied, can we discern the degree to which the external world is *genuinely* structured as conjoined antonymies versus that just being a *projection* on our part?

I'll venture the answer to all of these questions is no. For the first two questions, not only is the answer negative because many other local mechanisms within the other-side-of-language can be traced to other brain and body functions and states, but these other underpinnings themselves have embodied bases. Indeed, one could argue that our bodies, in which these other systems are rooted, are themselves embodied within something else. Our bodies are embodied in the biological and social systems we've evolved to espouse and inhabit. For instance, we're hardwired to be social to an exceptional degree not found even in other primate species, who themselves are already highly social relative to many other animals (Lieberman, 2013). We are also programmed to sleep during nighttime hours, probably because our dominant sense works best during daylight. This dominant sensory system is color, stereoscopic vision rather than something else (e.g., infrared), largely because primate vision developed in arboreal environments where a dominant food source (ripe fruit) is discernable within the visible color spectrum and depth perception is crucial for locomotion. Our primary locomotion is upright, bipedal walking, etc.

These systems in turn are embodied in biology (e.g., evolution, natural selection), which itself is embodied in the particular physical systems that govern our planet (e.g., climate, weather, local gravity, plate tectonics, seasonal and circadian cycles). These systems in turn are then embodied in more basic physical systems governing matter, space, energy, time, etc. (e.g., orbital mechanics, entropy, gravity, energy, the speed of light).

For the third question, we must face the conundrum concerning the presumed objectivity of conjoined antonymies versus their being a projected illusion on our part. True, from our perspective as humans, it does appear that many conjoined antonymies exist in the world, including the structure of most animals' bodies. And there indeed seems to be some objective reality to this – one need only look at most animals' external structure to see this pattern. But are we seeing this pattern mainly or only because we ourselves have that bilateral symmetrical body and brain? One can also find evidence that animals' bodies are *not* bilaterally symmetrical. Some animals patently do not have these patterns. For animals that do appear bilaterally symmetrical the pattern may only hold at low resolution. At high resolution the symmetry begins to break down. It also only seems to hold for mainly external body parts, and perhaps mostly or only for those parts involved in locomotion and perhaps sensation. Internally and functionally, many things are not symmetrical. Yet we predominantly see them as symmetrical.

We can also easily deconstruct nearly any oppositional concept in the human condition and demonstrate how its surface appearance as a conjoined antonymy can be countered. We tend to think of day and night, or light and dark, or black and white as conjoined antonymies. Yet these oppositional structures can easily be debunked with heightened scrutiny. Why, for instance, do we normally cleave the circadian cycle into two halves when it could easily be divided differently. Instead of day and night, for instance, we could have dark, twilight, light, peak light, light, twilight, dark, and peak dark, a division into eighths.

We could also divide the usual conjoined antonymy of *hot and cold* into something different. Consider, *hot, warm, neutral, cool, and cold*, a division into fifths. Five might seem an odd way to divide temperature, yet we have five fingers or toes on each limb. We also have clearly constructed a mathematical system based on ten, arguably because we have ten fingers on which we very likely practiced our first exercises in keeping count, as we still do today. So why not a projection based on five for temperature, or some other number for anything else?

The point to all this is that the twin possibilities that the purported conjoined antonymy structure of language (and in all the other conjoined antonymies we see) is projected from humans whose bodies are organized similarly, or that it's a more fundamental pattern found in nature, may simply not be discernable. Indeed, concomitant in this discussion is, of course, the view that these possibilities are not mutually exclusive.

So, as the famous story goes about the "little old lady" audience member at a public lecture (Hawking, 1988), who once challenged a famous scholar (by some accounts Bertrand Russell, by others William James) on the nature of cosmology, saying something like, "It's turtles all the way down," there may be some truth to the connections proposed here of language to the human body, and of the human body to everything else. Only in this case it might be, *it's the body all the way down.*

Epilogue
"A Clearing Revealing an Eclipse"

> Love is heavy and light,
> bright and dark,
> hot and cold,
> sick and healthy,
> asleep and awake –
> it's everything except what it is!
>
> William Shakespeare, Romeo and Juliet (1597)

I was corresponding recently with a friend about a lunar eclipse to soon take place – the longest-lasting one to occur in the twenty-first century. I brought the eclipse to the friend's attention because it was to be visible over central Europe but not western Canada. So my friend would be able to see it directly in her sky but I would not. Unfortunately, the European weather forecast issued shortly before the night of the eclipse called for cloudy skies. I was saddened and disappointed for my friend as she would miss this wonderful experience. I had been fortunate to view another lunar eclipse directly only a couple of years prior to this. So taken was I, as was my daughter, by the lovely spectacle that we named her then new horse, purchased coincidentally the day after, Lunar Eclipse.

In a delightful fluke, though, on the morning after the European eclipse I awakened to a very happy message – my friend described how, at the last minute, the clouds cleared unexpectedly and the eclipse became visible to her in all its full, copper-colored, splendid beauty. I wrote her back excitedly, expressing my delight at this turn of events and coining the spontaneous summary description:

"A clearing revealing an eclipse."[1]

This brief anecdote, and my description of the central event within it, silhouettes very nicely the final point I wish to emphasize in this book.

---

[1] A heartfelt expression of gratitude goes to Carina Rasse for enabling and inspiring this construction.

   In a fashion, this anecdote actually contains a pair of "clearings revealing eclipses." The first was the already described parting of the clouds to reveal the actual eclipse. But a second one occurred earlier – in my first revealing the news about the upcoming eclipse to my friend, only to then have the weather forecast occlude the possibility of seeing it.

Occasionally, wondrous things are revealed to us in the world of science and scholarship, only to themselves be shrouded under full or partial occlusion. Indeed, this is the very challenge, as well as joy, of scientific and scholarly discovery and dissemination – to keep facing and over-coming these occlusions and sharing what we find with other people, but to also find pleasure in this striptease for the mind.

But something special occurs in this respect, when the very thing we study is indeed the thing *doing* that scientific and scholarly discovery and dissemination – the human mind and its use of thought and language to understand and communicate about the world. Under these conditions, it's a little like *paying attention to that man behind the curtain,*[2] but then finding out *you* are the man behind the curtain, standing and looking at an infinity of reflections of yourself as you're sandwiched between facing double mirrors.

This book has presented the idea that language, akin to our human bodies and seemingly many other things in nature, has the structure of a conjoined antonymy. Two primary parts, oppositional in fundamental ways, yet united, working together to achieve some purpose. This pur-pose is also dependent on that conjoined antonymic structure – the purpose could not be accomplished if things were arranged differently.

For language, I've used and can add here a number of metaphors and analogies to capture this structure. One was brick and mortar.[3] Bricks are all about bulk, heft, and strength within themselves. They're not terribly concerned with connection (consider the derogatory labeling of an insen-sitive or oblivious person as being "thick as a brick"). Bricks are also fairly uniform. Mortar, on the other hand, is generally all about connection, adhesion, joinery, and strength *around* itself. It's the glue that holds the bricks together, allowing their separated strengths to join. Mortar also isn't uniform but rather molds to the shape of the bricks it surrounds and interconnects.[4]

Brick and mortar need one another in construction. Brick walls without mortar will eventually shift and topple. Mortar walls without bricks won't have the bulk and internal strength to stand. The two things together,

---

[2] In reference to a key scene in the old classic American film, *The Wizard of Oz* (LeRoy & Freed, 1939).

[3] Other metaphors used were food and recipes, photographic negatives and positives, matter and dark matter, construction materials and blueprints, etc.

[4] By many accounts, the etymology of "mortarboard" to refer to an academic hat worn in ceremonies related to academia is predominantly iconic – the hats physically resemble the square tool used by masons to hold and work with mortar. It is nonetheless an interesting coincidence that "mortar" is used in this context, in vague reference to completedness – cementing the knowledge, meaning, learning, etc., taking place during one's education and predominantly conducted through language.

though, meld their oppositional characteristics to construct solid and long-lasting and long-functioning structures.

I've also re-invoked in a fashion the old "bottom-up" and "top-down" formulation from earlier days in psycholinguistic explanation and theorizing. I did this with a mild trepidation, knowing how thinking has progressed beyond this era, some decades prior, when these terms dominated discussions about how language works. But I think the very general idea of one part of language meaning coming from sources as-sharable-as-possible between people, which can maximize the similarity of different people's experiences when language occurs between them, is probably necessary for language to work. This first part of meaning being anchored in some of our shared baser human neural functions, primarily sensation and action, and possibly emotion, which would be very similar across many or most people, also makes great sense. We generally move and sense things similarly given our shared human bodily structures and functionality. So, these sensory and motor arenas are probably one of our best shots at getting experiences to resonate similarly between people.

But another part of meaning is then necessitated to offset the limitations of this first part. The other meaning ingredient would have to bring different and potentially oppositional goods to bear on language functioning, including a bit of a fudging system to make us feel comfortable with the first meaning resonance system which may in reality function more messily than we realize. Creative accounting, as it were, to balance imperfect books. Luckily not illegal in this case. This other part would also be anchored in baser and different preexisting brain systems (e.g., social motivations and drives, emotions, varieties of kinds of perceptual and cognitive gestalt processes, adaptive forms of cognitive bias, and many others), but would also perhaps overall operate a bit less obviously compared to the scene-stealing sensory and motor embodied simulations.

One could also compare language functioning to the general process of sensation/perception in human vision. If one were to access a neural visual image capturing something seen in the world as that image exits the human retina, it would be barely recognizable as the subjective percept we'd eventually experience were we to naturally see that actual something. The image would be upside down, inverted, full of holes, messy with static, blurs and smudges, occluded with the shadows of blood vessels and neurons from the retina, only partly color coded, etc. But once our visual cortex cleans it up, the image appears as clean and clear as our subjective experience of normally functioning vision taking in any sight. Here, too, we can think of the clunkier but sloppily consistent-between-people sensory input as something like the embodied simulations which resonate between people during language usage. The tidying perceptual work taking place alongside that sensory input is then similar to the stealthier finish work performed by the other-side-of-meaning.

The book also couched this treatment of language-as-conjoined-antonymy amid a broader consideration of this dichotomous structure in nature. We can readily see many other instances, or at least appearances, of conjoined antonymies in the world around us. Animal bodies are essentially bilaterally symmetrical. Space and time seem to have this arrangement, as does sexual reproduction. We conceive an infinity of concepts which seem also to involve oppositional pairs (life–death, heaven–hell, good–evil, love–hate, male–female, hot–cold, right–wrong, happy–sad, inside–outside, etc.). We find aesthetic appeal in many things if they're symmetrical (Jacobsen & Hofel, 2003; Kersteen-Tucker, 1991; Pashler, 1990; Wenderoth, 1994).

The book also grappled with the dual possibilities that the world really is a deeply reaching continuance of nested conjoined antonymies versus the world only *appearing* to have this structure due to our projecting the structure upon it. Perhaps the latter possibility is just a happenstance of biology on Earth creating our bilaterally symmetrical bodies and brains and then our needing to use those bodies and brains to make sense of the world. One might also note how my very framing of the question about these possibilities itself demonstrates the issue – is it *either* this *or* that?

No firm conclusion was reached on this broader nature of conjoined antonymies in the world – i.e., the world is constructed of them versus one clever species on one planet, a species which happens to have a bilaterally symmetrical body and brain, just sees/conceives of the world that way. Other imaginable species with different bodies (e.g., asymmetrical ones, undivided ones, or bodies divided into analogous thirds, quarters, sixths) might conceive of things quite differently (and perhaps communicate accordingly).[5] And one could, of course, apply this same reasoning to viewing language as a conjoined antonymy – i.e., it is structured that way objectively versus we have the capacity and tendency of conceptualizing it that way, so it just looks that way to us.

But I feel some utility is nonetheless gained by considering language under this framework. Much advancement took place when conceptual metaphors and then later embodied simulations opened up our thinking about language, thought, embodiment, and related matters. Considering the potential for a connection between the gross physical structure of our bodies and brains, and the functional nature of our unique and

[5] The 2016 film *Arrival* (Cohen, Heisserer, Lunder, Metzger, Popelka, Wlodkowski & Villeneuve, 2016) imagined just such a possibility and conveyed it with a respectful treatment of linguistics as well, plus providing a heart-vise recognizeable to any fellow parent of an ill child.

predominant ability, language, an ability which put us squarely into our modern built worlds, and in a very short amount of time evolutionarily, seems a natural extension of these ideas and might be similarly illuminative.

Indeed, it might expand our ability to see things as structured differently than as conjoined antonymies – perhaps as complex aligned wholes. It could very well be, for instance, that we *do* have the tendency to project the conjoined antonymic structure onto things in the world, due to our bodies and minds, and our language, being structured this way. But projection aside, it could also be that the world just *is* structured this way.

We might see it that way, *and* it might be that way.

A clearing revealing an eclipse.

Nature and Art

Material and workmanship. There is no beauty unadorned and no excellence that would not become barbaric if it were not supported by artifice: This remedies the evil and improves the good. Nature scarcely ever gives us the very best; for that we must have recourse to art. Without this the best of natural dispositions is uncultured, and half is lacking to any excellence if training is absent. Every one has something unpolished without artificial training, and every kind of excellence needs some polish.

—Baltasar Gracian, *The Art of Worldly Wisdom*, xii (2005)

Have the Gift of Discovery

It is a proof of the highest genius, yet when was genius without a touch of madness? If discovery be a gift of genius, choice of means is a mark of sound sense. Discovery comes by special grace and very seldom. For many can follow up a thing when found, but to find it first is the gift of the few, and those the first in excellence and in age. Novelty flatters, and if successful gives the possessor double credit. In matters of judgment novelties are dangerous because leading to paradox, in matters of genius they deserve all praise. Yet both equally deserve applause if successful.

—Baltasar Gracian, *The Art of Worldly Wisdom*, cclxxxiii (2005)

Silken Words, Sugared Manners

Arrows pierce the body, insults the soul. Sweet pastry perfumes the breath. It is a great art in life to know how to sell wind. Most things are paid for in words, and by them you can remove impossibilities. Thus we deal in air, and a royal breath can produce courage and power. Always have your mouth full of sugar to sweeten your words, so that even your ill-wishers enjoy them. To please one must be peaceful.

—Baltasar Gracian, *The Art of Worldly Wisdom*, cclxvii (2005)

References

Ames, R. T. (2002). "Yin and Yang." In A. S. Cua, ed., *Encyclopedia of Chinese Philosophy*. London: 847.

Amit, E., Algom, D., and Trope, Y. (2009). "Distance-Dependent Processing of Pictures and Words." *Journal of Experimental Psychology: General* 138(3): 400–415.

Anderson, C., Kraus, M. W., Galinsky, A. D., and Keltner, D. (2012). "The Local-Ladder Effect: Social Status and Subjective Well-Being." *Psychological Science* 23(7): 764–771.

Arbib, M. A., and Rizzolatti, G. (1999). "Neural Expectations: A Possible Evolutionary Path from Manual Skills to Language." In P. Van Loocke, ed., *The Nature of Concepts: Evolution, Structure and Representation*. Florence, KY: 128–154.

Attardo, S. (2005). "Review of Metonymy and Pragmatic Inferencing." *Pragmatics and Cognition* 13(2): 434–438.

Attardo, S. (2009). "Review of Sarcasm and Other Mixed Messages: The Ambiguous Ways People Use Language." *Humor: International Journal of Humor Research* 22(4): 472–474.

Attardo, S., Hempelmann, C. F., and Di Maio, S. (2002). "Script Oppositions and Logical Mechanisms: Modeling Incongruities and Their Resolutions." *Humor: International Journal of Humor Research* 15(1): 3–46.

Austin, J. L. (1961). "The Meaning of a Word." In J. O. Urmson and G. J. Warnock, eds., *Philosophical Papers of J. L. Austin*. Oxford: 23–43.

Aziz-Aadeh, L. (2013). "Embodied Semantics for Language Related to Actions: A Review of fMRI and Neuropsychological Research." In Y. Coello and A. Bartolo, eds., *Language and Action in Cognitive Neuroscience*. New York: 278–283.

Bar-Anan, Y., Liberman, N., and Trope, Y. (2006). "The Association between Psychological Distance and Construal Level: Evidence from an Implicit Association Test." *Journal of Experimental Psychology: General* 135(4): 609–622.

Barnhart, C. L. (1972). *The World Book Dictionary*. Chicago.

Barr, D. J., and Keysar, B. (2002). "Anchoring Comprehension in Linguistic Precedents." *Journal of Memory and Language* 46(2): 391–418.

Barr, D. J., and Keysar, B. (2005). "Making Sense of How We Make Sense: The Paradox of Egocentrism in Language Use." In H. L. Colston and A. N. Katz, eds., *Figurative Language Comprehension: Social and Cultural Influences.* Mahwah, NJ: 21–42.

Barsalou, L. W. (2010). "Grounded Cognition: Past, Present, and Future." *Topics in Cognitive Science* 2(4): 716–724.

Barsalou, L. W. (2016). "On Staying Grounded and Avoiding Quixotic Dead Ends." *Psychonomic Bulletin and Review* 23(4): 1122–1142.

Baynham, M. (1996). "Humor as an Interpersonal Resource in Adult Numeracy Classes." *Language and Education* 10(2–3): 187–200.

Beck, S. D., and Weber, A. (2016). "Bilinguial and Monolingual Idiom Processing Is Cut from the Same Cloth: The Role of the L1 in Literal and Figurative Meaning Activation." *Frontiers in Psychology* 7, ArtID 1350.

Bell, N. (2012). "Formulaic Language, Creativity, and Language Play in a Second Language." *Annual Review of Applied Linguistics* 32: 189–205.

Bell, N. (2015). *We Are Not Amused: Failed Humor in Interaction.* Berlin.

Bell, N. (2017). *Multiple Perspectives on Language Play.* Berlin.

Berenson, T. (2016). "Here Are Trump and Rubio's Best Schoolyard Insults." *Time Magazine*, March 1, 2016 (http://time.com/4242827/donald-trump-marco-rubio-insults. Accessed January 19, 2019).

Bergen, B. K. (2012). *Louder than Words: The New Science of How the Mind Makes Meaning.* New York.

Berra, Y. (1998). *The Yogi Book: I Really Didn't Say Everything I Said.* New York.

Bianculli, D. (2017). "50 Years Later, The Biting Satire of 'The Smothers Brothers' Still Resonates." Broadcast on NPR, Fresh Air (https://n.pr/2GisVd E. Accessed April 15, 2019).

Blankenship, K. L., and Craig, T. Y. (2005). "The Role of Different Markers of Linguistic Powerlessness in Persuasion." *Journal of Language and Social Psychology* 24(1): 3–24.

Bloomfield, L. (1933). *Language.* New York.

Bolinger, D. (1950). "Rime, Assonance, and Morpheme Analysis." *Word* 6: 117–136.

Boroditsky, L. (2000). "Metaphoric Structuring: Understanding Time through Spatial Metaphors." *Cognition* 75: 1–27.

Boroditsky, L., and Ramscar, M. (2002). "The Roles of Body and Mind in Abstract Thoughts." *Psychological Science* 13(2): 185–189.

Boulenger, V., Hauk, O., and Pulvemuller, F. (2009). "Grasping Ideas with the Motor System: Semantic Somatotopy in Idiom Comprehension." *Cerebral Cortex* 19(8): 1905–1914.

Boulenger, V., Shtyrov, Y., and Pulvermüller, F. (2012). "When Do You Grasp the Idea? MEG Evidence for Instantaneous Idiom Understanding." *NeuroImage* 59: 3502–3513.

Bowdle, B., and Gentner, D. (2005). "The Career of Metaphor." *Psychological Review* 11: 193–216.

Brone, G., Feyaerts, K., and Veale, T. (2006). "Introduction: Cognitive Linguistic Approaches to Humor." *Humor: International Journal of Humor Research* 19(3): 203–228.

Bronte, C. (1847a). *Jane Eyre.* London.

Bronte, E. (1847b). *Wuthering Heights.* London.

Brooks, M. (director) (1974). Young Frankenstein. Motion picture. Twentieth Century Fox.

Brown, G. S. (29 December, 2018). "4 Can't-Miss Trips for 2019." ABC News: https://abcnews.go.com/GMA/Travel/miss-trips-2019/story?id=59929657. Accessed April 15, 2019.

Brown, P., and Levinson, S. (1987). Politeness: Some Universals in Language. Cambridge, UK.

Brown, R. (1958). Words and Things. New York.

Brown, R. M. (1973). Rubyfruit Jungle. New York.

Brown, R. W., Black, A. H., and Horowitz, A. E. (1955). "Phonetic Symbolism in Natural Languages." The Journal of Abnormal and Social Psychology 50(3): 388.

Bryant, B. (1960). "Love Hurts." Song, recorded by the Everly Brothers.

Burgers, C. F., van Mulken, M. J. P., and Schellens, P. J. (2013). "On Irony, Images and Creativity: A Corpus-Analytic Approach." In T. Veale, K. Feyaerts, and C. J. Forceville, eds., Creativity and the Agile Mind: A Multidisciplinary Approach to a Multifaceted Phenomenon. Berlin: 293–311.

Burgers, C., Konijn, E. A., and Steen, G. J. (2016). "Figurative Framing: Shaping Public Discourse through Metaphor, Hyperbole and Irony." Communication Theory 26(4): 410–430.

Burghardt, G. M. (2006). The Genesis of Animal Play: Testing the Limits. Cambridge, MA.

Burns, Z. C., Caruso, E. M., and Bartels, D. M. (2012). "Predicting Premeditation: Future Behavior Is Seen as More Intentional than Past Behavior." Journal of Experimental Psychology: General 141(2): 227–232.

Cacciari, C., Bolognini, N., Senna, I., Pellicciari, M. C., and Papagno, C. (2011). "Literal, Fictive and Metaphorical Motion Sentences Preserve the Motion Component of the Verb: A TMS Study." Brain and Language 119(3): 149–157.

Cain, K., and Towse, A. S. (2008). "To Get Hold of the Wrong End of the Stick: Reasons for Poor Idiom Understanding in Children with Reading Comprehension Difficulties." Journal of Speech, Language and Hearing Research 51(6): 1538–1549.

Cain, K., Towse, A. S., and Knight, R. S. (2009). "The Development of Idiom Comprehension: An Investigation of Semantic and Contextual Processing Skills." Journal of Experimental Child Psychology 102(3): 280–298.

Cameron, D. (2001). Working with Spoken Discourse. London: SAGE Publications.

Cameron, L. (2003). Metaphor in Educational Discourse. New York: Continuum.

Cardillo, E. R., Schmidt, G. L., Kranjec, A., and Chatterjee, A. (2010). "Stimulus Design Is an Obstacle Course: 560 Matched Literal and Metaphorical Sentences for Testing Neural Hypotheses about Metaphor." Behavior Research Methods 42: 651–664.

Cardillo, E. R., Watson, C. E., Schmidt, G. L., Kranjec, A., and Chatterjee, A. (2013). "From Novel to Familiar: Tuning the Brain for Metaphors." NeuroImage 59: 3212–3221.

Caruso, E. M., and Shafir, E. (2006). "Now That I Think about It, I'm in the Mood for Laughs: Decisions Focused on Mood." Journal of Behavioral Decision Making 19(2): 155–169.

Caruso, E. M., Gilbert, D. T., and Wilson, T. D. (2008). "A Wrinkle in Time: Asymmetric Valuation of Past and Future Events." *Psychological Science* 19(8): 796–801.

Caruso, E. M., Waytz, A., and Epley, N. (2010). "The Intentional Mind and the Hot Hand: Perceiving Intentions Makes Streaks Seem Likely to Continue." *Cognition* 116(1): 149–153.

Casasanto, D., and Dijkstra, K. (2010). "Motor Action and Emotional Memory." *Cognition* 115: 179–185.

Casey, P., Lownes, V., and Gil, D. (producers), and MacNaughton, I. (director) (1971). And Now for Something Completely Different. Motion picture. Columbia Pictures.

Chapman, G., Cleese, J., Gilliam, T., Idle, E., Innes, N., Jones, T., and Palin, M. (writers), and MacNaughton, I. (director) (1974). "The Light Entertainment War." TV series episode. In I. MacNaughton (producer), Monty Python's Flying Circus, BBC.

Chatterjee, A. (2008). "The Neural Organization of Spatial Thought and Language." *Seminars in Speech and Language* 29: 226–238.

Chatterjee, A. (2010). "Disembodying Cognition." *Language and Cognition* 2: 79–116.

Chen, E., Widick, P., and Chatterjee, A. (2008). "Functional–Anatomical Organization of Predicate Metaphor Processing." *Brain and Language* 107: 194–202.

Chevalier, T. (1999). *Girl with a Pearl Earring*. New York: Harper Collins.

Chopra, D., ed. (1998). *The Love Poems of Rumi*. New York: Harmony Books.

Cienki, A. (2016). "Cognitive Linguistics, Gesture Studies, and Multimodal Communication." *Cognitive Linguistics* 27(4): 603–618.

Cienki, A., and Muller, C. (2008b). "Metaphor, Gesture, and Thought." In R. W. Gibbs, ed., *The Cambridge Handbook of Metaphor and Thought*. New York: Cambridge University Press (pp. 483–501).

Cienki, A., and Muller, C., eds. (2008a). *Metaphor and Gesture*. Amsterdam: Benjamins.

Citron, F. M. M., and Goldberg, A. E. (2014). "Metaphorical Sentences are More Emotionally Engaging than Their Literal Counterparts." *Journal of Cognitive Neuroscience* 26: 2585–2595.

Clark, H. H. (1996). *Using Language*. Cambridge: Cambridge University Press.

Clark, H. H., and Schaefer, E. F. (1987). "Collaborating on Contributions to Conversations." *Language and Cognitive Processes* 2(1): 19–41.

Clayton, E. (2008). Aesop, Aristotle, and Animals: The Role of Fables in Human Life. *Humanitas* 21(1 and 2): 179–200.

Cline, A. (December 7, 2018). "Top George Carlin quotes on religion." Retrieved from: www.thoughtco.com/top-george-carlin-quotes-on-religion-4072040.

Cohen, D., Heisserer, E., Lunder, K., Metzger, T., Popelka, M., and Wlodkowski, S. (executive producers) and Villeneuve, D. (director) (2016). *Arrival*. Motion picture. Lava Bear Films.

Cokely, E. T., and Feltz, A. (2009). "Individual Differences, Judgment Biases, and Theory-of-Mind: Deconstructing the Intentional Action Side Effect Asymmetry." *Journal of Research in Personality* 43(1): 18–24.

Colston, H. L. (1997). "Salting a Wound or Sugaring a Pill: The Pragmatic Functions of Ironic Criticism." *Discourse Processes* 23(1): 25–45.

Colston, H. L. (2000a). "Dewey Defeats Truman: Interpreting Ironic Restatement." *Journal of Language and Social Psychology* 19(1): 46–65.

Colston, H. L. (2000b). "On Necessary Conditions for Verbal Irony Comprehension." *Pragmatics and Cognition* 8(2): 277–324.

Colston, H. L. (2002). "Contrast and Assimilation in Verbal Irony." *Journal of Pragmatics, 34*, 111–142.

Colston, H. L. (2015). *Using Figurative Language*. Cambridge, UK: Cambridge University Press.

Colston, H. L. (2017a, April). *Embodied simulations and verbal irony*. The Third International Symposium on Figurative Thought and Language, Osijek, Croatia.

Colston, H. L. (2017b). "Irony Performance and Perception: What Underlies Verbal, Situational and Other Ironies?" In A. Athanasiadou and H. Colston, eds., *Irony in Language Use and Communication*. Series: Figurative *Thought* and *Language*, vol. 1 (pp. 19–42). Amsterdam: Benjamins.

Colston, H. L. (2017c, October). "What Do Children Know and When Do They Know It?: Figurative Thought and Language in Development/Acquisition." Paper, Acquiring Figurative Meanings: International Linguistics Conference. Oslo, Norway.

Colston, H. L. (2018a, June). "Embodied Meaning in Embedded Metaphor: Variable Pragmatic Effects of Metaphorical and Non-Metaphorical Proverbs." Paper, Researching and Applying Metaphor 12 (RaAM-12). Hong Kong, China.

Colston, H. L. (2018b). "Irony as Indirectness Cross-Linguistically: On the Scope of Generic Mechanisms." In A. Capone, ed., *Indirect Reports and Pragmatics in the World Languages: Perspectives in Pragmatics, Philosophy and Psychology, vol. 19* (pp. 109–131). Switzerland: Springer.

Colston, H. L. (2018c, September). "Why There's a There There In, 'There's a Metaphor: Tragically Hip and Hockey Metaphors in Canadian English." Paper, Metaphor in Englishes Around the World, Third International Workshop, Klagenfurt, Austria.

Colston, H. L. (in press). "Figurative Language Development/Acquisition Research: Status and Ways Forward." *Journal of Pragmatics*.

Colston, H. L., and Brooks, E. N. (2008, May). "Pragmatic Effects of Metonymy." Poster session presented at the meeting of the Association for Psychological Science. Chicago, IL.

Colston, H. L., and Jindrich, P. L. (2000, June). "'Been There, Done That': Comprehending Asyndeton." Poster session presented at the meeting of the American Psychological Society. Miami, FL.

Colston, H. L., and A. N. Katz, eds. (2005). *Figurative Language Comprehension: Social and Cultural Influences*. Mahwah, NJ

Colston, H. L., and Keller, S. B. (1998). "You'll Never Believe This: Irony and Hyperbole in Expressing Surprise." *Journal of Psycholinguistic Research* 27(4): 499–513.

Colston, H. L., and Kinney, E. (2015, July). "Producing Figurative Pragmatic Effects: Endings Justifying Meanings." Paper, Thirteenth International Cognitive Linguistics Conference. Newcastle, UK.

Colston, H. L., and Kodet, A. (2008, April). "Embodiment in Word Meanings." Poster session presented at the meeting of the Midwestern Psychological Association. Chicago, IL.

Colston, H. L., and O'Brien, J. (2000a). "Contrast and Pragmatics in Figurative Language: Anything Understatement Can Do, Irony Can Do Better." *Journal of Pragmatics* 32(11): 1557–1583.

Colston, H. L., and O'Brien, J. (2000b). "Contrast of Kind Versus Contrast of Magnitude: The Pragmatic Accomplishments of Irony and Hyperbole." *Discourse Processes* 30(2): 179–199.

Colston, H., Sims, M., Pumphrey, M., Kinney, E., Evangelista, X., Vandermolen-Pater, N., Feeny, G. (in press). "Embodied Simulations and Verbal Irony Comprehension." In M. Brdar and R. Brdar-Szabo, eds. *Figurative Thought and Language in Action*. Amsterdam: Benjamins.

Conrad, J. (1899). *Heart of Darkness*. London: Blackwood's Magazine.

Culicover, P. A., and Nowak, A. (2002). "Markedness, Antisymmetry and the Complexity of Constructions." *Language Variation Yearbook* 2: 5–30.

Culicover, P. A., and Winkler, S. (2008). "English Focus Inversion." *Journal of Linguistics* 44(3): 625–658.

Culicover, P. W., and Jackendoff, R. (1999). "The View from the Periphery: The English Comparative Correlative." *Linguist Inquiry, 30*, 543–571.

Danesi, M. (2009). "Opposition Theory and the Interconnectedness of Language, Culture, and Cognition." *Sign Systems Studies, 37(1/2)*, 11–42.

Davis, R. (1961). "The Fitness of Names to Drawings: A Cross-Cultural Study in Tanganyika." *British Journal of Psychology, 52*, 259–268.

DePatie, D. H. (producer), and Jones, C., and Noble, M. (directors). (1963). *Transylvania 65000*. Motion picture. Warner Brothers.

Desai, R. H., Conant, L. L., Binder, J. R., Park, H., and Seidenberg, M. S. (2013). "A Piece of the Action: Modulation of Sensory-Motor Regions by Action Idioms and Metaphors." *NeuroImage, 83*, 862–869.

Desai, R., Binder, J., and Conant, L. (2011). "The Neural Career of Sensory-Motor Metaphors." *Journal of Cognitive Neuroscience, 23*, 2376–2386.

Dickens, C. (1859). *A Tale of Two Cities*. London: Chapman and Hill.

Doerr, A. (2014). *All the Light We Cannot See*. New York: Scribner.

Dove, G. O. (2009). "Beyond perceptual symbols: A call for representational pluralism." *Cognition, 110*, 412–431.

Dress, M. L., Kreuz, R. J., Link, K. E., and Caucci, G. M. (2008). "Regional variation in the use of sarcasm." *Journal of Language and Social Psychology, 27 (1)*, 71–85.

Dunbar, N. E., Banas, J. A., Rodriguez, D., Liu, S-J., and Abra, G. (2012). "Humor Use in Power-Differentiated Interactions." *Humor: International Journal of Humor Research, 25(4)*, 469–489.

Dunbar, R. (1996). *Grooming, Gossip, and the Evolution of Language*. Boston: Harvard University Press.

Eggers, D. (2012). *A Hologram for the King*. New York: Penguin Random House.

Enfield, N. J., and Stivers, T. (2007). *Person Reference in Interaction: Linguistic, Cultural and Social Perspectives*. Cambridge: Cambridge University Press.

Epley, N., Caruso, E., and Bazerman, M. H. (2006). "When Perspective Taking Increases Taking: Reactive Egoism in Social Interaction." *Journal of Personality and Social Psychology*, *91*(5), 872–889.

Epley, N., Keysar, B., Van Boven, L., and Gilovich, T. (2004). "Perspective Taking as Egocentric Anchoring and Adjustment." *Journal of Personality and Social Psychology*, *87(3)*, 327–339.

Escandell-Vidal, V., and Leonetti, M. (2014). "Fronting and Irony in Spanish." In A. Dufter, A. S. O. Toledo, eds., *Left Sentence Peripheries in Spanish: Diachronic, Variationist and Comparative Perspectives* (pp. 309–342). Amsterdam: Benjamins.

Escher, M. C. (2001). *M. C. Escher: The Graphic Work*. Cologne: Taschen.

Eskildsen, S. W. (2017). "The Emergence of Creativity in L2 English: A Usage-Based Case-Study." In N. Bell, ed., *Multiple Perspectives on Language Play* (pp. 281–316). Berlin: de Gruyter Mouton.

Fausey, C. M., and Boroditsky, L. (2010). "Subtle Linguistic Cues Influence Perceived Blame and Financial Liability." *Psychonomic Bulletin and Review*, *17* (5), 644–650.

Fausey, C. M., and Matlock, T. (2011). "Can Grammar Win Elections?" *Political Psychology*, *32*(4), 563–574.

Feingold, A., and Mazzella, R. (1991). "Psychometric Intelligence and Verbal Humor Ability." *Personality and Individual Differences*, *12(5)*, 427–435.

Fernardino, L., Contant, L. L., Binder, J. R., Blindauer, K., Hiner, B., Spangler, K., and Desai, R. H. (2013). "Where Is the Action? Action Sentence Processing in Parkinson's Disease." *Neuropsychologia*, *51*, 1510–1517.

Firth, A. (1996). "The Discursive Accomplishment of Normality: On "Lingua Franca" English and Conversation Analysis." *Journal of Pragmatics*, *26*(2), 237–259.

Fischer, M. H., and Zwaan, R. A. (2008). "Embodied Language: A Review of the Role of the Motor System in Language Comprehension." *Quarterly Journal of Experimental Psychology*, *61*, 825–850.

Forceville, C. J. and Urios-Aparisi, E., eds. (2009). *Multimodal Metaphor*. Berlin: Mouton de Gruyter.

Forster, E. M. (1971). *Maurice*. London: Edward Arnold.

Foster, S. (1848). *Oh! Susanna*. Song, recorded by The Singing Dogs.

Fowler, H. W., and Fowler, F. G. (1905). *The Works of Lucian of Samosata*. Oxford, UK: The Clarendon Press.

Fraley, B., and Aron, A. (2004). "The Effect of a Shared Humorous Experience on Closeness in Initial Encounters." *Personal Relationships*, *11(1)*, 61–78.

Franzen, J. (2010). *Freedom*. New York: Farrar, Straus and Giroux.

Gallese, V., and Lakoff, G. (2005). "The Brain's Concepts: The Role of the Sensory–Motor System in Conceptual Knowledge." *Cognitive Neuropsychology*, *22*, 455–479.

García Márquez, G. (1985). *Love in the Time of Cholera*. New York: Alfred A. Knopf.

Geffen, A. (producer), and Davis, M., Sommerfield, A, and McGown (directors) (2015). *Great Barrier Reef with David Attenborough*. Documentary, BBC.

Gibbs, R. W. (1981a). "Memory for Requests in Conversation." *Journal of Verbal Learning and Verbal Behavior, 20*(6), 630–640.

Gibbs, R. W. (1981b). "Your Wish is My Command: Convention and Context in Interpreting Indirect Requests." *Journal of Verbal Learning and Verbal Behavior, 20*(4), 431–444.

Gibbs, R. W. (1983). "Do People Always Process the Literal Meanings of Indirect Requests?" *Journal of Experimental Psychology: Learning, Memory, and Cognition, 9*(3), 524.

Gibbs, R. W. (1986). "On the Psycholinguistics of Sarcasm." *Journal of Experimental Psychology: General, 115(1)*, 3–15.

Gibbs, R. W. (1994). *The Poetics of Mind: Figurative Thought, Language, and Understanding*. Cambridge: Cambridge University Press.

Gibbs, R. W. (2000). "Irony in Talk among Friends." *Metaphor and Symbol, 15* (1–2), 5–27.

Gibbs, R. W. (2005). *Embodiment and Cognitive Science*. Cambridge, UK: Cambridge University Press.

Gibbs, R. W. (2006). "Metaphor Interpretation as Embodied Simulation." *Mind and Language, 21*, 434–458.

Gibbs, R. W. (2017). *Metaphor Wars: Conceptual Metaphors in Human Life*. New York: Cambridge University Press.

Gibbs, R. W., and Colston, H. L. (2007). *Irony in Language and Thought: A Cognitive Science Reader*. New York, NY: Taylor and Francis.

Gibbs, R. W., and Colston, H. L. (2012). *Interpreting Figurative Meaning*. Cambridge, UK: Cambridge University Press.

Gibbs, R. W., and McCarrell, N. S. (1990). "Why Boys Will Be Boys and Girls Will Be Girls: Understanding Colloquial Tautologies." *Journal of Psycholinguistic Research, 19*(2), 125–145.

Gibbs, R. W., and Mueller, R. A. G. (1988). "Conversational Sequences and Preference for Indirect Speech Acts." *Discourse Processes, 11(1)*, 101–116.

Gibbs, R. W., and O'Brien, J. (1991). "Psychological Aspects of Irony Understanding." *Journal of Pragmatics, 16*(6), 523–530.

Gibbs, R. W., Costa Lima, P. L., and Francozo, E. (2004). "Metaphor is Grounded in Embodied Experience." *Journal of Pragmatics, 36*, 1189–1210.

Gibbs, R., and Samermit, P. (2017). "How Does Irony Arise in Experience?" In A. Athanasiadou and H. L. Colston, eds., *Irony in Language Use and Communication* (pp. 43–60). Amsterdam: Benjamins.

Gilligan, V. (writer) and MacLaren, M. (director). (2012). "Gliding over all." Television series episode. In M. Bernstein (producer), Breaking Bad. New York: AMC.

Gilligan, V., Gould, P., Hutchinson, G., and Marion, H. (writers) and Gilligan, V. (director). (2018). "Wiedersehen." Television series episode. In M. Bernstein (producer), Better Call Saul. New York: AMC.

Giora, R. (1991). "On the Cognitive Aspects of the Joke." *Journal of Pragmatics, 16(5)*, 465–485.

Giora, R., Drucker, A., Fein, O., and Mendelson, I. (2015). "Default Sarcastic Interpretations: On the Priority of Nonsalient Interpretations." *Discourse Processes, 52(3)*, 173–200.

Giora, R., Fein, O., Ganzi, J., Levi, N. A., and Sabah, H. (2005). "On Negation as Mitigation: The Case of Negative Irony." *Discourse Processes*, *39*(1), 81–100.

Giora, R., Givoni, S., and Fein, O. (2015). "Defaultness Reigns: The Case of Sarcasm." *Metaphor and Symbol*, *30(4)*, 290–313.

Glenberg, A. M. (2010). "Embodiment as a Unifying Perspective for Psychology." *Wiley Interdisciplinary Reviews: Cognitive Science*, *1*, 586–596.

Glenberg, A. M., and Gallese, V. (2012). "Action-Based Language: A Theory of Language Acquisition, Comprehension, and Production." *Cortex*, *48(7)*, 905–922.

Glenberg, A. M., and Kaschak, M. P. (2002). "Grounding Language in Action." *Psychonomic Bulletin and Review*, *9*(3), 558–565.

Goatly, A. (1997). *The Language of Metaphors*. London, UK: Routledge.

Goldberg, A. E. (1995). *Constructions: A Construction Grammar Approach to Argument Structure*. University of Chicago Press.

Goldberg, A. E. (2003). "Constructions: A New Theoretical Approach to Language." *Trends in Cognitive Sciences*, *7(5)*, 219–224.

Golden, A. (1997). *Memoirs of a Geisha*. New York: Alfred A. Knopf.

Gracian, B. (2005). *The Art of Worldly Wisdom* (translated by J. Jacobs). New York: Dover Publications.

Gruskoff, M. (producer), and Brooks, M. (director). (1974). Young Frankenstein. Motion picture. Los Angeles: Twentieth Century-Fox.

Guardian News and Media Ltd. (2008). *Great Speeches of the Twentieth Century*. London: Cornerstone.

Hakemulder, F., Kuijpers, M. M., Tan, E. S., Balint, K., and Doicaru, M. M., eds. (2017). *Narrative Absorption, Vol. 27: Linguistic Approaches to Literature*. Amsterdam: Benjamins.

Hamilton, J. (2006). *When Madeline was Young*. New York: Doubleday.

Hann, D. (2017). "Building Rapport and a Sense of Communal Identity through Play in a Second Language Classroom." In N. Bell, ed., *Multiple Perspectives on Language Play* (pp. 219–244). Berlin: de Gruyter Mouton.

Hanne, M., and Hawken, S. J. (2007). "Metaphors for Illness in Contemporary Media." *Medical Humanities*, *33*, 93–99.

Hao, Y., and Veale, T. (2009). "Support structures for linguistic creativity: A computational analysis of creative irony in similes." Proceedings of the 31st Annual Meeting of the Cognitive Science Society. Retrieved from: www.cognitivesciencesociety.org/cogsci-archival-conference-information.

Hao, Y., and Veale, T. (2010). "An Ironic Fist in a Velvet Glove: Creative Mis-representation in the Construction of Ironic Similes." *Minds and Machines: Journal for Artificial Intelligence, Philosophy and Cognitive Science*, *20(4)*, 635–650.

Harris, R. A. (2013). *A Handbook of Rhetorical Devices*. Virtual Salt.

Haugh, M. (2017). "Jocular Language Play, Social Action and (Dis)Affiliation in Conversational Interaction." In N. Bell, ed., *Multiple Perspectives on Language Play* (pp. 143–168). Berlin: de Gruyter Mouton.

Hauk, O., and Pulvemuller, F. (2004). "Neurophysiological Distinction of Action Words in the Fronto-Central Cortex." *Human Brain Mapping*, *21(3)*, 191–201.

Hawking, S. (1988). *A Brief History of Time*. New York: Bantam Books.

Hawthorne, N. (1850). *The Scarlet Letter*. Boston: Ticknor and Fields.

Helzer, E. G., Connor-Smith, J. K., and Reed, M. A. (2009). "Traits, States, and Attentional Gates: Temperament and Threat Relevance as Predictors of Attentional Bias to Social Threat." *Anxiety, Stress and Coping, 22*(1), 57–76.

Heritage, S. (October 11, 2018). "'S'all good, man': How *Better Call Saul* became superior to *Breaking Bad*." *The Guardian*, Culture Section.

Holland, M. K., and Wertheimer, M. (1964). "Some Physiognomic Aspects of Naming, or, *Maluma* and *Takete* Revisited." *Perceptual and Motor Skills, 19*, 111–117.

Holmes, J. (2000). "Politeness, Power and Provocation: How Humor Functions in the Workplace." *Discourse Studies, 2*(2), 159–185.

Holmes, J., and Marra, M. (2002). "Having a Laugh at Work: How Humor Contributes to Workplace Culture." *Journal of Pragmatics, 34(12)*, 1683–710.

Holt, E. (2017). "'This System's So Slow': Negotiating Sequences of Laughter and Laughables in Call-Center Interaction." In N. Bell, ed., *Multiple Perspectives on Language Play* (pp. 93–118). Berlin: de Gruyter Mouton.

Honeck, R. P. (1997). *A Proverb in Mind: The Cognitive Science of Proverbial Wit and Wisdom*. Mahwah, NJ: Erlbaum.

Horton, W. S., and Keysar, B. (1996). "When Do Speakers Take into Account Common Ground?" *Cognition, 59*(1), 91–117.

Hosinger, E. (2013). "Representing Idioms: Syntactic and Contextual Effects on Idiom Processing." *Language and Speech, 56(3)*, 373–394.

Houston, K. (2013). *Shady Characters: The Secret Life of Punctuation, Symbols and Other Typographical Marks*. New York and London: W. W. Norton and Company.

Hugo, V. (1831). *The Hunchback of Notre Dame*. New York: Alfred A. Knopf.

Huth, T. (2017). "Playing with Turns, Playing with Action? A Social-Interactionist Perspective." In N. Bell, ed., *Multiple Perspectives on Language Play* (pp. 47–72). Berlin: de Gruyter Mouton.

Idema, W. L. (2009). *The White Snake and Her Son: A Translation of the Previous Scroll of Thunder Peak with Related Texts*. Indianapolis, IN: Hackett Publishing.

Idema, W. L. (2012). "Old Tales for New Times: Some Comments on the Cultural Translation of China's Four Great Folktales in the Twentieth Century." *Taiwan Journal of East Asian Studies, 9(1)*, 25–46.

Jackendoff, R. (1999). "Possible Stages in the Evolution of the Language Capacity." *Trends in Cognitive Sciences, 3(7)*, 272–279.

Jacobsen, T., and Hofel, L. (2003). "Descriptive and Evaluative Judgment Processes: Behavioral and Electrophysiological Indices of Processing Symmetry and Aesthetics." *Cognitive, Affective, and Behavioral Neuroscience, 3 (4)*, 289–299.

James, L., and Pinker, S. (2010). "Rationales for Indirect Speech: The Theory of the Strategic Speaker." *Psychological Review, 117(3)*, 785–807.

Jamrozik, A., McQuire, M., Cardillo, E. R., and Chatterjee, A. (2016). "Metaphor: Bridging Embodiment to Abstraction." *Psychonomic Bulletin and Review, 23(4)*, 1080–1089.

Jones, H. (1985). "No One is to Blame." Song, recorded by H. Jones.

Jones, S. (2002). *Antonymy: A Corpus-Based Perspective*. New York: Routledge.

Kable, J. W., Kan, I. P., Wilson, A., Thompson-Schill, S. L., and Chatterjee, A. (2005). "Conceptual Representations of Action in the Lateral Temporal Cortex." *Journal of Cognitive Neuroscience, 17*, 1855–1870.

Kable, J. W., Lease-Spellmeyer, J., and Chatterjee, A. (2002). "Neural Substrates of Action Event Knowledge." *Journal of Cognitive Neuroscience, 14*, 795–805.

Kasser, T., and Ryan, R. M. (1993). "A Dark Side of the American Dream: Correlates of Financial Success as a Central Life Aspiration." *Journal of Personality and Social Psychology, 65*(2), 410.

Katz, A. (2017). "The Standard Experimental Approach to the Study of Irony: Let Us Not Be Hasty in Throwing out the Baby with the Bathwater." In A. Athanasiadou and H. L. Colston, eds., *Irony in Language Use and Communication* (pp. 237–254). Amsterdam: Benjamins.

Katz, S. (1992). "Mystical Speech and Mystical Meaning." In S. T. Katz, ed., *Mysticism and Language* (pp. 3–41). New York: Oxford University Press.

Kecskes, I. (2007). "Formulaic Language in English Lingua Franca." In I. Kecskes and L. R. Horn, eds., *Explorations in Pragmatics: Linguistic, Cognitive and Intercultural Aspects* (pp. 191–218). Berlin: Mouton de Gruyter.

Kecskes, I., and L. Horn, eds. (2007). *Explorations in Pragmatics: Linguistic, Cognitive and Intercultural Aspects*. Berlin: de Gruyter Mouton.

Kecskes, I., and Mey, J. (2008). *Mouton Series in Pragmatics: Vol. 4. Intention, Common Ground and the Egocentric Speaker–Hearer*. Berlin: De Gruyter Mouton.

Kecskes, I., and Papp, T. (2003). "How to Demonstrate the Conceptual Effect of L2 on L1? Methods and Techniques." In V. Cook, ed., *Effects of the Second Language on the First*. Clevedon, UK: Multilingual Matters.

Kemmerer, D., Castillo, J. G., Talavage, T., Patterson, S., and Wiley, C. (2008). "Neuroanatomical Distribution of Five Semantic Components of Verbs: Evidence from fMRI." *Brain and Language, 107(1)*, 16–43.

Kerns, J. G., Cohen, J. D., MacDonald III, A. W., Cho, R. Y., Stenger, V. A., and Carter, C. S. (2004). "Anterior Cingulate Conflict Monitoring and Adjustments in Control." *Science, 303*(5660), 1023–1026.

Kerouac, J. (1957). *On the Road*. New York City: Viking Press.

Kersteen-Tucker, Z. (1991). "Long-Term Repetition Priming with Symmetrical Polygons and Words." *Memory and Cognition, 19(1)*, 37–43.

Keysar, B. (1994). "Discourse Context Effects: Metaphorical and Literal Interpretations." *Discourse Processes, 18*(3), 247–269.

Keysar, B. (2007). "Communication and Miscommunication: The Role of Egocentric Processes." *Intercultural Pragmatics, 4*(1), 71–84.

Keysar, B. (2008). "Egocentric Processes in Communication and Miscommunication." In I. Kecskes and J. Mey, eds., *Mouton Series in Pragmatics: Vol. 4. Intention, Common Ground and the Egocentric Speaker–Hearer* (pp. 277–296). Berlin, Germany: De Gruyter.

Keysar, B., and Henly, A. S. (2002). "Speakers' Overestimation of Their Effectiveness." *Psychological Science, 13*(3), 207–212.

Keysar, B., Barr, D. J., Balin, J. A., and Brauner, J. S. (2000). "Taking Perspective in Conversation: The Role of Mutual Knowledge in Comprehension." *Psychological Science, 11*(1), 32–38.

Keysar, B., Barr, D. J., Balin, J. A., and Paek, T. S. (1998). "Definite Reference and Mutual Knowledge: Process Models of Common Ground in Comprehension." *Journal of Memory and Language, 39*(1), 1–20.

Keysar, B., Barr, D., and Horton, W. S. (1998). "The Egocentric Basis of Language Use: Insights from a Processing Approach." *Current Directions in Psychological Science, 7(2)*, 46–50.

Kidd, S. M. (2003). *The Secret Life of Bees*. London: Penguin Books.

Kiley, T., Harris, S., Pasetta, M., Gary, S., and Davis, B. (directors) (1967–1970). The Smothers Brothers Comedy Hour. Television series. New York: CBS.

Kingsolver, B. (1998). *The Poisonwood Bible*. New York, NY: Harper Perennial.

Kingsolver, B. (2002). *Small Wonder: Essays*. New York: Harper Collins.

Köhler, W. (1929). *Gestalt Psychology*. New York, NY: Liveright.

Köhler, W. (1947). *Gestalt Psychology* (2nd ed.). New York, NY: Liveright.

Konopka, A. E., and Bock, K. (2009). "Lexical or Syntactic Control of Sentence Formulation? Structural Generalizations from Idiom Production." *Cognitive Psychology, 58(1)*, 68–101.

Koshoibekova. M. (2015). "The Legend of Dong Yong and the Seventh Fairy: The Heartbreaking Tale of an Orphan and The Daughter of the Jade Emperor." *The World of Chinese*. Retrieved from: www.theworldofchinese.com/2015/04/the-legend-of-dong-yong-and-the-seventh-fairy.

Kövecses, Z. (1986). *Metaphors of Anger, Pride, and Love*. Philadelphia: John Benjamins.

Kovecses, Z. (2011). "Recent Developments in Metaphor Theory: Are the New Views Rival Ones?" *Review of Cognitive Linguistics, 9*(1), 11–25.

Kovecses, Z. (2013). "The Metaphor-Metonymy Relationship: Correlation Metaphors Are Based on Metonymy." *Metaphor and Symbol, 28(2)*, 75–88.

Kunneman, F., Liebrecht, C., van Mulken, M., and van den Bosch, A. (2015). "Signaling Sarcasm: From Hyperbole to Hashtag." *Information Processing and Management, 51(4)*, 500–509.

Lacey, S., Stilla, R., and Sathian, K. (2012). "Metaphorically Feeling: Comprehending Textural Metaphors Activates Somatosensory Cortex." *Brain and Language, 120*, 416–421.

Lakoff, G., and Johnson, M. (1980). *Metaphors We Live By*. Chicago, IL: University of Chicago Press.

Lauro, L. J. R., Mattavelli, G., Papagno, C., and Tettamanti, M. (2013). "She Runs, the Road Runs, My Mind Runs, Bad Blood Runs between Us: Literal and Figurative Motion Verbs: An fMRI Study." *Neuroimage, 83*, 361–371.

Lawrence, D. H. (1928). *Lady Chatterley's Lover*. London: Penguin Books.

Lefkowitz, N., and Hedgcock, J. S. (2017). "Anti-Language: Linguistic Innovation, Identity Construction and Group Affiliation among Emerging Speech Communities." In N. Bell, ed., *Multiple Perspectives on Language Play* (pp. 347–376). Berlin: de Gruyter Mouton.

Lennon, J., and McCartney, P. (1967). "All you need is love." Song, recorded by The Beatles.

Leroux, G. (1911). *The Phantom of the Opera*. Paris: Pierre Laie.

LeRoy, M., and Freed, A. (producers), and Fleming, I (director) (1939). The *Wizard of Oz*. Motion picture. Los Angeles: Metro Goldwyn Mayer.

Lieberman, M. D. (2013). *Social: Why Our Brains Are Wired to Connect*. New York: Broadway Books.

Liu, D. (2008). *Idioms: Description, Comprehension, Acquisition, and Pedagogy*. New York: Routledge.

Loftus, E. F. (1975). "Leading Questions and the Eyewitness Report." *Cognitive Psychology, 7(4)*, 560–572.

Loftus, E. F. (1993). "Psychologists in the Eyewitness World." *American Psychologist, 48(5)*, 550–552.

Loftus, E. F. (2003). "Make-Believe Memories." *Cognitive Psychology, 58(1)*, 867–873.

Loftus, E. F., Miller, D. G., and Burns, H. J. (1978). "Semantic Integration of Verbal Information into a Visual Memory." *Journal of Experimental Psychology: Human Learning and Memory, 4*(1), 19.

Lorenz, K. (1943). "Die angeborenen Formen möglicher Erfahrung." *Z. Tierpsychol*, 5, 233–519.

Lucariello, J. (1994). "Situational Irony: A Concept of Events Gone Awry." *Journal of Experimental Psychology: General, 123(2)*, 129–145.

Lusch, V. R., and Colston, H. L. (2000, June). "A Gender Difference in Asyndeton." Poster session presented at the meeting of the American Psychological Society,Miami, FL.

Lyons, J. (1995). *Linguistic Semantics: An Introduction*. Cambridge, UK: Cambridge University Press.

Maglio, S. J., and Trope, Y. (2012). "Disembodiment: Abstract Construal Attenuates the Influence of Contextual Bodily State in Judgment." *Journal of Experimental Psychology: General, 141*(2), 211–216.

Mahon, B. Z., and Caramazza, A. (2008). "A Critical Look at the Embodied Cognition Hypothesis and a New Proposal for Grounding Conceptual Content." *Journal of Physiology, 102*, 59–70.

Mann, T. (1912). *Death in Venice*. Frankfurt: S. Fischer Verlag.

Mark, E. (2016, April 15). *"Song of everlasting sorrow."* *Ancient History Encyclopedia*. Retrieved from: www.ancient.eu/article/888.

Markel, N. N., and Hamp, E. P. (1960). "Connotative Meanings of Certain Phoneme Sequences." *Studies in Linguistics, 15*(1), 47–61.

Martin, R. (2007). *The Psychology of Humor: An Integrative Approach*. Boston: Elsevier Academic Press.

Martins, A. P. (2018, December 29). "Top 10 Weird Gifts for Christmas 2018." Retrieved from: www.NBCnews.com.

Mashal, N., Faust, M., Hendler, T., and Jung-Beeman, M. (2007). "An fMRI Investigation of the Neural Correlates Underlying the Processing of Novel Metaphoric Expressions." *Brain and Language, 100*, 115–126.

Maslow, A. H. (1943). "A Theory of Human Motivation." *Psychological Review, 50(4)*, 370–396.

Mather, V., and Rogers, K. (September 23, 2015.) "Behind the Yogi-isms: Those Said and Unsaid." *New York Times*.

Maurer, D., Pathman, T., and Mondloch, C. J. (2006). "The Shape of Boubas: Sound–Shape Correspondences in Toddlers and Adults." *Developmental Science, 9(3)*, 316–322.

McCullough, C. (1977). *The Thorn Birds*. New York: Harper and Row.

McEwan, I. (2001). *Atonement*. London: Jonathan Cape.

McGill, V. J., and Parry, W. T. (1948). "The Unity of Opposites: A Dialectical Principle." *Science and Society, 12(4)*, 418–444.

McGraw, P. A., and Warren, C. (2010). "Benign Violations: Making Immoral Behavior Funny." *Psychological Science, 21(8)*, 1141–1149.

Mearns, H. (1899). *Antigonish*. Retrieved from: https://en.wikipedia.org/wiki/Antigonish_(poem).

Mervosh, S. (2018). 'Mr. President, That's a Good One': Congressman Replies to Trump's Vulgar Tweet. *New York Times*, Politics.

Mesmer-Magnus, J., Glew, D. J., and Viswesvaran, C. (2012). "A Meta-Analysis of Positive Humor in the Workplace." *Journal of Managerial Psychology, 27(2)*, 155–190.

Mitchell, M. (1936). *Gone with the Wind*. London: Macmillan Publishers.

Morgan, D. (December 29, 2018). "The 10 best films of 2018." Retrieved from: www.CBSnews.com.

Morrow, L. (2005). *The Best Year of Their Lives: Kennedy, Johnson and Nixon in 1948: Learning the Secrets of Power*. New York: Basic Books.

Muller, C., and Cienki, A. (2009). "Words, Gestures, and Beyond: Forms of Multimodal Metaphor in the Use of Spoken Language." In C. J. Forceville, and E. Urios-Aparisi, eds., *Multimodal Metaphor* (pp. 297–328). Berlin: Mouton de Gruyter.

Nabakov, V. (1955). *Lolita*. Paris: Olympia Press.

New York Times (December 14, 2011). "Obama's speech to troops at Fort Bragg." Politics section.

Nezlek, J. B., Feist, G. J., Wilson, C. F., and Plesko, R. M. (2001). "Day-to-Day Variability in Empathy as a Function of Daily Events and Mood." *Journal of Research in Personality, 35(4)*, 401–423.

Nezlek, J. G., Schultz, A., Lopes, P., and Smith, V. C. (2007). "Naturally Occurring Variability in State Empathy." In T. Farrow, P. Woodruff, eds., *Empathy in Mental Illness* (pp. 187–200). New York: Cambridge University Press.

Nguyen, V. T. (2015). *The Sympathizer*. New York: Grove Press.

Nielsen, A., and Rendall, D. (2011). "The Sound of Round: Evaluating the Sound-Symbolic Role of Consonants in the Classic *Takete-Maluma* Phenomenon." *Canadian Journal of Experimental Psychology/Revue canadienne de psychologie expérimentale, 65(2)*, 115.

Norrick, N. R. (2003). "Issues in Conversational Joking." *Journal of Pragmatics, 35(9)*, 1333–1359.

Norrick, N. R. (2009). "A Theory of Humor in Interaction." *Journal of Literary Theory, 3(2)*, 261–284.

Norrick, N. R. (2017). "Language Play in Conversation." In N. Bell, ed., *Multiple Perspectives on Language Play* (pp. 11–46). Berlin: de Gruyter Mouton.

Nussbaum, M. (1995). *Love's Knowledge*. Oxford: Oxford University Press.

Obert, A., Gierski, F., Calmus, A., Portefaix, C., Declercq, C., Pierot, L., and Caillies, S. (2014). "Differential Bilateral Involvement of the Parietal Gyrus during Predicative Metaphor Processing: An Auditory fMRI Study." *Brain and Language, 137,* 112–119.

Ogden, C. K. (1932). *Opposition: A Linguistic and Psychological Analysis.* London: Paul, Trench and Trubner.

Ondaatje, M. (1992). *The English Patient.* Toronto: McClelland and Stewart.

Onysko, A. (2016). "A Note on the Relation between Cognitive Linguistics and Wordplay." In S. Knospe, A. Onysko, and Goth, M., eds., *Crossing Languages to Play with Words: Multidisciplinary Perspectives* (pp. 71–78). Berlin: de Gruyter Mouton.

Oring, E. (2011). "Parsing the Joke: The General Theory of Verbal Humor and Appropriate Incongruity." *Humor: International Journal of Humor Research, 24 (2),* 151–158.

Otsuji, E., and Pennycook, A. (2017). "Cities, Conviviality and Double-Edged Language Play." In N. Bell, ed., *Multiple Perspectives on Language Play* (pp. 199–218). Berlin: de Gruyter Mouton.

Panther, K. U., and Thornburg, L. (1998). "A Cognitive Approach to Inferencing in Conversation." *Journal of Pragmatics, 30(6),* 755–769.

Panther, K. U., and Thornburg, L., eds. (2003). *Metonymy and Pragmatic Inferencing.* Amsterdam: Benjamins.

Panther, K. U., & Thornberg, L. L. (2012). "Antonymy in Language Structure and Use." In M. Brdar, I. Raffaelli, & M. Z. Fuchs, eds., *Cognitive Linguistics between Universality and Variation.* Newcastle upon Tyne: Cambridge Scholars.

Panther, K-U., and Radden, G., eds. (1999). *Metonymy in Language and Thought.* Amsterdam: Benjamins.

Parault, S. J., and Schwanenflugel, P. J. (2006). "Sound-Symbolism: A Piece in the Puzzle of Word Learning." *Journal of Psycholinguistic Research, 35(4),* 329–351.

Pashler, H. (1990). "Coordinate Frame for Symmetry Detection and Object Recognition." *Journal of Experimental Psychology: Human Perception and Performance, 16(1),* 150–163.

Pasternak, B. (1957). *Doctor Zhivago.* New York: Pantheon Books.

Pecher, D., and Zwaan, R. A., eds. (2005). *Grounding Cognition: The Role of Perception and Action in Memory, Language, and Thinking.* Cambridge: Cambridge University Press.

Penny, M. (2014). *Outside, Inside.* Montreal: McGill-Queen's University Press.

Perez-Sobrino, P. (2014). "Meaning Construction in Verbomusical Environments: Conceptual Disintegration and Metonymy." *Journal of Pragmatics, 70,* 130–151.

Pexman, P. M., and Zvaigzne, M. T. (2004). "Does irony go better with friends?" *Metaphor and Symbol, 19(2),* 143–163.

Picard, U., and Silberman, S. (producers), and Buñuel, L. (writer and director) (1974). *The Phantom of Liberty.* Motion picture. Paris: Twentieth Century Fox.

Pickering, M. J., and Garrod, S. (2013). "An Integrated Theory of Language Production and Comprehension." *Behavioral and Brain Sciences, 36(4),* 329–347.

Pitzl, M. (2018). *Creativity in English as a Lingua Franca: Idiom and Metaphor.* Berlin: de Gruyter Mouton.

Pogrebin, M., and Poole, E. (1988). "Humor in the Briefing Room: A Study of the Strategic Uses of Humor among Police." *Journal of Contemporary Ethnography, 17(2)*, 183–210.

Pomerantz, A. (1978). "Compliment Responses: Notes on the Co-operation of Multiple Constraints." In J. Schenkein, ed., *Studies in the Organization of Conversational Interaction.* New York: Academic.

Pomerantz, A. (1984). "Agreeing and Disagreeing with Assessments: Some Features of Preferred/Dispreferred Turn Shapes." In J. M. Atkinson and J. Heritage, eds., *Structures of Social Action: Studies in Conversation Analysis.* Cambridge: Cambridge University Press.

Pomerantz, A., and Bell, N. (2007). "Learning to Play, Playing to Learn: FL Learners as Multicompetent Language Users." *Applied Linguistics, 28(4)*, 556–578.

Proulx, A. (1993). *The Shipping News.* New York: Simon and Schuster.

Ramachandran, V. S., and Hubbard, E. M. (2001). "Synaesthesia – A Window into Perception, Thought and Language." *Journal of Consciousness Studies, 8*, 3–34.

Raposo, A., Moss, H. E., Stamatakis, E. A., and Tyler, L. K. (2009). "Modulation of Motor and Premotor Cortices by Actions, Action Words and Action Sentences." *Neuropsychologia, 47*, 388–396.

Rasse, C. (2016). "Feeling for others: Environmental justice, emotion, and moral imagination in ethnic American literature." Unpublished master's thesis. Klagenfurt, Austria: Alpen-Adria-Universitat.

Rasse, C. (2017). Review of the book *Narrative Absorption*, vol. 27, "Linguistic Approaches to Literature." *Scientific Study of Literature, 7(2)*, 257–261.

Richardson, D. C., Spivey, M. J., Barsalou, L. W., and McRae, K. (2003). "Spatial Representations Activated during Real-Time Comprehension of Verbs." *Cognitive Science, 27*, 767–780.

Richter, G. (2015). "Trump: Anti-Rubio Ad Is 'Nothing Personal,' Just Payback." Retrieved from: www.Newsmax.com.

Riettta, T. (director). (2019). "Credit Card Envy." Television Commercial. Edmonton, Canada.

Ritchie, G. (1999). "Developing the Incongruity-Resolution Theory." In K. Binsted and G. Ritchie, eds., *Proceedings of the AISB Symposium on Creative Language: Stories and Humour* (pp. 78–85). Edinburgh: Society for the Study of Artificial Intelligence and the Simulation of Behaviour.

Ritchie, L. D. (2008). "X IS A JOURNEY: Embodied Simulation in Metaphor Interpretation." *Metaphor and Symbol, 23(3)*, 174–199.

Rizzolatti, G., and Arbib, M. A. (1999). "'From Grasping to Speech: Imitation Might Provide a Missing Link': Reply." *Trends in Neurosciences, 22(4)*, 152.

Roberts, R. M., and Kreuz, R. J. (1994). "Why Do People Use Figurative Language?" *Psychological Science, 5(3)*, 159–163.

Robinson, K. S. (2012). *2312.* New York: Orbit, Hachette Book Group.

Ruiz de Mendoza Ibanez, F. J., and Marial Uson, R. (2007). "High-Level Metaphor and Metonymy in Meaning Construction." In G. Radden,

K-M. Kopcke, T. Berg, and P. Siemund, eds., *Aspects of Meaning Construction*. Amsterdam: Benjamins.

Russo, R. (2002). *The Whore's Child and Other Stories*. New York: Alfred A. Knopf.

Sacks, Harvey, Schegloff, Emanuel A., and Jefferson, Gail (1974). "A Simplest Systematics for the Organization of Turn-Taking for Conversation." *Language*, *50*, 696–735.

Sanford, D. (2014). "Idiom as the Intersection of Conceptual and Syntactic Schemas." *Language and Cognition: An Interdisciplinary Journal of Language and Cognitive Science*, *6(4)*, 492–509.

Savickiene, I., and Dressler, W.U., eds. (2007). *The Acquisition of Diminutives: A Crosslinguistic Perspective*. Amsterdam, The Netherlands: John Benjamins Publishing Company.

Saygin, A., McCullough, S., Alac, M., and Emmorey, K. (2010). "Modulation of BOLD Response in Motion-Sensitive Lateral Temporal Cortex by Real and Fictive Motion Sentences." *Journal of Cognitive Neuroscience*, *22*, 2480–2890.

Schegloff, E. A., Jefferson, G. and Sacks, H. (1977). "The Preference for Self-Correction in the Organisation of Repair in Conversation." *Language*, *53 (2)*, 361–382.

Schlink, B. (1995). *The Reader*. New York: Vintage International.

Schneider, K. P., and Strubel-Burgdorf, S. (2012). "Diminutive *–let* in English." *SKASE Journal of Theoretical Linguistics*, *9(10)*, 15–32.

Schomp, V. (2010). *The Ancient Chinese: Myths of the World*. New York: Benchmark Books.

Schourup, L. (2011). "The Discourse Marker Now: A Relevance-Theoretic Approach." *Journal of Pragmatics*, *43*(8), 2110–2129.

Schuessler, A. (2007). *ABC Etymological Dictionary of Old Chinese*. Honolulu: University of Hawaii Press.

Searle, J. R. (1969). *Speech Acts: An Essay in the Philosophy of Language*. Cambridge, UK: Cambridge University Press.

Searle, J. R. (1975). "Indirect Speech Acts." In P. Cole and J. L. Morgan, eds., *In P. Cole and J. L. Morgan, eds., Syntax and Semantics* (Vol. 3, pp. 59–82). Cambridge, UK: Cambridge University Press.

Searle, J. R. (1979). *Expression and Meaning: Studies in the Theory of Speech Acts*. New York, NY: Cambridge University Press.

Seidlhofer, B. (2009). "Common Ground and Different Realities: World Englishes and English as a Lingua Franca." *World Englishes*, *28*(2), 236–245.

Shakespeare, W. (1596). "A Midsummer Night's Dream." In D. Bevington, ed., *The Complete Works of William Shakespeare, Volume II* (scene 1, line 134). New York: Bantam Books.

Shakespeare, W. (1993). *Romeo and Juliet*. Mineola, N.Y.: Dover Publications.

Shelley, C. (2001). "The Bicoherence Theory of Situational Irony." *Cognitive Science*, *25*, 775–818.

Sherman-Palladino, A., and Kirshner, R. (writers), and Chemel, L. S. (director) (2007). "Santa's Secret Stuff." Television series episode. In G. Abrams (Producer), Gilmore Girls. Burbank: The WB.

Sicherl, E. (2018). "A Comparison of Diminutive Expressions in English and Slovene as Exemplified by Roald Dahl's *Matilda*." *Languages in Contrast, 18(1)*, 283–306.

Sicherl, E., Žele, A. (2011). "Nominal Diminutives in Slovene and English." *Linguistica, 51*, 135–142

Sidhu, D. M., Pexman, P. M., and Saint-Aubin, J. (2016). "From the Bob/Kirk Effect to the Benoit/Éric Effect: Testing the Mechanism of Name Sound Symbolism in Two Languages." *Acta Psychologica, 169*, 88–99.

Silverstein, J. (December 29, 2018). "The biggest unsolved mysteries of 2018." Retrieved from: www.CBSnews.com.

Sinkeviciute, V. (2017). "'Everything He Says to Me It's Like He Stabs Me in the Face': Frontstage and Backstage Reactions to Teasing." In N. Bell, ed., *Multiple Perspectives on Language Play* (pp. 169–198). Berlin: de Gruyter Mouton.

Smith, R. (2018). *The Biology of Beauty: The Science behind Human Attractiveness.* Santa Barbara: Praeger/ABC-CLIO.

Smothers, T., and Smothers, R. (1965). "Mom Always Liked You Best." Recorded by T. Smothers and R. Smothers.

Solska, A. (2012). "Relevance-Theoretic Comprehension Procedure and Processing Multiple Meanings in Paradigmatic Puns." In E. Walaszewska and A. Piskorska, eds., *Relevance Theory: More than Understanding.* Newcastle upon Tyne: Cambridge Scholars.

Sontag, S. (1979). *Illness as Metaphor.* New York: Farrar, Straus and Giroux.

Sontag, S. (1989). *Aids and Its Metaphors.* New York: Farrar, Straus and Giroux.

Sperber, D., and Wilson, D. (1986). *Relevance: Communication and Cognition.* Oxford, UK: Blackwell.

Sperber, D., and Wilson, D. (1995). *Relevance: Communication and Cognition* (2nd ed.). Oxford, UK: Blackwell.

Stover, H. (2011). "Awareness in Metaphor Understanding." *Review of Cognitive Linguistics, 9(1)*, 65–82.

Styne, J., and Cahn, S. (1947). "It's Magic." Recorded by D. Day.

Sullivan, K. (2013). *Frames and Constructions In Metaphoric Language.* Amsterdam: Benjamins.

Sullivan, K. (2016). "Integrating Constructional Semantics and Conceptual Metaphor." *Constructions and Frames, 8(2)*, 141–165.

Sweetser, E. (2017). "Metaphor and Metonymy in Advertising: Building Viewpoint in Multimodal Multi-Space Blends." *Journal of Pragmatics, 122*, 65–76.

Takanashi, H. (2007). "Orthographic Puns: The Case of Japanese *Kyoka*." *Humor: International Journal of Humor Research, 20(3)*, 235–239.

Thibodeau, P. H., and Boroditsky, L. (2011). "Metaphors We Think With: The Role of Metaphor in Reasoning." *PLoS ONE, 6(2)*, ArtID e16782

Trope, Y., and Liberman, N. (2010). "Construal-Level Theory of Psychological Distance." *Psychological Review, 117*(2), 440–463.

Trump, D. J., [@realDonaldTrump] (November 12, 2017). Tweet. Retrieved from: https://twitter.com.

Tsur, R. (2009). "Metaphor and Figure-Ground Relationship: Comparisons from Poetry, Music, and the Visual Arts." In G. Brone and J. Vandaele, eds.,

Cognitive Poetics: Goals, Gains and Gaps (pp. 237–278). Berlin: Mouton de Gruyter.

Utsumi, A. (2000). "Verbal Irony as Implicit Display of Ironic Environment: Distinguishing Ironic Utterances from Nonirony." *Journal of Pragmatics, 32* (12), 1777–1806.

Uttich, K., and Lombrozo, T. (2010). "Norms Inform Mental State Ascriptions: A Rational Explanation for the Side-Effect Effect." *Cognition, 116*(1), 87–100.

Van Dam, J., and Bannink, A. (2017). "The First English (EFL) Lesson: Initial Settings or the Emergence of a Playful Classroom Culture." In N. Bell, ed., *Multiple Perspectives on Language Play* (pp. 245–280). Berlin: de Gruyter Mouton.

Veale, T. (2004). "Incongruity in Humor: Root-Cause or Epiphenomenon?" *Humor: International Journal of Humor Research, 17(4)*, 410–428.

Veale, T. (2009). "Hiding in Plain Sight: Figure-Ground Reversals in Humour." In G. Brone and J. Vandaele, eds., *Cognitive Poetics: Goals, Gains and Gaps* (pp. 279–286). Berlin: Mouton de Gruyter.

Veale, T. (2012). "A Computational Exploration of Creative Similes." In F. MacArther, Oncins-Martinez, J. L., Sanchez-Garcia, M., and Piquer-Piriz, A. M., eds., *Metaphor in Use: Context, Culture and Communication* (pp. 329–343). Amsterdam: Benjamins.

Veale, T. (2013). "Strategies and Tactics for Ironic Subversion." In M. Dynel, ed., *Developments in Linguistic Humour Theory* (pp. 321–339). Amsterdam: Benjamins.

Veale, T., and Alessandro, V. (2017). "Sparks Will Fly: Engineering Creative Script Conflicts." *Connection Science, 29(4)*, 332–349.

Veale, T., Feyaerts, K., and Brone, G. (2006). "The Cognitive Mechanisms of Adversarial Humor." *Humor: International Journal of Humor Research, 19(3)*, 305–338.

Vrabie, I. (2017). "The Conceptual Category of the Diminutive in English and Romanian: Existence, Recurrence, Status in Contemporary Language." *Bulletin of the Transilvania Univeristy of Brasov, Series IV: Philology and Cultural Studies, 10 (59)*, 37–46.

Wallentin, M., Lund, T. E., Östergaard, S., Östergaard, L., and Roepstorff, A. (2005). "Motion Verb Sentences Activate Left Posterior Middle Temporal Cortex despite Static Context." *NeuroReport, 16*, 649–652.

Wallentin, M., Nielsen, A. H., Vuust, P., Dohn, A., Roepstorff, A., and Lund, T. E. (2011). "BOLD Response to Motion Verbs in Left Posterior Middle Temporal Gyrus during Story Comprehension." *Brain and Language, 119*, 221–225.

Wallentin, M., Östergaard, S., Lund, T. E., Östergaard, L., and Roepstorff, A. (2005). "Concrete Spatial Language: See What I Mean?" *Brain and Language, 92*, 221–233.

Wang, S. (1995). *The Story of the Western Wing*. Oakland, CA: University of California Press.

Ward, G. L., and Hirschberg, J. (1991). "A Pragmatic Analysis of Tautological Utterances." *Journal of Pragmatics, 15*(6), 507–520.

Watson, C. E., Cardillo, E. R., Ianni, G. R., and Chatterjee, A. (2013). "Action Concepts in the Brain: An Activation Likelihood Estimation Meta-Analysis." *Journal of Cognitive Neuroscience, 25*, 1191–1205.

Welch, A. (December 29, 2018). "Google's top trending health questions of 2018." Retrieved from: www.CBSnews.com.

Wenderoth, P. (1994). "The Salience of Vertical Symmetry." *Perception, 23(2)*, 221–236.

Westbury, C. (2005). "Implicit Sound Symbolism in Lexical Access: Evidence from an Interference Task." *Brain and Language, 93(1)*, 10–19.

Westbury, C. (2018). "Implicit Sound Symbolism Effect in Lexical Access, Revisited: A Requiem for the Interference Task Paradigm." *Journal of Articles in Support of the Null Hypothesis, 15(1)*, 1–12.

Westbury, C., Hollis, G., Sidhu, D. M., and Pexman, P. M. (2018). "Weighing Up the Evidence for Sound Symbolism: Distributional Properties Predict Cue Strength." *Journal of Memory and Language, 99*, 122–150.

White, H. D. (2011). "Relevance Theory and Citations." *Journal of Pragmatics, 43* (14), 3345–3361.

Williams, K. D. (2001). *Ostracism: The Power of Silence*. New York, NY: Guildford Press.

Williams, L. E., and Bargh, J. A. (2008). "Experiencing Physical Warmth Promotes Interpersonal Warmth." *Science, 322*(5901), 606–607.

Williams, M. (December 29, 2018). "12 best and worst movies of 2018: All the films you need to see and avoid." Retrieved from: www.ABCnews.com.

Wilson, D. (2011). "Parallels and Differences in the Treatment of Metaphor in Relevance Theory and Cognitive Linguistics." *Studia Linguistica Universitatis Iagellonicae Cracoviensis, 128*, 195–213.

Wilson, D., and Sperber, D. (2012). *Meaning and Relevance*. Cambridge, UK: Cambridge University Press.

Wilson, N. L., and Gibbs, R. W. (2007). "Real and Imagined Body Movement Primes Metaphor Comprehension." *Cognitive Science, 31*(4), 721–731.

Wilson, N. L., and Gibbs, R. W., Jr. (2007). "Real and Imagined Body Movement Primes Metaphor Comprehension." *Cognitive Science, 31*, 721–731.

Winter, B., and Srinivasan, M. (June 2018). "Is metaphorical asymmetry actually based on concreteness? The role of word frequency." Presentation at the Researching and Applying Metaphor (RaAM) conference, Hong Kong, China.

Yu, A. (2001). *Rereading the Stone: Desire and the Making of Fiction in the Dream of the Red Chamber*. Princeton, NJ: Princeton University Press.

Yuan, H., and Chunde, Z. (2008). *Princess Peacock: Tales from the Other Peoples of China*. Westport, CT: Greenwood Publishing Group.

Zayts, O., and Schnurr, S. (2017). "Laughter as 'Serious Business': Clients' Laughter in Prenatal Screening for Down's Syndrome." In N. Bell, ed., *Multiple Perspectives on Language Play* (pp. 119–142). Berlin: de Gruyter Mouton.

Zharikov, S., and Gentner, D. (2002). "Why Do Metaphors Seem Deeper than Similes?" In W. D. Gray and C. Schunn, eds., *Proceedings of the Twenty-Fourth Annual Conference of the Cognitive Science Society* (pp. 976–981). Mahwah: Erlbaum.

Zwaan, R. A., and Taylor, L. J. (2006). "Seeing, Acting, Understanding: Motor Resonance in Language Comprehension." *Journal of Experimental Psychology: General, 135*, 1–11.

Index

For EU product safety concerns, contact us at Calle de José Abascal, 56–1°,
28003 Madrid, Spain or eugpsr@cambridge.org.

www.ingramcontent.com/pod-product-compliance
Ingram Content Group UK Ltd.
Pitfield, Milton Keynes, MK11 3LW, UK
UKHW020357140625
459647UK00020B/2522